ARNOLD
POETICAL WORKS

Oxford University Press, Ely House, London W. 1

GLASGOW NEW YORK TORONTO MELBOURNE WELLINGTON
CAPE TOWN SALISBURY IBADAN NAIROBI LUSAKA ADDIS ABABA
BOMBAY CALCUTTA MADRAS KARACHI LAHORE DACCA
KUALA LUMPUR SINGAPORE HONG KONG TOKYO

ARNOLD

POETICAL WORKS

Edited by
C. B. TINKER
and
H. F. LOWRY

LONDON
OXFORD UNIVERSITY PRESS
NEW YORK TORONTO

MATTHEW ARNOLD

Born: Laleham, 24 December 1822
Died: Liverpool, 15 April 1888

The Poems of Matthew Arnold, 1840 to 1867 were first
included in the series of Oxford Standard Authors in 1909
and reprinted seven times. In 1942 a new edition included
the poems published by Arnold since 1868, and this edition
was reprinted in 1945. The present edition, first published
in 1950, supersedes those mentioned above and contains
Arnold's complete poetical works. It was reprinted in 1953,
1957, 1961, 1963, 1966, and 1969

PRINTED IN GREAT BRITAIN

EDITORS' PREFACE

THE classification and order of the poems in this edition are those of the Library Edition of 1888, the last which could have had the advantage of the poet's arrangement of the material in it. Two poems, 'Horatian Echo' and 'Kaiser Dead', though printed in magazines during the poet's lifetime, were not included among the collected poems until the Popular Edition of 1890. To this final collection, the text of which is in general followed here, we have added the ten cancelled poems which the author excluded from his works, and the prefaces of 1853 and 1854 on the nature of poetry. A few verses never printed by Arnold himself may be found in *The Poetry of Matthew Arnold: A Commentary*, published by the present editors in 1940 (at pp. 335 ff., preceded by his translations from Homer at p. 329).

We had hoped that publication of the *Commentary* might bring news of additional unprinted manuscripts before the publishing of the edition of the poems themselves. In this hope we have been disappointed. Our search, since 1940, for such manuscripts has been almost entirely fruitless. It seems incredible that more should not have survived. Two of the printed editions, however, containing alterations in the poet's hand, have been discovered and used: the edition of 1854, given to the author's young son, Thomas, and the edition of 1881, later presented to John Singer Sargent by Lady Sandhurst.

We have printed Arnold's explanatory notes in their original form. He was somewhat free in his abridgement of the quotations of which he made use. For a more extended account of his sources, our *Commentary* may be consulted (e.g. pp. 109 ff. and 205 ff.).

The footnotes are intended to supply a full record of the successive alterations of the text from the manuscripts (when such are known) onwards through the various editions. Changes of spelling are recorded, but not the alterations in punctuation to which Arnold was addicted. To have included a complete enumeration of these successive changes (the reasons for which it is often difficult to discover) would have burdened our pages with footnotes which would have confused the general reader and have been of use to few or none who might consult them.

Once again we must acknowledge the generosity of Mr. Arnold Whitridge, who has permitted us to make full use of the material in his possession and to reprint such portions of it as were necessary to this edition. To the museums at Grasmere and Keswick we have elsewhere expressed our indebtedness, to Mrs. Norman Thwaites, and to the many friends and scholars who have helped us by criticism and suggestion. For assistance in the preparation of this volume we are indebted to Mr. Curt N. Taylor and, particularly, to the skill and extensive knowledge of Mr. Frederick Page, of the Oxford University Press.

C. B. T.
H. F. L.

October 1949

CONTENTS

EARLY POEMS

Sonnets

CONTENTS

CONTENTS

CONTENTS

CONTENTS

CONTENTS

VOLUMES OF POETRY
PUBLISHED BY ARNOLD

(A list of the poems in each of the editions specified below is given in
Thomas B. Smart, *The Bibliography of Matthew Arnold*, London, 1892)

THE STRAYED REVELLER: 1849

The / Strayed Reveller, / and / Other Poems. / By A. / London: / B. Fellowes,
Ludgate Street. / 1849.

EMPEDOCLES ON ETNA: 1852

Empedocles on Etna, / and / Other Poems. / By A. / London: / B. Fellowes,
Ludgate Street. / 1852.

POEMS: 1853

Poems. / By / Matthew Arnold. / A New Edition. / London: / Longman,
Brown, Green, and Longmans. / MDCCCLIII.

Second Edition: 1854

Poems. / By / Matthew Arnold. / Second Edition. / London: / Longman,
Brown, Green, and Longmans. / MDCCCLIV.

Third Edition: 1857

Poems. / By / Matthew Arnold. / Third Edition. / London: Longman,
Brown, Green, Longmans, & Roberts. / 1857.

POEMS. *Second Series*: 1855

Poems. / By / Matthew Arnold. / Second Series. / London: / Longman, Brown,
Green, and Longmans. / MDCCCLV.

MEROPE: 1858

Merope. / A Tragedy. / By / Matthew Arnold. / London : / Longman, Brown,
Green, Longmans, & Roberts. / MDCCCLVIII.

NEW POEMS: 1867

New Poems / by / Matthew Arnold / London / Macmillan and Co. / MDCCCLXVII.

Second Edition: 1868

New Poems / by / Matthew Arnold / Second Edition / London / Macmillan
and Co. / MDCCCLXVIII.

VOLUMES OF POETRY PUBLISHED BY ARNOLD

POEMS: 1869
(*Two Volumes*)

Poems / by / Matthew Arnold / the First Volume / Narrative and Elegiac Poems / London / Macmillan and Co. / MDCCCLXIX [*All rights reserved*]

Poems / by / Matthew Arnold / the Second Volume / Dramatic and Lyric Poems / [*&c., as above*]

POEMS: 1877
(*Two volumes*)

Poems / by / Matthew Arnold / the First Volume / Early Poems, Narrative Poems, / and Sonnets / New and Complete Edition / London / Macmillan and Co. / MDCCCLXXVII

Poems / by / Matthew Arnold / the Second Volume / Lyric, Dramatic, and Elegiac Poems / [*&c., as above*]

New Edition: 1881

(This edition agrees, in the main, with the edition of 1877. For differences between the two editions, see Smart, p. 10.)

POEMS: 1885
(*Library Edition*)

VOL. I
Poems / by / Matthew Arnold / Early Poems, Narrative Poems / and Sonnets / London / Macmillan and Co. / 1885

VOL. II
Poems / by / Matthew Arnold / Lyric and Elegiac Poems / London / Macmillan and Co. / 1885

VOL. III
Poems / by / Matthew Arnold / Dramatic and Later Poems / London / Mac. millan and Co. / 1885

New Edition: 1888

Poems / by / Matthew Arnold / Early Poems, Narrative Poems / and Sonnets / London / Macmillan and Co. / and New York / 1888 / *All rights reserved*

[Vol. II. 'Lyric and Elegiac Poems'; Vol. III. 'Dramatic and Later Poems'.]

POETICAL WORKS: 1890
(*Popular Edition*)

Poetical Works / of / Matthew Arnold / London / Macmillan and Co. / and New York / 1890 / *All rights reserved*

(Contains 'Horatian Echo' and 'Kaiser Dead', which, though appearing in periodicals, had not been included in any of the above editions.)

(*Selections*)

SELECTED POEMS: 1878

Selected Poems / of / Matthew Arnold / [*Vignette*] / London / Macmillan and Co. / 1878

(A new edition of the *Selected Poems* was printed in October 1878. Reprinted 1880, 1882, 1883, 1884, 1885, 1886, 1887, May and September 1888, and 1889.)

(*Publication of Prize Poems*)

Alaric at Rome. / A prize poem, / recited in Rugby School, / June XII, MDCCCXL. / [*Arms of the School.*] / Rugby: Combe and Crossley. / MDCCCXL.

Cromwell: / a prize poem, / recited in the Theatre, Oxford; / June 28, 1843. / By / Matthew Arnold, / Balliol College. / [*Arms of Oxford.*] / Oxford: / Printed and published by J. Vincent. / MDCCCXLIII.

(A second edition of *Cromwell* was reprinted by T. & G. Shrimpton, Broad Street, Oxford, in 1863; and the poem was also included in *Oxford Prize Poems*, 1846, published by J. H. Parker, J. Vincent, and H. Slatter.)

LIST OF KNOWN MANUSCRIPTS
OF ARNOLD'S POEMS

(Alphabetically arranged, according to titles used in this edition. For the distinction between the terms Yale Manuscript and Yale Papers see Tinker & Lowry, *The Poetry of Matthew Arnold, A Commentary*, pp. 8–10.)

Calais Sands (in the possession of Arnold Whitridge, Esq.)

Caution to Poets, A (Yale Manuscript. Fair copy in Arnold's letters to Clough)

Dover Beach (draft of 22 lines only; formerly in the collection of Thomas A. Wise. Now British Museum?)

Empedocles on Etna (two stanzas only, not used in printed poem. Yale Manuscript. MS. of three stanzas (Act I, Scene ii, ll. 397–411). Arnold's papers, in possession of Mrs. Norman Thwaites)

Faded Leaves ('Longing' and 'Too Late' only. Arnold Whitridge, Esq.)

Geist's Grave (in the possession of Arthur Houghton, Esq.)

Haworth Churchyard (fair copies of lines 48–54 and 66–71 only. Yale Papers)

Horatian Echo (Yale Papers)

Kaiser Dead (British Red Cross Sale, at Christie's, April 1918)

Lines written in Kensington Gardens (Yale Manuscript)

Memorial Verses, 1850 (Yale Papers)

New Rome (Arnold's diary for 1873)

Persistency of Poetry (fair copy in Arnold's note-book for 1867)

Philomela (written on the fly-leaf of a copy of Latham's *English Language*, London, 1848, in the possession of the Reverend Roger Wodehouse)

Question, A (fair copy of the first seven lines in 'Dora Wordsworth, her Book')

Rugby Chapel (Yale Papers)

Second Best, The (Yale Manuscript)

Shakespeare (British Museum)

Sohrab and Rustum (three portions only preserved: (1) lines 1–108 in the museum at Dove Cottage, Grasmere; (2) lines 109–467 in the possession of Arnold Whitridge, Esq.; (3) lines 468–524 in the Keswick Museum)

Stagirius (Yale Papers)

Stanzas from Carnac (in a journal of Mrs. Thomas Arnold, the poet's mother, now in the possession of Miss Dorothy Ward)

Stanzas in Memory of Edward Quillinan (Rotha Quillinan's album)

Terrace at Berne, The (four lines only, a revision of stanza 12, never adopted, Yale Papers)

Tristram and Iseult (a portion of Part III only, a draft of the first 63 lines. Yale Manuscript)

World's Triumphs, The (written on the inside front cover of Eckermann's *Gespräche mit Goethe*, vol. iii, Magdeburg, 1848, in the possession of Arnold Whitridge, Esq.)

Written in Emerson's Essays (Yale Manuscript)

Youth and Calm (Rotha Quillinan's album)

PREFACE

[First published 1853. Reprinted 1854 and 1857.]

IN two small volumes of Poems, published anonymously, one in 1849, the other in 1852, many of the Poems which compose the present volume have already appeared. The rest are now published for the first time.

I have, in the present collection, omitted the Poem from which 5 the volume published in 1852 took its title. I have done so, not because the subject of it was a Sicilian Greek born between two and three thousand years ago, although many persons would think this a sufficient reason. Neither have I done so because I had, in my own opinion, failed in the delineation which I intended to 10 effect. I intended to delineate the feelings of one of the last of the Greek religious philosophers, one of the family of Orpheus and Musaeus, having survived his fellows, living on into a time when the habits of Greek thought and feeling had begun fast to change, character to dwindle, the influence of the Sophists to prevail. Into 15 the feelings of a man so situated there entered much that we are accustomed to consider as exclusively modern; how much, the fragments of Empedocles himself which remain to us are sufficient at least to indicate. What those who are familiar only with the great monuments of early Greek genius suppose to be its exclusive 20 characteristics, have disappeared; the calm, the cheerfulness, the disinterested objectivity have disappeared: the dialogue of the mind with itself has commenced; modern problems have presented themselves; we hear already the doubts, we witness the discouragement, of Hamlet and of Faust. 25

The representation of such a man's feelings must be interesting, if consistently drawn. We all naturally take pleasure, says Aristotle, in any imitation or representation whatever: this is the basis of our love of Poetry: and we take pleasure in them, he adds, because all knowledge is naturally agreeable to us; not to the philosopher 30 only, but to mankind at large. Every representation therefore which is consistently drawn may be supposed to be interesting, inasmuch as it gratifies this natural interest in knowledge of all kinds. What is *not* interesting, is that which does not add to our knowledge of any kind; that which is vaguely conceived and loosely drawn; a representation which is general, indeterminate, 5 and faint, instead of being particular, precise, and firm.

Any accurate representation may therefore be expected to be interesting; but, if the representation be a poetical one, more than this is demanded. It is demanded, not only that it shall interest, but also that it shall inspirit and rejoice the reader: that it shall convey 10 a charm, and infuse delight. For the Muses, as Hesiod says, were born that they might be 'a forgetfulness of evils, and a truce from cares': and it is not enough that the Poet should add to the knowledge of men, it is required of him also that he should add to their happiness. 'All Art,' says Schiller, 'is dedicated to Joy, and there is no 15 higher and no more serious problem, than how to make men happy. The right Art is that alone, which creates the highest enjoyment.'

A poetical work, therefore, is not yet justified when it has been shown to be an accurate, and therefore interesting representation; it has to be shown also that it is a representation from which men 20 can derive enjoyment. In presence of the most tragic circumstances, represented in a work of Art, the feeling of enjoyment, as is well known, may still subsist: the representation of the most utter calamity, of the liveliest anguish, is not sufficient to destroy it: the more tragic the situation, the deeper becomes the enjoyment; 25 and the situation is more tragic in proportion as it becomes more terrible.

What then are the situations, from the representation of which, though accurate, no poetical enjoyment can be derived? They are those in which the suffering finds no vent in action; in which a 30 continuous state of mental distress is prolonged, unrelieved by incident, hope, or resistance; in which there is everything to be endured, nothing to be done. In such situations there is inevitably something morbid, in the description of them something monotonous. When they occur in actual life, they are painful, not tragic; 35 the representation of them in poetry is painful also.

To this class of situations, poetically faulty as it appears to me, that of Empedocles, as I have endeavoured to represent him, belongs; and I have therefore excluded the Poem from the present collection.

And why, it may be asked, have I entered into this explanation respecting a matter so unimportant as the admission or exclusion of the Poem in question? I have done so, because I was anxious to 5 avow that the sole reason for its exclusion was that which has been stated above; and that it has not been excluded in deference to the opinion which many critics of the present day appear to entertain against subjects chosen from distant times and countries: against the choice, in short, of any subjects but modern ones. 10

'The Poet,' it is said,[1] and by an intelligent critic, 'the Poet who would really fix the public attention must leave the exhausted past, and draw his subjects from matters of present import, and *therefore* both of interest and novelty.'

Now this view I believe to be completely false. It is worth 15 examining, inasmuch as it is a fair sample of a class of critical dicta everywhere current at the present day, having a philosophical form and air, but no real basis in fact; and which are calculated to vitiate the judgement of readers of poetry, while they exert, so far as they are adopted, a misleading influence on the practice of those who 20 write it.

What are the eternal objects of Poetry, among all nations and at all times? They are actions; human actions; possessing an inherent interest in themselves, and which are to be communicated in an interesting manner by the art of the Poet. Vainly will the 25 latter imagine that he has everything in his own power; that he can make an intrinsically inferior action equally delightful with a more excellent one by his treatment of it; he may indeed compel us to admire his skill, but his work will possess, within itself, an incurable defect. 30

The Poet, then, has in the first place to select an excellent action; and what actions are the most excellent? Those, certainly, which most powerfully appeal to the great primary human affections: to those elementary feelings which subsist permanently in the race,

[1] In *The Spectator* of April 2nd, 1853. The words quoted were not used with reference to poems of mine. *1854 first*

11 intelligent] apparently intelligent *1853*

and which are independent of time. These feelings are permanent
and the same; that which interests them is permanent and the same
also. The modernness or antiquity of an action, therefore, has
nothing to do with its fitness for poetical representation; this
5 depends upon its inherent qualities. To the elementary part of our
nature, to our passions, that which is great and passionate is eternally
interesting; and interesting solely in proportion to its greatness and
to its passion. A great human action of a thousand years ago is
more interesting to it than a smaller human action of to-day, even
10 though upon the representation of this last the most consummate
skill may have been expended, and though it has the advantage of
appealing by its modern language, familiar manners, and contemporary allusions, to all our transient feelings and interests.
These, however, have no right to demand of a poetical work that
15 it shall satisfy them; their claims are to be directed elsewhere.
Poetical works belong to the domain of our permanent passions:
let them interest these, and the voice of all subordinate claims upon
them is at once silenced.

Achilles, Prometheus, Clytemnestra, Dido—what modern poem
20 presents personages as interesting, even to us moderns, as these
personages of an 'exhausted past'? We have the domestic epic
dealing with the details of modern life which pass daily under our
eyes; we have poems representing modern personages in contact
with the problems of modern life, moral, intellectual, and social;
25 these works have been produced by poets the most distinguished
of their nation and time; yet I fearlessly assert that Hermann and
Dorothea, Childe Harold, Jocelyn, The Excursion, leave the reader
cold in comparison with the effect produced upon him by the latter
books of the Iliad, by the Oresteia, or by the episode of Dido. And
30 why is this? Simply because in the three last-named cases the action
is greater, the personages nobler, the situations more intense: and
this is the true basis of the interest in a poetical work, and this alone.

It may be urged, however, that past actions may be interesting
in themselves, but that they are not to be adopted by the modern
35 Poet, because it is impossible for him to have them clearly present
to his own mind, and he cannot therefore feel them deeply, nor

29 Oresteia] Orestea, *1853-4*   30 last-named] latter *1853-4*

represent them forcibly. But this is not necessarily the case. The externals of a past action, indeed, he cannot know with the precision of a contemporary; but his business is with its essentials. The outward man of Oedipus or of Macbeth, the houses in which they lived, the ceremonies of their courts, he cannot accurately 5 figure to himself; but neither do they essentially concern him. His business is with their inward man; with their feelings and behaviour in certain tragic situations, which engage their passions as men; these have in them nothing local and casual; they are as accessible to the modern Poet as to a contemporary. 10

The date of an action, then, signifies nothing: the action itself, its selection and construction, this is what is all-important. This the Greeks understood far more clearly than we do. The radical difference between their poetical theory and ours consists, as it appears to me, in this: that, with them, the poetical character of the 15 action in itself, and the conduct of it, was the first consideration; with us, attention is fixed mainly on the value of the separate thoughts and images which occur in the treatment of an action. They regarded the whole; we regard the parts. With them, the action predominated over the expression of it; with us, the expres- 20 sion predominates over the action. Not that they failed in expression, or were inattentive to it; on the contrary, they are the highest models of expression, the unapproached masters of the *grand style:* but their expression is so excellent because it is so admirably kept in its right degree of prominence; because it is so simple and so well 25 subordinated; because it draws its force directly from the pregnancy of the matter which it conveys. For what reason was the Greek tragic poet confined to so limited a range of subjects? Because there are so few actions which unite in themselves, in the highest degree, the conditions of excellence: and it was not thought that on any but 30 an excellent subject could an excellent Poem be constructed. A few actions, therefore, eminently adapted for tragedy, maintained almost exclusive possession of the Greek tragic stage; their significance appeared inexhaustible; they were as permanent problems, perpetually offered to the genius of every fresh poet. This too is 35 the reason of what appears to us moderns a certain baldness of expression in Greek tragedy; of the triviality with which we often

reproach the remarks of the chorus, where it takes part in the
dialogue: that the action itself, the situation of Orestes, or Merope,
or Alcmaeon, was to stand the central point of interest, unforgotten,
absorbing, principal; that no accessories were for a moment to dis-
5 tract the spectator's attention from this; that the tone of the parts
was to be perpetually kept down, in order not to impair the
grandiose effect of the whole. The terrible old mythic story on
which the drama was founded stood, before he entered the theatre,
traced in its bare outlines upon the spectator's mind; it stood in his
10 memory, as a group of statuary, faintly seen, at the end of a long
and dark vista: then came the Poet, embodying outlines, develop-
ing situations, not a word wasted, not a sentiment capriciously
thrown in: stroke upon stroke, the drama proceeded: the light
deepened upon the group; more and more it revealed itself to the
15 rivetted gaze of the spectator: until at last, when the final words
were spoken, it stood before him in broad sunlight, a model of
immortal beauty.

This was what a Greek critic demanded; this was what a Greek
poet endeavoured to effect. It signified nothing to what time an
20 action belonged; we do not find that the Persae occupied a particularly high rank among the dramas of Aeschylus, because it
represented a matter of contemporary interest: this was not what
a cultivated Athenian required; he required that the permanent
elements of his nature should be moved; and dramas of which the
25 action, though taken from a long-distant mythic time, yet was
calculated to accomplish this in a higher degree than that of the
Persae, stood higher in his estimation accordingly. The Greeks
felt, no doubt, with their exquisite sagacity of taste, that an action
of present times was too near them, too much mixed up with what
30 was accidental and passing, to form a sufficiently grand, detached,
and self-subsistent object for a tragic poem: such objects belonged
to the domain of the comic poet, and of the lighter kinds of poetry.
For the more serious kinds, for *pragmatic* poetry, to use an excellent
expression of Polybius, they were more difficult and severe in the
35 range of subjects which they permitted. Their theory and practice

35 *1853 inserts after* permitted, *and omits below, the sentence:* 'But for all
kinds of poetry alike . . . careful construction of the poem.'

alike, the admirable treatise of Aristotle, and the unrivalled works of their poets, exclaim with a thousand tongues—'All depends upon the subject; choose a fitting action, penetrate yourself with the feeling of its situations; this done, everything else will follow.'

But for all kinds of poetry alike there was one point on which they were rigidly exacting; the adaptability of the subject to the kind of poetry selected, and the careful construction of the poem.

How different a way of thinking from this is ours! We can hardly at the present day understand what Menander meant, when he told a man who inquired as to the progress of his comedy that he had finished it, not having yet written a single line, because he had constructed the action of it in his mind. A modern critic would have assured him that the merit of his piece depended on the brilliant things which arose under his pen as he went along. We have poems which seem to exist merely for the sake of single lines and passages; not for the sake of producing any total-impression. We have critics who seem to direct their attention merely to detached expressions, to the language about the action, not to the action itself. I verily think that the majority of them do not in their hearts believe that there is such a thing as a total-impression to be derived from a poem at all, or to be demanded from a poet; they think the term a common-place of metaphysical criticism. They will permit the Poet to select any action he pleases, and to suffer that action to go as it will, provided he gratifies them with occasional bursts of fine writing, and with a shower of isolated thoughts and images. That is, they permit him to leave their poetical sense ungratified, provided that he gratifies their rhetorical sense and their curiosity. Of his neglecting to gratify these, there is little danger; he needs rather to be warned against the danger of attempting to gratify these alone; he needs rather to be perpetually reminded to prefer his action to everything else; so to treat this, as to permit its inherent excellences to develop themselves, without interruption from the intrusion of his personal peculiarities: most fortunate, when he most entirely succeeds in effacing himself, and in enabling a noble action to subsist as it did in nature.

But the modern critic not only permits a false practice; he

absolutely prescribes false aims.—'A true allegory of the state of one's own mind in a representative history,' the Poet is told, 'is perhaps the highest thing that one can attempt in the way of poetry.' —And accordingly he attempts it. An allegory of the state of one's
5 own mind, the highest problem of an art which imitates actions! No assuredly, it is not, it never can be so: no great poetical work has ever been produced with such an aim. Faust itself, in which something of the kind is attempted, wonderful passages as it contains, and in spite of the unsurpassed beauty of the scenes which
10 relate to Margaret, Faust itself, judged as a whole, and judged strictly as a poetical work, is defective: its illustrious author, the greatest poet of modern times, the greatest critic of all times, would have been the first to acknowledge it; he only defended his work, indeed, by asserting it to be 'something incommensurable.'
15 The confusion of the present times is great, the multitude of voices counselling different things bewildering, the number of existing works capable of attracting a young writer's attention and of becoming his models, immense: what he wants is a hand to guide him through the confusion, a voice to prescribe to him the aim
20 which he should keep in view, and to explain to him that the value of the literary works which offer themselves to his attention is relative to their power of helping him forward on his road towards this aim. Such a guide the English writer at the present day will nowhere find. Failing this, all that can be looked for, all indeed
25 that can be desired, is, that his attention should be fixed on excellent models; that he may reproduce, at any rate, something of their excellence, by penetrating himself with their works and by catching their spirit, if he cannot be taught to produce what is excellent independently.
30 Foremost among these models for the English writer stands Shakespeare: a name the greatest perhaps of all poetical names; a name never to be mentioned without reverence. I will venture, however, to express a doubt, whether the influence of his works, excellent and fruitful for the readers of poetry, for the great
35 majority, has been of unmixed advantage to the writers of it. Shakespeare indeed chose excellent subjects; the world could afford no better than Macbeth, or Romeo and Juliet, or Othello: he had

no theory respecting the necessity of choosing subjects of present import, or the paramount interest attaching to allegories of the state of one's own mind; like all great poets, he knew well what constituted a poetical action; like them, wherever he found such an action, he took it; like them, too, he found his best in past times. 5
But to these general characteristics of all great poets he added a special one of his own; a gift, namely, of happy, abundant, and ingenious expression, eminent and unrivalled: so eminent as irresistibly to strike the attention first in him, and even to throw into comparative shade his other excellences as a poet. Here has 10
been the mischief. These other excellences were his fundamental excellences *as a poet;* what distinguishes the artist from the mere amateur, says Goethe, is *Architectonicè* in the highest sense; that power of execution, which creates, forms, and constitutes: not the profoundness of single thoughts, not the richness of imagery, 15
not the abundance of illustration. But these attractive accessories of a poetical work being more easily seized than the spirit of the whole, and these accessories being possessed by Shakespeare in an unequalled degree, a young writer having recourse to Shakespeare as his model runs great risk of being vanquished and absorbed 20
by them, and, in consequence, of reproducing, according to the measure of his power, these, and these alone. Of this preponderating quality of Shakespeare's genius, accordingly, almost the whole of modern English poetry has, it appears to me, felt the influence. To the exclusive attention on the part of his imitators to this it is 25
in a great degree owing, that of the majority of modern poetical works the details alone are valuable, the composition worthless. In reading them one is perpetually reminded of that terrible sentence on a modern French poet—*il dit tout ce qu'il veut, mais malheureusement il n'a rien à dire.* 30
   Let me give an instance of what I mean. I will take it from the works of the very chief among those who seem to have been formed in the school of Shakespeare: of one whose exquisite genius and pathetic death render him for ever interesting. I will take the poem of Isabella, or the Pot of Basil, by Keats. I choose this rather 35
than the Endymion, because the latter work (which a modern critic has classed with the Fairy Queen!), although undoubtedly there

blows through it the breath of genius, is yet as a whole so utterly incoherent, as not strictly to merit the name of a poem at all. The poem of Isabella, then, is a perfect treasure-house of graceful and felicitous words and images: almost in every stanza there occurs one of those vivid and picturesque turns of expression, by which the object is made to flash upon the eye of the mind, and which thrill the reader with a sudden delight. This one short poem contains, perhaps, a greater number of happy single expressions which one could quote than all the extant tragedies of Sophocles. But the action, the story? The action in itself is an excellent one; but so feebly is it conceived by the Poet, so loosely constructed, that the effect produced by it, in and for itself, is absolutely null. Let the reader, after he has finished the poem of Keats, turn to the same story in the Decameron: he will then feel how pregnant and interesting the same action has become in the hands of a great artist, who above all things delineates his object; who subordinates expression to that which it is designed to express.

I have said that the imitators of Shakespeare, fixing their attention on his wonderful gift of expression, have directed their imitation to this, neglecting his other excellences. These excellences, the fundamental excellences of poetical art, Shakespeare no doubt possessed them—possessed many of them in a splendid degree; but it may perhaps be doubted whether even he himself did not sometimes give scope to his faculty of expression to the prejudice of a higher poetical duty. For we must never forget that Shakespeare is the great poet he is from his skill in discerning and firmly conceiving an excellent action, from his power of intensely feeling a situation, of intimately associating himself with a character; not from his gift of expression, which rather even leads him astray, degenerating sometimes into a fondness for curiosity of expression, into an irritability of fancy, which seems to make it impossible for him to say a thing plainly, even when the press of the action demands the very directest language, or its level character the very simplest. Mr. Hallam, than whom it is impossible to find a saner and more judicious critic, has had the courage (for at the present day it needs courage) to remark, how extremely and faultily difficult Shakespeare's language often is. It is so: you may find main scenes

in some of his greatest tragedies, King Lear for instance, where the
language is so artificial, so curiously tortured, and so difficult, that
every speech has to be read two or three times before its meaning
can be comprehended. This over-curiousness of expression is
indeed but the excessive employment of a wonderful gift—of the 5
power of saying a thing in a happier way than any other man;
nevertheless, it is carried so far that one understands what M.
Guizot meant, when he said that Shakespeare appears in his language
to have tried all styles except that of simplicity. He has not the
severe and scrupulous self-restraint of the ancients, partly no doubt, 10
because he had a far less cultivated and exacting audience: he has
indeed a far wider range than they had, a far richer fertility of
thought; in this respect he rises above them: in his strong con-
ception of his subject, in the genuine way in which he is penetrated
with it, he resembles them, and is unlike the moderns: but in the 15
accurate limitation of it, the conscientious rejection of superfluities,
the simple and rigorous development of it from the first line of his
work to the last, he falls below them, and comes nearer to the
moderns. In his chief works, besides what he has of his own, he
has the elementary soundness of the ancients; he has their important 20
action and their large and broad manner: but he has not their purity
of method. He is therefore a less safe model; for what he has of his
own is personal, and inseparable from his own rich nature; it may
be imitated and exaggerated, it cannot be learned or applied as an
art; he is above all suggestive; more valuable, therefore, to young 25
writers as men than as artists. But clearness of arrangement, rigour
of development, simplicity of style—these may to a certain extent
be learned: and these may, I am convinced, be learned best from
the ancients, who although infinitely less suggestive than Shakespeare, are thus, to the artist, more instructive. 30

What, then, it will be asked, are the ancients to be our sole
models? the ancients with their comparatively narrow range
of experience, and their widely different circumstances? Not,
certainly, that which is narrow in the ancients, nor that in which
we can no longer sympathize. An action like the action of the 35
Antigone of Sophocles, which turns upon the conflict between the
heroine's duty to her brother's corpse and that to the laws of her

country, is no longer one in which it is possible that we should feel
a deep interest. I am speaking too, it will be remembered, not of
the best sources of intellectual stimulus for the general reader, but
of the best models of instruction for the individual writer. This
5 last may certainly learn of the ancients, better than anywhere else,
three things which it is vitally important for him to know:—the
all-importance of the choice of a subject; the necessity of accurate
construction; and the subordinate character of expression. He will
learn from them how unspeakably superior is the effect of the one
10 moral impression left by a great action treated as a whole, to the
effect produced by the most striking single thought or by the
happiest image. As he penetrates into the spirit of the great classical works, as he becomes gradually aware of their intense significance, their noble simplicity, and their calm pathos, he will be
15 convinced that it is this effect, unity and profoundness of moral
impression, at which the ancient Poets aimed; that it is this which
constitutes the grandeur of their works, and which makes them
immortal. He will desire to direct his own efforts towards producing the same effect. Above all, he will deliver himself from the
20 jargon of modern criticism, and escape the danger of producing
poetical works conceived in the spirit of the passing time, and which
partake of its transitoriness.

The present age makes great claims upon us: we owe it service,
it will not be satisfied without our admiration. I know not how it
25 is, but their commerce with the ancients appears to me to produce,
in those who constantly practise it, a steadying and composing
effect upon their judgement, not of literary works only, but of men
and events in general. They are like persons who have had a very
weighty and impressive experience: they are more truly than others
30 under the empire of facts, and more independent of the language
current among those with whom they live. They wish neither to
applaud nor to revile their age: they wish to know what it is, what
it can give them, and whether this is what they want. What they
want, they know very well; they want to educe and cultivate what
35 is best and noblest in themselves: they know, too, that this is no
easy task—χαλεπὸν, as Pittacus said, χαλεπὸν ἐσθλὸν ἔμμεναι—
and they ask themselves sincerely whether their age and its literature

can assist them in the attempt. If they are endeavouring to practise any art, they remember the plain and simple proceedings of the old artists, who attained their grand results by penetrating themselves with some noble and significant action, not by inflating themselves with a belief in the pre-eminent importance and great- 5 ness of their own times. They do not talk of their mission, nor of interpreting their age, nor of the coming Poet; all this, they know, is the mere delirium of vanity; their business is not to praise their age, but to afford to the men who live in it the highest pleasure which they are capable of feeling. If asked to afford this by means 10 of subjects drawn from the age itself, they ask what special fitness the present age has for supplying them: they are told that it is an era of progress, an age commissioned to carry out the great ideas of industrial development and social amelioration. They reply that with all this they can do nothing; that the elements they need for 15 the exercise of their art are great actions, calculated powerfully and delightfully to affect what is permanent in the human soul; that so far as the present age can supply such actions, they will gladly make use of them; but that an age wanting in moral grandeur can with difficulty supply such, and an age of spiritual discomfort with 20 difficulty be powerfully and delightfully affected by them.

A host of voices will indignantly rejoin that the present age is inferior to the past neither in moral grandeur nor in spiritual health. He who possesses the discipline I speak of will content himself with remembering the judgements passed upon the present age, in this 25 respect, by the two men, the one of strongest head, the other of widest culture, whom it has produced; by Goethe and by Niebuhr. It will be sufficient for him that he knows the opinions held by these two great men respecting the present age and its literature; and that he feels assured in his own mind that their aims and demands 30 upon life were such as he would wish, at any rate, his own to be; and their judgement as to what is impeding and disabling such as he may safely follow. He will not, however, maintain a hostile attitude towards the false pretensions of his age; he will content himself with not being overwhelmed by them. He will esteem 35

26–27 the two men . . . culture] the men of strongest head and widest culture *1853, 1854*

himself fortunate if he can succeed in banishing from his mind all feelings of contradiction, and irritation, and impatience; in order to delight himself with the contemplation of some noble action of a heroic time, and to enable others, through his representation
5 of it, to delight in it also.

I am far indeed from making any claim, for myself, that I possess this discipline; or for the following Poems, that they breathe its spirit. But I say, that in the sincere endeavour to learn and practise, amid the bewildering confusion of our times, what is sound and
10 true in poetical art, I seemed to myself to find the only sure guidance, the only solid footing, among the ancients. They, at any rate, knew what they wanted in Art, and we do not. It is this uncertainty which is disheartening, and not hostile criticism. How often have I felt this when reading words of disparagement or of
15 cavil: that it is the uncertainty as to what is really to be aimed at which makes our difficulty, not the dissatisfaction of the critic, who himself suffers from the same uncertainty. *Non me tua fervida terrent Dicta: Dii me terrent, et Jupiter hostis.*

Two kinds of *dilettanti,* says Goethe, there are in poetry: he
20 who neglects the indispensable mechanical part, and thinks he has done enough if he shows spirituality and feeling; and he who seeks to arrive at poetry merely by mechanism, in which he can acquire an artiṣan's readiness, and is without soul and matter. And he adds, that the first does most harm to Art, and the last to himself. If we
25 must be *dilettanti:* if it is impossible for us, under the circumstances amidst which we live, to think clearly, to feel nobly, and to delineate firmly: if we cannot attain to the mastery of the great artists—let us, at least, have so much respect for our Art as to prefer it to ourselves: let us not bewilder our successors: let us
30 transmit to them the practice of Poetry, with its boundaries and wholesome regulative laws, under which excellent works may again, perhaps, at some future time, be produced, not yet fallen into oblivion through our neglect, not yet condemned and cancelled by the influence of their eternal enemy, Caprice.

FOX HOW, AMBLESIDE,
    October 1, 1853.

I HAVE allowed the Preface to the former edition of these Poems to stand almost without change, because I still believe it to be, in the main, true. I must not, however, be supposed insensible to the force of much that has been alleged against portions of it, or un- aware that it contains many things incompletely stated, many 5 things which need limitation. It leaves, too, untouched the question, how far, and in what manner, the opinions there expressed respect- ing the choice of subjects apply to lyric poetry; that region of the poetical field which is chiefly cultivated at present. But neither have I time now to supply these deficiencies, nor is this the proper place 10 for attempting it: on one or two points alone I wish to offer, in the briefest possible way, some explanation.

An objection has been ably urged to the classing together, as subjects equally belonging to a past time, Oedipus and Macbeth. And it is no doubt true that to Shakespeare, standing on the verge 15 of the middle ages, the epoch of Macbeth was more familiar than that of Oedipus. But I was speaking of actions as they presented themselves to us moderns: and it will hardly be said that the Euro- pean mind, since Voltaire, has much more affinity with the times of Macbeth than with those of Oedipus. As moderns, it seems to 20 me, we have no longer any direct affinity with the circumstances and feelings of either; as individuals, we are attracted towards this or that personage, we have a capacity for imagining him, irrespec- tive of his times, solely according to a law of personal sympathy; and those subjects for which we feel this personal attraction most 25 strongly, we may hope to treat successfully. Alcestis or Joan of Arc, Charlemagne or Agamemnon—one of these is not really nearer to us now than another; each can be made present only by an act of poetic imagination: but this man's imagination has an affinity for one of them, and that man's for another. 30

It has been said that I wish to limit the Poet in his choice of sub- jects to the period of Greek and Roman antiquity: but it is not so:

26 Alcestis] Prometheus *1854*

I only counsel him to choose for his subjects great actions, without regarding to what time they belong. Nor do I deny that the poetic faculty can and does manifest itself in treating the most trifling action, the most hopeless subject. But it is a pity that power should
5 be wasted; and that the Poet should be compelled to impart interest and force to his subject, instead of receiving them from it, and thereby doubling his impressiveness. There is, it has been excellently said, an immortal strength in the stories of great actions: the most gifted poet, then, may well be glad to supplement with it
10 that mortal weakness, which, in presence of the vast spectacle of life and the world, he must for ever feel to be his individual portion.

Again, with respect to the study of the classical writers of antiquity: it has been said that we should emulate rather than imitate them. I make no objection: all I say is, let us study them.
15 They can help to cure us of what is, it seems to me, the great vice of our intellect, manifesting itself in our incredible vagaries in literature, in art, in religion, in morals; namely, that it is *fantastic*, and wants *sanity*. Sanity—that is the great virtue of the ancient literature: the want of that is the great defect of the modern, in
20 spite of all its variety and power. It is impossible to read carefully the great ancients, without losing something of our caprice and eccentricity: and to emulate them we must at least read them.

LONDON,
June 1, 1854.

(Small Arabic numbers in the text of the poems direct the reader's attention not to footnotes but to notes by the author, pp. 487–502.)

EARLY POEMS

SONNETS

QUIET WORK

*[**First** published 1849. Reprinted 1853, '54, '57, '69, and thereafter]*

ONE lesson, Nature, let me learn of thee,
One lesson which in every wind is blown,
One lesson of two duties kept at one
Though the loud world proclaim their enmity—

Of toil unsever'd from tranquillity!   5
Of labour, that in lasting fruit outgrows
Far noisier schemes, accomplish'd in repose,
Too great for haste, too high for rivalry!

Yes, while on earth a thousand discords ring,
Man's fitful uproar mingling with his toil,   10
Still do thy sleepless ministers move on,

---

1 *1849*: Two lessons, Nature,   2 *1849*: Two lessons that in every wind are blown;   *1853–7*: One lesson which   3 *1849*: Two blending duties, harmonis'd in one,   *1853–7*: two duties serv'd in one,   *MS. alteration (in 1854 volume) not adopted*: kept in one] at one   6 *1849*: Of labour, that in one short hour outgrows   *1853–7*: that in still advance outgrows   *MS. alterations (in 1854 volume), not adopted*:

> that in fruit by far outgoes
> by far outgrows
> in lasting fruit outgrows
> with mute advance outgoes

7 *1849*: Man's noisy schemes,   *MS. alterations (in 1854 volume), not adopted*:

> Man's noisy feats
> work
> Much noisier work,

10 *1849*: Man's weak complainings   *1853–80*: Man's senseless uproar *MS. alterations (in 1854 volume), not adopted*:

> Our senseless uproar mingling with our toil,
> Man's senseless uproar mingling with his toil,

11 *1869–80*: quiet ministers

B   *1*

Their glorious tasks in silence perfecting;
Still working, blaming still our vain turmoil,
Labourers that shall not fail, when man is gone.

TO A FRIEND

[*First published 1849. Reprinted 1853, '54, '57, '69, and thereafter*]

WHO prop, thou ask'st, in these bad days, my mind?—
He much, the old man, who, clearest-soul'd of men,
Saw The Wide Prospect, and the Asian Fen,[1]
And Tmolus hill, and Smyrna bay, though blind.

Much he, whose friendship I not long since won,   5
That halting slave, who in Nicopolis
Taught Arrian, when Vespasian's brutal son
Clear'd Rome of what most shamed him. But be his

My special thanks, whose even-balanced soul,
From first youth tested up to extreme old age,   10
Business could not make dull, nor passion wild;

Who saw life steadily, and saw it whole;
The mellow glory of the Attic stage,
Singer of sweet Colonus, and its child.

SHAKESPEARE

[*First published 1849. Reprinted 1853, '54, '57, '69, and thereafter*]

OTHERS abide our question. Thou art free.
We ask and ask—Thou smilest and art still,
Out-topping knowledge. For the loftiest hill,
Who to the stars uncrowns his majesty,

12 *1849*: glorious course   13 *1849*: chiding still
    TO A FRIEND. 4 *1849–57*: Tmolus'... Smyrna's   6 *Letter to Clough*:
Of that lame slave,
    SHAKESPEARE. 3 *1869*: So some sovran hill   4 *MS., 1849–57*:
That to the stars

Planting his steadfast footsteps in the sea,   5
Making the heaven of heavens his dwelling-place,
Spares but the cloudy border of his base
To the foil'd searching of mortality;

And thou, who didst the stars and sunbeams know,
Self-school'd, self-scann'd, self-honour'd, self-secure,   10
Didst tread on earth unguess'd at.—Better so!

All pains the immortal spirit must endure,
All weakness which impairs, all griefs which bow,
Find their sole speech in that victorious brow.

WRITTEN IN EMERSON'S ESSAYS

[First published 1849. Reprinted 1853, '77, and thereafter]

'O MONSTROUS, dead, unprofitable world,
That thou canst hear, and hearing, hold thy way!
A voice oracular hath peal'd to-day,
To-day a hero's banner is unfurl'd;

Hast thou no lip for welcome?'—So I said.   5
Man after man, the world smiled and pass'd by;
A smile of wistful incredulity
As though one spake of life unto the dead—

7 *MS. alteration (in 1854 volume), not adopted:* Spares often but the
border   *1869:* Spares but the border, often, of his base   9 *MS.
alteration (in 1854 volume), not adopted:* whose wit to highest heaven did go
1869: whose head did stars   11 *MS. 1849–69:* Didst walk on Earth
MS. alterations (in 1854 volume), not adopted, save for exception noted:
Didst pass
stand *1877*
live
13 *MS. 1849–54:* weakness that   *MS., 1849–54:* griefs that
14 *1849–77:* sole voice
WRITTEN IN EMERSON'S ESSAYS. 8 *1849–77:* of noise unto the dead:

Scornful, and strange, and sorrowful, and full
Of bitter knowledge. Yet the will is free;　　　　　10
Strong is the soul, and wise, and beautiful;

The seeds of godlike power are in us still;
Gods are we, bards, saints, heroes, if we will!—
Dumb judges, answer, truth or mockery?

WRITTEN IN BUTLER'S SERMONS

[First published 1849. Reprinted 1877 and thereafter]

AFFECTIONS, Instincts, Principles, and Powers,
Impulse and Reason, Freedom and Control—
So men, unravelling God's harmonious whole,
Rend in a thousand shreds this life of ours.

Vain labour! Deep and broad, where none may see,　　5
Spring the foundations of that shadowy throne
Where man's one nature, queen-like, sits alone,
Centred in a majestic unity;

And rays her powers, like sister-islands seen
Linking their coral arms under the sea,　　　　　10
Or cluster'd peaks with plunging gulfs between

Spann'd by aërial arches all of gold,
Whereo'er the chariot wheels of life are roll'd
In cloudy circles to eternity.

TO THE DUKE OF WELLINGTON

ON HEARING HIM MISPRAISED

[First published 1849. Reprinted 1877 and thereafter]

BECAUSE thou hast believed, the wheels of life
Stand never idle, but go always round;
Not by their hands, who vex the patient ground,
Moved only; but by genius, in the strife

WRITTEN IN BUTLER'S SERMONS. 6 *1849*: the shadowy

Of all its chafing torrents after thaw,   5
Urged; and to feed whose movement, spinning sand,
The feeble sons of pleasure set their hand;
And, in this vision of the general law,

Hast labour'd, but with purpose; hast become
Laborious, persevering, serious, firm—   10
For this, thy track, across the fretful foam

Of vehement actions without scope or term,
Call'd history, keeps a splendour; due to wit,
Which saw one clue to life, and follow'd it.

IN HARMONY WITH NATURE

TO A PREACHER

[*First published 1849. Reprinted 1877 and thereafter*]

'In harmony with Nature?' Restless fool,
Who with such heat dost preach what were to thee,
When true, the last impossibility—
To be like Nature strong, like Nature cool!

Know, man hath all which Nature hath, but more,   5
And in that *more* lie all his hopes of good.
Nature is cruel, man is sick of blood;
Nature is stubborn, man would fain adore;

Nature is fickle, man hath need of rest;
Nature forgives no debt, and fears no grave;   10
Man would be mild, and with safe conscience blest.

Man must begin, know this, where Nature ends;
Nature and man can never be fast friends.
Fool, if thou canst not pass her, rest her slave!

To THE DUKE OF WELLINGTON. 9 *1849*: Hast labour'd with the foremost,   14 *1849*: *one* clue
   IN HARMONY WITH NATURE. *Title, 1849*: To an Independent Preacher,
who preached that we should be 'In Harmony with Nature'.

SONNETS

TO GEORGE CRUIKSHANK

ON SEEING, IN THE COUNTRY, HIS PICTURE OF 'THE BOTTLE'

[First published 1849. Reprinted 1853, '54, '57, '69, and thereafter]

ARTIST, whose hand, with horror wing'd, hath torn
From the rank life of towns this leaf! and flung
The prodigy of full-blown crime among
Valleys and men to middle fortune born,

Not innocent, indeed, yet not forlorn—   5
Say, what shall calm us when such guests intrude
Like comets on the heavenly solitude?
Shall breathless glades, cheer'd by shy Dian's horn,

Cold-bubbling springs, or caves?—Not so! The soul
Breasts her own griefs; and, urged too fiercely, says: 10
'Why tremble? True, the nobleness of man

May be by man effaced; man can control
To pain, to death, the bent of his own days.
Know thou the worst! So much, not more, he *can*.'

TO A REPUBLICAN FRIEND, 1848

[First published 1849. Reprinted 1853, '54, '57, '69, and thereafter]

GOD knows it, I am with you. If to prize
Those virtues, prized and practised by too few,
But prized, but loved, but eminent in you,
Man's fundamental life; if to despise

TO GEORGE CRUIKSHANK. *Title, 1849–57*: To George Cruikshank, Esq.
On Seeing for the First Time His Picture of 'The Bottle,' in the Country.
1869 (only): *Human Limits*. On Seeing George Cruikshank's Picture of 'The
Bottle,' in the Country.

TO A REPUBLICAN FRIEND, 1848. *Title: date first inserted in 1853.*

The barren optimistic sophistries   5
Of comfortable moles, whom what they do
Teaches the limit of the just and true
(And for such doing they require not eyes);

If sadness at the long heart-wasting show
Wherein earth's great ones are disquieted;   10
If thoughts, not idle, while before me flow

The armies of the homeless and unfed—
If these are yours, if this is what you are,
Then am I yours, and what you feel, I share.

CONTINUED

[First published 1849. Reprinted 1853, '54, '57, '69, and thereafter]

YET, when I muse on what life is, I seem
Rather to patience prompted, than that proud
Prospect of hope which France proclaims so loud—
France, famed in all great arts, in none supreme;

Seeing this vale, this earth, whereon we dream,   5
Is on all sides o'ershadow'd by the high
Uno'erleap'd Mountains of Necessity,
Sparing us narrower margin than we deem.

Nor will that day dawn at a human nod,
When, bursting through the network superposed   10
By selfish occupation—plot and plan,

Lust, avarice, envy—liberated man,
All difference with his fellow-mortal closed,
Shall be left standing face to face with God.

8 *1849–57*: And for such doing have no need of eyes: *1869*: (And for such doing they require no eyes);
    CONTINUED. 13 *1849–57*: his fellow man compos'd,

RELIGIOUS ISOLATION

TO THE SAME FRIEND

[*First published 1849. Reprinted 1853, '54, '57, '69, and thereafter*]

CHILDREN (as such forgive them) have I known,
Ever in their own eager pastime bent
To make the incurious bystander, intent
On his own swarming thoughts, an interest own—

Too fearful or too fond to play alone.   5
Do thou, whom light in thine own inmost soul
(Not less thy boast) illuminates, control
Wishes unworthy of a man full-grown.

What though the holy secret, which moulds thee,
Mould not the solid earth? though never winds   10
Have whisper'd it to the complaining sea,

Nature's great law, and law of all men's minds?—
To its own impulse every creature stirs;
Live by thy light, and earth will live by hers!

MYCERINUS[2]

[*First published 1849. Reprinted 1853, '54, '57, '69, and thereafter*]

'NOT by the justice that my father spurn'd,
Not for the thousands whom my father slew,
Altars unfed and temples overturn'd,
Cold hearts and thankless tongues, where thanks are due;
Fell this dread voice from lips that cannot lie,   5
Stern sentence of the Powers of Destiny.

RELIGIOUS ISOLATION. *Under title,* 1849–57: To the Same.   1869:
To a Friend.   10 1849–81: Moulds not   *MS. alteration (in* 1881
volume): Mould

MYCERINUS. 4 1849–77: thanks were due   5 1849–57: this late
voice

I will unfold my sentence and my crime.
My crime—that, rapt in reverential awe,
I sate obedient, in the fiery prime
Of youth, self-govern'd, at the feet of Law;   10
Ennobling this dull pomp, the life of kings,
By contemplation of diviner things.

'My father loved injustice, and lived long;
Crown'd with gray hairs he died, and full of sway.
I loved the good he scorn'd, and hated wrong—   15
The Gods declare my recompence to-day.
I look'd for life more lasting, rule more high;
And when six years are measured, lo, I die!

'Yet surely, O my people, did I deem
Man's justice from the all-just Gods was given;   20
A light that from some upper fount did beam,
Some better archetype, whose seat was heaven;
A light that, shining from the blest abodes,
Did shadow somewhat of the life of Gods.

'Mere phantoms of man's self-tormenting heart,   25
Which on the sweets that woo it dares not feed!
Vain dreams, which quench our pleasures, then depart,
When the duped soul, self-master'd, claims its meed;
When, on the strenuous just man, Heaven bestows,
Crown of his struggling life, an unjust close!   30

'Seems it so light a thing, then, austere Powers,
To spurn man's common lure, life's pleasant things?
Seems there no joy in dances crown'd with flowers,
Love, free to range, and regal banquetings?
Bend ye on these, indeed, an unmoved eye,   35
Not Gods but ghosts, in frozen apathy?

'Or is it that some Force, too wise, too strong,
Even for yourselves to conquer or beguile,
Sweeps earth, and heaven, and men, and gods along,

27 *1849–69*: dreams, that   37 *1849–69*: that some Power,   *1877–*
81: too stern, too strong,   39 *1849–57*: Whirls earth   *1869–81*:
Bears earth

Like the broad volume of the insurgent Nile?   40
And the great powers we serve, themselves may be
Slaves of a tyrannous necessity?

'Or in mid-heaven, perhaps, your golden cars,
Where earthly voice climbs never, wing their flight,
And in wild hunt, through mazy tracts of stars,   45
Sweep in the sounding stillness of the night?
Or in deaf ease, on thrones of dazzling sheen,
Drinking deep draughts of joy, ye dwell serene?

'Oh, wherefore cheat our youth, if thus it be,
Of one short joy, one lust, one pleasant dream?   50
Stringing vain words of powers we cannot see,
Blind divinations of a will supreme;
Lost labour! when the circumambient gloom
But hides, if Gods, Gods careless of our doom?

'The rest I give to joy. Even while I speak,   55
My sand runs short; and—as yon star-shot ray,
Hemm'd by two banks of cloud, peers pale and weak,
Now, as the barrier closes, dies away—
Even so do past and future intertwine,
Blotting this six years' space, which yet is mine.   60

'Six years—six little years—six drops of time!
Yet suns shall rise, and many moons shall wane,
And old men die, and young men pass their prime,
And languid pleasure fade and flower again,
And the dull Gods behold, ere these are flown,   65
Revels more deep, joy keener than their own.

'Into the silence of the groves and woods
I will go forth; though something would I say—
Something—yet what, I know not; for the Gods
The doom they pass revoke not, nor delay;   70
And prayers, and gifts, and tears, are fruitless all,
And the night waxes, and the shadows fall.

40 *1849–57*: the broad rushing   *1849*: the column'd Nile;   *1853–*
7: the insurged Nile   68 *1849–57*: but something

'Ye men of Egypt, ye have heard your king!
I go, and I return not. But the will
Of the great Gods is plain; and ye must bring   75
Ill deeds, ill passions, zealous to fulfil
Their pleasure, to their feet; and reap their praise,
The praise of Gods, rich boon! and length of days.'

—So spake he, half in anger, half in scorn;
And one loud cry of grief and of amaze   80
Broke from his sorrowing people; so he spake,
And turning, left them there; and with brief pause,
Girt with a throng of revellers, bent his way
To the cool region of the groves he loved.
There by the river-banks he wander'd on,   85
From palm-grove on to palm-grove, happy trees,
Their smooth tops shining sunward, and beneath
Burying their unsunn'd stems in grass and flowers;
Where in one dream the feverish time of youth
Might fade in slumber, and the feet of joy   90
Might wander all day long and never tire.
Here came the king, holding high feast, at morn,
Rose-crown'd; and ever, when the sun went down,
A hundred lamps beam'd in the tranquil gloom,
From tree to tree all through the twinkling grove,   95
Revealing all the tumult of the feast—
Flush'd guests, and golden goblets foam'd with wine;
While the deep-burnish'd foliage overhead
Splinter'd the silver arrows of the moon.
   It may be that sometimes his wondering soul   100
From the loud joyful laughter of his lips
Might shrink half startled, like a guilty man
Who wrestles with his dream; as some pale shape
Gliding half hidden through the dusky stems,
Would thrust a hand before the lifted bowl,   105
Whispering: *A little space, and thou art mine!*
It may be on that joyless feast his eye

87 *1849–69*: sunwards,

Dwelt with mere outward seeming; he, within,
Took measure of his soul, and knew its strength,
And by that silent knowledge, day by day,   110
Was calm'd, ennobled, comforted, sustain'd.
It may be; but not less his brow was smooth,
And his clear laugh fled ringing through the gloom,
And his mirth quail'd not at the mild reproof
Sigh'd out by winter's sad tranquillity;   115
Nor, pall'd with its own fulness, ebb'd and died
In the rich languor of long summer-days;
Nor wither'd when the palm-tree plumes, that roof'd
With their mild dark his grassy banquet-hall,
Bent to the cold winds of the showerless spring;   120
No, nor grew dark when autumn brought the clouds.
    So six long years he revell'd, night and day.
And when the mirth wax'd loudest, with dull sound
Sometimes from the grove's centre echoes came,
To tell his wondering people of their king;   125
In the still night, across the steaming flats,
Mix'd with the murmur of the moving Nile.

THE CHURCH OF BROU

[First published 1853. Reprinted 1854, '57, '69, '81, and thereafter. In 1877
Part III was printed as a separate poem, 'A Tomb among the Mountains']

I

The Castle

Down the Savoy valleys sounding,
    Echoing round this castle old,
'Mid the distant mountain-chalets
    Hark! what bell for church is toll'd?

THE CASTLE. 4 *After the first stanza there was, from 1853 to 1857, a short*
rule to mark off the first four lines as a distinct portion of the poem. Similar marks
were used instead of asterisks in the later portions requiring to be so set off.

In the bright October morning   5
   Savoy's Duke had left his bride.
From the castle, past the drawbridge,
   Flow'd the hunters' merry tide.

Steeds are neighing, gallants glittering;
   Gay, her smiling lord to greet,   10
From her mullion'd chamber-casement
   Smiles the Duchess Marguerite.

From Vienna, by the Danube,
   Here she came, a bride, in spring.
Now the autumn crisps the forest;   15
   Hunters gather, bugles ring.

Hounds are pulling, prickers swearing,
   Horses fret, and boar-spears glance.
Off!—They sweep the marshy forests,
   Westward, on the side of France.   20

Hark! the game's on foot; they scatter!—
   Down the forest-ridings lone,
Furious, single horsemen gallop——
   Hark! a shout—a crash—a groan!

Pale and breathless, came the hunters;   25
   On the turf dead lies the boar—
God! the Duke lies stretch'd beside him,
   Senseless, weltering in his gore.

     *   *   *   *

In the dull October evening,
   Down the leaf-strewn forest-road,   30
To the castle, past the drawbridge,
   Came the hunters with their load.

In the hall, with sconces blazing,
   Ladies waiting round her seat,
Clothed in smiles, beneath the daïs   35
   Sate the Duchess Marguerite.

Hark! below the gates unbarring!
  Tramp of men and quick commands!
'—'Tis my lord come back from hunting—'
  And the Duchess claps her hands.   40

Slow and tired, came the hunters—
  Stopp'd in darkness in the court.
'—Ho, this way, ye laggard hunters!
  To the hall! What sport? What sport?'—

Slow they enter'd with their master;   45
  In the hall they laid him down.
On his coat were leaves and blood-stains,
  On his brow an angry frown.

Dead her princely youthful husband
  Lay before his youthful wife,   50
Bloody, 'neath the flaring sconces—
  And the sight froze all her life.

*   *   *   *

In Vienna, by the Danube,
  Kings hold revel, gallants meet.
Gay of old amid the gayest   55
  Was the Duchess Marguerite.

In Vienna, by the Danube,
  Feast and dance her youth beguiled.
Till that hour she never sorrow'd;
  But from then she never smiled.   60

'Mid the Savoy mountain valleys
  Far from town or haunt of man,
Stands a lonely church, unfinish'd,
  Which the Duchess Maud began;

Old, that Duchess stern began it,   65
  In gray age, with palsied hands;
But she died while it was building,
  And the Church unfinish'd stands—

67 *1853–4*: as it was

14

Stands as erst the builders left it,
　　When she sank into her grave;　　　　70
Mountain greensward paves the chancel,
　　Harebells flower in the nave.

'—In my castle all is sorrow,'
　　Said the Duchess Marguerite then;
'Guide me, some one, to the mountain!　　75
　　We will build the Church again.'—

Sandall'd palmers, faring homeward,
　　Austrian knights from Syria came.
'—Austrian wanderers bring, O warders!
　　Homage to your Austrian dame.'—　　80

From the gate the warders answer'd:
　　'—Gone, O knights, is she you knew!
Dead our Duke, and gone his Duchess;
　　Seek her at the Church of Brou!'—

Austrian knights and march-worn palmers　85
　　Climb the winding mountain-way—
Reach the valley, where the Fabric
　　Rises higher day by day.

Stones are sawing, hammers ringing;
　　On the work the bright sun shines,　　90
In the Savoy mountain-meadows,
　　By the stream, below the pines.

On her palfrey white the Duchess
　　Sate and watch'd her working train—
Flemish carvers, Lombard gilders,　　　95
　　German masons, smiths from Spain.

Clad in black, on her white palfrey,
　　Her old architect beside—
There they found her in the mountains,
　　Morn and noon and eventide.　　　　100

70 *1853–7*: she sunk　　　75 *1853–7*: 'Guide me, vassals,

There she sate, and watch'd the builders,
   Till the Church was roof'd and done.
Last of all, the builders rear'd her
   In the nave a tomb of stone.

On the tomb two forms they sculptured,   105
   Lifelike in the marble pale—
One, the Duke in helm and armour;
   One, the Duchess in her veil.

Round the tomb the carved stone fretwork
   Was at Easter-tide put on.   110
Then the Duchess closed her labours;
   And she died at the St. John.

II

The Church

Upon the glistening leaden roof
 Of the new Pile, the sunlight shines;
   The stream goes leaping by.
The hills are clothed with pines sun-proof;
'Mid bright green fields, below the pines,   5
   Stands the Church on high.
What Church is this, from men aloof?—
'Tis the Church of Brou.

At sunrise, from their dewy lair
Crossing the stream, the kine are seen   10
   Round the wall to stray—
The churchyard wall that clips the square
Of open hill-sward fresh and green
   Where last year they lay.
But all things now are order'd fair   15
Round the Church of Brou.

THE CHURCH. 13 *1853–7*: Of shaven hill-sward trim

On Sundays, at the matin-chime,
The Alpine peasants, two and three,
    Climb up here to pray;
Burghers and dames, at summer's prime,   20
Ride out to church from Chambery,
    Dight with mantles gay.
But else it is a lonely time
Round the Church of Brou.

On Sundays, too, a priest doth come   25
From the wall'd town beyond the pass,
    Down the mountain-way;
And then you hear the organ's hum,
You hear the white-robed priest say mass,
    And the people pray.   30
But else the woods and fields are dumb
Round the Church of Brou.

And after church, when mass is done,
The people to the nave repair
    Round the tomb to stray;   35
And marvel at the Forms of stone,
And praise the chisell'd broideries rare—
    Then they drop away.
The princely Pair are left alone
In the Church of Brou.   40

III

The Tomb

So rest, for ever rest, O princely Pair!
In your high church, 'mid the still mountain-air,
Where horn, and hound, and vassals, never come.
Only the blessed Saints are smiling dumb,
From the rich painted windows of the nave,   5
On aisle, and transept, and your marble grave;

THE TOMB. *Title, 1877*: A Tomb among the Mountains.

Where thou, young Prince! shalt never more arise
From the fringed mattress where thy Duchess lies,
On autumn-mornings, when the bugle sounds,
And ride across the drawbridge with thy hounds   10
To hunt the boar in the crisp woods till eve;
And thou, O Princess! shalt no more receive,
Thou and thy ladies, in the hall of state,
The jaded hunters with their bloody freight,
Coming benighted to the castle-gate.   15

   So sleep, for ever sleep, O marble Pair!
Or, if ye wake, let it be then, when fair
On the carved western front a flood of light
Streams from the setting sun, and colours bright
Prophets, transfigured Saints, and Martyrs brave,   20
In the vast western window of the nave;
And on the pavement round the Tomb there glints
A chequer-work of glowing sapphire-tints,
And amethyst, and ruby—then unclose
Your eyelids on the stone where ye repose,   25
And from your broider'd pillows lift your heads,
And rise upon your cold white marble beds;
And, looking down on the warm rosy tints,
Which chequer, at your feet, the illumined flints,
Say: *What is this? we are in bliss—forgiven—*   30
Behold the pavement of the courts of Heaven!
Or let it be on autumn nights, when rain
Doth rustlingly above your heads complain
On the smooth leaden roof, and on the walls
Shedding her pensive light at intervals   35
The moon through the clere-story windows shines,
And the wind washes through the mountain-pines.
Then, gazing up 'mid the dim pillars high,

17 *1853*: And if ye wake   27 *1869*: And raise you on   29 *1853–7*: That chequer,   37 *1853*: washes in the mountain pines.   *1854, 1857*: wails among the mountain pines.   *1869, 1877*: washes 'mid the mountain pines.   38 *1853–77*: gazing up through   *MS. in 1854 volume (adopted 1881)* up 'mid

The foliaged marble forest where ye lie,
Hush, ye will say, *it is eternity!*   40
This is the glimmering verge of Heaven, and these
The columns of the heavenly palaces!
And, in the sweeping of the wind, your ear
The passage of the Angels' wings will hear,
And on the lichen-crusted leads above   45
The rustle of the eternal rain of love.

A MODERN SAPPHO

[First published 1849. Reprinted 1853, '69, and thereafter]

THEY are gone—all is still! Foolish heart, dost thou quiver?
  Nothing stirs on the lawn but the quick lilac-shade.
Far up shines the house, and beneath flows the river—
  Here lean, my head, on this cold balustrade!

Ere he come—ere the boat by the shining-branch'd border   5
  Of dark elms shoot round, dropping down the proud stream,
Let me pause, let me strive, in myself make some order,
  Ere their boat-music sound, ere their broider'd flags gleam.

Last night we stood earnestly talking together;
  She enter'd—that moment his eyes turn'd from me!   10
Fasten'd on her dark hair, and her wreath of white heather—
  As yesterday was, so to-morrow will be.

Their love, let me know, must grow strong and yet stronger,
  Their passion burn more, ere it ceases to burn.
They must love—while they must! but the hearts that love   15
    longer
  Are rare—ah! most loves but flow once, and return.

A MODERN SAPPHO. 2 *1849, 1853*: Nothing moves   3 *1849,*
1853: gleams the house   4 *1849–69*: cool balustrade   6 *1849,*
1853: come round,   7 *1849, 1853*: find some order,   8 *1849,*
1853: *inserted after this line*:
    Is it hope makes me linger? the dim thought, that sorrow
    Means parting? that only in absence lies pain?
    It was well with me once if I saw him: to-morrow
    May bring one of the old happy moments again.

I shall suffer—but they will outlive their affection;
   I shall weep—but their love will be cooling; and he,
As he drifts to fatigue, discontent, and dejection,
   Will be brought, thou poor heart, how much nearer to thee! 20

For cold is his eye to mere beauty, who, breaking
   The strong band which passion around him hath furl'd,
Disenchanted by habit, and newly awaking,
   Looks languidly round on a gloom-buried world.

Through that gloom he will see but a shadow appearing,   25
   Perceive but a voice as I come to his side—
But deeper their voice grows, and nobler their bearing,
   Whose youth in the fires of anguish hath died.

So, to wait!—But what notes down the wind, hark! are driving?
   'Tis he! 'tis their flag, shooting round by the trees!   30
—Let my turn, if it *will* come, be swift in arriving!
   Ah! hope cannot long lighten torments like these.

Hast thou yet dealt him, O life, thy full measure?
   World, have thy children yet bow'd at his knee?
Hast thou with myrtle-leaf crown'd him, O pleasure?   35
   —Crown, crown him quickly, and leave him for me!

REQUIESCAT

[*First published 1853. Reprinted 1853, '54, '57, '69, and thereafter*]

     Strew on her roses, roses,
       And never a spray of yew!
     In quiet she reposes;
       Ah, would that I did too!

A Modern Sappho. 22 *1849, 1853*: band which beauty   *1869*: The
strong spell which passion upon him hath hurl'd,   29 *1849, 1853*:
Then—to wait.   30 *1849, 1853*: 'tis the boat   31 *1849*: Let my
turn, if it will come,   *1869*: Let *my* turn

REQUIESCAT

Her mirth the world required;   5
     She bathed it in smiles of glee.
But her heart was tired, tired,
     And now they let her be.

Her life was turning, turning,
     In mazes of heat and sound.   10
But for peace her soul was yearning,
     And now peace laps her round.

Her cabin'd, ample spirit,
     It flutter'd and fail'd for breath.
To-night it doth inherit   15
     The vasty hall of death.

YOUTH AND CALM

[*First published 1852, as second paragraph of a poem entitled 'Lines written by a Death-bed'. Reprinted, as below, 1867 and thereafter*]

'Tis death! and peace, indeed, is here,
And ease from shame, and rest from fear.
There's nothing can dismarble now
The smoothness of that limpid brow.
But is a calm like this, in truth,   5
The crowning end of life and youth,
And when this boon rewards the dead,
Are all debts paid, has all been said?
And is the heart of youth so light,
Its step so firm, its eye so bright,   10
Because on its hot brow there blows
A wind of promise and repose
From the far grave, to which it goes;
Because it hath the hope to come,

YOUTH AND CALM. *Title, 1852: Lines written by a Death-bed.*   2 *1852:* But ah, though peace   3 *1852:* Though nothing can   5 *1852:* Yet is a calm   *MS. Rotha Quillinan's Album (Dec. 28, 1851):* Yet ah, is Calm alone, in truth,   8 *1868:* as all [*sic*]   10 *1852–88:* eye so bright (*later* eyes *here rejected*)   *MS. Album:* step so gay,   11 *MS. Album:* on its hot hour   14 *1852–81:* Because it has

One day, to harbour in the tomb?   15
Ah no, the bliss youth dreams is one
For daylight, for the cheerful sun,
For feeling nerves and living breath—
Youth dreams a bliss on this side death.
It dreams a rest, if not more deep,   20
More grateful than this marble sleep;
It hears a voice within it tell:
Calm's not life's crown, though calm is well.
'Tis all perhaps which man acquires,
But 'tis not what our youth desires.   25

A MEMORY-PICTURE

[First published 1849. Reprinted 1853, '54, '57, '69, and thereafter]

LAUGH, my friends, and without blame
Lightly quit what lightly came;
Rich to-morrow as to-day,
Spend as madly as you may!
I, with little land to stir,   5
Am the exacter labourer.
　　Ere the parting hour go by,
　　Quick, thy tablets, Memory!

19 *MS. Album*: dreams a joy   20 *MS. Album*: It asks a rest,
24 *MS. Album*: perhaps that

A MEMORY-PICTURE. *Title, 1849–57*: To my Friends, who ridiculed a
tender Leave-taking.   *1853–69: Printed as first poem in the* 'Switzerland'
group.   Refrain: 1849–54: Ere the parting kiss be dry,   8 *1849–57*:
inserted after this line:

But my Youth reminds me—'Thou
Hast liv'd light as these live now:
As these are, thou too wert such:
Much hast had, hast squander'd much.'
Fortune's now less frequent heir,
Ah! I husband what's grown rare.
　　Ere the parting kiss be dry, [hour go by *1857*]
　　Quick, thy tablets, Memory!

*In 1869 this and the preceding stanza were cancelled; the first stanza was
restored in 1877.*

A MEMORY-PICTURE

Once I said: 'A face is gone
If too hotly mused upon;   10
And our best impressions are
Those that do themselves repair.'
Many a face I so let flee,
Ah! is faded utterly.
　　Ere the parting hour go by,   15
　　Quick, thy tablets, Memory!

Marguerite says: 'As last year went,
So the coming year'll be spent;
Some day next year, I shall be,
Entering heedless, kiss'd by thee.'   20
Ah, I hope!—yet, once away,
What may chain us, who can say?
　　Ere the parting hour go by,
　　Quick, thy tablets, Memory!

Paint that lilac kerchief, bound   25
Her soft face, her hair around;
Tied under the archest chin
Mockery ever ambush'd in.
Let the fluttering fringes streak
All her pale, sweet-rounded cheek.   30
　　Ere the parting hour go by,
　　Quick, thy tablets, Memory!

Paint that figure's pliant grace
As she tow'rd me lean'd her face,
Half refused and half resign'd   35
Murmuring: 'Art thou still unkind?'
Many a broken promise then
Was new made—to break again.
　　Ere the parting hour go by,
　　Quick, thy tablets, Memory!   40

9 *1849–69*: Young, I said:　　*1877*: Long I said:　　13 *1849–57*:
Many a face I then let by,　　*1869*: Many a face I then let flee,
34 *1849–57*: towards　　*1869–81*: toward

23

Paint those eyes, so blue, so kind,
Eager tell-tales of her mind;
Paint, with their impetuous stress
Of inquiring tenderness,
Those frank eyes, where deep I see   45
An angelic gravity.
  Ere the parting hour go by,
    Quick, thy tablets, Memory!

What, my friends, these feeble lines
Show, you say, my love declines?   50
To paint ill as I have done,
Proves forgetfulness begun?
Time's gay minions, pleased you see,
Time, your master, governs me;
  Pleased, you mock the fruitless cry: 55
    'Quick, thy tablets, Memory!'

Ah, too true! Time's current strong
Leaves us fixt to nothing long.
Yet, if little stays with man,
Ah, retain we all we can!   60
If the clear impression dies,
Ah, the dim remembrance prize!
  Ere the parting hour go by,
    Quick, thy tablets, Memory!

A DREAM

[*First published 1853. Reprinted 1854, '57, '81, and thereafter*]

WAS it a dream? We sail'd, I thought we sail'd,
Martin and I, down a green Alpine stream,
Border'd, each bank, with pines; the morning sun,
On the wet umbrage of their glossy tops,

45 *1849–69*: deep doth lie   *1877–8*: deep doth be   *1880*: deep
will be   58 *1849–57, 1877, 1878*: us true   *1869*: us firm
1881: us join'd   *MS. alteration in 1881 (not adopted)*: us fixt
  A DREAM. *From 1853 to 1857 this was the third poem of the* 'Switzerland'
group.   3 *1853–7*: Under o'erhanging pines;

On the red pinings of their forest-floor,   5
Drew a warm scent abroad; behind the pines
The mountain-skirts, with all their sylvan change
Of bright-leaf'd chestnuts and moss'd walnut-trees
And the frail scarlet-berried ash, began.
Swiss chalets glitter'd on the dewy slopes,   10
And from some swarded shelf, high up, there came
Notes of wild pastoral music—over all
Ranged, diamond-bright, the eternal wall of snow.
Upon the mossy rocks at the stream's edge,
Back'd by the pines, a plank-built cottage stood,   15
Bright in the sun; the climbing gourd-plant's leaves
Muffled its walls, and on the stone-strewn roof
Lay the warm golden gourds; golden, within,
Under the eaves, peer'd rows of Indian corn.
We shot beneath the cottage with the stream.   20
On the brown, rude-carved balcony, two forms
Came forth—Olivia's, Marguerite! and thine.
Clad were they both in white, flowers in their breast;
Straw hats bedeck'd their heads, with ribbons blue,
Which danced, and on their shoulders, fluttering, play'd.   25
They saw us, they conferr'd; their bosoms heaved,
And more than mortal impulse fill'd their eyes.
Their lips moved; their white arms, waved eagerly,
Flash'd once, like falling streams; we rose, we gazed.
One moment, on the rapid's top, our boat   30
Hung poised—and then the darting river of Life
(Such now, methought, it was), the river of Life,
Loud thundering, bore us by; swift, swift it foam'd,
Black under cliffs it raced, round headlands shone.
Soon the plank'd cottage by the sun-warm'd pines   35
Faded—the moss—the rocks; us burning plains,
Bristled with cities, us the sea received.

23 *1853*: their breasts;   25 *1853–7*: Which wav'd,   *MS.*
alteration (in 1854 volume), not adopted: Which stirr'd,   32 *added in*
1881.   35 *1853–81*: 'mid the sun-warm'd   *MS. alteration (in 1881*
volume), not adopted: by the sun-warm'd

THE NEW SIRENS

[*First published 1849. Reprinted in* MACMILLAN'S MAGAZINE,
December 1876; then in 1877 and thereafter]

In the cedarn shadow sleeping,
Where cool grass and fragrant glooms
Forth at noon had lured me, creeping
From your darken'd palace rooms—
I, who in your train at morning   5
Stroll'd and sang with joyful mind,
Heard, in slumber, sounds of warning;
Heard the hoarse boughs labour in the wind.

Who are they, O pensive Graces,
—For I dream'd they wore your forms—   10
Who on shores and sea-wash'd places
Scoop the shelves and fret the storms?
Who, when ships are that way tending,
Troop across the flushing sands,
To all reefs and narrows wending,   15
With blown tresses, and with beckoning hands?

Yet I see, the howling levels
Of the deep are not your lair;
And your tragic-vaunted revels
Are less lonely than they were.   20
Like those Kings with treasure steering
From the jewell'd lands of dawn,
Troops, with gold and gifts, appearing,
Stream all day through your enchanted lawn.

Title, 1849, 1876: The New Sirens, A Palinode.   1 *1849, 1876*:
cedar shadow   *1877*: cedar-shadow   3 *1849*: Oft at noon
have   *1876–81*: Late at eve had   7 *1849*: Heard, at evening,
8 *1876–81*: Saw the hoarse boughs
    21 ff. *1849*: In a Tyrian galley steering
               From the golden springs of dawn,
               Troops, like Eastern kings, appearing,

And we too, from upland valleys,   25
Where some Muse with half-curved frown
Leans her ear to your mad sallies
Which the charm'd winds never drown;
By faint music guided, ranging
The scared glens, we wander'd on,   30
Left our awful laurels hanging,
And came heap'd with myrtles to your throne.

From the dragon-warder'd fountains
Where the springs of knowledge are,
From the watchers on the mountains,   35
And the bright and morning star;
We are exiles, we are falling,
We have lost them at your call—
O ye false ones, at your calling
Seeking ceiled chambers and a palace-hall!   40

Are the accents of your luring
More melodious than of yore?
Are those frail forms more enduring
Than the charms Ulysses bore?
That we sought you with rejoicings,   45
Till at evening we descry
At a pause of Siren voicings
These vext branches and this howling sky? . . .

*   *   *   *

Oh, your pardon! The uncouthness
Of that primal age is gone,   50
And the skin of dazzling smoothness
Screens not now a heart of stone.
Love has flush'd those cruel faces;
And those slacken'd arms forgo
The delight of death-embraces,   55
And yon whitening bone-mounds do not grow.

54 *1849, 1876*: your slacken'd arms forego   55 *1849*: of fierce embraces
56 *1849*: And those whitening

'Ah,' you say; 'the large appearance
Of man's labour is but vain,
And we plead as staunch adherence
Due to pleasure as to pain.'   60
Pointing to earth's careworn creatures,
'Come,' you murmur with a sigh:
'Ah! we own diviner features,
Loftier bearing, and a prouder eye.

'Come,' you say, 'the hours were dreary;   65
Dull did life in torpor fade;
Time is lame, and we grew weary
In the slumbrous cedarn shade.
Round our hearts with long caresses,
With low sighings, Silence stole,   70
And her load of steaming tresses
Fell, like Ossa, on the climbing soul.

'Come,' you say, 'the soul is fainting
Till she search and learn her own,
And the wisdom of man's painting   75
Leaves her riddle half unknown.
Come,' you say, 'the brain is seeking,
While the sovran heart is dead;
Yet this glean'd, when Gods were speaking,
Rarer secrets than the toiling head.   80

57 _1849_, _1876_: 'Come,' you say   59 _1849_: firm adherence   61 _1849_:
some world-worn creatures   65 _1849_: are dreary   66 _1849_: Life
is long, and will not fade: _1877_: Life without love does but fade:
_1881_: Dull, without love, life doth fade: 67 _1849_: Time is lame, and
we grow weary   _1876–81_: Vain it wastes, and we grew weary   MS.
alteration 1881: Vain it wore, and we grew weary   68 _1849_: this slumbrous
70 _1849_: With low sighs hath Silence stole;   72 _1849_: Weighs, like
Ossa, on the aery soul.   _1876–81_: Weigh'd, like Ossa, on the aery soul.
MS. _alteration (in 1881 volume)_: Fell like . . . on the climbing soul.
78 _1849_: When the princely heart is dead: _1876–81_: While the princely
heart is dead;   MS. _alteration (in 1881 volume)_: sovran heart

'Come,' you say, 'opinion trembles,
Judgment shifts, convictions go;
Life dries up, the heart dissembles—
Only, what we feel, we know.
Hath your wisdom felt emotions?   85
Will it weep our burning tears?
Hath it drunk of our love-potions
Crowning moments with the wealth of years?'

—I am dumb. Alas, too soon all
Man's grave reasons disappear!   90
Yet, I think, at God's tribunal
Some large answer you shall hear.
But, for me, my thoughts are straying
Where at sunrise, through your vines,
On these lawns I saw you playing,   95
Hanging garlands on your odorous pines;

When your showering locks enwound you,
And your heavenly eyes shone through;
When the pine-boughs yielded round you,
And your brows were starr'd with dew;   100
And immortal forms, to meet you,
Down the statued alleys came,
And through golden horns, to greet you,
Blew such music as a God may frame.

Yes, I muse! And if the dawning   105
Into daylight never grew,
If the glistering wings of morning
On the dry noon shook their dew,
If the fits of joy were longer,
Or the day were sooner done,   110
Or, perhaps, if hope were stronger,

85 *1849–77*: wisdom known   88 *1849–81*: weight of years?'
MS. alteration (in 1881 volume): wealth of years   94 *1849*: the vines
96 *1849, 1876*: on the odorous

No weak nursling of an earthly sun . . .
    Pluck, pluck cypress, O pale maidens,
      Dusk the hall with yew!

    *   *   *   *

    For a bound was set to meetings,   115
    And the sombre day dragg'd on;
    And the burst of joyful greetings,
    And the joyful dawn, were gone.
    For the eye grows fill'd with gazing,
    And on raptures follow calms;   120
    And those warm locks men were praising,
Droop'd, unbraided, on your listless arms.

    Storms unsmooth'd your folded valleys,
    And made all your cedars frown;
    Leaves were whirling in the alleys   125
    Which your lovers wander'd down.
    —Sitting cheerless in your bowers,
    The hands propping the sunk head,
    Still they gall you, the long hours,
And the hungry thought, that must be fed!   130

    Is the pleasure that is tasted
    Patient of a long review?
    Will the fire joy hath wasted,
    Mused on, warm the heart anew?
    —Or, are those old thoughts returning,   135
    Guests the dull sense never knew,
    Stars, set deep, yet inly burning,
Germs, your untrimm'd passion overgrew?

---

115 *1849*: But a bound   119 *1849, 1876*: was fill'd   125 *1849*:
Leaves are whirling   129 *1849–81*: Do they gall you, the long hours,
        And the hungry thought, that must be fed?
MS. alteration (in 1881 volume): Still they gall

Once, like us, you took your station
Watchers for a purer fire;   140
But you droop'd in expectation,
And you wearied in desire.
When the first rose flush was steeping
All the frore peak's awful crown,
Shepherds say, they found you sleeping   145
In some windless valley, farther down.

Then you wept, and slowly raising
Your dozed eyelids, sought again,
Half in doubt, they say, and gazing
Sadly back, the seats of men;—   150
Snatch'd a turbid inspiration
From some transient earthly sun,
And proclaim'd your vain ovation
For those mimic raptures you had won. . . .

  *   *   *   *

With a sad, majestic motion,   155
With a stately, slow surprise,
From their earthward-bound devotion
Lifting up your languid eyes—
Would you freeze my too loud boldness,
Dumbly smiling as you go,   160
One faint frown of distant coldness
Flitting fast across each marble brow?

Do I brighten at your sorrow,
O sweet Pleaders?—doth my lot
Find assurance in to-morrow   165
Of one joy, which you have not?

139 *1849, 1876*: Once, like me,   146 *1849*: In a windless valley,
further down.   151 *1849*: an earthly inspiration   152 *1849*:
human Sun,   154 *1849*: For the mimic raptures you had won.
Pluck, pluck cypress, O pale maidens,
Dusk the hall with yew!
159 *1849–81*: my louder boldness,   *MS. alteration (in 1881 volume)*:
my too loud

O, speak once, and shame my sadness!
Let this sobbing, Phrygian strain,
Mock'd and baffled by your gladness,
Mar the music of your feasts in vain!　　　　170

*　　　*　　　*　　　*

Scent, and song, and light, and flowers!
Gust on gust, the harsh winds blow—
Come, bind up those ringlet showers!
Roses for that dreaming brow!
Come, once more that ancient lightness,　　　　175
Glancing feet, and eager eyes!
Let your broad lamps flash the brightness
Which the sorrow-stricken day denies!

Through black depths of serried shadows,
Up cold aisles of buried glade;　　　　180
In the midst of river-meadows
Where the looming kine are laid;
From your dazzled windows streaming,
From your humming festal room,
Deep and far, a broken gleaming　　　　185
Reels and shivers on the ruffled gloom.

Where I stand, the grass is glowing;
Doubtless you are passing fair!
But I hear the north wind blowing,
And I feel the cold night-air.　　　　190
Can I look on your sweet faces,
And your proud heads backward thrown,
From this dusk of leaf-strewn places
With the dumb woods and the night alone?

167 ff. *1849*: 　　　　let my sadness
　　　　　　　And this sobbing Phrygian strain,
　　　　　　　Sham'd and baffled by your gladness,
　　　　　　　Blame the music of your feasts in vain.

168 *1876*: throbbing, Phrygian strain,　　　　172 *1849*: the hoarse winds
181 *1849–81*: In the mist　　　182 *1876–81*: the looming deer　　*MS.*
alteration (in 1881 volume): looming kine　　184 *1849*: From the humming

Yet, indeed, this flux of guesses—   195
Mad delight, and frozen calms—
Mirth to-day and vine-bound tresses,
And to-morrow—folded palms;
Is this all? this balanced measure?
Could life run no happier way?   200
Joyous, at the height of pleasure,
Passive at the nadir of dismay?

But, indeed, this proud possession,
This far-reaching, magic chain,
Linking in a mad succession   205
Fits of joy and fits of pain—
Have you seen it at the closing?
Have you track'd its clouded ways?
Can your eyes, while fools are dozing,
Drop, with mine, adown life's latter days?   210

When a dreary dawn is wading
Through this waste of sunless greens,
When the flushing hues are fading
On the peerless cheek of queens;
When the mean shall no more sorrow,   215
And the proudest no more smile;
As old age, youth's fatal morrow,
Spreads its cold light wider all that while?

Then, when change itself is over,
When the slow tide sets one way,   220
Shall you find the radiant lover,
Even by moments, of to-day?

195 *1849–77*: But, indeed,   200 *1849*: easier way?
201 *1849*: Happy, at the noon   202 *1849*: Passive, at the midnight
211 *1849–81*: a dreary light   213 *1849–81*: flashing lights
217–18 *1849–81*: While the dawning of the morrow
                 Widens slowly westward all that while?

C   33

The eye wanders, faith is failing—
O, loose hands, and let it be!
Proudly, like a king bewailing,⁣   225
O, let fall one tear, and set us free!

All true speech and large avowal
Which the jealous soul concedes;
All man's heart which brooks bestowal,
All frank faith which passion breeds—⁣   230
These we had, and we gave truly;
Doubt not, what we had, we gave!
False we were not, nor unruly;
Lodgers in the forest and the cave.

Long we wander'd with you, feeding⁣   235
Our rapt souls on your replies,
In a wistful silence reading
All the meaning of your eyes.
By moss-border'd statues sitting,
By well-heads, in summer days.⁣   240
But we turn, our eyes are flitting—
See, the white east, and the morning rays!

And you too, O worshipp'd Graces,
Sylvan Gods of this fair shade!
Is there doubt on divine faces?⁣   245
Are the blessed Gods dismay'd?
Can men worship the wan features,
The sunk eyes, the wailing tone,
Of unsphered, discrowned creatures,
Souls as little godlike as their own?⁣   250

Come, loose hands! The winged fleetness
Of immortal feet is gone;
And your scents have shed their sweetness,
And your flowers are overblown.

236 *1849*: sad souls   243 *1849*: O weeping Graces,   246 *1849*:
the happy Gods

And your jewell'd gauds surrender   255
  Half their glories to the day;
  Freely did they flash their splendour,
Freely gave it—but it dies away.

  In the pines the thrush is waking—
  Lo, yon orient hill in flames!   260
  Scores of true love knots are breaking
  At divorce which it proclaims.
  When the lamps are paled at morning,
  Heart quits heart and hand quits hand.
  Cold in that unlovely dawning,   265
Loveless, rayless, joyless you shall stand!

  Pluck no more red roses, maidens,
  Leave the lilies in their dew—
  Pluck, pluck cypress, O pale maidens,
  Dusk, oh, dusk the hall with yew!   270
  —Shall I seek, that I may scorn her,
  Her I loved at eventide?
  Shall I ask, what faded mourner
Stands, at daybreak, weeping by my side?
  Pluck, pluck cypress, O pale maidens!   275
    Dusk the hall with yew!

THE VOICE

[*First published 1849. Reprinted 1877 and thereafter*]

  As the kindling glances,
    Queen-like and clear,
  Which the bright moon lances
    From her tranquil sphere
  At the sleepless waters   5
    Of a lonely mere,
On the wild whirling waves, mournfully, mournfully,
    Shiver and die.

267 *1849*: Strew no more

As the tears of sorrow
   Mothers have shed—   10
Prayers that to-morrow
   Shall in vain be sped
When the flower they flow for
   Lies frozen and dead—
Fall on the throbbing brow, fall on the burning breast,   15
      Bringing no rest.

     Like bright waves that fall
     With a lifelike motion
On the lifeless margin of the sparkling Ocean;
A wild rose climbing up a mouldering wall—   20
A gush of sunbeams through a ruin'd hall—
Strains of glad music at a funeral—
     So sad, and with so wild a start
     To this deep-sober'd heart,
     So anxiously and painfully,   25
     So drearily and doubtfully,
And oh, with such intolerable change
     Of thought, such contrast strange,
O unforgotten voice, thy accents come,
Like wanderers from the world's extremity,   30
     Unto their ancient home!

In vain, all, all in vain,
They beat upon mine ear again,
Those melancholy tones so sweet and still.
Those lute-like tones which in the bygone year   35
     Did steal into mine ear—
Blew such a thrilling summons to my will,
   Yet could not shake it;
Made my tost heart its very life-blood spill,
   Yet could not break it.   40

24 *1849*: this long sober'd heart,   29 *1849, 1877*: thy whispers
come,   35 *1849*: in long distant years   36 *1849*: mine ears
39 *1849*: Drain'd all the life my full heart had to spill;

YOUTH'S AGITATIONS

[*First published 1852. Reprinted 1867 and thereafter*]

WHEN I shall be divorced, some ten years hence,
From this poor present self which I am now;
When youth has done its tedious vain expense
Of passions that for ever ebb and flow;

Shall I not joy youth's heats are left behind,   5
And breathe more happy in an even clime?—
Ah no, for then I shall begin to find
A thousand virtues in this hated time!

Then I shall wish its agitations back,
And all its thwarting currents of desire;   10
Then I shall praise the heat which then I lack,
And call this hurrying fever, generous fire;

And sigh that one thing only has been lent
To youth and age in common—discontent.

THE WORLD'S TRIUMPHS

[*First published 1852. Reprinted 1853, '54, '57, '69, and thereafter*]

So far as I conceive the world's rebuke
To him address'd who would recast her new,
Not from herself her fame of strength she took,
But from their weakness who would work her rue.

'Behold,' she cries, 'so many rages lull'd,   5
So many fiery spirits quite cool'd down;
Look how so many valours, long undull'd,
After short commerce with me, fear my frown!

YOUTH'S AGITATIONS. *Title, 1852*: Sonnet.
THE WORLD'S TRIUMPHS. *Title, 1852*: Sonnet.   **2** *MS.*: her *over it*
4 *MS.*: from their baseness

'Thou too, when thou against my crimes wouldst cry,
Let thy foreboded homage check thy tongue!'—   10
The world speaks well; yet might her foe reply:
'Are wills so weak?—then let not mine wait long!

'Hast thou so rare a poison?—let me be
Keener to slay thee, lest thou poison me!'

STAGIRIUS[3]

[First published 1849. Reprinted 1855, '77, and thereafter]

THOU, who dost dwell alone—
Thou, who dost know thine own—
Thou, to whom all are known
From the cradle to the grave—
    Save, oh! save.   5
From the world's temptations,
    From tribulations,
From that fierce anguish
Wherein we languish,
From that torpor deep   10
Wherein we lie asleep,
Heavy as death, cold as the grave,
    Save, oh! save.

When the soul, growing clearer,
    Sees God no nearer;   15
When the soul, mounting higher,
    To God comes no nigher;
But the arch-fiend Pride
Mounts at her side,
Foiling her high emprise,   20
Sealing her eagle eyes,

9 *MS.*: Thus thou, when thou   10 *MS.*: foreboded treason
STAGIRIUS. *Title, 1849*: Stagyrus   *1855*: Desire.   14–17 *MS.*:
When the soul rising higher, to God comes no nigher—
When the mind waxing clearer sees God no nearer—
20 *MS., 1855*: emprize,

38

And, when she fain would soar,
Makes idols to adore,
Changing the pure emotion
Of her high devotion,   25
To a skin-deep sense
Of her own eloquence;
Strong to deceive, strong to enslave—
        Save, oh! save.

From the ingrain'd fashion   30
Of this earthly nature
That mars thy creature;
From grief that is but passion,
From mirth that is but feigning,
From tears that bring no healing,   35
From wild and weak complaining,
        Thine old strength revealing,
        Save, oh! save.
From doubt, where all is double;
Where wise men are not strong,   40
Where comfort turns to trouble,
Where just men suffer wrong;
Where sorrow treads on joy,
Where sweet things soonest cloy,
Where faiths are built on dust,   45
Where love is half mistrust,
Hungry, and barren, and sharp as the sea—
        Oh! set us free.
O let the false dream fly,
Where our sick souls do lie   50
    Tossing continually!
        O where thy voice doth come
        Let all doubts be dumb,

24 *MS.*: Freezing *is written above* Changing *as an alternative reading.*
33, 34 *In the MS. these two lines are transposed.*   37 *MS.*: Thy true
strength   39 *MS.*: Doubts,   40 *MS.*: Where good men
43 *MS.*: puts out joy—

Let all words be mild,
All strifes be reconciled,   55
All pains beguiled!
Light bring no blindness,
Love no unkindness,
Knowledge no ruin,
Fear no undoing!   60
From the cradle to the grave,
    Save, oh! save.

HUMAN LIFE

[First published 1852. Reprinted 1867 and thereafter]

WHAT mortal, when he saw,
Life's voyage done, his heavenly Friend,
Could ever yet dare tell him fearlessly:
'I have kept uninfringed my nature's law;
The inly-written chart thou gavest me,   5
To guide me, I have steer'd by to the end'?

Ah! let us make no claim,
On life's incognisable sea,
To too exact a steering of our way;
Let us not fret and fear to miss our aim,   10
If some fair coast have lured us to make stay,
Or some friend hail'd us to keep company.

Ay! we would each fain drive
At random, and not steer by rule.
Weakness! and worse, weakness bestow'd in vain!   15
Winds from our side the unsuiting consort rive,
We rush by coasts where we had lief remain;
Man cannot, though he would, live chance's fool.

No! as the foaming swath
Of torn-up water, on the main,   20
Falls heavily away with long-drawn roar

HUMAN LIFE. 11 *1852–81*: has lured us   *MS. alteration (in 1881*
volume): have   19 *1852, 1867*: swathe

On either side the black deep-furrow'd path
Cut by an onward-labouring vessel's prore,
And never touches the ship-side again;

Even so we leave behind,   25
As, charter'd by some unknown Powers,
We stem across the sea of life by night,
The joys which were not for our use design'd;—
The friends to whom we had no natural right,
The homes that were not destined to be ours.   30

TO A GIPSY CHILD BY THE SEA-SHORE

DOUGLAS, ISLE OF MAN

[First published 1849. Reprinted 1855, '69, and thereafter]

WHO taught this pleading to unpractised eyes?
Who hid such import in an infant's gloom?
Who lent thee, child, this meditative guise?
Who mass'd, round that slight brow, these clouds of doom?

27 *1868, 1869*: We stem across the sea by night,
      TO A GIPSY CHILD BY THE SEA-SHORE. 1–20 *1869 only: first stanza
cancelled; next four rewritten as follows:*

> The port lies bright under the August sun,
> Gay shine the waters and the cluster'd pier;
> Blithely, this morn, old Ocean's work is done,
> And blithely do these sea-birds hover near.
>
> Poor child, whom the light air of childish joy
> Wafts not from thine own thoughts—of graver strain,
> Surely, than those which should thine age employ—
> A weight of meditation mixt with pain!
>
> Blithe all else stirs, thou stirrest not!—averse
> From thine own mother's breast, that knows not thee,
> With eyes which seek thine eyes thou dost converse,
> And thy dark mournful vision rests on me.
>
> Glooms that go deep as thine I have not known,
> Moods of fantastic sadness, nothing worth!
> Musings, that ere they could grow ripe were flown,
> And grief that heal'd at every smile of earth.

4 *1855*: What clouds thy forehead, and fore-dates thy doom?

Lo! sails that gleam a moment and are gone;⠀⠀⠀⠀⠀5
The swinging waters, and the cluster'd pier.
Not idly Earth and Ocean labour on,
Nor idly do these sea-birds hover near.

But thou, whom superfluity of joy
Wafts not from thine own thoughts, nor longings vain,⠀⠀10
Nor weariness, the full-fed soul's annoy—
Remaining in thy hunger and thy pain;

Thou, drugging pain by patience; half averse
From thine own mother's breast, that knows not thee;
With eyes which sought thine eyes thou didst converse,⠀⠀15
And that soul-searching vision fell on me.

Glooms that go deep as thine I have not known:
Moods of fantastic sadness, nothing worth.
Thy sorrow and thy calmness are thine own:
Glooms that enhance and glorify this earth.⠀⠀⠀⠀20

What mood wears like complexion to thy woe?
His, who in mountain glens, at noon of day,
Sits rapt, and hears the battle break below?
—Ah! thine was not the shelter, but the fray.

Some exile's, mindful how the past was glad?⠀⠀⠀⠀25
Some angel's, in an alien planet born?
—No exile's dream was ever half so sad,
Nor any angel's sorrow so forlorn.

Is the calm thine of stoic souls, who weigh
Life well, and find it wanting, nor deplore;⠀⠀⠀⠀30
But in disdainful silence turn away,
Stand mute, self-centred, stern, and dream no more?

15 *1849*: eyes that⠀⠀⠀⠀21-2 *1869*:
⠀⠀⠀⠀⠀⠀⠀Whose mood shall fancy liken to thy woe?
⠀⠀⠀⠀⠀⠀⠀Some dreamer's, who, far off, a summer's day,
25-6 *1849, 1855*: What exile's, changing bitter thoughts with glad?
⠀⠀⠀⠀⠀⠀⠀What seraph's, in some alien planet born?
25 *1869*: his past⠀⠀⠀⠀27 *1869*: Never was exile's memory half so sad,
28 *1869*: And **never** angel's

Or do I wait, to hear some gray-hair'd king
Unravel all his many-colour'd lore;
Whose mind hath known all arts of governing,   35
Mused much, loved life a little, loathed it more?

Down the pale cheek long lines of shadow slope,
Which years, and curious thought, and suffering give.
—Thou hast foreknown the vanity of hope,
Foreseen thy harvest—yet proceed'st to live.   40

O meek anticipant of that sure pain
Whose sureness gray-hair'd scholars hardly learn!
What wonder shall time breed, to swell thy strain?
What heavens, what earth, what sun shalt thou discern?

Ere the long night, whose stillness brooks no star,   45
Match that funereal aspect with her pall,
I think, thou wilt have fathom'd life too far,
Have known too much——or else forgotten all.

The Guide of our dark steps a triple veil
Betwixt our senses and our sorrow keeps;   50
Hath sown with cloudless passages the tale
Of grief, and eased us with a thousand sleeps.

Ah! not the nectarous poppy lovers use,
Not daily labour's dull, Lethæan spring,
Oblivion in lost angels can infuse   55
Of the soil'd glory, and the trailing wing.

And though thou glean, what strenuous gleaners may,
In the throng'd fields where winning comes by strife;
And though the just sun gild, as mortals pray,
Some reaches of thy storm-vext stream of life;   60

37–8 *1869*:
          Down thy pale cheek those lines of shadow slope,
          Which years, to most, and care, and suffering, give;—
44 *1849–88*: what suns   55 *1869*: lorn angels   58 *1869*: In
earth's throng'd fields   59 *1849–69*: as all men pray,

43

TO A GIPSY CHILD BY THE SEA-SHORE

Though that blank sunshine blind thee; though the cloud
That sever'd the world's march and thine, be gone;
Though ease dulls grace, and Wisdom be too proud
To halve a lodging that was all her own—

Once, ere the day decline, thou shalt discern,   65
Oh once, ere night, in thy success, thy chain!
Ere the long evening close, thou shalt return,
And wear this majesty of grief again.

A QUESTION
TO FAUSTA

[First published 1849. Reprinted 1877 and thereafter]

JOY comes and goes, hope ebbs and flows
    Like the wave;
Change doth unknit the tranquil strength of men.
    Love lends life a little grace,
    A few sad smiles; and then,   5
    Both are laid in one cold place,
      In the grave.

Dreams dawn and fly, friends smile and die
    Like spring flowers;
Our vaunted life is one long funeral.   10
    Men dig graves with bitter tears
    For their dead hopes; and all,
    Mazed with doubts and sick with fears,
      Count the hours.

We count the hours! These dreams of ours,   15
    False and hollow,
Do we go hence and find they are not dead?
    Joys we dimly apprehend,
    Faces that smiled and fled,
    Hopes born here, and born to end,   20
      Shall we follow?

62 *1849, 1855*: is gone   63 *1869*: and wisdom is   64 *1869*: To
halve a house that should be all her own—   65 *1869–81*: Once, ere thy
day go down,   *MS. alteration (in 1881 volume)*: Once, ere the day decline,
A QUESTION. *Title, 1849*: To Fausta.   17 *1849*: Shall we go

IN UTRUMQUE PARATUS

[First published 1849. Reprinted 1869 and thereafter]

IF, in the silent mind of One all-pure,
    At first imagined lay
The sacred world; and by procession sure
From those still deeps, in form and colour drest,
Seasons alternating, and night and day,   5
The long-mused thought to north, south, east, and west,
    Took then its all-seen way;

O waking on a world which thus-wise springs!
    Whether it needs thee count
Betwixt thy waking and the birth of things   10
Ages or hours—O waking on life's stream!
By lonely pureness to the all-pure fount
(Only by this thou canst) the colour'd dream
    Of life remount!

Thin, thin the pleasant human noises grow,   15
    And faint the city gleams;
Rare the lone pastoral huts—marvel not thou!
The solemn peaks but to the stars are known,
But to the stars, and the cold lunar beams;
Alone the sun arises, and alone   20
    Spring the great streams.

But, if the wild unfather'd mass no birth
    In divine seats hath known;
In the blank, echoing solitude if Earth,
Rocking her obscure body to and fro,   25
Ceases not from all time to heave and groan,
Unfruitful oft, and at her happiest throe
    Forms, what she forms, alone;

O seeming sole to awake, thy sun-bathed head
    Piercing the solemn cloud   30
Round thy still dreaming brother-world outspread!

IN UTRUMQUE PARATUS

O man, whom Earth, thy long-vext mother, bare
Not without joy—so radiant, so endow'd
(Such happy issue crown'd her painful care)—
    Be not too proud!   35

Oh when most self-exalted, most alone,
    Chief dreamer, own thy dream!
Thy brother-world stirs at thy feet unknown,
Who hath a monarch's hath no brother's part;
Yet doth thine inmost soul with yearning teem.   40
—Oh, what a spasm shakes the dreamer's heart!
    'I, too, but seem.'

THE WORLD AND THE QUIETIST

TO CRITIAS

[*First published 1849. Reprinted 1855, '77, and thereafter*]

    'WHY, when the world's great mind
      Hath finally inclined,
Why,' you say, Critias, 'be debating still?
    Why, with these mournful rhymes
    Learn'd in more languid climes,   5
    Blame our activity
    Who, with such passionate will,
    Are what we mean to be?'

    Critias, long since, I know
    (For Fate decreed it so),   10
Long since the world hath set its heart to live;
    Long since, with credulous zeal

IN UTRUMQUE PARATUS. 36 *1869 only: last stanza discarded and new ending supplied:*

    Thy native world stirs at thy feet unknown,
      Yet there thy secret lies!
    Out of this stuff, these forces, thou art grown,
    And proud self-severance from them were disease.
    O scan thy native world with pious eyes!
    High as thy life be risen, 'tis from these;
      And these, too, rise.

It turns life's mighty wheel,
Still doth for labourers send
  Who still their labour give,   15
And still expects an end.

Yet, as the wheel flies round,
With no ungrateful sound
Do adverse voices fall on the world's ear.
  Deafen'd by his own stir   20
  The rugged labourer
  Caught not till then a sense
  So glowing and so near
    Of his omnipotence.

So, when the feast grew loud   25
In Susa's palace proud,
A white-robed slave stole to the Great King's side.
  He spake—the Great King heard;
  Felt the slow-rolling word
  Swell his attentive soul;   30
  Breathed deeply as it died,
    And drain'd his mighty bowl.

HORATIAN ECHO[4]

(TO AN AMBITIOUS FRIEND)

[*Written in 1847. First published in* THE CENTURY GUILD HOBBY HORSE, *July 1887. Reprinted 1890*]

OMIT, omit, my simple friend,
Still to enquire how parties tend,
Or what we fix with foreign powers.
If France and we are really friends,
And what the Russian Czar intends,   5
  Is no concern of ours.

THE WORLD AND THE QUIETIST. 27 *1849, 1855*: to the Monarch's side.
28 *1849, 1855*: He spoke: the Monarch heard: *1877*: He spoke—the
Great King heard

Us not the daily quickening race
Of the invading populace
Shall draw to swell that shouldering herd;
Mourn will we not your closing hour,   10
Ye imbeciles in present power,
        Doom'd, pompous, and absurd!

And let us bear, that they debate
Of all the engine-work of state,
Of commerce, laws, and policy,   15
The secrets of the world's machine,
And what the rights of man may mean,
        With readier tongue than we.

Only, that with no finer art
They cloak the troubles of the heart   20
With pleasant smile, let us take care;
Nor with a lighter hand dispose
Fresh garlands of this dewy rose,
        To crown Eugenia's hair.

Of little threads our life is spun,   25
And he spins ill, who misses one.
But is thy fair Eugenia cold?
Yet Helen had an equal grace,
And Juliet's was as fair a face,
        And now their years are told.   30

The day approaches, when we must
Be crumbling bones and windy dust;
And scorn us as our mistress may,
Her beauty will no better be
Than the poor face she slights in thee,   35
        When dawns that day, that day.

THE SECOND BEST

[*First published 1852. Reprinted 1867 and thereafter*]

MODERATE tasks and moderate leisure,
Quiet living, strict-kept measure
Both in suffering and in pleasure—
    'Tis for this thy nature yearns.

But so many books thou readest, 5
But so many schemes thou breedest,
But so many wishes feedest,
    That thy poor head almost turns.

And (the world's so madly jangled,
Human things so fast entangled) 10
Nature's wish must now be strangled
    For that best which she discerns.

So it *must* be! yet, while leading
A strain'd life, while overfeeding,
Like the rest, his wit with reading, 15
    No small profit that man earns,

Who through all he meets can steer him,
Can reject what cannot clear him,
Cling to what can truly cheer him;
    Who each day more surely learns 20

That an impulse, from the distance
Of his deepest, best existence,
To the words, 'Hope, Light, Persistence,'
    Strongly sets and truly burns.

13 *1852*: So it must be: **24** *1852–68*: Strongly stirs

CONSOLATION

[*First published 1852. Reprinted 1853, '54, '57, '69, and thereafter*]

MIST clogs the sunshine.
Smoky dwarf houses
Hem me round everywhere;
A vague dejection
Weighs down my soul.　　　　　5

Yet, while I languish,
Everywhere countless
Prospects unroll themselves,
And countless beings
Pass countless moods.　　　　　10

Far hence, in Asia,
On the smooth convent-roofs,
On the gilt terraces,
Of holy Lassa,
Bright shines the sun.　　　　　15

Grey time-worn marbles
Hold the pure Muses;
In their cool gallery,
By yellow Tiber,
They still look fair.　　　　　20

Strange unloved uproar*
Shrills round their portal;
Yet not on Helicon
Kept they more cloudless
Their noble calm.　　　　　25

* Written during the siege of Rome by the French, 1849. [M. A.]

1853, 1854: these lines printed as a motto to the poem:
　　　　The wide earth is still
　　Wider than one man's passion: there's no mood,
　　No meditation, no delight, no sorrow,
　　Cas'd in one man's dimensions, can distil
　　Such pregnant and infectious quality,
　　Six yards round shall not ring it.—

13 *1852–81:* gold terraces,

Through sun-proof alleys
In a lone, sand-hemm'd
City of Africa,
A blind, led beggar,
Age-bow'd, asks alms.   30

No bolder robber
Erst abode ambush'd
Deep in the sandy waste;
No clearer eyesight
Spied prey afar.   35

Saharan sand-winds
Sear'd his keen eyeballs;
Spent is the spoil he won.
For him the present
Holds only pain.   40

Two young, fair lovers,
Where the warm June-wind,
Fresh from the summer fields
Plays fondly round them,
Stand, tranced in joy.   45

With sweet, join'd voices,
And with eyes brimming:
'Ah,' they cry, 'Destiny,
Prolong the present!
Time, stand still here!'   50

The prompt stern Goddess
Shakes her head, frowning;
Time gives his hour-glass
Its due reversal;
Their hour is gone.   55

With weak indulgence
Did the just Goddess
Lengthen their happiness,
She lengthen'd also
Distress elsewhere.   60

CONSOLATION

The hour, whose happy
Unalloy'd moments
I would eternalise,
Ten thousand mourners
Well pleased see end.   65

The bleak, stern hour,
Whose severe moments
I would annihilate,
Is pass'd by others
In warmth, light, joy.   70

Time, so complain'd of,
Who to no one man
Shows partiality,
Brings round to all men
Some undimm'd hours.   75

RESIGNATION

TO FAUSTA

[*First published 1849. Reprinted 1855, '69, and thereafter*

To die be given us, or attain!
Fierce work it were, to do again.
So pilgrims, bound for Mecca, pray'd
At burning noon; so warriors said,
Scarf'd with the cross, who watch'd the miles   5
Of dust which wreathed their struggling files
Down Lydian mountains; so, when snows
Round Alpine summits, eddying rose,
The Goth, bound Rome-wards; so the Hun,
Crouch'd on his saddle, while the sun   10
Went lurid down o'er flooded plains
Through which the groaning Danube strains
To the drear Euxine;—so pray all,
Whom labours, self-ordain'd, enthrall;

RESIGNATION. 6 *1849–77*: dust that   10 *1849–69*: when the sun

Because they to themselves propose   15
On this side the all-common close
A goal which, gain'd, may give repose.
So pray they; and to stand again
Where they stood once, to them were pain;
Pain to thread back and to renew   20
Past straits, and currents long steer'd through.

But milder natures, and more free—
Whom an unblamed serenity
Hath freed from passions, and the state
Of struggle these necessitate;   25
Whom schooling of the stubborn mind
Hath made, or birth hath found, resign'd—
These mourn not, that their goings pay
Obedience to the passing day.
These claim not every laughing Hour   30
For handmaid to their striding power;
Each in her turn, with torch uprear'd,
To await their march; and when appear'd,
Through the cold gloom, with measured race,
To usher for a destined space   35
(Her own sweet errands all forgone)
The too imperious traveller on.
These, Fausta, ask not this; nor thou,
Time's chafing prisoner, ask it now!

  We left, just ten years since, you say,   40
That wayside inn we left to-day.[5]
Our jovial host, as forth we fare,
Shouts greeting from his easy chair.
High on a bank our leader stands,
Reviews and ranks his motley bands,   45
Makes clear our goal to every eye—
The valley's western boundary.
A gate swings to! our tide hath flow'd
Already from the silent road.
The valley-pastures, one by one,   50

Are threaded, quiet in the sun;
And now beyond the rude stone bridge
Slopes gracious up the western ridge.
Its woody border, and the last
Of its dark upland farms is past—   55
Cool farms, with open-lying stores,
Under their burnish'd sycamores;
All past! and through the trees we glide,
Emerging on the green hill-side.
There climbing hangs, a far-seen sign,   60
Our wavering, many-colour'd line;
There winds, upstreaming slowly still
Over the summit of the hill.
And now, in front, behold outspread
Those upper regions we must tread!   65
Mild hollows, and clear heathy swells,
The cheerful silence of the fells.
Some two hours' march with serious air,
Through the deep noontide heats we fare;
The red-grouse, springing at our sound,   70
Skims, now and then, the shining ground;
No life, save his and ours, intrudes
Upon these breathless solitudes.
O joy! again the farms appear.
Cool shade is there, and rustic cheer;   75
There springs the brook will guide us down,
Bright comrade, to the noisy town.
Lingering, we follow down; we gain
The town, the highway, and the plain.
And many a mile of dusty way,   80
Parch'd and road-worn, we made that day;
But, Fausta, I remember well,
That as the balmy darkness fell
We bathed our hands with speechless glee,
That night, in the wide-glimmering sea.   85

56 *1849*: Lone farms,

Once more we tread this self-same road,
Fausta, which ten years since we trod;
Alone we tread it, you and I,
Ghosts of that boisterous company.
Here, where the brook shines, near its head,   90
In its clear, shallow, turf-fringed bed;
Here, whence the eye first sees, far down,
Capp'd with faint smoke, the noisy town;
Here sit we, and again unroll,
Though slowly, the familiar whole.   95
The solemn wastes of heathy hill
Sleep in the July sunshine still;
The self-same shadows now, as then,
Play through this grassy upland glen;
The loose dark stones on the green way   100
Lie strewn, it seems, where then they lay;
On this mild bank above the stream,
(You crush them!) the blue gentians gleam.
Still this wild brook, the rushes cool,
The sailing foam, the shining pool!   105
These are not changed; and we, you say,
Are scarce more changed, in truth, than they.

The gipsies, whom we met below,
They, too, have long roam'd to and fro;
They ramble, leaving, where they pass,   110
Their fragments on the cumber'd grass.
And often to some kindly place
Chance guides the migratory race,
Where, though long wanderings intervene,
They recognise a former scene.   115
The dingy tents are pitch'd; the fires
Give to the wind their wavering spires;
In dark knots crouch round the wild flame
Their children, as when first they came;
They see their shackled beasts again   120
Move, browsing, up the gray-wall'd lane.

Signs are not wanting, which might raise
The ghost in them of former days—
Signs are not wanting, if they would;
Suggestions to disquietude.   125
For them, for all, time's busy touch,
While it mends little, troubles much.
Their joints grow stiffer—but the year
Runs his old round of dubious cheer;
Chilly they grow—yet winds in March,   130
Still, sharp as ever, freeze and parch;
They must live still—and yet, God knows,
Crowded and keen the country grows;
It seems as if, in their decay,
The law grew stronger every day.   135
So might they reason, so compare,
Fausta, times past with times that are.
But no!—they rubb'd through yesterday
In their hereditary way,
And they will rub through, if they can,   140
To-morrow on the self-same plan,
Till death arrive to supersede,
For them, vicissitude and need.

The poet, to whose mighty heart
Heaven doth a quicker pulse impart,   145
Subdues that energy to scan
Not his own course, but that of man.
Though he move mountains, though his day
Be pass'd on the proud heights of sway,
Though he hath loosed a thousand chains,   150
Though he hath borne immortal pains,
Action and suffering though he know—
He hath not lived, if he lives so.
He sees, in some great-historied land,
A ruler of the people stand,   155
Sees his strong thought in fiery flood

123 *1849–69*: The ghosts   142 *1849–69*: Till death arrives

56

Roll through the heaving multitude;
Exults—yet for no moment's space
Envies the all-regarded place.
Beautiful eyes meet his—and he   160
Bears to admire uncravingly;
They pass—he, mingled with the crowd,
Is in their far-off triumphs proud.
From some high station he looks down,
At sunset, on a populous town;   165
Surveys each happy group, which fleets,
Toil ended, through the shining streets,
Each with some errand of its own—
And does not say: *I am alone.*
He sees the gentle stir of birth   170
When morning purifies the earth;
He leans upon a gate and sees
The pastures, and the quiet trees.
Low, woody hill, with gracious bound,
Folds the still valley almost round;   175
The cuckoo, loud on some high lawn,
Is answer'd from the depth of dawn;
In the hedge straggling to the stream,
Pale, dew-drench'd, half-shut roses gleam;
But, where the farther side slopes down,   180
He sees the drowsy new-waked clown
In his white quaint-embroider'd frock
Make, whistling, tow'rd his mist-wreathed flock—
Slowly, behind his heavy tread,
The wet, flower'd grass heaves up its head.   185
Lean'd on his gate, he gazes—tears
Are in his eyes, and in his ears
The murmur of a thousand years.
Before him he sees life unroll,
A placid and continuous whole—   190

166 *1849, 1855*: that fleets,   180 *1849–69*: further
183 *1849, 1855*: towards   *1869–81*: toward   184 *1849, 1855*: the
heavy tread

57

That general life, which does not cease,
Whose secret is not joy, but peace;
That life, whose dumb wish is not miss'd
If birth proceeds, if things subsist;
The life of plants, and stones, and rain,   195
The life he craves—if not in vain
Fate gave, what chance shall not control,
His sad lucidity of soul.

You listen—but that wandering smile,
Fausta, betrays you cold the while!   200
Your eyes pursue the bells of foam
Wash'd, eddying, from this bank, their home.
Those gipsies, so your thoughts I scan,
Are less, the poet more, than man.
They feel not, though they move and see;   205
Deeper the poet feels; but he
Breathes, when he will, immortal air,
Where Orpheus and where Homer are.
In the day's life, whose iron round
Hems us all in, he is not bound;   210
He leaves his kind, o'erleaps their pen,
And flees the common life of men.
He escapes thence, but we abide—
Not deep the poet sees, but wide.

The world in which we live and move   215
Outlasts aversion, outlasts love,
Outlasts each effort, interest, hope,
Remorse, grief, joy;—and were the scope
Of these affections wider made,
Man still would see, and see dismay'd,   220
Beyond his passion's widest range,
Far regions of eternal change.
Nay, and since death, which wipes out man,
Finds him with many an unsolved plan,

206 *1849–77: Deeply the Poet*   211, 212 *These lines were added in*
1881.

58

With much unknown, and much untried,   225
Wonder not dead, and thirst not dried,
Still gazing on the ever full
Eternal mundane spectacle—
This world in which we draw our breath,
In some sense, Fausta, outlasts death.   230

Blame thou not, therefore, him who dares
Judge vain beforehand human cares;
Whose natural insight can discern
What through experience others learn;
Who needs not love and power, to know   235
Love transient, power an unreal show;
Who treads at ease life's uncheer'd ways—
Him blame not, Fausta, rather praise!
Rather thyself for some aim pray
Nobler than this, to fill the day;   240
Rather that heart, which burns in thee,
Ask, not to amuse, but to set free;
Be passionate hopes not ill resign'd
For quiet, and a fearless mind.
And though fate grudge to thee and me   245
The poet's rapt security,
Yet they, believe me, who await
No gifts from chance, have conquer'd fate.
They, winning room to see and hear,
And to men's business not too near,   250
Through clouds of individual strife
Draw homeward to the general life.
Like leaves by suns not yet uncurl'd;
To the wise, foolish; to the world,
Weak;—yet not weak, I might reply,   255
Not foolish, Fausta, in His eye,
To whom each moment in its race,
Crowd as we will its neutral space,
Is but a quiet watershed

252 *1849*, *1855*: homewards   257 *1849*: Each moment as it flies,
to whom,   258 *1849*: its neutral room,

Whence, equally, the seas of life and death are fed.   260

Enough, we live!—and if a life,
With large results so little rife,
Though bearable, seem hardly worth
This pomp of worlds, this pain of birth;
Yet, Fausta, the mute turf we tread,   265
The solemn hills around us spread,
This stream which falls incessantly,
The strange-scrawl'd rocks, the lonely sky,
If I might lend their life a voice,
Seem to bear rather than rejoice.   270
And even could the intemperate prayer
Man iterates, while these forbear,
For movement, for an ampler sphere,
Pierce Fate's impenetrable ear;
Not milder is the general lot   275
Because our spirits have forgot,
In action's dizzying eddy whirl'd,
The something that infects the world.

267 *1849, 1855*: stream that

NARRATIVE POEMS

SOHRAB AND RUSTUM [6]

AN EPISODE

[First published 1853. Reprinted 1854, '57, '69, and thereafter]

AND the first grey of morning fill'd the east,
And the fog rose out of the Oxus stream.
But all the Tartar camp along the stream
Was hush'd, and still the men were plunged in sleep;
Sohrab alone, he slept not; all night long   5
He had lain wakeful, tossing on his bed;
But when the grey dawn stole into his tent,
He rose, and clad himself, and girt his sword,
And took his horseman's cloak, and left his tent,
And went abroad into the cold wet fog,   10
Through the dim camp to Peran-Wisa's tent.
   Through the black Tartar tents he pass'd, which stood
Clustering like bee-hives on the low flat strand
Of Oxus, where the summer-floods o'erflow
When the sun melts the snows in high Pamere;   15
Through the black tents he pass'd, o'er that low strand,
And to a hillock came, a little back
From the stream's brink—the spot where first a boat,
Crossing the stream in summer, scrapes the land.
The men of former times had crown'd the top   20
With a clay fort; but that was fall'n, and now
The Tartars built there Peran-Wisa's tent,
A dome of laths, and o'er it felts were spread.
And Sohrab came there, and went in, and stood
Upon the thick piled carpets in the tent,   25
And found the old man sleeping on his bed
Of rugs and felts, and near him lay his arms.

1 *MS.*: rays of morning streak'd *cancelled.*   10 *MS.*: cold dim
air *cancelled.*   11 *MS.*: hush'd camp   19 *MS.*: meets the land
cancelled.

And Peran-Wisa heard him, though the step
Was dull'd; for he slept light, an old man's sleep;
And he rose quickly on one arm, and said:— 30
     'Who art thou? for it is not yet clear dawn.
Speak! is there news, or any night alarm?'
     But Sohrab came to the bedside, and said:—
'Thou know'st me, Peran-Wisa! it is I.
The sun is not yet risen, and the foe 35
Sleep; but I sleep not; all night long I lie
Tossing and wakeful, and I come to thee.
For so did King Afrasiab bid me seek
Thy counsel, and to heed thee as thy son,
In Samarcand, before the army march'd; 40
And I will tell thee what my heart desires.
Thou know'st if, since from Ader-baijan first
I came among the Tartars and bore arms,
I have still served Afrasiab well, and shown,
At my boy's years, the courage of a man. 45
This too thou know'st, that while I still bear on
The conquering Tartar ensigns through the world,
And beat the Persians back on every field,
I seek one man, one man, and one alone—
Rustum, my father; who I hoped should greet, 50
Should one day greet, upon some well-fought field,
His not unworthy, not inglorious son.
So I long hoped, but him I never find.
Come then, hear now, and grant me what I ask.
Let the two armies rest to-day; but I 55
Will challenge forth the bravest Persian lords
To meet me, man to man; if I prevail,
Rustum will surely hear it; if I fall—
Old man, the dead need no one, claim no kin.
Dim is the rumour of a common fight, 60
Where host meets host, and many names are sunk;
But of a single combat fame speaks clear.'

42 *1853, 1854*: Thou knowest   *After* 59 *MS.*: But I shall conquer, that
my heart forebodes *cancelled.*

He spoke; and Peran-Wisa took the hand
Of the young man in his, and sigh'd, and said:--
  'O Sohrab, an unquiet heart is thine!   65
Canst thou not rest among the Tartar chiefs,
And share the battle's common chance with us
Who love thee, but must press for ever first,
In single fight incurring single risk,
To find a father thou hast never seen?   70
That were far best, my son, to stay with us
Unmurmuring; in our tents, while it is war,
And when 'tis truce, then in Afrasiab's towns.
But, if this one desire indeed rules all,
To seek out Rustum—seek him not through fight!   75
Seek him in peace, and carry to his arms,
O Sohrab, carry an unwounded son!
But far hence seek him, for he is not here.
For now it is not as when I was young,
When Rustum was in front of every fray;   80
But now he keeps apart, and sits at home,
In Seistan, with Zal, his father old.
Whether that his own mighty strength at last
Feels the abhorr'd approaches of old age,
Or in some quarrel with the Persian King.   85
There go!—Thou wilt not? Yet my heart forebodes
Danger or death awaits thee on this field.
Fain would I know thee safe and well, though lost
To us; fain therefore send thee hence, in peace
To seek thy father, not seek single fights   90
In vain;—but who can keep the lion's cub
From ravening, and who govern Rustum's son?
Go, I will grant thee what thy heart desires.'
  So said he, and dropp'd Sohrab's hand, and left
His bed, and the warm rugs whereon he lay;   95
And o'er his chilly limbs his woollen coat

71-3 *First inserted in 1854.*   74 *1853*: Or, if indeed this one
desire rules all,   86-7 *MS.*: *These two lines were a later insertion in
the MS.*

He pass'd, and tied his sandals on his feet,
And threw a white cloak round him, and he took
In his right hand a ruler's staff, no sword;
And on his head he set his sheep-skin cap,   100
Black, glossy, curl'd, the fleece of Kara-Kul;
And raised the curtain of his tent, and call'd
His herald to his side, and went abroad.

    The sun by this had risen, and clear'd the fog
From the broad Oxus and the glittering sands.   105
And from their tents the Tartar horsemen filed
Into the open plain; so Haman bade—
Haman, who next to Peran-Wisa ruled
The host, and still was in his lusty prime.
From their black tents, long files of horse, they stream'd;   110
As when some grey November morn the files,
In marching order spread, of long-neck'd cranes
Stream over Casbin and the southern slopes
Of Elburz, from the Aralian estuaries,
Or some frore Caspian reed-bed, southward bound   115
For the warm Persian sea-board—so they stream'd.
The Tartars of the Oxus, the King's guard,
First, with black sheep-skin caps and with long spears;
Large men, large steeds; who from Bokhara come
And Khiva, and ferment the milk of mares.   120
Next, the more temperate Toorkmuns of the south,
The Tukas, and the lances of Salore,
And those from Attruck and the Caspian sands;
Light men and on light steeds, who only drink
The acrid milk of camels, and their wells.   125
And then a swarm of wandering horse, who came
From far, and a more doubtful service own'd;
The Tartars of Ferghana, from the banks
Of the Jaxartes, men with scanty beards
And close-set skull-caps; and those wilder hordes   130

100–1 *These two lines were a later insertion in the MS.*   100 *MS.,*
1853–7: he plac'd   104 *MS.*: By this the sun   117 *MS.*: Tartars
of Bokhara *cancelled.*

64

Who roam o'er Kipchak and the northern waste,
Kalmucks and unkempt Kuzzaks, tribes who stray
Nearest the Pole, and wandering Kirghizzes,
Who come on shaggy ponies from Pamere;
These all filed out from camp into the plain.   135
And on the other side the Persians form'd;—
First a light cloud of horse, Tartars they seem'd,
The Ilyats of Khorassan; and behind,
The royal troops of Persia, horse and foot,
Marshall'd battalions bright in burnish'd steel.   140
But Peran-Wisa with his herald came,
Threading the Tartar squadrons to the front,
And with his staff kept back the foremost ranks.
And when Ferood, who led the Persians, saw
That Peran-Wisa kept the Tartars back,   145
He took his spear, and to the front he came,
And check'd his ranks, and fix'd them where they stood.
And the old Tartar came upon the sand
Betwixt the silent hosts, and spake, and said:—
   'Ferood, and ye, Persians and Tartars, hear!   150
Let there be truce between the hosts to-day.
But choose a champion from the Persian lords
To fight our champion Sohrab, man to man.'
   As, in the country, on a morn in June,
When the dew glistens on the pearled ears,   155
A shiver runs through the deep corn for joy—
So, when they heard what Peran-Wisa said,
A thrill through all the Tartar squadrons ran
Of pride and hope for Sohrab, whom they loved.
   But as a troop of pedlars, from Cabool,   160
Cross underneath the Indian Caucasus,

---

131 *MS.: The first phrase read successively,* come from Kipchak; dwell
in Kipchak; rove o'er Kipchak, *and, at last,* roam o'er   132 *1853–7:*
unkemp'd   142 *MS.:* Swift through the Tartar; swift *above* slow
deleted.   148 *MS.:* the old Tartar *deleted for* Peran Wisa; *then original
reading restored.*   149 *MS.:* and spoke   151 *1881:* Let their [*sic*]
161 *MS.:* Wind *deleted for* Climb

That vast sky-neighbouring mountain of milk snow;
Crossing so high, that, as they mount, they pass
Long flocks of travelling birds dead on the snow,
Choked by the air, and scarce can they themselves   165
Slake their parch'd throats with sugar'd mulberries—
In single file they move, and stop their breath,
For fear they should dislodge the o'erhanging snows—
So the pale Persians held their breath with fear.

   And to Ferood his brother chiefs came up   170
To counsel; Gudurz and Zoarrah came,
And Feraburz, who ruled the Persian host
Second, and was the uncle of the King;
These came and counsell'd, and then Gudurz said:—

   'Ferood, shame bids us take their challenge up,   175
Yet champion have we none to match this youth.
He has the wild stag's foot, the lion's heart.
But Rustum came last night; aloof he sits
And sullen, and has pitch'd his tents apart.
Him will I seek, and carry to his ear   180
The Tartar challenge, and this young man's name.
Haply he will forget his wrath, and fight.
Stand forth the while, and take their challenge up.'

   So spake he; and Ferood stood forth and cried:—
'Old man, be it agreed as thou hast said!   185
Let Sohrab arm, and we will find a man.'

   He spake: and Peran-Wisa turn'd, and strode
Back through the opening squadrons to his tent.
But through the anxious Persians Gudurz ran,
And cross'd the camp which lay behind, and reach'd,   190
Out on the sands beyond it, Rustum's tents.
Of scarlet cloth they were, and glittering gay,

163 *MS., 1853–77*: Winding so high   163–6 *MS.*: *These four lines,
a later insertion, written on the right-hand margin.*   167 *MS.*: In single
file they pass *deleted for* In single file they wind; *then deleted for the present
reading.*   168 *MS.*: oer' [*sic*] *inserted later.*   178 *MS.*: Rustum
deleted for Rostom; *then original spelling restored. And so regularly hereafter
in MS.*   184 *1853–69*: stood forth and said:—   187 *1853–69*:
He spoke

Just pitch'd; the high pavilion in the midst
Was Rustum's, and his men lay camp'd around.
And Gudurz enter'd Rustum's tent, and found   195
Rustum; his morning meal was done, but still
The table stood before him, charged with food—
A side of roasted sheep, and cakes of bread,
And dark green melons; and there Rustum sate
Listless, and held a falcon on his wrist,   200
And play'd with it; but Gudurz came and stood
Before him; and he look'd, and saw him stand,
And with a cry sprang up and dropp'd the bird,
And greeted Gudurz with both hands, and said:—
    'Welcome! these eyes could see no better sight.   205
What news? but sit down first, and eat and drink.'
    But Gudurz stood in the tent-door, and said:—
'Not now! a time will come to eat and drink,
But not to-day; to-day has other needs.
The armies are drawn out, and stand at gaze;   210
For from the Tartars is a challenge brought
To pick a champion from the Persian lords
To fight their champion—and thou know'st his name—
Sohrab men call him, but his birth is hid.
O Rustum, like thy might is this young man's!   215
He has the wild stag's foot, the lion's heart;
And he is young, and Iran's chiefs are old,
Or else too weak; and all eyes turn to thee.
Come down and help us, Rustum, or we lose!'
    He spoke; but Rustum answer'd with a smile:—   220
'Go to! if Iran's chiefs are old, then I
Am older; if the young are weak, the King
Errs strangely; for the King, for Kai Khosroo,
Himself is young, and honours younger men,
And lets the aged moulder to their graves.   225
Rustum he loves no more, but loves the young—

193 *MS.*: New pitch'd *cancelled.*   197 *MS., 1853–7*: stood beside him
197 *MS.*: with cates *deleted for present reading.*   198 *MS.*: cakes *over*
loaves *deleted.*   216 *MS.*: hath *deleted for* has

The young may rise at Sohrab's vaunts, not I.
For what care I, though all speak Sohrab's fame?
For would that I myself had such a son,
And not that one slight helpless girl I have—   230
A son so famed, so brave, to send to war,
And I to tarry with the snow-hair'd Zal,
My father, whom the robber Afghans vex,
And clip his borders short, and drive his herds,
And he has none to guard his weak old age.   235
There would I go, and hang my armour up,
And with my great name fence that weak old man,
And spend the goodly treasures I have got,
And rest my age, and hear of Sohrab's fame,
And leave to death the hosts of thankless kings,   240
And with these slaughterous hands draw sword no more.'

    He spoke, and smiled; and Gudurz made reply:—
'What then, O Rustum, will men say to this,
When Sohrab dares our bravest forth, and seeks
Thee most of all, and thou, whom most he seeks,   245
Hidest thy face? Take heed lest men should say:
Like some old miser, Rustum hoards his fame,
And shuns to peril it with younger men.'

    And, greatly moved, then Rustum made reply:—
'O Gudurz, wherefore dost thou say such words?   250
Thou knowest better words than this to say.
What is one more, one less, obscure or famed,
Valiant or craven, young or old, to me?
Are not they mortal, am not I myself?
But who for men of nought would do great deeds?   255
Come, thou shalt see how Rustum hoards his fame!
But I will fight unknown, and in plain arms;

228 *MS.*: What irks it me that men speak Sohrab's praise? *deleted; then half a line written above,* I am not wrong'd when, *deleted; then, on next page, at top,* For what care I, that Sohrab's fame quench theirs? *Then deleted, and, below, after the comma, the present reading.*   231 *MS.*: A son so prais'd, *deleted for* A son so fam'd; *then* A son so prais'd [?]; *then,* fam'd *restored.* 232 *MS.*: white-hair'd Zal *cancelled.*   234 *MS.*: borders round *cancelled.* 236 *MS.*: would I stay, *cancelled.*

Let not men say of Rustum, he was match'd
In single fight with any mortal man.'
    He spoke, and frown'd; and Gudurz turn'd, and ran   260
Back quickly through the camp in fear and joy—
Fear at his wrath, but joy that Rustum came.
But Rustum strode to his tent-door, and call'd
His followers in, and bade them bring his arms,
And clad himself in steel; the arms he chose   265
Were plain, and on his shield was no device,
Only his helm was rich, inlaid with gold,
And, from the fluted spine atop, a plume
Of horsehair waved, a scarlet horsehair plume.
So arm'd, he issued forth; and Ruksh, his horse,   270
Follow'd him like a faithful hound at heel—
Ruksh, whose renown was noised through all the earth,
The horse, whom Rustum on a foray once
Did in Bokhara by the river find
A colt beneath its dam, and drove him home,   275
And rear'd him; a bright bay, with lofty crest,
Dight with a saddle-cloth of broider'd green
Crusted with gold, and on the ground were work'd
All beasts of chase, all beasts which hunters know.
So follow'd, Rustum left his tents, and cross'd   280
The camp, and to the Persian host appear'd.
And all the Persians knew him, and with shouts
Hail'd; but the Tartars knew not who he was.
And dear as the wet diver to the eyes
Of his pale wife who waits and weeps on shore,   285
By sandy Bahrein, in the Persian Gulf,
Plunging all day in the blue waves, at night,
Having made up his tale of precious pearls,

262 *MS.*: and joy, *cancelled.*   275 *MS.*: beside its dam, *cancelled.*
276 *MS.*: train'd him; *cancelled.*   280 *MS.*: Rustum issued forth *cancelled.*
284 *MS.*: wet fisher *cancelled.*   285 *MS.*: weeps ashore, *cancelled.*
286 *MS.*: At twilight, on a stormy eve in March, *cancelled.*   287–8 *MS.*:
               Running fast homeward with the turn of tide
               Beaches the pinnace in a darkening cove
deleted for the present passage, which is written in above the respective lines.

Rejoins her in their hut upon the sands—
So dear to the pale Persians Rustum came.   290
    And Rustum to the Persian front advanced,
And Sohrab arm'd in Haman's tent, and came.
And as afield the reapers cut a swath
Down through the middle of a rich man's corn,
And on each side are squares of standing corn,   295
And in the midst a stubble, short and bare—
So on each side were squares of men, with spears
Bristling, and in the midst, the open sand.
And Rustum came upon the sand, and cast
His eyes toward the Tartar tents, and saw   300
Sohrab come forth, and eyed him as he came.
    As some rich woman, on a winter's morn,
Eyes through her silken curtains the poor drudge
Who with numb blacken'd fingers makes her fire—
At cock-crow, on a starlit winter's morn,   305
When the frost flowers the whiten'd window-panes—
And wonders how she lives, and what the thoughts
Of that poor drudge may be; so Rustum eyed
The unknown adventurous youth, who from afar
Came seeking Rustum, and defying forth   310
All the most valiant chiefs; long he perused
His spirited air, and wonder'd who he was.
For very young he seem'd, tenderly rear'd;
Like some young cypress, tall, and dark, and straight,
Which in a queen's secluded garden throws   315
Its slight dark shadow on the moonlit turf,
By midnight, to a bubbling fountain's sound—
So slender Sohrab seem'd, so softly rear'd.
And a deep pity enter'd Rustum's soul
As he beheld him coming; and he stood,   320
And beckon'd to him with his hand, and said:—
    'O thou young man, the air of Heaven is soft,

293 *MS.*, *1853–7*: swathe   300 *1853–69*: towards   302 *MS.*
rich lady *cancelled*.   309 *MS.*: who through the world *cancelled*
310 *MS.*: Went seeking *cancelled*.   312 *MS.*: His face and air *cancelled*

And warm, and pleasant; but the grave is cold!
Heaven's air is better than the cold dead grave.
Behold me! I am vast, and clad in iron,   325
And tried; and I have stood on many a field
Of blood, and I have fought with many a foe—
Never was that field lost, or that foe saved.
O Sohrab, wherefore wilt thou rush on death?
Be govern'd! quit the Tartar host, and come   330
To Iran, and be as my son to me,
And fight beneath my banner till I die!
There are no youths in Iran brave as thou.'

   So he spake, mildly; Sohrab heard his voice,
The mighty voice of Rustum, and he saw   335
His giant figure planted on the sand,
Sole, like some single tower, which a chief
Hath builded on the waste in former years
Against the robbers; and he saw that head,
Streak'd with its first grey hairs;—hope filled his soul, 340
And he ran forward and embraced his knees,
And clasp'd his hand within his own, and said:—

   'O, by thy father's head! by thine own soul!
Art thou not Rustum? speak! art thou not he?'

   But Rustum eyed askance the kneeling youth,   345
And turn'd away, and spake to his own soul:—

   'Ah me, I muse what this young fox may mean!
False, wily, boastful, are these Tartar boys.
For if I now confess this thing he asks,
And hide it not, but say: *Rustum is here!*   350
He will not yield indeed, nor quit our foes,
But he will find some pretext not to fight,
And praise my fame, and proffer courteous gifts,
A belt or sword perhaps, and go his way.
And on a feast-tide, in Afrasiab's hall,   355

338 *MS.*: Hath *deleted for* Has   *1853–7*: Has builded   *MS.*: former
days *cancelled.*   341 *1853–7*: forwards   346 *1853–69*: spoke
to his   352 *MS.*: Then will he find *cancelled.*   355 *1853–4*: on a
feast day

In Samarcand, he will arise and cry:
"I challenged once, when the two armies camp'd
Beside the Oxus, all the Persian lords
To cope with me in single fight; but they
Shrank, only Rustum dared; then he and I 360
Changed gifts, and went on equal terms away."
So will he speak, perhaps, while men applaud;
Then were the chiefs of Iran shamed through me.'
 And then he turn'd, and sternly spake aloud:—
'Rise! wherefore dost thou vainly question thus 365
Of Rustum? I am here, whom thou hast call'd
By challenge forth; make good thy vaunt, or yield!
Is it with Rustum only thou wouldst fight?
Rash boy, men look on Rustum's face and flee!
For well I know, that did great Rustum stand 370
Before thy face this day, and were reveal'd,
There would be then no talk of fighting more.
But being what I am, I tell thee this—
Do thou record it in thine inmost soul:
Either thou shalt renounce thy vaunt and yield, 375
Or else thy bones shall strew this sand, till winds
Bleach them, or Oxus with his summer-floods,
Oxus in summer wash them all away.'
 He spoke; and Sohrab answer'd, on his feet:—
'Art thou so fierce? Thou wilt not fright me so! 380
I am no girl, to be made pale by words.
Yet this thou hast said well, did Rustum stand
Here on this field, there were no fighting then.
But Rustum is far hence, and we stand here.
Begin! thou art more vast, more dread than I, 385
And thou art proved, I know, and I am young—
But yet success sways with the breath of Heaven.
And though thou thinkest that thou knowest sure
Thy victory, yet thou canst not surely know.
For we are all, like swimmers in the sea, 390
Poised on the top of a huge wave of fate,
Which hangs uncertain to which side to fall.

And whether it will heave us up to land,
Or whether it will roll us out to sea,
Back out to sea, to the deep waves of death,　　　　395
We know not, and no search will make us know;
Only the event will teach us in its hour.'

He spoke, and Rustum answer'd not, but hurl'd
His spear; down from the shoulder, down it came,
As on some partridge in the corn a hawk,　　　　400
That long has tower'd in the airy clouds,
Drops like a plummet; Sohrab saw it come,
And sprang aside, quick as a flash; the spear
Hiss'd, and went quivering down into the sand,
Which it sent flying wide;—then Sohrab threw　　　　405
In turn, and full struck Rustum's shield; sharp rang,
The iron plates rang sharp, but turn'd the spear.
And Rustum seized his club, which none but he
Could wield; an unlopp'd trunk it was, and huge,
Still rough—like those which men in treeless plains　　　　410
To build them boats fish from the flooded rivers,
Hyphasis or Hydaspes, when, high up
By their dark springs, the wind in winter-time
Hath made in Himalayan forests wrack,
And strewn the channels with torn boughs—so huge　　　　415
The club which Rustum lifted now, and struck
One stroke; but again Sohrab sprang aside,
Lithe as the glancing snake, and the club came
Thundering to earth, and leapt from Rustum's hand.
And Rustum follow'd his own blow, and fell　　　　420
To his knees, and with his fingers clutch'd the sand;
And now might Sohrab have unsheathed his sword,
And pierced the mighty Rustum while he lay

408 *MS.*: Then *cancelled.*　　　　409 *MS.*: it was, still rough *cancelled.*
1881: and unlopp'd [*sic*]　　　410 *MS.*: Still rough *inserted above.*　　　410
MS.: men who dwell in treeless plains *cancelled.*　　　411 *MS.*: To saw them
planks *cancelled.*　　　　414 *MS.*: Hath *deleted for* Has *inserted above.*
1853–69: Has　　　415 *MS.*: so rough *cancelled.*　　　421 *MS.*: grasp'd
the sand *cancelled.*

Dizzy, and on his knees, and choked with sand;
But he look'd on, and smiled, nor bared his sword,   425
But courteously drew back, and spoke, and said:—

'Thou strik'st too hard! that club of thine will float
Upon the summer-floods, and not my bones.
But rise, and be not wroth! not wroth am I;
No, when I see thee, wrath forsakes my soul.   430
Thou say'st, thou art not Rustum; be it so!
Who art thou then, that canst so touch my soul?
Boy as I am, I have seen battles too—
Have waded foremost in their bloody waves,
And heard their hollow roar of dying men;   435
But never was my heart thus touch'd before.
Are they from Heaven, these softenings of the heart?
O thou old warrior, let us yield to Heaven!
Come, plant we here in earth our angry spears,
And make a truce, and sit upon this sand,   440
And pledge each other in red wine, like friends,
And thou shalt talk to me of Rustum's deeds.
There are enough foes in the Persian host,
Whom I may meet, and strike, and feel no pang;
Champions enough Afrasiab has, whom thou   445
Mayst fight; fight *them*, when they confront thy spear!
But oh, let there be peace 'twixt thee and me!'

He ceased, but while he spake, Rustum had risen,
And stood erect, trembling with rage; his club
He left to lie, but had regain'd his spear,   450
Whose fiery point now in his mail'd right-hand
Blazed bright and baleful, like that autumn-star,
The baleful sign of fevers; dust had soil'd
His stately crest, and dimm'd his glittering arms.
His breast heaved, his lips foam'd, and twice his voice   455
Was choked with rage; at last these words broke way:—

'Girl! nimble with thy feet, not with thy hands!
Curl'd minion, dancer, coiner of sweet words!

425 *MS.*: drew his sword *cancelled.*
446 *MS., 1853–7: no italics.*

Fight, let me hear thy hateful voice no more!
Thou art not in Afrasiab's gardens now   460
With Tartar girls, with whom thou art wont to dance;
But on the Oxus-sands, and in the dance
Of battle, and with me, who make no play
Of war; I fight it out, and hand to hand.
Speak not to me of truce, and pledge, and wine!   465
Remember all thy valour; try thy feints
And cunning! all the pity I had is gone;
Because thou hast shamed me before both the hosts
With thy light skipping tricks, and thy girl's wiles.' *from*
  He spoke, and Sohrab kindled at his taunts,   470
And he too drew his sword; at once they rush'd
Together, as two eagles on one prey
Come rushing down together from the clouds,
One from the east, one from the west; their shields
Dash'd with a clang together, and a din   475
Rose, such as that the sinewy woodcutters
Make often in the forest's heart at morn,
Of hewing axes, crashing trees—such blows
Rustum and Sohrab on each other hail'd.
And you would say that sun and stars took part   480
In that unnatural conflict; for a cloud
Grew suddenly in Heaven, and dark'd the sun
Over the fighters' heads; and a wind rose
Under their feet, and moaning swept the plain,
And in a sandy whirlwind wrapp'd the pair.   485
In gloom they twain were wrapp'd, and they alone;
For both the on-looking hosts on either hand
Stood in broad daylight, and the sky was pure,
And the sun sparkled on the Oxus stream.
But in the gloom they fought, with bloodshot eyes   490
And labouring breath; first Rustum struck the shield
Which Sohrab held stiff out; the steel-spiked spear

477 *MS.*: forest's depth   484 *MS.*: Eddying and moaning round, and
swept the plain,   488 *MS.*: bright daylight   492 *MS.*:
held advanc'd   spiked *struck out, but written in again above.*

Rent the tough plates, but fail'd to reach the skin,
And Rustum pluck'd it back with angry groan.
Then Sohrab with his sword smote Rustum's helm,   495
Nor clove its steel quite through; but all the crest
He shore away, and that proud horsehair plume,
Never till now defiled, sank to the dust;
And Rustum bow'd his head; but then the gloom
Grew blacker, thunder rumbled in the air,   500
And lightnings rent the cloud; and Ruksh, the horse,
Who stood at hand, utter'd a dreadful cry;—
No horse's cry was that, most like the roar
Of some pain'd desert-lion, who all day
Hath trail'd the hunter's javelin in his side,   505
And comes at night to die upon the sand.
The two hosts heard that cry, and quaked for fear,
And Oxus curdled as it cross'd his stream.
But Sohrab heard, and quail'd not, but rush'd on,
And struck again; and again Rustum bow'd   510
His head; but this time all the blade, like glass,
Sprang in a thousand shivers on the helm,
And in the hand the hilt remain'd alone.
Then Rustum raised his head; his dreadful eyes
Glared, and he shook on high his menacing spear,   515
And shouted: *Rustum!*—Sohrab heard that shout,
And shrank amazed; back he recoil'd one step,
And scann'd with blinking eyes the advancing form;
And then he stood bewilder'd; and he dropp'd
His covering shield, and the spear pierced his side. 520
He reel'd, and staggering back, sank to the ground;
And then the gloom dispersed, and the wind fell,
And the bright sun broke forth, and melted all

493 *MS.*: but miss'd, *deleted for* fail'd, *which is struck out, then written in
again.*   498 *MS.*: never defac'd till now, sham'd to the dust.
1853–7: sunk to   500 *MS.*: Grew deeper, thunder crash'd along the sky,
505 *1853–81*: Has trail'd   508 *MS.*: as it reach'd   509 *MS.*: but
sprang on   513 *1853–7*: in his hand   517 *MS.*: one pace,
521 *1853–7*: sunk to the ground

The cloud; and the two armies saw the pair—
Saw Rustum standing, safe upon his feet, 525
And Sohrab, wounded, on the bloody sand.

Then, with a bitter smile, Rustum began:—
'Sohrab, thou thoughtest in thy mind to kill
A Persian lord this day, and strip his corpse,
And bear thy trophies to Afrasiab's tent. 530
Or else that the great Rustum would come down
Himself to fight, and that thy wiles would move
His heart to take a gift, and let thee go.
And then that all the Tartar host would praise
Thy courage or thy craft, and spread thy fame, 535
To glad thy father in his weak old age.
Fool, thou art slain, and by an unknown man!
Dearer to the red jackals shalt thou be
Than to thy friends, and to thy father old.'

And, with a fearless mien, Sohrab replied:— 540
'Unknown thou art; yet thy fierce vaunt is vain.
Thou dost not slay me, proud and boastful man!
No! Rustum slays me, and this filial heart.
For were I match'd with ten such men as thee,
And I were that which till to-day I was, 545
They should be lying here, I standing there.
But that belovéd name unnerved my arm—
That name, and something, I confess, in thee,
Which troubles all my heart, and made my shield
Fall; and thy spear transfix'd an unarm'd foe. 550
And now thou boastest, and insult'st my fate.
But hear thou this, fierce man, tremble to hear:
The mighty Rustum shall avenge my death!
My father, whom I seek through all the world,
He shall avenge my death, and punish thee!' 555

As when some hunter in the spring hath found
A breeding eagle sitting on her nest,

544-5 *1853–77*:
For were I match'd with ten such men as thou,
And I were he who till to-day I was,

Upon the craggy isle of a hill-lake,
And pierced her with an arrow as she rose,
And follow'd her to find her where she fell   560
Far off;—anon her mate comes winging back
From hunting, and a great way off descries
His huddling young left sole; at that, he checks
His pinion, and with short uneasy sweeps
Circles above his eyry, with loud screams   565
Chiding his mate back to her nest; but she
Lies dying, with the arrow in her side,
In some far stony gorge out of his ken,
A heap of fluttering feathers—never more
Shall the lake glass her, flying over it;   570
Never the black and dripping precipices
Echo her stormy scream as she sails by—
As that poor bird flies home, nor knows his loss,
So Rustum knew not his own loss, but stood
Over his dying son, and knew him not.   575

But, with a cold incredulous voice, he said:—
'What prate is this of fathers and revenge?
The mighty Rustum never had a son.'

And, with a failing voice, Sohrab replied:—
'Ah yes, he had! and that lost son am I.   580
Surely the news will one day reach his ear,
Reach Rustum, where he sits, and tarries long,
Somewhere, I know not where, but far from here;
And pierce him like a stab, and make him leap
To arms, and cry for vengeance upon thee.   585
Fierce man, bethink thee, for an only son!
What will that grief, what will that vengeance be?
Oh, could I live, till I that grief had seen!
Yet him I pity not so much, but her,
My mother, who in Ader-baijan dwells   590
With that old king, her father, who grows grey
With age, and rules over the valiant Koords.
Her most I pity, who no more will see

576 *1881* (*only*): And, with a cold

78

Sohrab returning from the Tartar camp,
With spoils and honour, when the war is done.   595
But a dark rumour will be bruited up,
From tribe to tribe, until it reach her ear;
And then will that defenceless woman learn
That Sohrab will rejoice her sight no more,
But that in battle with a nameless foe,   600
By the far-distant Oxus, he is slain.'

   He spoke; and as he ceased, he wept aloud,
Thinking of her he left, and his own death.
He spoke; but Rustum listen'd, plunged in thought.
Nor did he yet believe it was his son   605
Who spoke, although he call'd back names he knew;
For he had had sure tidings that the babe,
Which was in Ader-baijan born to him,
Had been a puny girl, no boy at all—
So that sad mother sent him word, for fear   610
Rustum should seek the boy, to train in arms.
And so he deem'd that either Sohrab took,
By a false boast, the style of Rustum's son;
Or that men gave it him, to swell his fame.
So deem'd he; yet he listen'd, plunged in thought   615
And his soul set to grief, as the vast tide
Of the bright rocking Ocean sets to shore
At the full moon; tears gather'd in his eyes;
For he remember'd his own early youth,
And all its bounding rapture; as, at dawn,   620
The shepherd from his mountain-lodge descries
A far, bright city, smitten by the sun,
Through many rolling clouds—so Rustum saw
His youth; saw Sohrab's mother, in her bloom;
And that old king, her father, who loved well   625
His wandering guest, and gave him his fair child
With joy; and all the pleasant life they led,
They three, in that long-distant summer-time—
The castle, and the dewy woods, and hunt

611 *1853–69*: take the boy

And hound, and morn on those delightful hills   630
In Ader-baijan. And he saw that youth,
Of age and looks to be his own dear son,
Piteous and lovely, lying on the sand,
Like some rich hyacinth which by the scythe
Of an unskilful gardener has been cut,   635
Mowing the garden grass-plots near its bed,
And lies, a fragrant tower of purple bloom,
On the mown, dying grass—so Sohrab lay,
Lovely in death, upon the common sand.
And Rustum gazed on him with grief, and said:—   640
  'O Sohrab, thou indeed art such a son
Whom Rustum, wert thou his, might well have loved.
Yet here thou errest, Sohrab, or else men
Have told thee false—thou art not Rustum's son.
For Rustum had no son; one child he had—   645
But one—a girl; who with her mother now
Plies some light female task, nor dreams of us—
Of us she dreams not, nor of wounds, nor war.'
  But Sohrab answer'd him in wrath; for now
The anguish of the deep-fix'd spear grew fierce,   650
And he desired to draw forth the steel,
And let the blood flow free, and so to die—
But first he would convince his stubborn foe;
And, rising sternly on one arm, he said:—
  'Man, who art thou who dost deny my words?   655
Truth sits upon the lips of dying men,
And falsehood, while I lived, was far from mine.
I tell thee, prick'd upon this arm I bear
That seal which Rustum to my mother gave,
That she might prick it on the babe she bore.'   660
  He spoke; and all the blood left Rustum's cheeks,
And his knees totter'd, and he smote his hand
Against his breast, his heavy mailed hand,
That the hard iron corslet clank'd aloud;
And to his heart he press'd the other hand,   665
And in a hollow voice he spake, and said:—

'Sohrab, that were a proof which could not lie!
If thou show this, then art thou Rustum's son.'
    Then, with weak hasty fingers, Sohrab loosed
His belt, and near the shoulder bared his arm,   670
And show'd a sign in faint vermilion points
Prick'd; as a cunning workman, in Pekin,
Pricks with vermilion some clear porcelain vase,
An emperor's gift—at early morn he paints,
And all day long, and, when night comes, the lamp   675
Lights up his studious forehead and thin hands—
So delicately prick'd the sign appear'd
On Sohrab's arm, the sign of Rustum's seal.
It was that griffin, which of old rear'd Zal,
Rustum's great father, whom they left to die,   680
A helpless babe, among the mountain-rocks;
Him that kind creature found, and rear'd, and loved—
Then Rustum took it for his glorious sign.
And Sohrab bared that image on his arm,
And himself scann'd it long with mournful eyes,   685
And then he touch'd it with his hand and said:—
    'How say'st thou? Is that sign the proper sign
Of Rustum's son, or of some other man's?'
    He spoke; but Rustum gazed, and gazed, and stood
Speechless; and then he utter'd one sharp cry: 690
O boy—thy father!—and his voice choked there.
And then a dark cloud pass'd before his eyes,
And his head swam, and he sank down to earth.
But Sohrab crawl'd to where he lay, and cast
His arms about his neck, and kiss'd his lips,   695
And with fond faltering fingers stroked his cheeks,
Trying to call him back to life; and life
Came back to Rustum, and he oped his eyes,
And they stood wide with horror; and he seized
In both his hands the dust which lay around,   700
And threw it on his head, and smirch'd his hair,—

684 *1853–77*: that figure
693 *1853–7*: sunk down

His hair, and face, and beard, and glittering arms;
And strong convulsive groanings shook his breast,
And his sobs choked him; and he clutch'd his sword,
To draw it, and for ever let life out.   705
But Sohrab saw his thought, and held his hands,
And with a soothing voice he spake, and said:—

'Father, forbear! for I but meet to-day
The doom which at my birth was written down
In Heaven, and thou art Heaven's unconscious hand.   710
Surely my heart cried out that it was thou,
When first I saw thee; and thy heart spoke too,
I know it! but fate trod those promptings down
Under its iron heel; fate, fate engaged
The strife, and hurl'd me on my father's spear.   715
But let us speak no more of this! I find
My father; let me feel that I have found!
Come, sit beside me on this sand, and take
My head betwixt thy hands, and kiss my cheeks,
And wash them with thy tears, and say: *My son!*   720
Quick! quick! for number'd are my sands of life,
And swift; for like the lightning to this field
I came, and like the wind I go away—
Sudden, and swift, and like a passing wind.
But it was writ in Heaven that this should be.'   725
So said he, and his voice released the heart
Of Rustum, and his tears broke forth; he cast
His arms round his son's neck, and wept aloud,
And kiss'd him. And awe fell on both the hosts,
When they saw Rustum's grief; and Ruksh, the horse,   730
With his head bowing to the ground and mane
Sweeping the dust, came near, and in mute woe
First to the one then to the other moved
His head, as if inquiring what their grief
Might mean; and from his dark, compassionate eyes,   735
The big warm tears roll'd down, and caked the sand.
But Rustum chid him with stern voice, and said:—

707 *1853–77*: he spoke   709 *1853–69*: doom that

'Ruksh, now thou grievest; but, O Ruksh, thy feet
Should first have rotted on their nimble joints,
Or ere they brought thy master to this field!'   740
    But Sohrab look'd upon the horse and said;—
'Is this, then, Ruksh? How often, in past days,
My mother told me of thee, thou brave steed,
My terrible father's terrible horse! and said,
That I should one day find thy lord and thee.   745
Come, let me lay my hand upon thy mane!
O Ruksh, thou art more fortunate than I;
For thou hast gone where I shall never go,
And snuff'd the breezes of my father's home.
And thou hast trod the sands of Seistan,   750
And seen the River of Helmund, and the Lake
Of Zirrah; and the aged Zal himself
Has often stroked thy neck, and given thee food,
Corn in a golden platter soak'd with wine,
And said: *O Ruksh! bear Rustum well!*—but I   755
Have never known my grandsire's furrow'd face,
Nor seen his lofty house in Seistan,
Nor slaked my thirst at the clear Helmund stream;
But lodged among my father's foes, and seen
Afrasiab's cities only, Samarcand,   760
Bokhara, and lone Khiva in the waste,
And the black Toorkmun tents; and only drunk
The desert rivers, Moorghab and Tejend,
Kohik, and where the Kalmuks feed their sheep,
The northern Sir; and this great Oxus stream,   765
The yellow Oxus, by whose brink I die.'
    Then, with a heavy groan, Rustum bewail'd:—
'Oh, that its waves were flowing over me!
Oh, that I saw its grains of yellow silt
Roll tumbling in the current o'er my head!'   770

739 *1853–7:* Should then have rotted on thy nimble joints,   *1869–*
81: Should then have rotted on their nimble joints,   740 *1853–78,*
1881: When first they bore   *1885:* Or ere they brought (*as in present
reading*)   767 *1853–77:* And, with a heavy groan, Rustum replied:—

But, with a grave mild voice, Sohrab replied:—
'Desire not that, my father! thou must live.
For some are born to do great deeds, and live,
As some are born to be obscured, and die.
Do thou the deeds I die too young to do,   775
And reap a second glory in thine age;
Thou art my father, and thy gain is mine.
But come! thou seest this great host of men
Which follow me; I pray thee, slay not these!
Let me entreat for them; what have they done?   780
They follow'd me, my hope, my fame, my star.
Let them all cross the Oxus back in peace.
But me thou must bear hence, not send with them,
But carry me with thee to Seistan,
And place me on a bed, and mourn for me,   785
Thou, and the snow-hair'd Zal, and all thy friends.
And thou must lay me in that lovely earth,
And heap a stately mound above my bones,
And plant a far-seen pillar over all.
That so the passing horseman on the waste   790
May see my tomb a great way off, and cry:
Sohrab, the mighty Rustum's son, lies there,
Whom his great father did in ignorance kill!
And I be not forgotten in my grave.'

        And, with a mournful voice, Rustum replied:—   795
'Fear not! as thou hast said, Sohrab, my son,
So shall it be; for I will burn my tents,
And quit the host, and bear thee hence with me,
And carry thee away to Seistan,
And place thee on a bed, and mourn for thee,   800
With the snow-headed Zal, and all my friends.
And I will lay thee in that lovely earth,
And heap a stately mound above thy bones,
And plant a far-seen pillar over all,
And men shall not forget thee in thy grave.   805
And I will spare thy host; yea, let them go!

    771 *1853–77*: And, with   791 *1853–69*: and say:

84

Let them all cross the Oxus back in peace!
What should I do with slaying any more?
For would that all whom I have ever slain
Might be once more alive; my bitterest foes,   810
And they who were call'd champions in their time,
And through whose death I won that fame I have—
And I were nothing but a common man,
A poor, mean soldier, and without renown,
So thou mightest live too, my son, my son!   815
Or rather would that I, even I myself,
Might now be lying on this bloody sand,
Near death, and by an ignorant stroke of thine,
Not thou of mine! and I might die, not thou;
And I, not thou, be borne to Seistan;   820
And Zal might weep above my grave, not thine;
And say: *O son, I weep thee not too sore,*
For willingly, I know, thou met'st thine end!
But now in blood and battles was my youth,
And full of blood and battles is my age,   825
And I shall never end this life of blood.'

   Then, at the point of death, Sohrab replied:—
'A life of blood indeed, thou dreadful man!
But thou shalt yet have peace; only not now,
Not yet! but thou shalt have it on that day,   830
When thou shalt sail in a high-masted ship,
Thou and the other peers of Kai Khosroo,
Returning home over the salt blue sea,
From laying thy dear master in his grave.'

   And Rustum gazed in Sohrab's face, and said:—   835
'Soon be that day, my son, and deep that sea!
Till then, if fate so wills, let me endure.'

   He spoke; and Sohrab smiled on him, and took
The spear, and drew it from his side, and eased
His wound's imperious anguish; but the blood   840
Came welling from the open gash, and life

809 *1890 (only)*: all that I have ever slain   818 *In 1854 the word*
of *was inadvertently dropped.*   835 *1853–7*: gazed on

Flow'd with the stream;—all down his cold white side
The crimson torrent ran, dim now and soil'd,
Like the soil'd tissue of white violets
Left, freshly gather'd, on their native bank,   845
By children whom their nurses call with haste
Indoors from the sun's eye; his head droop'd low,
His limbs grew slack; motionless, white, he lay—
White, with eyes closed; only when heavy gasps,
Deep heavy gasps quivering through all his frame,   850
Convulsed him back to life, he open'd them,
And fix'd them feebly on his father's face;
Till now all strength was ebb'd, and from his limbs
Unwillingly the spirit fled away,
Regretting the warm mansion which it left,   855
And youth, and bloom, and this delightful world.
      So, on the bloody sand, Sohrab lay dead;
And the great Rustum drew his horseman's cloak
Down o'er his face, and sate by his dead son.
As those black granite pillars, once high-rear'd   860
By Jemshid in Persepolis, to bear
His house, now 'mid their broken flights of steps
Lie prone, enormous, down the mountain side—
So in the sand lay Rustum by his son.
      And night came down over the solemn waste,   865
And the two gazing hosts, and that sole pair,
And darken'd all; and a cold fog, with night,
Crept from the Oxus. Soon a hum arose,
As of a great assembly loosed, and fires
Began to twinkle through the fog; for now   870
Both armies moved to camp, and took their meal;
The Persians took it on the open sands
Southward, the Tartars by the river marge;
And Rustum and his son were left alone.
      But the majestic river floated on,   875

843 *1853*: torrent pour'd,   846 *1853–77*: By romping children
whom their nurses call   847 *1853–7*: From the hot fields at noon:
1869: From the hot field at noon:

Out of the mist and hum of that low land,
Into the frosty starlight, and there moved,
Rejoicing, through the hush'd Chorasmian waste,
Under the solitary moon;—he flow'd
Right for the polar star, past Orgunjè,   880
Brimming, and bright, and large; then sands begin
To hem his watery march, and dam his streams,
And split his currents; that for many a league
The shorn and parcell'd Oxus strains along
Through beds of sand and matted rushy isles—   885
Oxus, forgetting the bright speed he had
In his high mountain-cradle in Pamere,
A foil'd circuitous wanderer—till at last
The long'd-for dash of waves is heard, and wide
His luminous home of waters opens, bright   890
And tranquil, from whose floor the new-bathed stars
Emerge, and shine upon the Aral Sea.

THE SICK KING IN BOKHARA

[*First published 1849. Reprinted 1855, 1869, and thereafter*]

Hussein

O MOST just Vizier, send away
The cloth-merchants, and let them be,
Them and their dues, this day! the King
Is ill at ease, and calls for thee.

The Vizier

O merchants, tarry yet a day   5
Here in Bokhara! but at noon,
To-morrow, come, and ye shall pay
Each fortieth web of cloth to me,
As the law is, and go your way.
O Hussein, lead me to the King!   10
Thou teller of sweet tales, thine own,

Ferdousi's, and the others', lead!
How is it with my lord?

Hussein

Alone,
Ever since prayer-time, he doth wait,
O Vizier! without lying down,   15
In the great window of the gate,
Looking into the Registàn,
Where through the sellers' booths the slaves
Are this way bringing the dead man.—
O Vizier, here is the King's door!   20

The King

O Vizier, I may bury him?

The Vizier

O King, thou know'st, I have been sick
These many days, and heard no thing
(For Allah shut my ears and mind),
Not even what thou dost, O King!   25
Wherefore, that I may counsel thee,
Let Hussein, if thou wilt, make haste
To speak in order what hath chanced.

The King

O Vizier, be it as thou say'st!

Hussein

Three days since, at the time of prayer   30
A certain Moollah, with his robe
All rent, and dust upon his hair,
Watch'd my lord's coming forth, and push'd
The golden mace-bearers aside,
And fell at the King's feet, and cried: 35

'Justice, O King, and on myself!
On this great sinner, who did break
The law, and by the law must die!
Vengeance, O King!'

But the King spake:
'What fool is this, that hurts our ears   40
With folly? or what drunken slave?
My guards, what, prick him with your spears!
Prick me the fellow from the path!'
As the King said, so it was done,
And to the mosque my lord pass'd on.   45

But on the morrow, when the King
Went forth again, the holy book
Carried before him, as is right,
And through the square his way he took;
My man comes running, fleck'd with blood   50
From yesterday, and falling down
Cries out most earnestly: 'O King,
My lord, O King, do right, I pray!

'How canst thou, ere thou hear, discern
If I speak folly? but a king,   55
Whether a thing be great or small,
Like Allah, hears and judges all.

'Wherefore hear thou! Thou know'st, how fierce
In these last days the sun hath burn'd;
That the green water in the tanks   60
Is to a putrid puddle turn'd;
And the canal, which from the stream
Of Samarcand is brought this way,
Wastes, and runs thinner every day.

---

37 *1849–69*: who hath broke   39 *1849–69*: spoke: 44 *1849–*
77: so was it done   49 *1849–77*: through the square his path he took;
62 *1849–81*: that from the stream

'Now I at nightfall had gone forth   65
Alone, and in a darksome place
Under some mulberry-trees I found
A little pool; and in short space,
With all the water that was there
I fill'd my pitcher, and stole home   70
Unseen; and having drink to spare,
I hid the can behind the door,
And went up on the roof to sleep.

'But in the night, which was with wind
And burning dust, again I creep   75
Down, having fever, for a drink.

'Now meanwhile had my brethren found
The water-pitcher, where it stood
Behind the door upon the ground,
And call'd my mother; and they all,   80
As they were thirsty, and the night
Most sultry, drain'd the pitcher there;
That they sate with it, in my sight,
Their lips still wet, when I came down.

'Now mark! I, being fever'd, sick   85
(Most unblest also), at that sight
Brake forth, and cursed them—dost thou hear?—
One was my mother——Now, do right!'

But my lord mused a space, and said:
'Send him away, Sirs, and make on!   90
It is some madman!' the King said.
As the King bade, so was it done.

The morrow, at the self-same hour,
In the King's path, behold, the man,
Not kneeling, sternly fix'd! he stood   95
Right opposite, and thus began,

68 *1849–69*: in brief space   92 *1849–69*: As the King said,

90

Frowning grim down: 'Thou wicked King,
Most deaf where thou shouldst most give ear!
What, must I howl in the next world,
Because thou wilt not listen here?   100

'What, wilt thou pray, and get thee grace,
And all grace shall to me be grudged?
Nay but, I swear, from this thy path
I will not stir till I be judged!'

Then they who stood about the King   105
Drew close together and conferr'd;
Till that the King stood forth and said:
'Before the priests thou shalt be heard.'

But when the Ulemas were met,
And the thing heard, they doubted **not;**   110
But sentenced him, as the law is,
To die by stoning on the spot.

Now the King charged us secretly:
'Stoned must he be, the law stands so.
Yet, if he seek to fly, give way;   115
Hinder him not, but let him go.'

So saying, the King took a stone,
And cast it softly;—but the man,
With a great joy upon his face,
Kneel'd down, and cried not, neither ran.   120

So they, whose lot it was, cast stones,
That they flew thick and bruised him sore.
But he praised Allah with loud voice,
And remain'd kneeling as before.

My lord had cover'd up his face;   125
But when one told him, 'He is dead,'
Turning him quickly to go in,
'Bring thou to me his corpse,' he said.

109 *1849*: Ulema   116 *1849, 1855*: Forbid him **not,**

And truly, while I speak, O King,
I hear the bearers on the stair;   130
Wilt thou they straightway bring him in?
—Ho! enter ye who tarry there!

The Vizier

O King, in this I praise thee not!
Now must I call thy grief not wise.
Is he thy friend, or of thy blood,   135
To find such favour in thine eyes?

Nay, were he thine own mother's son,
Still, thou art king, and the law stands.
It were not meet the balance swerved,
The sword were broken in thy hands.   140

But being nothing, as he is,
Why for no cause make sad thy face?—
Lo, I am old! three kings, ere thee,
Have I seen reigning in this place.

But who, through all this length of time,   145
Could bear the burden of his years,
If he for strangers pain'd his heart
Not less than those who merit tears?

Fathers we *must* have, wife and child,
And grievous is the grief for these;   150
This pain alone, which *must* be borne,
Makes the head white, and bows the knees.

But other loads than this his own
One man is not well made to bear.
Besides, to each are his own friends,   155
To mourn with him, and show him care.

Look, this is but one single place,
Though it be great; all the earth round,
If a man bear to have it so,
Things which might vex him shall be found.   160

Upon the Russian frontier, where
The watchers of two armies stand
Near one another, many a man,
Seeking a prey unto his hand,

Hath snatch'd a little fair-hair'd slave;   165
They snatch also, towards Mervè,
The Shiah dogs, who pasture sheep,
And up from thence to Orgunjè.

And these all, labouring for a lord,
Eat not the fruit of their own hands;   170
Which is the heaviest of all plagues,
To that man's mind, who understands.

The kaffirs also (whom God curse!)
Vex one another, night and day;
There are the lepers, and all sick;   175
There are the poor, who faint alway.

All these have sorrow, and keep still,
Whilst other men make cheer, and sing.
Wilt thou have pity on all these?
No, nor on this dead dog, O King!   180

The King

O Vizier, thou art old, I young!
Clear in these things I cannot see.
My head is burning, and a heat
Is in my skin which angers me.

But hear ye this, ye sons of men!   185
They that bear rule, and are obey'd,
Unto a rule more strong than theirs
Are in their turn obedient made.

In vain therefore, with wistful eyes
Gazing up hither, the poor man,   190
Who loiters by the high-heap'd booths,
Below there, in the Registàn,

161 *1849*: Upon the northern frontier,   168 *1849*: Urghendjè.

Says: 'Happy he, who lodges there!
With silken raiment, store of rice,
And for this drought, all kinds of fruits,   195
Grape-syrup, squares of colour'd ice,

'With cherries serv'd in drifts of snow.'
In vain hath a king power to build
Houses, arcades, enamell'd mosques;
And to make orchard-closes, fill'd   200

With curious fruit-trees brought from far;
With cisterns for the winter-rain,
And, in the desert, spacious inns
In divers places—if that pain

Is not more lighten'd, which he feels,   205
If his will be not satisfied;
And that it be not, from all time
The law is planted, to abide.

Thou wast a sinner, thou poor man!
Thou wast athirst; and didst not see,   210
That, though we take what we desire,
We must not snatch it eagerly.

And I have meat and drink at will,
And rooms of treasures, not a few.
But I am sick, nor heed I these;   215
And what I would, I cannot do.

Even the great honour which I have,
When I am dead, will soon grow still;
So have I neither joy, nor fame.
But what I can do, that I will.   220

I have a fretted brick-work tomb
Upon a hill on the right hand,
Hard by a close of apricots,
Upon the road of Samarcand;

201 *1849, 1855*: fruit trees, bought from   209, 210 *1849, 1855*: Thou wert
211 *1849–69*: though we snatch

Thither, O Vizier, will I bear   225
This man my pity could not save,
And, plucking up the marble flags,
There lay his body in my grave.

Bring water, nard, and linen rolls!
Wash off all blood, set smooth each limb!   230
Then say: 'He was not wholly vile,
Because a king shall bury him.'

BALDER DEAD[7]

[First published 1855. Reprinted 1869 and thereafter]

I. SENDING

So on the floor lay Balder dead; and round
Lay thickly strewn swords, axes, darts, and spears,
Which all the Gods in sport had idly thrown
At Balder, whom no weapon pierced or clove;
But in his breast stood fixt the fatal bough   5
Of mistletoe, which Lok the Accuser gave
To Hoder, and unwitting Hoder threw—
'Gainst that alone had Balder's life no charm.
    And all the Gods and all the Heroes came,
And stood round Balder on the bloody floor,   10
Weeping and wailing; and Valhalla rang
Up to its golden roof with sobs and cries;
And on the tables stood the untasted meats,
And in the horns and gold-rimm'd skulls the wine.
And now would night have fall'n and found them yet 15
Wailing; but otherwise was Odin's will.
And thus the father of the ages spake:—
    'Enough of tears, ye Gods, enough of wail!
Not to lament in was Valhalla made.

227 *1849*: And, tearing up
    BALDER DEAD. *Title, 1855*: Balder Dead / An Episode.
I. *Sending.* 14 *1855–81*: sculls

If any here might weep for Balder's death,　　　　20
I most might weep, his father; such a son
I lose to-day, so bright, so loved a God.
But he has met that doom, which long ago
The Nornies, when his mother bare him, spun,
And fate set seal, that so his end must be.　　　　25
Balder has met his death, and ye survive—
Weep him an hour, but what can grief avail?
For ye yourselves, ye Gods, shall meet your doom,
All ye who hear me, and inhabit Heaven,
And I too, Odin too, the Lord of all.　　　　30
But ours we shall not meet, when that day comes,
With women's tears and weak complaining cries—
Why should we meet another's portion so?
Rather it fits you, having wept your hour,
With cold dry eyes, and hearts composed and stern,　　　　35
To live, as erst, your daily life in Heaven.
By me shall vengeance on the murderer Lok,
The foe, the accuser, whom, though Gods, we hate,
Be strictly cared for, in the appointed day.
Meanwhile, to-morrow, when the morning dawns,　　　　40
Bring wood to the seashore to Balder's ship,
And on the deck build high a funeral-pile,
And on the top lay Balder's corpse, and put
Fire to the wood, and send him out to sea
To burn; for that is what the dead desire.'　　　　45
　　So spake the King of Gods, and straightway rose,
And mounted his horse Sleipner, whom he rode;
And from the hall of Heaven he rode away
To Lidskialf, and sate upon his throne,
The mount, from whence his eye surveys the world.　　　　50
And far from Heaven he turn'd his shining orbs
To look on Midgard, and the earth, and men.
And on the conjuring Lapps he bent his gaze
Whom antler'd reindeer pull over the snow;

28 *1855*: For you　32 *1855, 1869*: woman's tears　46 *1855, 1869*: So
having spoke, the King of Gods arose

And on the Finns, the gentlest of mankind,   55
Fair men, who live in holes under the ground;
Nor did he look once more to Ida's plain,
Nor tow'rd Valhalla, and the sorrowing Gods;
For well he knew the Gods would heed his word,
And cease to mourn, and think of Balder's pyre.   60
   But in Valhalla all the Gods went back
From around Balder, all the Heroes went;
And left his body stretch'd upon the floor.
And on their golden chairs they sate again,
Beside the tables, in the hall of Heaven;   65
And before each the cooks who served them placed
New messes of the boar Serimner's flesh,
And the Valkyries crown'd their horns with mead.
So they, with pent-up hearts and tearless eyes,
Wailing no more, in silence ate and drank,   70
While twilight fell, and sacred night came on.
   But the blind Hoder left the feasting Gods
In Odin's hall, and went through Asgard streets,
And past the haven where the Gods have moor'd
Their ships, and through the gate, beyond the wall;   75
Though sightless, yet his own mind led the God.
Down to the margin of the roaring sea
He came, and sadly went along the sand,
Between the waves and black o'erhanging cliffs
Where in and out the screaming seafowl fly;   80
Until he came to where a gully breaks
Through the cliff-wall, and a fresh stream runs down
From the high moors behind, and meets the sea.
There, in the glen, Fensaler stands, the house
Of Frea, honour'd mother of the Gods,   85
And shows its lighted windows to the main.
There he went up, and pass'd the open doors;
And in the hall he found those women old,
The prophetesses, who by rite eterne
On Frea's hearth feed high the sacred fire   90

58 *1855*: towards

Both night and day; and by the inner wall
Upon her golden chair the Mother sate,
With folded hands, revolving things to come.
To her drew Hoder near, and spake, and said:—

  'Mother, a child of bale thou bar'st in me!   95
For, first, thou barest me with blinded eyes,
Sightless and helpless, wandering weak in Heaven;
And, after that, of ignorant witless mind
Thou barest me, and unforeseeing soul;
That I alone must take the branch from Lok,   100
The foe, the accuser, whom, though Gods, we hate,
And cast it at the dear-loved Balder's breast
At whom the Gods in sport their weapons threw—
'Gainst that alone had Balder's life no charm.
Now therefore what to attempt, or whither fly,   105
For who will bear my hateful sight in Heaven?
Can I, O mother, bring them Balder back?
Or—for thou know'st the fates, and things allow'd—
Can I with Hela's power a compact strike,
And make exchange, and give my life for his?'   110

  He spoke: the mother of the Gods replied:—
'Hoder, ill-fated, child of bale, my son,
Sightless in soul and eye, what words are these?
That one, long portion'd with his doom of death,
Should change his lot, and fill another's life,   115
And Hela yield to this, and let him go!
On Balder Death hath laid her hand, not thee;
Nor doth she count this life a price for that.
For many Gods in Heaven, not thou alone,
Would freely die to purchase Balder back,   120
And wend themselves to Hela's gloomy realm.
For not so gladsome is that life in Heaven
Which Gods and heroes lead, in feast and fray,
Waiting the darkness of the final times,
That one should grudge its loss for Balder's sake,   125
Balder their joy, so bright, so loved a God.
But fate withstands, and laws forbid this way.

Yet in my secret mind one way I know,
Nor do I judge if it shall win or fail;
But much must still be tried, which shall but fail.'   130
    And the blind Hoder answer'd her, and said:—
'What way is this, O mother, that thou show'st?
Is it a matter which a God might try?'
    And straight the mother of the Gods replied:—
'There is a road which leads to Hela's realm,   135
Untrodden, lonely, far from light and Heaven.
Who goes that way must take no other horse
To ride, but Sleipner, Odin's horse, alone.
Nor must he choose that common path of Gods
Which every day they come and go in Heaven,   140
O'er the bridge Bifrost, where is Heimdall's watch,
Past Midgard fortress, down to earth and men.
But he must tread a dark untravell'd road
Which branches from the north of Heaven, and ride
Nine days, nine nights, toward the northern ice,   145
Through valleys deep-engulph'd, with roaring streams.
And he will reach on the tenth morn a bridge
Which spans with golden arches Giall's stream,
Not Bifrost, but that bridge a damsel keeps,
Who tells the passing troops of dead their way   150
To the low shore of ghosts, and Hela's realm.
And she will bid him northward steer his course.
Then he will journey through no lighted land,
Nor see the sun arise, nor see it set;
But he must ever watch the northern Bear,   155
Who from her frozen height with jealous eye
Confronts the Dog and Hunter in the south,
And is alone not dipt in Ocean's stream.
And straight he will come down to Ocean's strand—
Ocean, whose watery ring enfolds the world,   160
And on whose marge the ancient giants dwell.
But he will reach its unknown northern shore,

135 _1855–81_: There is a way   _MS. alteration (in 1881 volume)_: a road
145 _1855_: towards

Far, far beyond the outmost giant's home,
At the chink'd fields of ice, the waste of snow.
And he must fare across the dismal ice   165
Northward, until he meets a stretching wall
Barring his way, and in the wall a grate.
But then he must dismount, and on the ice
Tighten the girths of Sleipner, Odin's horse,
And make him leap the grate, and come within.   170
And he will see stretch round him Hela's realm,
The plains of Niflheim, where dwell the dead,
And hear the roaring of the streams of Hell.
And he will see the feeble, shadowy tribes,
And Balder sitting crown'd, and Hela's throne.   175
Then must he not regard the wailful ghosts
Who all will flit, like eddying leaves, around;
But he must straight accost their solemn queen,
And pay her homage, and entreat with prayers,
Telling her all that grief they have in Heaven   180
For Balder, whom she holds by right below;
If haply he may melt her heart with words,
And make her yield, and give him Balder back.'

    She spoke; but Hoder answer'd her and said:—
'Mother, a dreadful way is this thou show'st;   185
No journey for a sightless God to go!'

    And straight the mother of the Gods replied:—
'Therefore thyself thou shalt not go, my son.
But he whom first thou meetest when thou com'st
To Asgard, and declar'st this hidden way,   190
Shall go; and I will be his guide unseen.'

    She spoke, and on her face let fall her veil,
And bow'd her head, and sate with folded hands,
But at the central hearth those women old,
Who while the Mother spake had ceased their toil, 195
Began again to heap the sacred fire.
And Hoder turn'd, and left his mother's house,
Fensaler, whose lit windows look to sea;

165 *1855*: And he will fare   176 *1855, 1869*: Then he must not

And came again down to the roaring waves,
And back along the beach to Asgard went,   200
Pondering on that which Frea said should be.
    But night came down, and darken'd Asgard streets.
Then from their loathéd feast the Gods arose,
And lighted torches, and took up the corpse
Of Balder from the floor of Odin's hall,   205
And laid it on a bier, and bare him home
Through the fast-darkening streets to his own house,
Breidablik, on whose columns Balder graved
The enchantments that recall the dead to life.
For wise he was, and many curious arts,   210
Postures of runes, and healing herbs he knew;
Unhappy! but that art he did not know,
To keep his own life safe, and see the sun.
There to his hall the Gods brought Balder home,
And each bespake him as he laid him down:—   215
    'Would that ourselves, O Balder, we were borne
Home to our halls, with torchlight, by our kin,
So thou might'st live, and still delight the Gods!'
    They spake; and each went home to his own house.
But there was one, the first of all the Gods   220
For speed, and Hermod was his name in Heaven;
Most fleet he was, but now he went the last,
Heavy in heart for Balder, to his house,
Which he in Asgard built him, there to dwell,
Against the harbour, by the city-wall.   225
Him the blind Hoder met, as he came up
From the sea cityward, and knew his step;
Nor yet could Hermod see his brother's face,
For it grew dark; but Hoder touch'd his arm.
And as a spray of honeysuckle flowers   230
Brushes across a tired traveller's face
Who shuffles through the deep dew-moisten'd dust,
On a May evening, in the darken'd lanes,
And starts him, that he thinks a ghost went by—
So Hoder brush'd by Hermod's side, and said:—   235

'Take Sleipner, Hermod, and set forth with dawn
To Hela's kingdom, to ask Balder back;
And they shall be thy guides, who have the power.'

He spake, and brush'd soft by, and disappear'd.
And Hermod gazed into the night, and said:—   240

'Who is it utters through the dark his hest
So quickly, and will wait for no reply?
The voice was like the unhappy Hoder's voice.
Howbeit I will see, and do his hest;
For there rang note divine in that command.'   245

So speaking, the fleet-footed Hermod came
Home, and lay down to sleep in his own house;
And all the Gods lay down in their own homes.
And Hoder too came home, distraught with grief,
Loathing to meet, at dawn, the other Gods;   250
And he went in, and shut the door, and fixt
His sword upright, and fell on it, and died.

But from the hill of Lidskialf Odin rose,
The throne, from which his eye surveys the world;
And mounted Sleipner, and in darkness rode   255
To Asgard. And the stars came out in heaven,
High over Asgard, to light home the King.
But fiercely Odin gallop'd, moved in heart;
And swift to Asgard, to the gate, he came.
And terribly the hoofs of Sleipner rang   260
Along the flinty floor of Asgard streets,
And the Gods trembled on their golden beds
Hearing the wrathful Father coming home—
For dread, for like a whirlwind, Odin came.
And to Valhalla's gate he rode, and left   265
Sleipner; and Sleipner went to his own stall;
And in Valhalla Odin laid him down.

But in Breidablik, Nanna, Balder's wife,
Came with the Goddesses who wrought her will,
And stood by Balder lying on his bier.   270
And at his head and feet she station'd Scalds

270 *1855*: stood round Balder

102

Who in their lives were famous for their song;
These o'er the corpse intoned a plaintive strain,
A dirge—and Nanna and her train replied.
And far into the night they wail'd their dirge.   275
But when their souls were satisfied with wail,
They went, and laid them down, and Nanna went
Into an upper chamber, and lay down;
And Frea seal'd her tired lids with sleep.

  And 'twas when night is bordering hard on dawn,   280
When air is chilliest, and the stars sunk low;
Then Balder's spirit through the gloom drew near,
In garb, in form, in feature as he was,
Alive; and still the rays were round his head
Which were his glorious mark in Heaven; he stood   285
Over against the curtain of the bed,
And gazed on Nanna as she slept, and spake:—

  'Poor lamb, thou sleepest, and forgett'st thy woe!
Tears stand upon the lashes of thine eyes,
Tears wet the pillow by thy cheek; but thou,   290
Like a young child, hast cried thyself to sleep.
Sleep on; I watch thee, and am here to aid.
Alive I kept not far from thee, dear soul!
Neither do I neglect thee now, though dead.
For with to-morrow's dawn the Gods prepare   295
To gather wood, and build a funeral-pile
Upon my ship, and burn my corpse with fire,
That sad, sole honour of the dead; and thee
They think to burn, and all my choicest wealth,
With me, for thus ordains the common rite.   300
But it shall not be so; but mild, but swift,
But painless shall a stroke from Frea come,
To cut thy thread of life, and free thy soul,
And they shall burn thy corpse with mine, not thee.
And well I know that by no stroke of death,   305
Tardy or swift, would'st thou be loath to die,
So it restored thee, Nanna, to my side,
Whom thou so well hast loved; but I can smooth

Thy way, and this, at least, my prayers avail.
Yes, and I fain would altogether ward   310
Death from thy head, and with the Gods in Heaven
Prolong thy life, though not by thee desired—
But right bars this, not only thy desire.
Yet dreary, Nanna, is the life they lead
In that dim world, in Hela's mouldering realm;   315
And doleful are the ghosts, the troops of dead,
Whom Hela with austere control presides.
For of the race of Gods is no one there,
Save me alone, and Hela, solemn queen;
And all the nobler souls of mortal men   320
On battle-field have met their death, and now
Feast in Valhalla, in my father's hall;
Only the inglorious sort are there below,
The old, the cowards, and the weak are there—
Men spent by sickness, or obscure decay.   325
But even there, O Nanna, we might find
Some solace in each other's look and speech,
Wandering together through that gloomy world,
And talking of the life we led in Heaven,
While we yet lived, among the other Gods.'   330
   He spake, and straight his lineaments began
To fade; and Nanna in her sleep stretch'd out
Her arms towards him with a cry—but he
Mournfully shook his head, and disappear'd.
And as the woodman sees a little smoke   335
Hang in the air, afield, and disappear,
So Balder faded in the night away.
And Nanna on her bed sank back; but then
Frea, the mother of the Gods, with stroke
Painless and swift, set free her airy soul,   340
Which took, on Balder's track, the way below;
And instantly the sacred morn appear'd.

320 *1881 only*: For all the   338 *1855*: sunk back

2. JOURNEY TO THE DEAD

FORTH from the east, up the ascent of Heaven,
Day drove his courser with the shining mane;
And in Valhalla, from his gable-perch,
The golden-crested cock began to crow.
Hereafter, in the blackest dead of night,   5
With shrill and dismal cries that bird shall crow,
Warning the Gods that foes draw nigh to Heaven;
But now he crew at dawn, a cheerful note,
To wake the Gods and Heroes to their tasks.
And all the Gods, and all the Heroes, woke.   10
And from their beds the Heroes rose, and donn'd
Their arms, and led their horses from the stall,
And mounted them, and in Valhalla's court
Were ranged; and then the daily fray began.
And all day long they there are hack'd and hewn,   15
'Mid dust, and groans, and limbs lopp'd off, and blood;
But all at night return to Odin's hall,
Woundless and fresh; such lot is theirs in Heaven.
And the Valkyries on their steeds went forth
Tow'rd earth and fights of men; and at their side   20
Skulda, the youngest of the Nornies, rode;
And over Bifrost, where is Heimdall's watch,
Past Midgard fortress, down to earth they came;
There through some battle-field, where men fall fast,
Their horses fetlock-deep in blood, they ride,   25
And pick the bravest warriors out for death,
Whom they bring back with them at night to Heaven
To glad the Gods, and feast in Odin's hall.
    But the Gods went not now, as otherwhile,
Into the tilt-yard, where the Heroes fought,   30
To feast their eyes with looking on the fray;
Nor did they to their judgment-place repair
By the ash Igdrasil, in Ida's plain,
Where they hold council, and give laws for men.
But they went, Odin first, the rest behind,   35

20 *1855–81*: Toward Earth

To the hall Gladheim, which is built of gold;
Where are in circle ranged twelve golden chairs,
And in the midst one higher, Odin's throne.
There all the Gods in silence sate them down;
And thus the Father of the ages spake:—   40

'Go quickly, Gods, bring wood to the seashore,
With all, which it beseems the dead to have,
And make a funeral-pile on Balder's ship;
On the twelfth day the Gods shall burn his corpse.
But Hermod, thou take Sleipner, and ride down   45
To Hela's kingdom, to ask Balder back.'

So said he; and the Gods arose, and took
Axes and ropes, and at their head came Thor,
Shouldering his hammer, which the giants know.
Forth wended they, and drave their steeds before.   50
And up the dewy mountain-tracks they fared
To the dark forests, in the early dawn;
And up and down, and side and slant they roam'd.
And from the glens all day an echo came
Of crashing falls; for with his hammer Thor   55
Smote 'mid the rocks the lichen-bearded pines,
And burst their roots, while to their tops the Gods
Made fast the woven ropes, and haled them down,
And lopp'd their boughs, and clove them on the sward,
And bound the logs behind their steeds to draw,   60
And drave them homeward; and the snorting steeds
Went straining through the crackling brushwood down,
And by the darkling forest-paths the Gods
Follow'd, and on their shoulders carried boughs.
And they came out upon the plain, and pass'd   65
Asgard, and led their horses to the beach,
And loosed them of their loads on the seashore,
And ranged the wood in stacks by Balder's ship;
And every God went home to his own house.

But when the Gods were to the forest gone,   70
Hermod led Sleipner from Valhalla forth

50 1855: drove   61 1855: drove

And saddled him; before that, Sleipner brook'd
No meaner hand than Odin's on his mane,
On his broad back no lesser rider bore;
Yet docile now he stood at Hermod's side,   75
Arching his neck, and glad to be bestrode,
Knowing the God they went to seek, how dear.
But Hermod mounted him, and sadly fared
In silence up the dark untravell'd road
Which branches from the north of Heaven, and went 80
All day; and daylight waned, and night came on.
And all that night he rode, and journey'd so,
Nine days, nine nights, toward the northern ice,
Through valleys deep-engulph'd, by roaring streams.
And on the tenth morn he beheld the bridge   85
Which spans with golden arches Giall's stream,
And on the bridge a damsel watching arm'd,
In the strait passage, at the farther end,
Where the road issues between walling rocks.
Scant space that warder left for passers by;—   90
But as when cowherds in October drive
Their kine across a snowy mountain-pass
To winter-pasture on the southern side,
And on the ridge a waggon chokes the way,
Wedged in the snow; then painfully the hinds   95
With goad and shouting urge their cattle past,
Plunging through deep untrodden banks of snow
To right and left, and warm steam fills the air—
So on the bridge that damsel block'd the way,
And question'd Hermod as he came, and said:—   100

   'Who art thou on thy black and fiery horse
Under whose hoofs the bridge o'er Giall's stream
Rumbles and shakes? Tell me thy race and home.
But yestermorn, five troops of dead pass'd by,
Bound on their way below to Hela's realm,   105
Nor shook the bridge so much as thou alone.

And thou hast flesh and colour on thy cheeks,
Like men who live, and draw the vital air;
Nor look'st thou pale and wan, like men deceased,
Souls bound below, my daily passers here.'   110
    And the fleet-footed Hermod answer'd her:—
'O damsel, Hermod am I call'd, the son
Of Odin; and my high-roof'd house is built
Far hence, in Asgard, in the city of Gods;
And Sleipner, Odin's horse, is this I ride.   115
And I come, sent this road on Balder's track;
Say then, if he hath cross'd thy bridge or no?'
    He spake; the warder of the bridge replied:—
'O Hermod, rarely do the feet of Gods
Or of the horses of the Gods resound   120
Upon my bridge; and, when they cross, I know.
Balder hath gone this way, and ta'en the road
Below there, to the north, tow'rd Hela's realm.
From here the cold white mist can be discern'd,
Nor lit with sun, but through the darksome air   125
By the dim vapour-blotted light of stars,
Which hangs over the ice where lies the road.
For in that ice are lost those northern streams,
Freezing and ridging in their onward flow,
Which from the fountain of Vergelmer run,   130
The spring that bubbles up by Hela's throne.
There are the joyless seats, the haunt of ghosts,
Hela's pale swarms; and there was Balder bound.
Ride on! pass free! but he by this is there.'
    She spake, and stepp'd aside, and left him room.   135
And Hermod greeted her, and gallop'd by
Across the bridge; then she took post again.
But northward Hermod rode, the way below;
And o'er a darksome tract, which knows no sun,
But by the blotted light of stars, he fared.   140
And he came down to Ocean's northern strand,
At the drear ice, beyond the giants' home.

123 *1855–81*: toward Hela's   125 *1855–77*: Not lit

Thence on he journey'd o'er the fields of ice
Still north, until he met a stretching wall
Barring his way, and in the wall a grate.   145
Then he dismounted, and drew tight the girths,
On the smooth ice, of Sleipner, Odin's horse,
And made him leap the grate, and came within.
And he beheld spread round him Hela's realm,
The plains of Niflheim, where dwell the dead,   150
And heard the thunder of the streams of Hell.
For near the wall the river of Roaring flows,
Outmost; the others near the centre run—
The Storm, the Abyss, the Howling, and the Pain;
These flow by Hela's throne, and near their spring.   155
And from the dark flock'd up the shadowy tribes;—
And as the swallows crowd the bulrush-beds
Of some clear river, issuing from a lake,
On autumn-days, before they cross the sea;
And to each bulrush-crest a swallow hangs   160
Quivering, and others skim the river-streams,
And their quick twittering fills the banks and shores—
So around Hermod swarm'd the twittering ghosts.
Women, and infants, and young men who died
Too soon for fame, with white ungraven shields;   165
And old men, known to glory, but their star
Betray'd them, and of wasting age they died,
Not wounds; yet, dying, they their armour wore,
And now have chief regard in Hela's realm.
Behind flock'd wrangling up a piteous crew,   170
Greeted of none, disfeatured and forlorn—
Cowards, who were in sloughs interr'd alive;
And round them still the wattled hurdles hung,
Wherewith they stamp'd them down, and trod them deep,
To hide their shameful memory from men.   175
But all he pass'd unhail'd, and reach'd the throne
Of Hela, and saw, near it, Balder crown'd,

160–1 *1855–81*:   a swallow hangs
                    Swinging,

And Hela set thereon, with countenance stern;
And thus bespake him first the solemn queen:—
    'Unhappy, how hast thou endured to leave   180
The light, and journey to the cheerless land
Where idly flit about the feeble shades?
How didst thou cross the bridge o'er Giall's stream,
Being alive, and come to Ocean's shore?
Or how o'erleap the grate that bars the wall?'   185
    She spake: but down off Sleipner Hermod sprang,
And fell before her feet, and clasp'd her knees;
And spake, and mild entreated her, and said:—
    'O Hela, wherefore should the Gods declare
Their errands to each other, or the ways   190
They go? the errand and the way is known.
Thou know'st, thou know'st, what grief we have in Heaven
For Balder, whom thou hold'st by right below.
Restore him! for what part fulfils he here?
Shall he shed cheer over the cheerless seats,   195
And touch the apathetic ghosts with joy?
Not for such end, O queen, thou hold'st thy realm.
For Heaven was Balder born, the city of Gods
And Heroes, where they live in light and joy.
Thither restore him, for his place is there!'   200
    He spoke; and grave replied the solemn queen:—
'Hermod, for he thou art, thou son of Heaven!
A strange unlikely errand, sure, is thine.
Do the Gods send to me to make them blest?
Small bliss my race hath of the Gods obtained.   205
Three mighty children to my father Lok
Did Angerbode, the giantess, bring forth—
Fenris the wolf, the Serpent huge, and me.
Of these the Serpent in the sea ye cast,
Who since in your despite hath wax'd amain,   210
And now with gleaming ring enfolds the world;
Me on this cheerless nether world ye threw,
And gave me nine unlighted realms to rule;

    178 *1881 (only)*: Hela sat

While on his island in the lake afar,
Made fast to the bored crag, by wile not strength   215
Subdued, with limber chains lives Fenris bound.
Lok still subsists in Heaven, our father wise,
Your mate, though loathed, and feasts in Odin's hall;
But him too foes await, and netted snares,
And in a cave a bed of needle-rocks,   220
And o'er his visage serpents dropping gall.
Yet he shall one day rise, and burst his bonds,
And with himself set us his offspring free,
When he guides Muspel's children to their bourne.
Till then in peril or in pain we live,   225
Wrought by the Gods—and ask the Gods our aid?
Howbeit, we abide our day; till then,
We do not as some feebler haters do—
Seek to afflict our foes with petty pangs,
Helpless to better us, or ruin them.   230
Come then! if Balder was so dear beloved,
And this is true, and such a loss is Heaven's—
Hear, how to Heaven may Balder be restored.
Show me through all the world the signs of grief!
Fails but one thing to grieve, here Balder stops!   235
Let all that lives and moves upon the earth
Weep him, and all that is without life weep;
Let Gods, men, brutes, beweep him; plants and stones!
So shall I know the lost was dear indeed,
And bend my heart, and give him back to Heaven.'   240
    She spake; and Hermod answer'd her, and said:—
'Hela, such as thou say'st, the terms shall be.
But come, declare me this, and truly tell:
May I, ere I depart, bid Balder hail,
Or is it here withheld to greet the dead?'   245
    He spake, and straightway Hela answered him:—
'Hermod, greet Balder if thou wilt, and hold
Converse; his speech remains, though he be dead.'
    And straight to Balder Hermod turn'd, and spake:—

234 *1855, 1869*: though all [*sic*]

'Even in the abode of death, O Balder, hail!   250
Thou hear'st, if hearing, like as speech, is thine,
The terms of thy releasement hence to Heaven;
Fear nothing but that all shall be fulfill'd.
For not unmindful of thee are the Gods,
Who see the light, and blest in Asgard dwell;   255
Even here they seek thee out, in Hela's realm.
And sure of all the happiest far art thou
Who ever have been known in earth or Heaven;
Alive, thou wast of Gods the most beloved,
And now thou sittest crown'd by Hela's side,   260
Here, and hast honour among all the dead.'
    He spake; and Balder utter'd him reply,
But feebly, as a voice far off; he said:—
    'Hermod the nimble, gild me not my death!
Better to live a serf, a captured man,   265
Who scatters rushes in a master's hall,
Than be a crown'd king here, and rule the dead.
And now I count not of these terms as safe
To be fulfill'd, nor my return as sure,
Though I be loved, and many mourn my death;   270
For double-minded ever was the seed
Of Lok, and double are the gifts they give.
Howbeit, report thy message; and therewith,
To Odin, to my father, take this ring,
Memorial of me, whether saved or no;   275
And tell the Heaven-born Gods how thou hast seen
Me sitting here below by Hela's side,
Crown'd, having honour among all the dead.'
    He spake, and raised his hand, and gave the ring.
And with inscrutable regard the queen   280
Of Hell beheld them, and the ghosts stood dumb.
But Hermod took the ring, and yet once more
Kneel'd and did homage to the solemn queen;
Then mounted Sleipner, and set forth to ride
Back, through the astonish'd tribes of dead, to Heaven. 285

And to the wall he came, and found the grate
Lifted, and issued on the fields of ice.
And o'er the ice he fared to Ocean's strand,
And up from thence, a wet and misty road,
To the arm'd damsel's bridge, and Giall's stream.   290
Worse was that way to go than to return,
For him;—for others all return is barr'd.
Nine days he took to go, two to return,
And on the twelfth morn saw the light of Heaven.
And as a traveller in the early dawn   295
To the steep edge of some great valley comes,
Through which a river flows, and sees, beneath,
Clouds of white rolling vapours fill the vale,
But o'er them, on the farther slope, descries
Vineyards, and crofts, and pastures, bright with sun— 300
So Hermod, o'er the fog between, saw Heaven.
And Sleipner snorted, for he smelt the air
Of Heaven; and mightily, as wing'd, he flew.
And Hermod saw the towers of Asgard rise;
And he drew near, and heard no living voice   305
In Asgard; and the golden halls were dumb.
Then Hermod knew what labour held the Gods;
And through the empty streets he rode, and pass'd
Under the gate-house to the sands, and found
The Gods on the sea-shore by Balder's ship.   310

3. FUNERAL

THE Gods held talk together, group'd in knots,
Round Balder's corpse, which they had thither borne;
And Hermod came down tow'rds them from the gate.
And Lok, the father of the serpent, first
Beheld him come, and to his neighbour spake:—   5
  'See, here is Hermod, who comes single back
From Hell; and shall I tell thee how he seems?
Like as a farmer, who hath lost his dog,

306 *1855*: but the golden halls
3. *Funeral.* 3 *1855–81*: down towards

Some morn, at market, in a crowded town—
Through many streets the poor beast runs in vain,   10
And follows this man after that, for hours;
And, late at evening, spent and panting, falls
Before a stranger's threshold, not his home,
With flanks a-tremble, and his slender tongue
Hangs quivering out between his dust-smear'd jaws,   15
And piteously he eyes the passers by;
But home his master comes to his own farm,
Far in the country, wondering where he is—
So Hermod comes to-day unfollow'd home.'

   And straight his neighbour, moved with wrath, replied:—
'Deceiver! fair in form, but false in heart!   21
Enemy, mocker, whom, though Gods, we hate—
Peace, lest our father Odin hear thee gibe!
Would I might see him snatch thee in his hand,
And bind thy carcase, like a bale, with cords,   25
And hurl thee in a lake, to sink or swim!
If clear from plotting Balder's death, to swim;
But deep, if thou devisedst it, to drown,
And perish, against fate, before thy day.'

   So they two soft to one another spake.   30
But Odin look'd toward the land, and saw
His messenger; and he stood forth, and cried.
And Hermod came, and leapt from Sleipner down,
And in his father's hand put Sleipner's rein,
And greeted Odin and the Gods, and said:—   35

   'Odin, my father, and ye, Gods of Heaven!
Lo, home, having perform'd your will, I come.
Into the joyless kingdom have I been,
Below, and look'd upon the shadowy tribes
Of ghosts, and communed with their solemn queen;   40
And to your prayer she sends you this reply:
Show her through all the world the signs of grief!
Fails but one thing to grieve, there Balder stops!
Let Gods, men, brutes, beweep him; plants and stones:

9 *1855*: One morn,

So shall she know your loss was dear indeed,   45
And bend her heart, and give you Balder back.'

He spoke; and all the Gods to Odin look'd;
And straight the Father of the ages said:—

'Ye Gods, these terms may keep another day.
But now, put on your arms, and mount your steeds,   50
And in procession all come near, and weep
Balder; for that is what the dead desire.
When ye enough have wept, then build a pile
Of the heap'd wood, and burn his corpse with fire
Out of our sight; that we may turn from grief,   55
And lead, as erst, our daily life in Heaven.'

He spoke, and the Gods arm'd; and Odin donn'd
His dazzling corslet and his helm of gold,
And led the way on Sleipner; and the rest
Follow'd, in tears, their father and their king.   60
And thrice in arms around the dead they rode,
Weeping; the sands were wetted, and their arms,
With their thick-falling tears—so good a friend
They mourn'd that day, so bright, so loved a God.
And Odin came, and laid his kingly hands   65
On Balder's breast, and thus began the wail:—

'Farewell, O Balder, bright and loved, my son!
In that great day, the twilight of the Gods,
When Muspel's children shall beleaguer Heaven,
Then we shall miss thy counsel and thy arm.'   70

Thou camest near the next, O warrior Thor!
Shouldering thy hammer, in thy chariot drawn,
Swaying the long-hair'd goats with silver'd rein;
And over Balder's corpse these words didst say:—

'Brother, thou dwellest in the darksome land,   75
And talkest with the feeble tribes of ghosts,
Now, and I know not how they prize thee there—
But here, I know, thou wilt be miss'd and mourn'd.
For haughty spirits and high wraths are rife
Among the Gods and Heroes here in Heaven,   80
As among those whose joy and work is war;

And daily strifes arise, and angry words.
But from thy lips, O Balder, night or day,
Heard no one ever an injurious word
To God or Hero, but thou keptest back   85
The others, labouring to compose their brawls.
Be ye then kind, as Balder too was kind!
For we lose him, who smoothed all strife in Heaven.'

He spake, and all the Gods assenting wail'd.
And Freya next came nigh, with golden tears;   90
The loveliest Goddess she in Heaven, by all
Most honour'd after Frea, Odin's wife.
Her long ago the wandering Oder took
To mate, but left her to roam distant lands;
Since then she seeks him, and weeps tears of gold.   95
Names hath she many; Vanadis on earth
They call her, Freya is her name in Heaven;
She in her hands took Balder's head, and spake:—

'Balder, my brother, thou art gone a road
Unknown and long, and haply on that way   100
My long-lost wandering Oder thou hast met,
For in the paths of Heaven he is not found.
Oh, if it be so, tell him what thou wast
To his neglected wife, and what he is,
And wring his heart with shame, to hear thy word!   105
For he, my husband, left me here to pine,
Not long a wife, when his unquiet heart
First drove him from me into distant lands;
Since then I vainly seek him through the world,
And weep from shore to shore my golden tears,   110
But neither god nor mortal heeds my pain.
Thou only, Balder, wast for ever kind,
To take my hand, and wipe my tears, and say:
Weep not, O Freya, weep no goldente ars!
One day the wandering Oder will return,   115
Or thou wilt find him in thy faithful search
On some great road, or resting in an inn,

103, 112 *1855, 1869*: wert

Or at a ford, or sleeping by a tree.
So Balder said;—but Oder, well I know,
My truant Oder I shall see no more   120
To the world's end; and Balder now is gone,
And I am left uncomforted in Heaven.'
   She spake; and all the Goddesses bewail'd.
Last from among the Heroes one came near,
No God, but of the hero-troop the chief—   125
Regner, who swept the northern sea with fleets,
And ruled o'er Denmark and the heathy isles,
Living; but Ella captured him and slew;—
A king whose fame then fill'd the vast of Heaven,
Now time obscures it, and men's later deeds.   130
He last approach'd the corpse, and spake, and said:—
   'Balder, there yet are many Scalds in Heaven
Still left, and that chief Scald, thy brother Brage,
Whom we may bid to sing, though thou art gone.
And all these gladly, while we drink, we hear,   135
After the feast is done, in Odin's hall;
But they harp ever on one string, and wake
Remembrance in our soul of wars alone,
Such as on earth we valiantly have waged,
And blood, and ringing blows, and violent death.   140
But when thou sangest, Balder, thou didst strike
Another note, and, like a bird in spring,
Thy voice of joyance minded us, and youth,
And wife, and children, and our ancient home.
Yes, and I, too, remember'd then no more   145
My dungeon, where the serpents stung me dead,
Nor Ella's victory on the English coast—
But I heard Thora laugh in Gothland Isle,
And saw my shepherdess, Aslauga, tend
Her flock along the white Norwegian beach.   150
Tears started to mine eyes with yearning joy.
Therefore with grateful heart I mourn thee dead.'
   So Regner spake, and all the Heroes groan'd.

But now the sun had pass'd the height of Heaven,
And soon had all that day been spent in wail;   155
But then the Father of the ages said:—
    'Ye Gods, there well may be too much of wail!
Bring now the gather'd wood to Balder's ship;
Heap on the deck the logs, and build the pyre.'
    But when the Gods and Heroes heard, they brought   160
The wood to Balder's ship, and built a pile,
Full the deck's breadth, and lofty; then the corpse
Of Balder on the highest top they laid,
With Nanna on his right, and on his left
Hoder, his brother, whom his own hand slew.   165
And they set jars of wine and oil to lean
Against the bodies, and stuck torches near,
Splinters of pine-wood, soak'd with turpentine;
And brought his arms and gold, and all his stuff,
And slew the dogs who at his table fed,   170
And his horse, Balder's horse, whom most he loved,
And placed them on the pyre, and Odin threw
A last choice gift thereon, his golden ring.
The mast they fixt, and hoisted up the sails,
Then they put fire to the wood; and Thor   175
Set his stout shoulder hard against the stern
To push the ship through the thick sand;—sparks flew
From the deep trench she plough'd, so strong a God
Furrow'd it; and the water gurgled in.
And the ship floated on the waves, and rock'd.   180
But in the hills a strong east-wind arose,
And came down moaning to the sea; first squalls
Ran black o'er the sea's face, then steady rush'd
The breeze, and fill'd the sails, and blew the fire.
And wreathed in smoke the ship stood out to sea.   185
Soon with a roaring rose the mighty fire,
And the pile crackled; and between the logs

170 *1855*: the dogs which   172 *1855–81*: And threw them on the
pyre,   *MS. alteration, 1881*: put [*cancelled*] on the pyre, placed them
174 *1855*: They fixt the mast,

Sharp quivering tongues of flame shot out, and leapt,
Curling and darting, higher, until they lick'd
The summit of the pile, the dead, the mast,   190
And ate the shrivelling sails; but still the ship
Drove on, ablaze above her hull with fire.
And the Gods stood upon the beach, and gazed.
And while they gazed, the sun went lurid down
Into the smoke-wrapt sea, and night came on.   195
Then the wind fell, with night, and there was calm;
But through the dark they watch'd the burning ship
Still carried o'er the distant waters on,
Farther and farther, like an eye of fire.
And long, in the far dark, blazed Balder's pile;   200
But fainter, as the stars rose high, it flared,
The bodies were consumed, ash choked the pile.
And as, in a decaying winter-fire,
A charr'd log, falling, makes a shower of sparks—
So with a shower of sparks the pile fell in,   205
Reddening the sea around; and all was dark.

   But the Gods went by starlight up the shore
To Asgard, and sate down in Odin's hall
At table, and the funeral-feast began.
All night they ate the boar Serimner's flesh,   210
And from their horns, with silver rimm'd, drank mead,
Silent, and waited for the sacred morn.

   And morning over all the world was spread.
Then from their loathéd feast the Gods arose,
And took their horses, and set forth to ride   215
O'er the bridge Bifrost, where is Heimdall's watch,

Between 199 and 200 1855 has the following lines:
      And as in the dark night a travelling man
      Who bivouacs in a forest 'mid the hills,
      Sees suddenly a spire of flame shoot up
      Out of the black waste forest, far below,
      Which woodcutters have lighted near their lodge
      Against the wolves; and all night long it flares:—
200 *1855*: So flar'd, in the far darkness, Balder's pyre   *1869*: So showed
201 *1855*: as the stars rose high, it burn'd

To the ash Igdrasil, and Ida's plain;
Thor came on foot, the rest on horseback rode.
And they found Mimir sitting by his fount
Of wisdom, which beneath the ashtree springs;   220
And saw the Nornies watering the roots
Of that world-shadowing tree with honey-dew.
There came the Gods, and sate them down on stones;
And thus the Father of the ages said:—

'Ye Gods, the terms ye know, which Hermod brought.
Accept them or reject them! both have grounds.   226
Accept them, and they bind us, unfulfill'd,
To leave for ever Balder in the grave,
An unrecover'd prisoner, shade with shades.
But how, ye say, should the fulfilment fail?—   230
Smooth sound the terms, and light to be fulfill'd;
For dear-beloved was Balder while he lived
In Heaven and earth, and who would grudge him tears?
But from the traitorous seed of Lok they come,
These terms, and I suspect some hidden fraud.   235
Bethink ye, Gods, is there no other way?—
Speak, were not this a way, the way for Gods?
If I, if Odin, clad in radiant arms,
Mounted on Sleipner, with the warrior Thor
Drawn in his car beside me, and my sons,   240
All the strong brood of Heaven, to swell my train,
Should make irruption into Hela's realm,
And set the fields of gloom ablaze with light,
And bring in triumph Balder back to Heaven?'

He spake, and his fierce sons applauded loud.   245
But Frea, mother of the Gods, arose,
Daughter and wife of Odin; thus she said:—

'Odin, thou whirlwind, what a threat is this!
Thou threatenest what transcends thy might, even thine.
For of all powers the mightiest far art thou,   250
Lord over men on earth, and Gods in Heaven;
Yet even from thee thyself hath been withheld
One thing—to undo what thou thyself hast ruled.

For all which hath been fixt, was fixt by thee.
In the beginning, ere the Gods were born,   255
Before the Heavens were builded, thou didst slay
The giant Ymir, whom the abyss brought forth,
Thou and thy brethren fierce, the sons of Bor,
And cast his trunk to choke the abysmal void.
But of his flesh and members thou didst build   260
The earth and Ocean, and above them Heaven.
And from the flaming world, where Muspel reigns,
Thou sent'st and fetched'st fire, and madest lights,
Sun, moon, and stars, which thou hast hung in Heaven,
Dividing clear the paths of night and day.   265
And Asgard thou didst build, and Midgard fort;
Then me thou mad'st; of us the Gods were born.
Last, walking by the sea, thou foundest spars
Of wood, and framed'st men, who till the earth,
Or on the sea, the field of pirates, sail.   270
And all the race of Ymir thou didst drown,
Save one, Bergelmer;—he on shipboard fled
Thy deluge, and from him the giants sprang.
But all that brood thou hast removed far off,
And set by Ocean's utmost marge to dwell;   275
But Hela into Niflheim thou threw'st,
And gav'st her nine unlighted worlds to rule,
A queen, and empire over all the dead.
That empire wilt thou now invade, light up
Her darkness, from her grasp a subject tear?—   280
Try it; but I, for one, will not applaud.
Nor do I merit, Odin, thou should'st slight
Me and my words, though thou be first in Heaven;
For I too am a Goddess, born of thee,
Thine eldest, and of me the Gods are sprung;   285
And all that is to come I know, but lock
In mine own breast, and have to none reveal'd.
Come then! since Hela holds by right her prey,

259 *1855, 1869*: And threw his trunk   268 *1855, 1869*: Then, walking
287 *1855, 1869*: In my

But offers terms for his release to Heaven,
Accept the chance; thou canst no more obtain.   290
Send through the world thy messengers; entreat
All living and unliving things to weep
For Balder; if thou haply thus may'st melt
Hela, and win the loved one back to Heaven.'

She spake, and on her face let fall her veil,   295
And bow'd her head, and sate with folded hands.
Nor did the all-ruling Odin slight her word;
Straightway he spake, and thus address'd the Gods:

'Go quickly forth through all the world, and pray
All living and unliving things to weep   300
Balder, if haply he may thus be won.'

When the Gods heard, they straight arose, and took
Their horses, and rode forth through all the world;
North, south, east, west, they struck, and roam'd the world,
Entreating all things to weep Balder's death.   305
And all that lived, and all without life, wept.
And as in winter, when the frost breaks up,
At winter's end, before the spring begins,
And a warm west-wind blows, and thaw sets in—
After an hour a dripping sound is heard   310
In all the forests, and the soft-strewn snow
Under the trees is dibbled thick with holes,
And from the boughs the snowloads shuffle down;
And, in fields sloping to the south, dark plots
Of grass peep out amid surrounding snow,   315
And widen, and the peasant's heart is glad—
So through the world was heard a dripping noise
Of all things weeping to bring Balder back;
And there fell joy upon the Gods to hear.

But Hermod rode with Niord, whom he took   320
To show him spits and beaches of the sea
Far off, where some unwarn'd might fail to weep—
Niord, the God of storms, whom fishers know;
Not born in Heaven; he was in Vanheim rear'd,

With men, but lives a hostage with the Gods;   325
He knows each frith, and every rocky creek
Fringed with dark pines, and sands where seafowl scream—
They two scour'd every coast, and all things wept.
And they rode home together, through the wood
Of Jarnvid, which to east of Midgard lies   330
Bordering the giants, where the trees are iron;
There in the wood before a cave they came,
Where sate, in the cave's mouth, a skinny hag,
Toothless and old; she gibes the passers by.
Thok is she call'd, but now Lok wore her shape;   335
She greeted them the first, and laugh'd, and said:—
   'Ye Gods, good lack, is it so dull in Heaven,
That ye come pleasuring to Thok's iron wood?
Lovers of change ye are, fastidious sprites.
Look, as in some boor's yard a sweet-breath'd cow,   340
Whose manger is stuff'd full of good fresh hay,
Snuffs at it daintily, and stoops her head
To chew the straw, her litter, at her feet—
So ye grow squeamish, Gods, and sniff at Heaven!'
   She spake; but Hermod answer'd her and said:—   345
'Thok, not for gibes we come, we come for tears.
Balder is dead, and Hela holds her prey,
But will restore, if all things give him tears.
Begrudge not thine! to all was Balder dear.'
   Then, with a louder laugh, the hag replied:—   350
'Is Balder dead? and do ye come for tears?
Thok with dry eyes will weep o'er Balder's pyre.
Weep him all other things, if weep they will—
I weep him not! let Hela keep her prey.'
   She spake, and to the cavern's depth she fled,   355
Mocking; and Hermod knew their toil was vain.
And as seafaring men, who long have wrought
In the great deep for gain, at last come home,
And towards evening see the headlands rise
Of their dear country, and can plain descry   360

A fire of wither'd furze which boys have lit
Upon the cliffs, or smoke of burning weeds
Out of a till'd field inland;—then the wind
Catches them, and drives out again to sea;
And they go long days tossing up and down   365
Over the grey sea-ridges, and the glimpse
Of port they had makes bitterer far their toil—
So the Gods' cross was bitterer for their joy.

   Then, sad at heart, to Niord Hermod spake:—
'It is the accuser Lok, who flouts us all!   370
Ride back, and tell in Heaven this heavy news;
I must again below, to Hela's realm.'

   He spoke; and Niord set forth back to Heaven.
But northward Hermod rode, the way below,
The way he knew; and traversed Giall's stream,   375
And down to Ocean groped, and cross'd the ice,
And came beneath the wall, and found the grate
Still lifted; well was his return foreknown.
And once more Hermod saw around him spread
The joyless plains, and heard the streams of Hell.   380
But as he enter'd, on the extremest bound
Of Niflheim, he saw one ghost come near,
Hovering, and stopping oft, as if afraid—
Hoder, the unhappy, whom his own hand slew.
And Hermod look'd, and knew his brother's ghost,   385
And call'd him by his name, and sternly said:—

   'Hoder, ill-fated, blind in heart and eyes!
Why tarriest thou to plunge thee in the gulph
Of the deep inner gloom, but flittest here,
In twilight, on the lonely verge of Hell,   390
Far from the other ghosts, and Hela's throne?
Doubtless thou fearest to meet Balder's voice,
Thy brother, whom through folly thou didst slay.'

   He spoke; but Hoder answer'd him, and said:—
'Hermod the nimble, dost thou still pursue   395
The unhappy with reproach, even in the grave?
For this I died, and fled beneath the gloom,

Not daily to endure abhorring Gods,
Nor with a hateful presence cumber Heaven;
And canst thou not, even here, pass pitying by?   400
No less than Balder have I lost the light
Of Heaven, and communion with my kin;
I too had once a wife, and once a child,
And substance, and a golden house in Heaven—
But all I left of my own act, and fled   405
Below, and dost thou hate me even here?
Balder upbraids me not, nor hates at all,
Though he has cause, have any cause; but he,
When that with downcast looks I hither came,
Stretch'd forth his hand, and with benignant voice, 410
Welcome, he said, *if there be welcome here,*
Brother and fellow-sport of Lok with me!
And not to offend thee, Hermod, nor to force
My hated converse on thee, came I up
From the deep gloom, where I will now return;   415
But earnestly I long'd to hover near,
Not too far off, when that thou camest by;
To feel the presence of a brother God,
And hear the passage of a horse of Heaven,
For the last time—for here thou com'st no more.'   420

He spake, and turn'd to go to the inner gloom.
But Hermod stay'd him with mild words, and said:—

'Thou doest well to chide me, Hoder blind!
Truly thou say'st, the planning guilty mind
Was Lok's; the unwitting hand alone was thine.   425
But Gods are like the sons of men in this—
When they have woe, they blame the nearest cause.
Howbeit stay, and be appeased! and tell:
Sits Balder still in pomp by Hela's side,
Or is he mingled with the unnumber'd dead?'   430

And the blind Hoder answer'd him and spake:—
'His place of state remains by Hela's side,
But empty; for his wife, for Nanna came
Lately below, and join'd him; and the pair

Frequent the still recesses of the realm   435
Of Hela, and hold converse undisturb'd.
But they too, doubtless, will have breathed the balm,
Which floats before a visitant from Heaven,
And have drawn upward to this verge of Hell.'

He spake; and, as he ceased, a puff of wind   440
Roll'd heavily the leaden mist aside
Round where they stood, and they beheld two forms
Make toward them o'er the stretching cloudy plain.
And Hermod straight perceived them, who they were,
Balder and Nanna; and to Balder said:—   445

'Balder, too truly thou foresaw'st a snare!
Lok triumphs still, and Hela keeps her prey.
No more to Asgard shalt thou come, nor lodge
In thy own house, Breidablik, nor enjoy
The love all bear toward thee, nor train up   450
Forset, thy son, to be beloved like thee.
Here must thou lie, and wait an endless age.
Therefore for the last time, O Balder, hail!'

He spake; and Balder answer'd him, and said:—
'Hail and farewell! for here thou com'st no more.   455
Yet mourn not for me, Hermod, when thou sitt'st
In Heaven, nor let the other Gods lament,
As wholly to be pitied, quite forlorn.
For Nanna hath rejoin'd me, who, of old,
In Heaven, was seldom parted from my side;   460
And still the acceptance follows me, which crown'd
My former life, and cheers me even here.
The iron frown of Hela is relax'd
When I draw nigh, and the wan tribes of dead
Love me, and gladly bring for my award   465
Their ineffectual feuds and feeble hates—
Shadows of hates, but they distress them still.'

And the fleet-footed Hermod made reply:—
'Thou hast then all the solace death allows,

439 *1855*: upwards   443 *1855, 1869*: towards
450 *1855*: towards   465 *1855*: Trust me,

Esteem and function; and so far is well.   470
Yet here thou liest, Balder, underground,
Rusting for ever; and the years roll on,
The generations pass, the ages grow,
And bring us nearer to the final day
When from the south shall march the fiery band   475
And cross the bridge of Heaven, with Lok for guide,
And Fenris at his heel with broken chain;
While from the east the giant Rymer steers
His ship, and the great serpent makes to land;
And all are marshall'd in one flaming square   480
Against the Gods, upon the plains of Heaven,
I mourn thee, that thou canst not help us then.'
  He spake; but Balder answer'd him, and said:—
'Mourn not for me! Mourn, Hermod, for the Gods;
Mourn for the men on earth, the Gods in Heaven,   485
Who live, and with their eyes shall see that day!
The day will come, when fall shall Asgard's towers,
And Odin, and his sons, the seed of Heaven;
But what were I, to save them in that hour?
If strength might save them, could not Odin save,   490
My father, and his pride, the warrior Thor,
Vidar the silent, the impetuous Tyr?
I, what were I, when these can nought avail?
Yet, doubtless, when the day of battle comes,
And the two hosts are marshall'd, and in Heaven   495
The golden-crested cock shall sound alarm,
And his black brother-bird from hence reply,
And bucklers clash, and spears begin to pour—
Longing will stir within my breast, though vain.
But not to me so grievous, as, I know,   500
To other Gods it were, is my enforced
Absence from fields where I could nothing aid;
For I am long since weary of your storm
Of carnage, and find, Hermod, in your life

487 *1855, 1869*: when Asgard's towers shall fall,   490 *1855*: could save them, could not

Something too much of war and broils, which make   505
Life one perpetual fight, a bath of blood.
Mine eyes are dizzy with the arrowy hail;
Mine ears are stunn'd with blows, and sick for calm.
Inactive therefore let me lie, in gloom,
Unarm'd, inglorious; I attend the course   510
Of ages, and my late return to light,
In times less alien to a spirit mild,
In new-recover'd seats, the happier day.'

He spake; and the fleet Hermod thus replied:—
'Brother, what seats are these, what happier day?   515
Tell me, that I may ponder it when gone.'

And the ray-crowned Balder answer'd him:—
'Far to the south, beyond the blue, there spreads
Another Heaven, the boundless—no one yet
Hath reach'd it; there hereafter shall arise   520
The second Asgard, with another name.
Thither, when o'er this present earth and Heavens
The tempest of the latter days hath swept,
And they from sight have disappear'd, and sunk,
Shall a small remnant of the Gods repair;   525
Hoder and I shall join them from the grave.
There re-assembling we shall see emerge
From the bright Ocean at our feet an earth
More fresh, more verdant than the last, with fruits
Self-springing, and a seed of man preserved,   530
Who then shall live in peace, as now in war.
But we in Heaven shall find again with joy
The ruin'd palaces of Odin, seats
Familiar, halls where we have supp'd of old;
Re-enter them with wonder, never fill   535
Our eyes with gazing, and rebuild with tears.
And we shall tread once more the well-known plain
Of Ida, and among the grass shall find
The golden dice wherewith we play'd of yore;
And that will bring to mind the former life   540

539 *1855–69*: with which we play'd

And pastime of the Gods, the wise discourse
Of Odin, the delights of other days.
O Hermod, pray that thou may'st join us then!
Such for the future is my hope; meanwhile,
I rest the thrall of Hela, and endure   545
Death, and the gloom which round me even now
Thickens, and to its inner gulph recalls.
Farewell, for longer speech is not allow'd!'
   He spoke, and waved farewell, and gave his hand
To Nanna; and she gave their brother blind   550
Her hand, in turn, for guidance; and the three
Departed o'er the cloudy plain, and soon
Faded from sight into the interior gloom.
But Hermod stood beside his drooping horse,
Mute, gazing after them in tears; and fain,   555
Fain had he follow'd their receding steps,
Though they to death were bound, and he to Heaven,
Then; but a power he could not break withheld.
And as a stork which idle boys have trapp'd,
And tied him in a yard, at autumn sees   560
Flocks of his kind pass flying o'er his head
To warmer lands, and coasts that keep the sun;—
He strains to join their flight, and from his shed
Follows them with a long complaining cry—
So Hermod gazed, and yearn'd to join his kin.   565

  At last he sigh'd, and set forth back to Heaven.

TRISTRAM AND ISEULT[8]

[*First published 1852. Reprinted 1853, '54, '57, '69, and thereafter*]

I

𝔗ristram

Tristram

Is she not come? The messenger was sure.
Prop me upon the pillows once again—
Raise me, my page! this cannot long endure.
—Christ, what a night! how the sleet whips the pane!
What lights will those out to the northward be?   5

The Page

The lanterns of the fishing-boats at sea.

Tristram

Soft—who is that, stands by the dying fire?

The Page

Iseult.

Tristram

Ah! not the Iseult I desire.

*   *   *   *

What Knight is this so weak and pale,
Though the locks are yet brown on his noble head,   10
Propt on pillows in his bed,
Gazing seaward for the light
Of some ship that fights the gale
On this wild December night?

TRISTRAM AND ISEULT. *Title 1857*: Tristan and Iseult. *In 1869 Arnold reverted to spelling his hero's name* Tristram, *which had been used in the first three editions.*
9 *The asterisks here and elsewhere in the poem were inserted in 1853.*
12 *1852–7*: Gazing seawards

Over the sick man's feet is spread   15
A dark green forest-dress;
A gold harp leans against the bed,
Ruddy in the fire's light.
I know him by his harp of gold,
Famous in Arthur's court of old;   20
I know him by his forest-dress—
The peerless hunter, harper, knight,
Tristram of Lyoness.

What Lady is this, whose silk attire
Gleams so rich in the light of the fire?   25
The ringlets on her shoulders lying
In their flitting lustre vying
With the clasp of burnish'd gold
Which her heavy robe doth hold.
Her looks are mild, her fingers slight   30
As the driven snow are white;
But her cheeks are sunk and pale.
Is it that the bleak sea-gale
Beating from the Atlantic sea
On this coast of Brittany,   35
Nips too keenly the sweet flower?
Is it that a deep fatigue
Hath come on her, a chilly fear,
Passing all her youthful hour
Spinning with her maidens here,   40
Listlessly through the window-bars
Gazing seawards many a league,
From her lonely shore-built tower,
While the knights are at the wars?
Or, perhaps, has her young heart   45
Felt already some deeper smart,

Between 25 *and* 26 *1852 reads*:
> Never surely has been seen
> So slight a form in so rich a dress.

30, 31 *First inserted in 1853.*   32 *1853–69*: And her cheeks
33 *1854*: the black sea-gale

Of those that in secret the heart-strings rive,
Leaving her sunk and pale, though fair?
Who is this snowdrop by the sea?—
I know her by her mildness rare,   50
Her snow-white hands, her golden hair;
I know her by her rich silk dress,
And her fragile loveliness—
The sweetest Christian soul alive,
Iseult of Brittany.   55

Iseult of Brittany?—but where
Is that other Iseult fair,
That proud, first Iseult, Cornwall's queen?
She, whom Tristram's ship of yore
From Ireland to Cornwall bore,   60
To Tyntagel, to the side
Of King Marc, to be his bride?
She who, as they voyaged, quaff'd
With Tristram that spiced magic draught,
Which since then for ever rolls   65
Through their blood, and binds their souls,
Working love, but working teen?—
There were two Iseults who did sway
Each her hour of Tristram's day;
But one possess'd his waning time,   70
The other his resplendent prime.
Behold her here, the patient flower,
Who possess'd his darker hour!
Iseult of the Snow-White Hand
Watches pale by Tristram's bed.   75
She is here who had his gloom,
Where art thou who hadst his bloom?
One such kiss as those of yore
Might thy dying knight restore!

50 *1852*: her golden hair,   51 *First inserted in 1853.*
56–82 *First inserted in 1853.*   60, 61 *1853, 1854*:
                To Tyntagil from Ireland bore,
                To Cornwall's palace, to the side

Does the love-draught work no more?   80
Art thou cold, or false, or dead,
Iseult of Ireland?

     *   *   *   *

Loud howls the wind, sharp patters the rain,
And the knight sinks back on his pillows again.
He is weak with fever and pain,   85
And his spirit is not clear.
Hark! he mutters in his sleep,
As he wanders far from here,
Changes place and time of year,
And his closéd eye doth sweep   90
O'er some fair unwintry sea,
Not this fierce Atlantic deep,
While he mutters brokenly:—

Tristram

The calm sea shines, loose hang the vessel's sails;
Before us are the sweet green fields of Wales,   95
And overhead the cloudless sky of May.—
'*Ah, would I were in those green fields at play,*
Not pent on ship-board this delicious day!
Tristram, I pray thee, of thy courtesy,
Reach me my golden phial stands by thee,   100
But pledge me in it first for courtesy.—'
Ha! dost thou start? are thy lips blanch'd like mine?
Child, 'tis no true draught this, 'tis poison'd wine!
Iseult! . . . .

     *   *   *   *

Ah, sweet angels, let him dream!   105
Keep his eyelids! let him seem
Not this fever-wasted wight

93 *1852–77*: As he   97 *The italics here and elsewhere were introduced*
in 1853.   100 *1852–81*: golden cup that stands by thee
101 *1852–69*: And pledge   103 *1852–81*: 'tis no water this,

Thinn'd and paled before his time,
But the brilliant youthful knight
In the glory of his prime,   110
Sitting in the gilded barge,
At thy side, thou lovely charge,
Bending gaily o'er thy hand,
Iseult of Ireland!
And she too, that princess fair,   115
If her bloom be now less rare,
Let her have her youth again—
Let her be as she was then!
Let her have her proud dark eyes,
And her petulant quick replies—   120
Let her sweep her dazzling hand
With its gesture of command,
And shake back her raven hair
With the old imperious air!
As of old, so let her be,   125
That first Iseult, princess bright,
Chatting with her youthful knight
As he steers her o'er the sea,
Quitting at her father's will
The green isle where she was bred,   130
And her bower in Ireland,
For the surge-beat Cornish strand;
Where the prince whom she must wed
Dwells on loud Tyntagel's hill,
High above the sounding sea.   135
And that potion rare her mother
Gave her, that her future lord,
Gave her, that King Marc and she,

---

134 *1852–4*: Keeps his court in Tyntagil   *1857*: Dwells on proud
Tyntagel's hill,   *MS. alterations in 1854 volume [not adopted]*: Sits on
proud Tyntagel's hill,   135 *1852–69*: Fast beside the   136 *1852–78*:
golden cup her mother   *1880*: phial rare her mother   *The reading*
golden cup *was restored in 1881, only to be changed to* potion rare *in 1885.*
137 *1852*: Gave her, that her lord and she   138 *Added in 1853.*

Might drink it on their marriage-day,
And for ever love each other—   140
Let her, as she sits on board,
Ah, sweet saints, unwittingly!
See it shine, and take it up,
And to Tristram laughing say:
'Sir Tristram, of thy courtesy,   145
Pledge me in my golden cup!'
Let them drink it—let their hands
Tremble, and their cheeks be flame,
As they feel the fatal bands
Of a love they dare not name,   150
With a wild delicious pain,
Twine about their hearts again!
Let the early summer be
Once more round them, and the sea
Blue, and o'er its mirror kind   155
Let the breath of the May-wind,
Wandering through their drooping sails,
Die on the green fields of Wales!
Let a dream like this restore
What his eye must see no more!   160

Tristram

Chill blows the wind, the pleasaunce-walks are drear—
Madcap, what jest was this, to meet me here?
Were feet like those made for so wild a way?
The southern winter-parlour, by my fay,
Had been the likeliest trysting-place to-day!   165
'*Tristram!—nay, nay—thou must not take my hand!—*
Tristram!—sweet love!—we are betray'd—out-plann'd.
Fly—save thyself—save me!—I dare not stay.'—
One last kiss first!—''*Tis vain—to horse—away!*'

*   *   *   *

Ah! sweet saints, his dream doth move   170
Faster surely than it should,

From the fever in his blood!
All the spring-time of his love
Is already gone and past,
And instead thereof is seen   175
Its winter, which endureth still—
Tyntagel on its surge-beat hill,
The pleasaunce-walks, the weeping queen,
The flying leaves, the straining blast,
And that long, wild kiss—their last.   180
And this rough December-night,
And his burning fever-pain,
Mingle with his hurrying dream,
Till they rule it, till he seem
The press'd fugitive again,   185
The love-desperate banish'd knight
With a fire in his brain
Flying o'er the stormy main.
—Whither does he wander now?
Haply in his dreams the wind   190
Wafts him here, and lets him find
The lovely orphan child again
In her castle by the coast;
The youngest, fairest chatelaine,
Whom this realm of France can boast,   195
Our snowdrop by the Atlantic sea,
Iseult of Brittany.
And—for through the haggard air,
The stain'd arms, the matted hair
Of that stranger-knight ill-starr'd,   200
There gleam'd something, which recall'd
The Tristram who in better days
Was Launcelot's guest at Joyous Gard—
Welcomed here, and here install'd,
Tended of his fever here,   205
Haply he seems again to move

177 *1852–4*: The palace towers of Tyntagil,   195 *1852–81*: That
this realm   201 *1852–7*: that recall'd

His young guardian's heart with love;
In his exiled loneliness,
In his stately, deep distress,
Without a word, without a tear.   210
—Ah! 'tis well he should retrace
His tranquil life in this lone place:
His gentle bearing at the side
Of his timid youthful bride;
His long rambles by the shore   215
On winter-evenings, when the roar
Of the near waves came, sadly grand,
Through the dark, up the drown'd sand,
Or his endless reveries
In the woods, where the gleams play   220
On the grass under the trees,
Passing the long summer's day
Idle as a mossy stone
In the forest-depths alone,
The chase neglected, and his hound   225
Couch'd beside him on the ground.
—Ah! what trouble's on his brow?
Hither let him wander now;
Hither, to the quiet hours
Pass'd among these heaths of ours   230
By the grey Atlantic sea;
Hours, if not of ecstasy,
From violent anguish surely free!

Tristram

All red with blood the whirling river flows,
The wide plain rings, the dazed air throbs with blows.   235
Upon us are the chivalry of Rome—
Their spears are down, their steeds are bathed in foam.
'Up, Tristram, up,' men cry, 'thou moonstruck knight!
What foul fiend rides thee? On into the fight!'
—Above the din her voice is in my ears;   240

I see her form glide through the crossing spears.—
Iseult! . . . .

    *   *   *   *

    Ah! he wanders forth again;
    We cannot keep him; now, as then,
    There's a secret in his breast
    Which will never let him rest.   245
    These musing fits in the green wood
    They cloud the brain, they dull the blood!
    —His sword is sharp, his horse is good;
    Beyond the mountains will he see   250
    The famous towns of Italy,
    And label with the blessed sign
    The heathen Saxons on the Rhine.
    At Arthur's side he fights once more
    With the Roman Emperor.   255
    There's many a gay knight where he goes
    Will help him to forget his care;
    The march, the leaguer, Heaven's blithe air,
    The neighing steeds, the ringing blows—
    Sick pining comes not where these are.   260
    Ah! what boots it, that the jest
    Lightens every other brow,
    What, that every other breast
    Dances as the trumpets blow,
    If one's own heart beats not light   265
    On the waves of the toss'd fight,
    If oneself cannot get free
    From the clog of misery?
    Thy lovely youthful wife grows pale
    Watching by the salt sea-tide   270
    With her children at her side
    For the gleam of thy white sail.
    Home, Tristram, to thy halls again!

246 *1852–69*: That will never   266 *1852*: In the waves
269 *1881*: The lovely

To our lonely sea complain,
To our forests tell thy pain!   275

Tristram

All round the forest sweeps off, black in shade,
But it is moonlight in the open glade;
And in the bottom of the glade shine clear
The forest-chapel and the fountain near.
—I think, I have a fever in my blood;   280
Come, let me leave the shadow of this wood,
Ride down, and bathe my hot brow in the flood.
—Mild shines the cold spring in the moon's clear light;
God! 'tis *her* face plays in the waters bright.
'Fair love,' she says, 'canst thou forget so soon,   285
At this soft hour, under this sweet moon?'—
Iseult! . . . .

*   *   *   *

Ah, poor soul! if this be so,
Only death can balm thy woe.
The solitudes of the green wood   290
Had no medicine for thy mood;
The rushing battle clear'd thy blood
As little as did solitude.
—Ah! his eyelids slowly break
Their hot seals, and let him wake;   295
What new change shall we now see?
A happier? Worse it cannot be.

Tristram

Is my page here? Come, turn me to the fire!
Upon the window-panes the moon shines bright;
The wind is down—but she'll not come to-night.   300
Ah no! she is asleep in Cornwall now,
Far hence; her dreams are fair—smooth is her brow.

301 *1852–4:* In Tyntagil   302 *1852–4:* her dreams are fair—her
sleep is still.   *MS. alterations (in 1854 volume):* smooth is her brow.

Of me she recks not, nor my vain desire.
—I have had dreams, I have had dreams, my page,
Would take a score years from a strong man's age;   305
And with a blood like mine, will leave, I fear,
Scant leisure for a second messenger.
—My princess, art thou there? Sweet, do not wait!
To bed, and sleep! my fever is gone by;
To-night my page shall keep me company.   310
Where do the children sleep? kiss them for me!
Poor child, thou art almost as pale as I;
This comes of nursing long and watching late.
To bed—good night!

*   *   *   *

   She left the gleam-lit fireplace,   315
She came to the bed-side;
She took his hands in hers—her tears
Down on his wasted fingers rain'd.
She raised her eyes upon his face—
Not with a look of wounded pride,   320
A look as if the heart complained—
Her look was like a sad embrace;
The gaze of one who can divine
A grief, and sympathise.
Sweet flower! thy children's eyes   325
Are not more innocent than thine.

   But they sleep in shelter'd rest,
Like helpless birds in the warm nest,
On the castle's southern side;
Where feebly comes the mournful roar   330
Of buffeting wind and surging tide
Through many a room and corridor.
—Full on their window the moon's ray
Makes their chamber as bright as day.

303 *1852, 1853*: nor of my desire.   308 *1852–81*: Sweet, 'tis too late.
318 *1852–81*: on her slender fingers

It shines upon the blank white walls,   335
And on the snowy pillow falls,
And on two angel-heads doth play
Turn'd to each other—the eyes closed,
The lashes on the cheeks reposed.
Round each sweet brow the cap close-set   340
Hardly lets peep the golden hair;
Through the soft-open'd lips the air
Scarcely moves the coverlet.
One little wandering arm is thrown
At random on the counterpane,   345
And often the fingers close in haste
As if their baby-owner chased
The butterflies again.
This stir they have, and this alone;
But else they are so still!   350
—Ah, tired madcaps! you lie still;
But were you at the window now,
To look forth on the fairy sight
Of your illumined haunts by night,
To see the park-glades where you play   355
Far lovelier than they are by day,
To see the sparkle on the eaves,
And upon every giant-bough
Of those old oaks, whose wet red leaves
Are jewell'd with bright drops of rain—   360
How would your voices run again!
And far beyond the sparkling trees
Of the castle-park one sees
The bare heaths spreading, clear as day,
Moor behind moor, far, far away,   365
Into the heart of Brittany.
And here and there, lock'd by the land,
Long inlets of smooth glittering sea,
And many a stretch of watery sand
All shining in the white moon-beams—   370
But you see fairer in your dreams!

What voices are these on the clear night-air?
What lights in the court—what steps on the stair?

II
Iseult of Ireland

Tristram

RAISE the light, my page! that I may see her.—
　　Thou art come at last, then, haughty Queen!
Long I've waited, long I've fought my fever;
　　Late thou comest, cruel thou hast been.

Iseult

Blame me not, poor sufferer! that I tarried;　　　　5
　　Bound I was, I could not break the band.
Chide not with the past, but feel the present!
　　I am here—we meet—I hold thy hand.

Tristram

Thou art come, indeed—thou hast rejoin'd me;
　　Thou hast dared it—but too late to save.　　　　10
Fear not now that men should tax thine honour!
　　I am dying: build—(thou may'st)—my grave!

Iseult

Tristram, ah, for love of Heaven, speak kindly!
　　What, I hear these bitter words from thee?
Sick with grief I am, and faint with travel—　　　　15
　　Take my hand—dear Tristram, look on me!

Tristram

I forgot, thou comest from thy voyage—
　　Yes, the spray is on thy cloak and hair.
But thy dark eyes are not dimm'd, proud Iseult!
　　And thy beauty never was more fair.　　　　20

II. *Iseult of Ireland.* 6. *1852–7*: I was bound,　　11 *1852–69*: thy honour　　13 *1852–7*: Tristram, for the love of Heaven,　　*1857*: Tristan

Iseult

Ah, harsh flatterer! let alone my beauty!
I, like thee, have left my youth afar.
Take my hand, and touch these wasted fingers—
See my cheek and lips, how white they are!

Tristram

Thou art paler—but thy sweet charm, Iseult!   25
Would not fade with the dull years away.
Ah, how fair thou standest in the moonlight!
I forgive thee, Iseult!—thou wilt stay?

Iseult

Fear me not, I will be always with thee;
I will watch thee, tend thee, soothe thy pain;   30
Sing thee tales of true, long-parted lovers,
Join'd at evening of their days again.

Tristram

No, thou shalt not speak! I should be finding
Something alter'd in thy courtly tone.
Sit—sit by me! I will think, we've lived so   35
In the green wood, all our lives, alone.

Iseult

Alter'd, Tristram? Not in courts, believe me,
Love like mine is alter'd in the breast;
Courtly life is light and cannot reach it—
Ah! it lives, because so deep-suppress'd!   40

What, thou think'st men speak in courtly chambers
Words by which the wretched are consoled?
What, thou think'st this aching brow was cooler,
Circled, Tristram, by a band of gold?

Royal state with Marc, my deep-wrong'd husband—   45
    That was bliss to make my sorrows flee!
Silken courtiers whispering honied nothings—
    Those were friends to make me false to thee!

Ah, on which, if both our lots were balanced,
    Was indeed the heaviest burden thrown—   50
Thee, a pining exile in thy forest,
    Me, a smiling queen upon my throne?

Vain and strange debate, where both have suffer'd,
    Both have pass'd a youth consumed and sad,
Both have brought their anxious day to evening,   55
    And have now short space for being glad!

Join'd we are henceforth; nor will thy people,
    Nor thy younger Iseult take it ill,
That a former rival shares her office,
    When she sees her humbled, pale, and still.   60

I, a faded watcher by thy pillow,
    I, a statue on thy chapel-floor,
Pour'd in prayer before the Virgin-Mother,
    Rouse no anger, make no rivals more.

She will cry: 'Is this the foe I dreaded?   65
    This his idol? this that royal bride?
Ah, an hour of health would purge his eyesight!
    Stay, pale queen! for ever by my side.'

Hush, no words! that smile, I see, forgives me.
    I am now thy nurse, I bid thee sleep.   70
Close thine eyes—this flooding moonlight blinds them!—
    Nay, all 's well again! thou must not weep.

45-8 *This stanza appeared first in 1853; it was placed before the preceding stanza until 1877.*   51 *1852-7:* a weeping exile   54 *1852-77:* constrain'd and sad,   *1878-81:* repress'd and sad,   *MS. alterations 1881:* forlorn and sad, [*not adopted*].   59 *1852, 1853:* an ancient rival   63 *1852-77:* Pour'd in grief   65 *1852:* She will say—'Is this the form I dreaded?

Tristram

I am happy! yet I feel, there's something
    Swells my heart, and takes my breath away.
Through a mist I see thee; near—come nearer!   75
    Bend—bend down!—I yet have much to say.

Iseult

Heaven! his head sinks back upon the pillow—
    Tristram! Tristram! let thy heart not fail!
Call on God and on the holy angels!
    What, love, courage!—Christ! he is so pale.   80

Tristram

Hush, 'tis vain, I feel my end approaching!
    This is what my mother said should be,
When the fierce pains took her in the forest,
    The deep draughts of death, in bearing me.

'Son,' she said, 'thy name shall be of sorrow;   85
    Tristram art thou call'd for my death's sake.'
So she said, and died in the drear forest.
    Grief since then his home with me doth make.

I am dying.—Start not, nor look wildly!
    Me, thy living friend, thou canst not save.   90
But, since living we were ununited,
    Go not far, O Iseult! from my grave.

Close mine eyes, then seek the princess Iseult;
    Speak her fair, she is of royal blood!
Say, I will'd so, that thou stay beside me—   95
    She will grant it; she is kind and good.

Now to sail the seas of death I leave thee—
    One last kiss upon the living shore!

93 *1852–77*: Rise, go hence, and seek the princess Iseult:
95 *1852–7*: Say, I charg'd her, that ye live together:—   *1869–81*: Say,
I charg'd her, that thou stay beside me—   *MS. alteration 1881*: Say, I
charg'd thee, that thou stay beside her [*not adopted*].   97, 98 *1852*:
        Now stand clear before me in the moonlight.
      Fare, farewell, thou long, thou deeply lov'd!

Iseult

Tristram!—Tristram!—stay—receive me with thee!
Iseult leaves thee, Tristram! never more.　　　　　100

* 　　 * 　　 * 　　 *

You see them clear—the moon shines bright.
Slow, slow and softly, where she stood,
She sinks upon the ground;—her hood
Had fallen back; her arms outspread
Still hold her lover's hand; her head　　　　　105
Is bow'd, half-buried, on the bed.
O'er the blanch'd sheet her raven hair
Lies in disorder'd streams; and there,
Strung like white stars, the pearls still are,
And the golden bracelets, heavy and rare,　　　　　110
Flash on her white arms still.
The very same which yesternight
Flash'd in the silver sconces' light,
When the feast was gay and the laughter loud
In Tyntagel's palace proud.　　　　　115
But then they deck'd a restless ghost
With hot-flush'd cheeks and brilliant eyes,
And quivering lips on which the tide
Of courtly speech abruptly died,
And a glance which over the crowded floor,　　　　　120
The dancers, and the festive host,
Flew ever to the door.
That the knights eyed her in surprise,
And the dames whispered scoffingly:
'Her moods, good lack, they pass like showers!　　　　　125

99, 100 *1852*: Tristram!—Tristram—stay—I come! Ah Sorrow—
　　　　Fool! thou missest—we are both unmov'd!
105 *1852–81*: lover's hands　　　*1877*: Still holds　　　114, 115 *1852–4*:
　　　　When the feast was loud and the laughter shrill
　　　　In the banquet-hall of Tyntagil.
120 *1852–69*: glance that

But yesternight and she would be
As pale and still as wither'd flowers,
And now to-night she laughs and speaks
And has a colour in her cheeks;
Christ keep us from such fantasy!'—   130

Yes, now the longing is o'erpast,
Which, dogg'd by fear and fought by shame
Shook her weak bosom day and night,
Consumed her beauty like a flame,
And dimm'd it like the desert-blast.   135
And though the bed-clothes hide her face,
Yet were it lifted to the light,
The sweet expression of her brow
Would charm the gazer, till his thought
Erased the ravages of time,   140
Fill'd up the hollow cheek, and brought
A freshness back as of her prime—
So healing is her quiet now.
So perfectly the lines express
A tranquil, settled loveliness,   145
Her younger rival's purest grace.

The air of the December-night
Steals coldly around the chamber bright,
Where those lifeless lovers be;
Swinging with it, in the light   150
Flaps the ghostlike tapestry.
And on the arras wrought you see
A stately Huntsman, clad in green,
And round him a fresh forest-scene.

130 *1852, 1853*: Heaven keep us   131–46 *First inserted in 1869;
originally the first paragraph of* 'Lines by a Death-bed'.   135 *1869
(only)*: dimm'd her   136 *1852, 1869–81*: curtains hide her face,
MS. alteration (in 1881 volume): bed-clothes hide   145 *1852 (only)*:
placid, settled   146 *1852*: Her youngest rival's freshest grace.   *1869*:
Her younger rival's calmest grace.   149 *First inserted in 1853.*   151
1852: Shines the   152 *1852*: And there upon the wall you see

On that clear forest-knoll he stays,   155
With his pack round him, and delays.
He stares and stares, with troubled face,
At this huge, gleam-lit fireplace,
At that bright, iron-figured door,
And those blown rushes on the floor.   160
He gazes down into the room
With heated cheeks and flurried air,
And to himself he seems to say:
'What place is this, and who are they?
Who is that kneeling Lady fair?   165
And on his pillows that pale Knight
Who seems of marble on a tomb?
How comes it here, this chamber bright,
Through whose mullion'd windows clear
The castle-court all wet with rain,   170
The drawbridge and the moat appear,
And then the beach, and, mark'd with spray,
The sunken reefs, and far away
The unquiet bright Atlantic plain?
—What, has some glamour made me sleep,   175
And sent me with my dogs to sweep,
By night, with boisterous bugle-peal,
Through some old, sea-side, knightly hall,

155 *1852*: 'Tis noon with him, and yet he stays   *After* 156 *1852*
(*only*) *has these lines*:

        As rooted to the earth, nor sounds
        His lifted horn, nor cheers his hounds
        Into the tangled glen below.
        Yet in the sedgy bottom there
        Where the deep forest stream creeps slow
        Fring'd with dead leaves and mosses rare,
        The wild boar harbours close, and feeds.

157–60 *1852* (*only*): *these lines appear after line* 174.   158 *1852*: the
huge   159 *1852–7*: the bright   160 *1852*: the blown   163,
164 *First inserted in* 1853. *In* 1852 *the knight is not represented as speaking;*
neither marks of quotation nor italics are used.   175, 176 *1852*:

        Has then some glamour made him sleep,
        And sent him with his dogs to sweep,

Not in the free green wood at all?
That Knight's asleep, and at her prayer   180
That Lady by the bed doth kneel—
Then hush, thou boisterous bugle-peal!'
—The wild boar rustles in his lair;
The fierce hounds snuff the tainted air;
But lord and hounds keep rooted there.   185

Cheer, cheer thy dogs into the brake,
O Hunter! and without a fear
Thy golden-tassell'd bugle blow,
And through the glades thy pastime take—
For thou wilt rouse no sleepers here!   190
For these thou seest are unmoved;
Cold, cold as those who lived and loved
A thousand years ago.

III

Iseult of Brittany

A YEAR had flown, and o'er the sea away,
In Cornwall, Tristram and Queen Iseult lay;
In King Marc's chapel, in Tyntagel old—
There in a ship they bore those lovers cold.

The young surviving Iseult, one bright day,   5
Had wander'd forth. Her children were at play
In a green circular hollow in the heath
Which borders the sea-shore—a country path
Creeps over it from the till'd fields behind.
The hollow's grassy banks are soft-inclined,   10
And to one standing on them, far and near

III. *Iseult of Brittany.* 1, 2 *1852*:
         A year had flown, and in the chapel old
         Lay Tristram and queen Iseult dead and cold.
3, 4 *There is no equivalent of these lines in the edition of 1852. In 1853–4*
         At Tyntagil, in King Marc's chapel old:
         There in a ship they bore those lovers cold.

The lone unbroken view spreads bright and clear
Over the waste. This cirque of open ground
Is light and green; the heather, which all round
Creeps thickly, grows not here; but the pale grass   15
Is strewn with rocks, and many a shiver'd mass
Of vein'd white-gleaming quartz, and here and there
Dotted with holly-trees and juniper.
In the smooth centre of the opening stood
Three hollies side by side, and made a screen,   20
Warm with the winter-sun, of burnish'd green
With scarlet berries gemm'd, the fell-fare's food.
Under the glittering hollies Iseult stands,
Watching her children play; their little hands
Are busy gathering spars of quartz, and streams   25
Of stagshorn for their hats; anon, with screams
Of mad delight they drop their spoils, and bound
Among the holly-clumps and broken ground,
Racing full speed, and startling in their rush
The fell-fares and the speckled missel-thrush   30
Out of their glossy coverts;—but when now
Their cheeks were flush'd, and over each hot brow,
Under the feather'd hats of the sweet pair,
In blinding masses shower'd the golden hair—
Then Iseult call'd them to her, and the three   35
Cluster'd under the holly-screen, and she
Told them an old-world Breton history.

Warm in their mantles wrapt the three stood there,
Under the hollies, in the clear still air—
Mantles with those rich furs deep glistering   40
Which Venice ships do from swart Egypt bring.
Long they stay'd still—then, pacing at their ease,
Moved up and down under the glossy trees.
But still, as they pursued their warm dry road,
From Iseult's lips the unbroken story flow'd,   45
And still the children listen'd, their blue eyes

13 *1852*: This ring   27 *1881*: thy drop [*sic*]

150

Fix'd on their mother's face in wide surprise;
Nor did their looks stray once to the sea-side,
Nor to the brown heaths round them, bright and wide,
Nor to the snow, which, though 't was all away   50
From the open heath, still by the hedgerows lay,
Nor to the shining sea-fowl, that with screams
Bore up from where the bright Atlantic gleams,
Swooping to landward; nor to where, quite clear,
The fell-fares settled on the thickets near.   55
And they would still have listen'd, till dark night
Came keen and chill down on the heather bright;
But, when the red glow on the sea grew cold,
And the grey turrets of the castle old
Look'd sternly through the frosty evening-air,   60
Then Iseult took by the hand those children fair,
And brought her tale to an end, and found the path,
And led them home over the darkening heath.

And is she happy? Does she see unmoved
The days in which she might have lived and loved   65
Slip without bringing bliss slowly away,
One after one, to-morrow like to-day?
Joy has not found her yet, nor ever will—
Is it this thought which makes her mien so still,
Her features so fatigued, her eyes, though sweet,   70
So sunk, so rarely lifted save to meet
Her children's? She moves slow; her voice alone
Hath yet an infantine and silver tone,
But even that comes languidly; in truth,
She seems one dying in a mask of youth.   75
And now she will go home, and softly lay
Her laughing children in their beds, and play
Awhile with them before they sleep; and then
She'll light her silver lamp, which fishermen
Dragging their nets through the rough waves, afar,   80
Along this iron coast, know like a star,

69 *1852–69*: thought that   73 *1852–7*: Has yet

And take her broidery-frame, and there she'll sit
Hour after hour, her gold curls sweeping it;
Lifting her soft-bent head only to mind
Her children, or to listen to the wind.   85
And when the clock peals midnight, she will move
Her work away, and let her fingers rove
Across the shaggy brows of Tristram's hound
Who lies, guarding her feet, along the ground;
Or else she will fall musing, her blue eyes   90
Fixt, her slight hands clasp'd on her lap; then rise,
And at her prie-dieu kneel, until she have told
Her rosary-beads of ebony tipp'd with gold,
Then to her soft sleep—and to-morrow 'll be
To-day's exact repeated effigy.   95

Yes, it is lonely for her in her hall.
The children, and the grey-hair'd seneschal,
Her women, and Sir Tristram's aged hound,
Are there the sole companions to be found.
But these she loves; and noisier life than this   100
She would find ill to bear, weak as she is.
She has her children, too, and night and day
Is with them; and the wide heaths where they play,
The hollies, and the cliff, and the sea-shore,
The sand, the sea-birds, and the distant sails,   105
These are to her dear as to them; the tales
With which this day the children she beguiled
She gleaned from Breton grandames, when a child,
In every hut along this sea-coast wild.
She herself loves them still, and, when they are told,   110
Can forget all to hear them, as of old.

Dear saints, it is not sorrow, as I hear,
Not suffering, which shuts up eye and ear
To all that has delighted them before,

112–50 *Omitted in 1853, 1854; reinserted in 1857.*   113 *1852 and*
1857–69: that shuts   114 *1852 and 1857–69*: all which

And lets us be what we were once no more.   115
No, we may suffer deeply, yet retain
Power to be moved and soothed, for all our pain,
By what of old pleased us, and will again.
No, 'tis the gradual furnace of the world,
In whose hot air our spirits are upcurl'd   120
Until they crumble, or else grow like steel—
Which kills in us the bloom, the youth, the spring—
Which leaves the fierce necessity to feel,
But takes away the power—this can avail,
By drying up our joy in everything,   125
To make our former pleasures all seem stale.
This, or some tyrannous single thought, some fit
Of passion, which subdues our souls to it,
Till for its sake alone we live and move—
Call it ambition, or remorse, or love—   130
This too can change us wholly, and make seem
All which we did before, shadow and dream.

    And yet, I swear, it angers me to see
How this fool passion gulls men potently;
Being, in truth, but a diseased unrest,   135
And an unnatural overheat at best.
How they are full of languor and distress
Not having it; which when they do possess,
They straightway are burnt up with fume and care,
And spend their lives in posting here and there   140
Where this plague drives them; and have little ease,
Are furious with themselves, and hard to please.
Like that bald Cæsar, the famed Roman wight,
Who wept at reading of a Grecian knight
Who made a name at younger years than he;   145
Or that renown'd mirror of chivalry,
Prince Alexander, Philip's peerless son,

132 *1852 and 1857–69*: All that   142 *1852*: Can never end their tasks, are hard to please.   *1857–69*: Are fretful with themselves, and hard to please.   143 *1857–77*: bold Cæsar,

Who carried the great war from Macedon
Into the Soudan's realm, and thundered on
To die at thirty-five in Babylon.   150

What tale did Iseult to the children say,
Under the hollies, that bright winter's day?

She told them of the fairy-haunted land
Away the other side of Brittany,
Beyond the heaths, edged by the lonely sea;   155
Of the deep forest-glades of Broce-liande,
Through whose green boughs the golden sunshine creeps,
Where Merlin by the enchanted thorn-tree sleeps.
For here he came with the fay Vivian,
One April, when the warm days first began.   160
He was on foot, and that false fay, his friend,
On her white palfrey; here he met his end,
In these lone sylvan glades, that April-day.
This tale of Merlin and the lovely fay
Was the one Iseult chose, and she brought clear   165
Before the children's fancy him and her.

Blowing between the stems, the forest-air
Had loosen'd the brown locks of Vivian's hair,
Which play'd on her flush'd cheek, and her blue eyes
Sparkled with mocking glee and exercise.   170
Her palfrey's flanks were mired and bathed in sweat,
For they had travell'd far and not stopp'd yet.
A brier in that tangled wilderness
Had scored her white right hand, which she allows
To rest ungloved on her green riding-dress;   175
The other warded off the drooping boughs.
But still she chatted on, with her blue eyes
Fix'd full on Merlin's face, her stately prize.
Her 'haviour had the morning's fresh clear grace,
The spirit of the woods was in her face.   180
She look'd so witching fair, that learned wight

168 *1852–77*: the brown curls   173 *1852-81*: briar

Forgot his craft, and his best wits took flight;
And he grew fond, and eager to obey
His mistress, use her empire as she may.

They came to where the brushwood ceased, and day   185
Peer'd 'twixt the stems; and the ground broke away,
In a sloped sward down to a brawling brook;
And up as high as where they stood to look
On the brook's farther side was clear, but then
The underwood and trees began again.   190
This open glen was studded thick with thorns
Then white with blossom; and you saw the horns,
Through last year's fern, of the shy fallow-deer
Who come at noon down to the water here.
You saw the bright-eyed squirrels dart along   195
Under the thorns on the green sward; and strong
The blackbird whistled from the dingles near,
And the weird chipping of the woodpecker
Rang lonelily and sharp; the sky was fair,
And a fresh breath of spring stirr'd everywhere.   200
Merlin and Vivian stopp'd on the slope's brow,
To gaze on the light sea of leaf and bough
Which glistering plays all round them, lone and mild,
As if to itself the quiet forest smiled.
Upon the brow-top grew a thorn, and here   205
The grass was dry and moss'd, and you saw clear
Across the hollow; white anemonies
Starr'd the cool turf, and clumps of primroses
Ran out from the dark underwood behind.
No fairer resting-place a man could find.   210
'Here let us halt,' said Merlin then; and she
Nodded, and tied her palfrey to a tree.

They sate them down together, and a sleep
Fell upon Merlin, more like death, so deep.

189 *1852–69*: further   193 *1852–77*: the green fern   194 *1852–*
69: Which come   198 *1852–7*: light chipping   202 *1852–77*:
on the green sea   203 *1852–77*: Which glistering lay

Her finger on her lips, then Vivian rose,   215
And from her brown-lock'd head the wimple throws,
And takes it in her hand, and waves it over
The blossom'd thorn-tree and her sleeping lover.
Nine times she waved the fluttering wimple round,
And made a little plot of magic ground.   220
And in that daisied circle, as men say,
Is Merlin prisoner till the judgment-day;
But she herself whither she will can rove—
For she was passing weary of his love.

SAINT BRANDAN

[*First published in* FRASER'S MAGAZINE, *July 1860.
Reprinted 1867 and thereafter*]

SAINT BRANDAN sails the northern main;
The brotherhoods of saints are glad.
He greets them once, he sails again;
So late!—such storms!—The Saint is mad!

He heard, across the howling seas,   5
Chime convent-bells on wintry nights;
He saw, on spray-swept Hebrides,
Twinkle the monastery-lights.

But north, still north, Saint Brandan steer'd—
And now no bells, no convents more!   10
The hurtling Polar lights are near'd,
The sea without a human shore.

At last—(it was the Christmas night;
Stars shone after a day of storm)—
He sees float past an iceberg white,   15
And on it—Christ!—a living form.

SAINT BRANDAN. 15 *1860* (*Fraser's Magazine*): float near

That furtive mien, that scowling eye,
Of hair that red and tufted fell——
It is—Oh, where shall Brandan fly?—
The traitor Judas, out of hell!   20

Palsied with terror, Brandan sate;
The moon was bright, the iceberg near.
He hears a voice sigh humbly: 'Wait!
By high permission I am here.

'One moment wait, thou holy man!   25
On earth my crime, my death, they knew;
My name is under all men's ban—
Ah, tell them of my respite too!

'Tell them, one blessed Christmas-night—
(It was the first after I came,   30
Breathing self-murder, frenzy, spite,
To rue my guilt in endless flame)—

'I felt, as I in torment lay
'Mid the souls plagued by heavenly power
An angel touch mine arm, and say: 35
Go hence and cool thyself an hour!

' "Ah, whence this mercy, Lord?" I said.
The Leper recollect, said he,
Who ask'd the passers-by for aid,
In Joppa, and thy charity.   40

'Then I remember'd how I went,
In Joppa, through the public street,
One morn when the sirocco spent
Its storms of dust with burning heat;

'And in the street a leper sate,   45
Shivering with fever, naked, old;
Sand raked his sores from heel to pate,
The hot wind fever'd him five-fold.

18 *1860*: black and tufted

'He gazed upon me as I pass'd,
And murmur'd: *Help me, or I die!*—   50
To the poor wretch my cloak I cast,
Saw him look eased, and hurried by.

'Oh Brandan, think what grace divine,
What blessing must full goodness shower,
When fragment of it small, like mine,   55
Hath such inestimable power!

'Well-fed, well-clothed, well-friended, I
Did that chance act of good, that one!
Then went my way to kill and lie—
Forgot my good as soon as done.   60

'That germ of kindness, in the womb
Of mercy caught, did not expire;
Outlives my guilt, outlives my doom,
And friends me in the pit of fire.

'Once every year, when carols wake,   65
On earth, the Christmas-night's repose,
Arising from the sinners' lake,
I journey to these healing snows.

'I stanch with ice my burning breast,
With silence balm my whirling brain.   70
O Brandan! to this hour of rest
That Joppan leper's ease was pain.'——

Tears started to Saint Brandan's eyes;
He bow'd his head, he breathed a prayer—
Then look'd, and lo, the frosty skies!   75
The iceberg, and no Judas there!

54 *1860–7*: true goodness   55 *1860*: When semblance of it faint
1867: If semblance of it faint   *1868*: If fragment of it small
56 *1860*: inalienable power: 60 *1860*: my deed   75, 76 *1860–9*:
                        When he look'd up—tenantless lies
                        The iceberg in the frosty air!
76 *1877*: The iceberg and no tenant there!

THE NECKAN

[*First published 1853. Reprinted 1854, '57, '69, and thereafter*]

In summer, on the headlands,
  The Baltic Sea along,
Sits Neckan with his harp of gold,
  And sings his plaintive song.

Green rolls beneath the headlands,   5
  Green rolls the Baltic Sea;
And there, below the Neckan's feet,
  His wife and children be.

He sings not of the ocean,
  Its shells and roses pale;   10
Of earth, of earth the Neckan sings,
  He hath no other tale.

He sits upon the headlands,
  And sings a mournful stave
Of all he saw and felt on earth   15
  Far from the kind sea-wave.

Sings how, a knight, he wander'd
  By castle, field, and town—
But earthly knights have harder hearts
  Than the sea-children own.   20

Sings of his earthly bridal—
  Priest, knights, and ladies gay.
'—And who art thou,' the priest began,
  'Sir Knight, who wedd'st to-day?'—

'—I am no knight,' he answered;   25
  'From the sea-waves I come.'—
The knights drew sword, the ladies scream'd,
  The surpliced priest stood dumb.

16 *1853–7*: the green sea wave.

He sings how from the chapel
   He vanish'd with his bride,   30
And bore her down to the sea-halls,
   Beneath the salt sea-tide.

He sings how she sits weeping
   'Mid shells that round her lie.
'—False Neckan shares my bed,' she weeps;   35
   'No Christian mate have I.'—

He sings how through the billows
   He rose to earth again,
And sought a priest to sign the cross,
   That Neckan Heaven might gain.   40

He sings how, on an evening,
   Beneath the birch-trees cool,
He sate and play'd his harp of gold,
   Beside the river-pool.

Beside the pool sate Neckan—   45
   Tears fill'd his mild blue eye.
On his white mule, across the bridge,
   A cassock'd priest rode by.

'—Why sitt'st thou there, O Neckan,
   And play'st thy harp of gold?   50
Sooner shall this my staff bear leaves,
   Than thou shalt Heaven behold.'—

But, lo, the staff, it budded!
   It green'd, it branch'd, it waved.
'—O ruth of God,' the priest cried out,   55
   'This lost sea-creature saved!'

32 *1857 (only)*: **the** cold sea tide.   46 *1853–7*: cold blue eye.
MS. corrections (in 1854 volume) cold *deleted for* mild *and then for* kind
53–6 *This stanza was added in 1869.*

The cassock'd priest rode onwards,
   And vanished with his mule;
But Neckan in the twilight grey
   Wept by the river-pool.   60

He wept: 'The earth hath kindness,
   The sea, the starry poles;
Earth, sea, and sky, and God above—
   But, ah, not human souls!'

In summer, on the headlands,   65
   The Baltic Sea along,
Sits Neckan with his harp of gold,
   And sings this plaintive song.

THE FORSAKEN MERMAN

[First published 1849. Reprinted 1853, '54, '57, '69, and thereafter]

COME, dear children, let us away;
Down and away below!
Now my brothers call from the bay,
Now the great winds shoreward blow,
Now the salt tides seaward flow;   5
Now the wild white horses play,
Champ and chafe and toss in the spray.
Children dear, let us away!
This way, this way!

Call her once before you go—   10
Call once yet!
In a voice that she will know:
'Margaret! Margaret!'
Children's voices should be dear
(Call once more) to a mother's ear;   15

59 *1853–7*: And Neckan   61–4 *This stanza was added in 1869.*
61 *1869 (only)*: He said: *MS. (in 1854 volume), not adopted:* He
mused:
   THE FORSAKEN MERMAN. 4 *1849–57*: shorewards   5 *1849–57*:
seawards

Children's voices, wild with pain—
Surely she will come again!
Call her once and come away;
This way, this way!
'Mother dear, we cannot stay!   20
The wild white horses foam and fret.'
Margaret! Margaret!

Come, dear children, come away down;
Call no more!
One last look at the white-wall'd town,   25
And the little grey church on the windy shore,
Then come down!
She will not come though you call all day;
Come away, come away!

Children dear, was it yesterday   30
We heard the sweet bells over the bay?
In the caverns where we lay,
Through the surf and through the swell,
The far-off sound of a silver bell?
Sand-strewn caverns, cool and deep,   35
Where the winds are all asleep;
Where the spent lights quiver and gleam,
Where the salt weed sways in the stream,
Where the sea-beasts, ranged all round,
Feed in the ooze of their pasture-ground;   40
Where the sea-snakes coil and twine,
Dry their mail and bask in the brine;
Where great whales come sailing by,
Sail and sail, with unshut eye,
Round the world for ever and aye?   45
When did music come this way?
Children dear, was it yesterday?

Children dear, was it yesterday
(Call yet once) that she went away?

20 *From 1849 to 1869 the quotation consisted of this single line.*

Once she sate with you and me,   50
On a red gold throne in the heart of the sea,
And the youngest sate on her knee.
She comb'd its bright hair, and she tended it well,
When down swung the sound of a far-off bell.
She sigh'd, she look'd up through the clear green sea;   55
She said: 'I must go, for my kinsfolk pray
In the little grey church on the shore to-day.
'Twill be Easter-time in the world—ah me!
And I lose my poor soul, Merman! here with thee.'
I said: 'Go up, dear heart, through the waves;   60
Say thy prayer, and come back to the kind sea-caves!'
She smiled, she went up through the surf in the bay.
Children dear, was it yesterday?

Children dear, were we long alone?
'The sea grows stormy, the little ones moan;   65
Long prayers,' I said, 'in the world they say;
Come!' I said; and we rose through the surf in the bay.
We went up the beach, by the sandy down
Where the sea-stocks bloom, to the white-wall'd town;
Through the narrow paved streets, where all was still,   70
To the little grey church on the windy hill.
From the church came a murmur of folk at their prayers,
But we stood without in the cold blowing airs.
We climb'd on the graves, on the stones worn with rains,
And we gazed up the aisle through the small leaded panes. 75
She sate by the pillar; we saw her clear:
'Margaret, hist! come quick, we are here!
Dear heart,' I said, 'we are long alone;
The sea grows stormy, the little ones moan.'
But, ah, she gave me never a look,   80
For her eyes were seal'd to the holy book!
Loud prays the priest; shut stands the door.

54 *1849–69*: the far-off   82 *From 1849 to 1857 this line was enclosed*
within quotation-marks.

Come away, children, call no more!
Come away, come down, call no more!

Down, down, down!   85
Down to the depths of the sea!
She sits at her wheel in the humming town,
Singing most joyfully.
Hark what she sings: 'O joy, O joy,
For the humming street, and the child with its toy!   90
For the priest, and the bell, and the holy well;
For the wheel where I spun,
And the blessed light of the sun!'
And so she sings her fill,
Singing most joyfully,   95
Till the spindle drops from her hand,
And the whizzing wheel stands still.
She steals to the window, and looks at the sand,
And over the sand at the sea;
And her eyes are set in a stare;   100
And anon there breaks a sigh,
And anon there drops a tear,
From a sorrow-clouded eye,
And a heart sorrow-laden,
A long, long sigh;   105
For the cold strange eyes of a little Mermaiden
And the gleam of her golden hair.

Come away, away children;
Come children, come down!
The hoarse wind blows coldly;   110
Lights shine in the town.
She will start from her slumber
When gusts shake the door;
She will hear the winds howling,
Will hear the waves roar.   115

96 *1849–77*: the shuttle falls   110 *1849*: The salt tide rolls seaward.
1853–81: The hoarse wind blows colder,   *MS. alteration (in 1881*
volume): coldly;

We shall see, while above us
The waves roar and whirl,
A ceiling of amber,
A pavement of pearl.
Singing: 'Here came a mortal,   120
But faithless was she!
And alone dwell for ever
The kings of the sea.'

But, children, at midnight,
When soft the winds blow,   125
When clear falls the moonlight,
When spring-tides are low;
When sweet airs come seaward
From heaths starr'd with broom,
And high rocks throw mildly   130
On the blanch'd sands a gloom;
Up the still, glistening beaches,
Up the creeks we will hie,
Over banks of bright seaweed
The ebb-tide leaves dry.   135
We will gaze, from the sand-hills,
At the white, sleeping town;
At the church on the hill-side—
And then come back down.
Singing: 'There dwells a loved one,   140
But cruel is she!
She left lonely for ever
The kings of the sea.'

SONNETS

AUSTERITY OF POETRY

[First published 1867. Reprinted 1868 and thereafter]

THAT son of Italy who tried to blow,[9]
Ere Dante came, the trump of sacred song,
In his light youth amid a festal throng
Sate with his bride to see a public show.

Fair was the bride, and on her front did glow   5
Youth like a star; and what to youth belong—
Gay raiment, sparkling gauds, elation strong.
A prop gave way! crash fell a platform! lo,

'Mid struggling sufferers, hurt to death, she lay!
Shuddering, they drew her garments off—and found   10
A robe of sackcloth next the smooth, white skin.

Such, poets, is your bride, the Muse! young, gay,
Radiant, adorn'd outside; a hidden ground
Of thought and of austerity within.

A PICTURE AT NEWSTEAD

[First published 1867. Reprinted 1868 and thereafter]

WHAT made my heart, at Newstead, fullest swell?—
'Twas not the thought of Byron, of his cry
Stormily sweet, his Titan-agony;
It was the sight of that Lord Arundel

Who struck, in heat, his child he loved so well,   5
And his child's reason flicker'd, and did die.
Painted (he will'd it) in the gallery
They hang; the picture doth the story tell.

A PICTURE AT NEWSTEAD. 5 *1867 (only)*: the child   6 *1867 (only)*:
the child's

Behold the stern, mail'd father, staff in hand!
The little fair-hair'd son, with vacant gaze,   10
Where no more lights of sense or knowledge are!

Methinks the woe, which made that father stand
Baring his dumb remorse to future days,
Was woe than Byron's woe more tragic far.

RACHEL

[First published 1867. Reprinted 1868 and thereafter]

I

In Paris all look'd hot and like to fade.
Sere, in the garden of the Tuileries,
Sere with September, droop'd the chestnut-trees.
'Twas dawn; a brougham roll'd through the streets
    and made

Halt at the white and silent colonnade   5
Of the French Theatre. Worn with disease,
Rachel, with eyes no gazing can appease,
Sate in the brougham and those blank walls survey'd.

She follows the gay world, whose swarms have fled
To Switzerland, to Baden, to the Rhine;   10
Why stops she by this empty play-house drear?

Ah, where the spirit its highest life hath led,
All spots, match'd with that spot, are less divine;
And Rachel's Switzerland, her Rhine, is here!

II

Unto a lonely villa, in a dell
Above the fragrant warm Provençal shore,
The dying Rachel in a chair they bore
Up the steep pine-plumed paths of the Estrelle,

RACHEL. *2 1867–9*: Brown in the garden   *3 1867–9*: Brown with
September

And laid her in a stately room, where fell 5
The shadow of a marble Muse of yore,
The rose-crown'd queen of legendary lore,
Polymnia, full on her death-bed.—'Twas well!

The fret and misery of our northern towns,
In this her life's last day, our poor, our pain, 10
Our jangle of false wits, our climate's frowns,

Do for this radiant Greek-soul'd artist cease;
Sole object of her dying eyes remain
The beauty and the glorious art of Greece.

III

SPRUNG from the blood of Israel's scatter'd race,
At a mean inn in German Aarau born,
To forms from antique Greece and Rome uptorn,
Trick'd out with a Parisian speech and face,

Imparting life renew'd, old classic grace; 5
Then, soothing with thy Christian strain forlorn,
A-Kempis! her departing soul outworn,
While by her bedside Hebrew rites have place—

Ah, not the radiant spirit of Greece alone
She had—one power, which made her breast its home! 10
In her, like us, there clash'd, contending powers,

Germany, France, Christ, Moses, Athens, Rome.
The strife, the mixture in her soul, are ours;
Her genius and her glory are her own.

WORLDLY PLACE

[First published 1867. Reprinted 1868 and thereafter]

EVEN *in a palace, life may be led well!*
So spake the imperial sage, purest of men,
Marcus Aurelius. But the stifling den
Of common life, where, crowded up pell-mell,

WORLDLY PLACE. 2 *1867–9:* So spoke

Our freedom for a little bread we sell,   5
And drudge under some foolish master's ken
Who rates us if we peer outside our pen—
Match'd with a palace, is not this a hell?

Even in a palace! On his truth sincere,
Who spoke these words, no shadow ever came;   10
And when my ill-school'd spirit is aflame

Some nobler, ampler stage of life to win,
I'll stop, and say: 'There were no succour here!
The aids to noble life are all within.'

EAST LONDON

[First published 1867. Reprinted 1868 and thereafter]

'Twas August, and the fierce sun overhead
Smote on the squalid streets of Bethnal Green,
And the pale weaver, through his windows seen
In Spitalfields, look'd thrice dispirited.

I met a preacher there I knew, and said: 5
'Ill and o'erwork'd, how fare you in this scene?'—
'Bravely!' said he; 'for I of late have been
Much cheer'd with thoughts of Christ, *the living bread.*'

O human soul! as long as thou canst so
Set up a mark of everlasting light,   10
Above the howling senses' ebb and flow,

To cheer thee, and to right thee if thou roam—
Not with lost toil thou labourest through the night!
Thou mak'st the heaven thou hop'st indeed thy home.

WEST LONDON

[First published 1867. Reprinted 1868 and thereafter]

Crouch'd on the pavement, close by Belgrave Square,
A tramp I saw, ill, moody, and tongue-tied.
A babe was in her arms, and at her side
A girl; their clothes were rags, their feet were bare.

Some labouring men, whose work lay somewhere there,   5
Pass'd opposite; she touch'd her girl, who hied
Across, and begg'd, and came back satisfied.
The rich she had let pass with frozen stare.

Thought I: 'Above her state this spirit towers;
She will not ask of aliens, but of friends,   10
Of sharers in a common human fate.

'She turns from that cold succour, which attends
The unknown little from the unknowing great,
And points us to a better time than ours.'

EAST AND WEST
[First published 1867. Reprinted 1868 and thereafter]

IN the bare midst of Anglesey they show
Two springs which close by one another play;
And, 'Thirteen hundred years agone,' they say,
'Two saints met often where those waters flow.

'One came from Penmon westward, and a glow   5
Whiten'd his face from the sun's fronting ray;
Eastward the other, from the dying day,
And he with unsunn'd face did always go.'

Seiriol the Bright, Kybi the Dark! men said.
The seër from the East was then in light,   10
The seër from the West was then in shade.

Ah! now 'tis changed. In conquering sunshine bright
The man of the bold West now comes array'd;
He of the mystic East is touch'd with night.

THE BETTER PART
[First published 1867. Reprinted 1868 and thereafter]

LONG fed on boundless hopes, O race of man,
How angrily thou spurn'st all simpler fare!
'Christ,' some one says, 'was human as we are;
No judge eyes us from Heaven, our sin to scan;

THE BETTER PART. *Title 1867, 1868*: Anti-Desperation.

'We live no more, when we have done our span.'—   5
'Well, then, for Christ,' thou answerest, 'who can care?
From sin, which Heaven records not, why forbear?
Live we like brutes our life without a plan!'

So answerest thou; but why not rather say:
'Hath man no second life?—*Pitch this one high!*   10
Sits there no judge in Heaven, our sin to see?—

'*More strictly, then, the inward judge obey!*
Was Christ a man like us? *Ah! let us try
If we then, too, can be such men as he!*'

THE DIVINITY

[First published 1867. Reprinted 1868 and thereafter]

'YES, write it in the rock,' Saint Bernard said,
'Grave it on brass with adamantine pen!
'Tis God himself becomes apparent, when
God's wisdom and God's goodness are display'd,

'For God of these his attributes is made.'—   5
Well spake the impetuous Saint, and bore of men
The suffrage captive; now, not one in ten
Recalls the obscure opposer he outweigh'd.[10]

God's wisdom and God's goodness!—Ay, but fools
Mis-define these till God knows them no more.   10
Wisdom and goodness, they are God!—what schools

Have yet so much as heard this simpler lore?
This no Saint preaches, and this no Church rules;
'Tis in the desert, now and heretofore.

IMMORTALITY

[First published 1867. Reprinted 1868 and thereafter]

FOIL'D by our fellow-men, depress'd, outworn,
We leave the brutal world to take its way,
And, *Patience! in another life*, we say,
The world shall be thrust down, and we up-borne.

And will not, then, the immortal armies scorn   5
The world's poor, routed leavings? or will they,
Who fail'd under the heat of this life's day,
Support the fervours of the heavenly morn?

No, no! the energy of life may be
Kept on after the grave, but not begun;   10
And he who flagg'd not in the earthly strife,

From strength to strength advancing—only he,
His soul well-knit, and all his battles won,
Mounts, and that hardly, to eternal life.

THE GOOD SHEPHERD WITH THE KID

[First published 1867. Reprinted 1868 and thereafter]

He saves the sheep, the goats he doth not save.
So rang Tertullian's sentence, on the side
Of that unpitying Phrygian sect which cried:[11]
'Him can no fount of fresh forgiveness lave,

'Who sins, once wash'd by the baptismal wave.'—   5
So spake the fierce Tertullian. But she sigh'd,
The infant Church! of love she felt the tide
Stream on her from her Lord's yet recent grave.

And then she smiled; and in the Catacombs,
With eye suffused but heart inspired true,   10
On those walls subterranean, where she hid

Her head 'mid ignominy, death, and tombs,
She her Good Shepherd's hasty image drew—
And on his shoulders, not a lamb, a kid.

THE GOOD SHEPHERD WITH THE KID. 12 *1867–77*: in ignominy,

MONICA'S LAST PRAYER [12]

[*First published 1867. Reprinted 1868 and thereafter*]

'AH, could thy grave at home, at Carthage, be!'
Care not for that, and lay me where I fall!
Everywhere heard will be the judgment-call;
But at God's altar, oh! remember me.

Thus Monica, and died in Italy.   5
Yet fervent had her longing been, through all
Her course, for home at last, and burial
With her own husband, by the Libyan sea.

Had been! but at the end, to her pure soul
All tie with all beside seem'd vain and cheap,   10
And union before God the only care.

Creeds pass, rites change, no altar standeth whole.
Yet we her memory, as she pray'd, will keep,
Keep by this: *Life in God, and union there!*

1 *1867–9*: 'Oh, could

LYRIC POEMS

SWITZERLAND

1. MEETING

[*First published 1852. Reprinted 1853, '54, '57, '69, and thereafter*]

AGAIN I see my bliss at hand,
The town, the lake are here;
My Marguerite smiles upon the strand,[13]
Unalter'd with the year.

I know that graceful figure fair,   5
That cheek of languid hue;
I know that soft, enkerchief'd hair,
And those sweet eyes of blue.

Again I spring to make my choice;
Again in tones of ire   10
I hear a God's tremendous voice:
'Be counsell'd, and retire.'

Ye guiding Powers who join and part,
What would ye have with me?
Ah, warn some more ambitious heart,   15
And let the peaceful be!

2. PARTING

[*First published 1852. Reprinted 1853, '54, '57, '69, and thereafter*]

YE storm-winds of Autumn!
Who rush by, who shake
The window, and ruffle
The gleam-lighted lake;

1. *Meeting. Title, 1852–7*: The Lake; *from 1853 through 1869 was second poem of* 'Switzerland' *group.*
2. *Parting. Title 1853–7*: Switzerland IV. Parting;   *1869*: Switzerland 3. Parting.

Who cross to the hill-side   5
Thin-sprinkled with farms,
Where the high woods strip sadly
Their yellowing arms—
Ye are bound for the mountains!
Ah! with you let me go   10
Where your cold, distant barrier,
The vast range of snow,
Through the loose clouds lifts dimly
Its white peaks in air—
How deep is their stillness!   15
Ah, would I were there!

But on the stairs what voice is this I hear,
Buoyant as morning, and as morning clear?
Say, has some wet bird-haunted English lawn
Lent it the music of its trees at dawn?   20
Or was it from some sun-fleck'd mountain-brook
That the sweet voice its upland clearness took?
        Ah! it comes nearer—
        Sweet notes, this way!

    Hark! fast by the window   25
    The rushing winds go,
    To the ice-cumber'd gorges,
    The vast seas of snow!
    There the torrents drive upward
    Their rock-strangled hum;   30
    There the avalanche thunders
    The hoarse torrent dumb.
    —I come, O ye mountains!
    Ye torrents, I come!

But who is this, by the half-open'd door,   35
Whose figure casts a shadow on the floor?
The sweet blue eyes—the soft, ash-colour'd hair—
The cheeks that still their gentle paleness wear—

The lovely lips, with their arch smile that tells
The unconquer'd joy in which her spirit dwells— 40
    Ah! they bend nearer—
    Sweet lips, this way!

Hark! the wind rushes past us!
Ah! with that let me go
To the clear, waning hill-side, 45
Unspotted by snow,
There to watch, o'er the sunk vale,
The frore mountain-wall,
Where the niched snow-bed sprays down
Its powdery fall. 50
There its dusky blue clusters
The aconite spreads;
There the pines slope, the cloud-strips
Hung soft in their heads.
No life but, at moments, 55
The mountain-bee's hum.
—I come, O ye mountains!
Ye pine-woods, I come!

Forgive me! forgive me!
    Ah, Marguerite, fain 60
Would these arms reach to clasp thee!
    But see! 'tis in vain.

In the void air, towards thee,
    My stretch'd arms are cast;
But a sea rolls between us— 65
    Our different past!

To the lips, ah! of others
    Those lips have been prest,
And others, ere I was,
    Were strain'd to that breast; 70

64 *1852–69*: strain'd arms   70 *1852–69*: Were clasp'd

Far, far from each other
   Our spirits have grown;
And what heart knows another?
   Ah! who knows his own?

Blow, ye winds! lift me with you!   75
   I come to the wild.
Fold closely, O Nature!
   Thine arms round thy child.

To thee only God granted
   A heart ever new—   80
To all always open,
   To all always true.

Ah! calm me, restore me;
   And dry up my tears
On thy high mountain-platforms;   85
   Where morn first appears;

Where the white mists, for ever,
   Are spread and upfurl'd—
In the stir of the forces
   Whence issued the world.   90

3. A FAREWELL

[*First published 1852. Reprinted 1854, '57, '69, and thereafter*]

My horse's feet beside the lake,
Where sweet the unbroken moonbeams lay,
Sent echoes through the night to wake
Each glistening strand, each heath-fringed bay.

The poplar avenue was pass'd,   5
And the roof'd bridge that spans the stream;
Up the steep street I hurried fast,
Led by thy taper's starlike beam.

3. *A Farewell. Title 1854, 1857*: Switzerland V. A Farewell;   *1869*:
Switzerland 4. A Farewell.   8 *1852*: Lit by

I came! I saw thee rise!—the blood
Pour'd flushing to thy languid cheek.　　　　10
Lock'd in each other's arms we stood,
In tears, with hearts too full to speak.

Days flew;—ah, soon I could discern
A trouble in thine alter'd air!
Thy hand lay languidly in mine,　　　　15
Thy cheek was grave, thy speech grew rare;

I blame thee not!—this heart, I know,
To be long loved was never framed;
For something in its depths doth glow
Too strange, too restless, too untamed.　　　　20

And women—things that live and move
Mined by the fever of the soul—
They seek to find in those they love
Stern strength, and promise of control.

They ask not kindness, gentle ways—　　　　25
These they themselves have tried and known;
They ask a soul which never sways
With the blind gusts that shake their own.

I too have felt the load I bore
In a too strong emotion's sway;　　　　30
I too have wish'd, no woman more,
This starting, feverish heart away.

I too have long'd for trenchant force,
And will like a dividing spear;
Have praised the keen, unscrupulous course,　　　　35
Which knows no doubt, which feels no fear.

But in the world I learnt, what there
Thou too wilt surely one day prove,
That will, that energy, though rare,
Are yet far, far less rare than love.　　　　40

10 *1852*: Came flooding to　　　*1854–7*: Came flushing to
27 *1852–7*: that never　　　28 *1852–7*: which shake

Go, then!—till time and fate impress
This truth on thee, be mine no more!
They will!—for thou, I feel, not less
Than I, wast destined to this lore.

We school our manners, act our parts—   45
But He, who sees us through and through,
Knows that the bent of both our hearts
Was to be gentle, tranquil, true.

And though we wear out life, alas!
Distracted as a homeless wind,   50
In beating where we must not pass,
In seeking what we shall not find;

Yet we shall one day gain, life past,
Clear prospect o'er our being's whole;
Shall see ourselves, and learn at last   55
Our true affinities of soul.

We shall not then deny a course
To every thought the mass ignore;
We shall not then call hardness force,
Nor lightness wisdom any more.   60

Then, in the eternal Father's smile,
Our soothed, encouraged souls will dare
To seem as free from pride and guile,
As good, as generous, as they are.

Then we shall know our friends!—though much   65
Will have been lost—the help in strife,
The thousand sweet, still joys of such
As hand in hand face earthly life—

Though these be lost, there will be yet
A sympathy august and pure;   70
Ennobled by a vast regret,
And by contrition seal'd thrice sure.

43 *1852–69*: no less   44 *1852–7*: wert destin'd
63 *1854–69*: To *seem*   64 *1854–69*: they *are*.

And we, whose ways were unlike here,
May then more neighbouring courses ply;
May to each other be brought near,   75
And greet across infinity.

How sweet, unreach'd by earthly jars,
My sister! to maintain with thee
The hush among the shining stars,
The calm upon the moonlit sea!   80

How sweet to feel, on the boon air,
All our unquiet pulses cease!
To feel that nothing can impair
The gentleness, the thirst for peace—

The gentleness too rudely hurl'd   85
On this wild earth of hate and fear;
The thirst for peace a raving world
Would never let us satiate here.

4. ISOLATION. TO MARGUERITE

[First published 1857. Reprinted 1869 and thereafter]

WE were apart; yet, day by day,
I bade my heart more constant be.
I bade it keep the world away,
And grow a home for only thee;
Nor fear'd but thy love likewise grew,   5
Like mine, each day, more tried, more true.

The fault was grave! I might have known,
What far too soon, alas! I learn'd—
The heart can bind itself alone,
And faith may oft be unreturn'd.   10
Self-sway'd our feelings ebb and swell—
Thou lov'st no more;—Farewell! Farewell!

78 *1852–69*: to behold
    4. *Isolation. To Marguerite. Title 1857*: Switzerland VI. To Marguerite;
1869: Switzerland 6. Isolation. To Marguerite.   10 *1857–69*: faith is
often   *1877*: faith may well be

Farewell!—and thou, thou lonely heart,
Which never yet without remorse
Even for a moment didst depart 15
From thy remote and spheréd course
To haunt the place where passions reign—
Back to thy solitude again!

Back! with the conscious thrill of shame
Which Luna felt, that summer-night, 20
Flash through her pure immortal frame,
When she forsook the starry height
To hang over Endymion's sleep
Upon the pine-grown Latmian steep.

Yet she, chaste queen, had never proved 25
How vain a thing is mortal love,
Wandering in Heaven, far removed.
But thou hast long had place to prove
This truth—to prove, and make thine own:
'Thou hast been, shalt be, art, alone.' 30

Or, if not quite alone, yet they
Which touch thee are unmating things—
Ocean and clouds and night and day;
Lorn autumns and triumphant springs;
And life, and others' joy and pain, 35
And love, if love, of happier men.

Of happier men—for they, at least,
Have *dream'd* two human hearts might blend
In one, and were through faith released
From isolation without end 40
Prolong'd; nor knew, although not less
Alone than thou, their loneliness.

38 *1869: italics dropped.*

5. TO MARGUERITE—CONTINUED

[*First published 1852. Reprinted 1853, '54, '57, '69, and thereafter*]

YES! in the sea of life enisled,
With echoing straits between us thrown,
Dotting the shoreless watery wild,
We mortal millions live *alone*.
The islands feel the enclasping flow,   5
And then their endless bounds they know.

But when the moon their hollows lights,
And they are swept by balms of spring,
And in their glens, on starry nights,
The nightingales divinely sing;   10
And lovely notes, from shore to shore,
Across the sounds and channels pour—

Oh! then a longing like despair
Is to their farthest caverns sent;
For surely once, they feel, we were   15
Parts of a single continent!
Now round us spreads the watery plain—
Oh might our marges meet again!

Who order'd, that their longing's fire
Should be, as soon as kindled, cool'd?   20
Who renders vain their deep desire?—
A God, a God their severance ruled!
And bade betwixt their shores to be
The unplumb'd, salt, estranging sea.

Title 1852: To Marguerite,/In Returning a Volume of the Letters of
Ortis;   *1853*: Switzerland V. To Marguerite;   *1854*: Switzerland.
VI. To Marguerite;   *1857*: Switzerland VII. Isolation;   *1869*:
Switzerland 7. To Marguerite. Continued.

6. ABSENCE

[First published 1852. Reprinted 1853, '54, '57, '69, and thereafter]

In this fair stranger's eyes of grey
Thine eyes, my love! I see.
I shiver; for the passing day
Had borne me far from thee.

This is the curse of life! that not   5
A nobler, calmer train
Of wiser thoughts and feelings blot
Our passions from our brain;

But each day brings its petty dust
Our soon-choked souls to fill,   10
And we forget because we must
And not because we will.

I struggle towards the light; and ye,
Once-long'd-for storms of love!
If with the light ye cannot be,   15
I bear that ye remove.

I struggle towards the light—but oh,
While yet the night is chill,
Upon time's barren, stormy flow,
Stay with me, Marguerite, still!   20

7. THE TERRACE AT BERNE

(COMPOSED TEN YEARS AFTER THE PRECEDING)

[First published 1867. Reprinted 1868 and thereafter]

Ten years!—and to my waking eye
Once more the roofs of Berne appear;
The rocky banks, the terrace high,
The stream!—and do I linger here?

6. *Absence. Title 1852*: Absence;   *1853*: Switzerland **VI.** Absence;
1854: Switzerland VII. Absence;   *1857*: Switzerland VIII. Absence;
1869: Switzerland 5. Absence.   3 *1852–69*: I shudder:
7. *The Terrace at Berne. Title 1867*: The Terrace at Berne;   *1869* :
Switzerland **8.** The Terrace at Berne./(Composed **Ten** Years after the
Preceding.)

The clouds are on the Oberland,   5
The Jungfrau snows look faint and far;
But bright are those green fields at hand,
And through those fields comes down the Aar,

And from the blue twin-lakes it comes,
Flows by the town, the churchyard fair;   10
And 'neath the garden-walk it hums,
The house!—and is my Marguerite there?

Ah, shall I see thee, while a flush
Of startled pleasure floods thy brow,
Quick through the oleanders brush,   15
And clap thy hands, and cry: '*Tis thou!*

Or hast thou long since wander'd back,
Daughter of France! to France, thy home;
And flitted down the flowery track
Where feet like thine too lightly come?   20

Doth riotous laughter now replace
Thy smile; and rouge, with stony glare,
Thy cheek's soft hue; and fluttering lace
The kerchief that enwound thy hair?

Or is it over?—art thou dead?—   25
Dead!—and no warning shiver ran
Across my heart, to say thy thread
Of life was cut, and closed thy span!

Could from earth's ways that figure slight
Be lost, and I not feel 'twas so?   30
Of that fresh voice the gay delight
Fail from earth's air, and I not know?

Or shall I find thee still, but changed,
But not the Marguerite of thy prime?
With all thy being re-arranged,   35
Pass'd through the crucible of time;

With spirit vanish'd, beauty waned,
And hardly yet a glance, a tone,
A gesture—anything—retain'd
Of all that was my Marguerite's own?   40

I will not know! For wherefore try,
To things by mortal course that live,
A shadowy durability,
For which they were not meant, to give?

Like driftwood spars, which meet and pass   45
Upon the boundless ocean-plain,
So on the sea of life, alas!
Man meets man—meets, and quits again.

I knew it when my life was young;
I feel it still, now youth is o'er.   50
—The mists are on the mountain hung,
And Marguerite I shall see no more.

THE STRAYED REVELLER

[*First published 1849. Reprinted 1853, '54, '57, '69, and thereafter*]

THE PORTICO OF CIRCE'S PALACE.   EVENING

A Youth. Circe

The Youth

FASTER, faster,
O Circe, Goddess,
Let the wild, thronging train,
The bright procession
Of eddying forms,   5
Sweep through my soul!

45 MS. (*dated 1879, not adopted*): Like ships that meet and speak and
pass   48 *1867–9*: Man nears man, meets, and leaves again.
51 *1867–9*: the mountains
  THE STRAYED REVELLER. *Indication of place and time first added in 1853.*

Thou standest, smiling
Down on me! thy right arm,
Lean'd up against the column there,
Props thy soft cheek;   10
Thy left holds, hanging loosely,
The deep cup, ivy-cinctured,
I held but now.

Is it, then, evening
So soon? I see, the night-dews,   15
Cluster'd in thick beads, dim
The agate brooch-stones
On thy white shoulder;
The cool night-wind, too,
Blows through the portico,   20
Stirs thy hair, Goddess,
Waves thy white robe!

Circe

Whence art thou, sleeper?

The Youth

When the white dawn first
Through the rough fir-planks   25
Of my hut, by the chestnuts,
Up at the valley-head,
Came breaking, Goddess!
I sprang up, I threw round me
My dappled fawn-skin;   30
Passing out, from the wet turf,
Where they lay, by the hut door,
I snatch'd up my vine-crown, my fir-staff,
All drench'd in dew—
Came swift down to join   35
The rout early gather'd
In the town, round the temple,
Iacchus' white fane
On yonder hill.

Quick I pass'd, following   40
The wood-cutters' cart-track
Down the dark valley;—I saw
On my left, through the beeches,
Thy palace, Goddess,
Smokeless, empty!   45
Trembling, I enter'd; beheld
The court all silent,
The lions sleeping,
On the altar this bowl.
I drank, Goddess!   50
And sank down here, sleeping,
On the steps of thy portico.

Circe

Foolish boy! Why tremblest thou?
Thou lovest it, then, my wine?
Wouldst more of it? See, how glows,   55
Through the delicate, flush'd marble,
The red, creaming liquor,
Strown with dark seeds!
Drink, then! I chide thee not,
Deny thee not my bowl.   60
Come, stretch forth thy hand, then—so!
Drink—drink again!

The Youth

Thanks, gracious one!
Ah, the sweet fumes again!
More soft, ah me,   65
More subtle-winding
Than Pan's flute-music!
Faint—faint! Ah me,
Again the sweet sleep!

51 *1853–69*: And sunk

187

Circe

Hist! Thou—within there! 70
Come forth, Ulysses!
Art tired with hunting?
While we range the woodland,
See what the day brings.

Ulysses

Ever new magic! 75
Hast thou then lured hither,
Wonderful Goddess, by thy art,
The young, languid-eyed Ampelus,
Iacchus' darling—
Or some youth beloved of Pan, 80
Of Pan and the Nymphs?
That he sits, bending downward
His white, delicate neck
To the ivy-wreathed marge
Of thy cup; the bright, glancing vine-leaves 85
That crown his hair,
Falling forward, mingling
With the dark ivy-plants—
His fawn-skin, half untied,
Smear'd with red wine-stains? Who is he, 90
That he sits, overweigh'd
By fumes of wine and sleep,
So late, in thy portico?
What youth, Goddess,—what guest
Of Gods or mortals? 95

Circe

Hist! he wakes!
I lured him not hither, Ulysses.
Nay, ask him!

87 *1849–57*: forwards

The Youth

Who speaks? Ah, who comes forth
To thy side, Goddess, from within?   100
How shall I name him?
This spare, dark-featured,
Quick-eyed stranger?
Ah, and I see too
His sailor's bonnet,   105
His short coat, travel-tarnish'd,
With one arm bare!—
Art thou not he, whom fame
This long time rumours
The favour'd guest of Circe, brought by the waves?
Art thou he, stranger?   111
The wise Ulysses,
Laertes' son?

Ulysses

I am Ulysses.
And thou, too, sleeper?   115
Thy voice is sweet.
It may be thou hast follow'd
Through the islands some divine bard,
By age taught many things,
Age and the Muses;   120
And heard him delighting
The chiefs and people
In the banquet, and learn'd his songs,
Of Gods and Heroes,
Of war and arts,   125
And peopled cities,
Inland, or built
By the grey sea.—If so, then hail!
I honour and welcome thee.

122 *1877*: and the people

The Youth

The Gods are happy.　　　　　　130
They turn on all sides
Their shining eyes,
And see below them
The earth and men.

They see Tiresias　　　　　　135
Sitting, staff in hand,
On the warm, grassy
Asopus bank,
His robe drawn over
His old, sightless head,　　　　　140
Revolving inly
The doom of Thebes.

They see the Centaurs
In the upper glens
Of Pelion, in the streams,　　　　145
Where red-berried ashes fringe
The clear-brown shallow pools,
With streaming flanks, and heads
Rear'd proudly, snuffing
The mountain wind.　　　　　　150

They see the Indian
Drifting, knife in hand,
His frail boat moor'd to
A floating isle thick-matted
With large-leaved, low-creeping melon-plants, 155
And the dark cucumber.
He reaps, and stows them,
Drifting—drifting;—round him,
Round his green harvest-plot,
Flow the cool lake-waves,　　　　160
The mountains ring them.

They see the Scythian
On the wide stepp, unharnessing
His wheel'd house at noon.
He tethers his beast down, and makes his meal—
Mares' milk, and bread   166
Baked on the embers;—all around
The boundless, waving grass-plains stretch, thick-starr'd
With saffron and the yellow hollyhock
And flag-leaved iris-flowers.   170
Sitting in his cart
He makes his meal; before him, for long miles,
Alive with bright green lizards,
And the springing bustard-fowl,
The track, a straight black line,   175
Furrows the rich soil; here and there
Clusters of lonely mounds
Topp'd with rough-hewn,
Grey, rain-blear'd statues, overpeer
The sunny waste.   180

They see the ferry
On the broad, clay-laden
Lone Chorasmian stream;—thereon,
With snort and strain,
Two horses, strongly swimming, tow   185
The ferry-boat, with woven ropes
To either bow
Firm harness'd by the mane; a chief,
With shout and shaken spear,
Stands at the prow, and guides them; but astern
The cowering merchants, in long robes,   191
Sit pale beside their wealth
Of silk-bales and of balsam-drops,
Of gold and ivory,
Of turquoise-earth and amethyst,   195
Jasper and chalcedony,

169 *1869–77*: holyhock

And milk-barr'd onyx-stones.
The loaded boat swings groaning
In the yellow eddies;
The Gods behold them.   200
They see the Heroes
Sitting in the dark ship
On the foamless, long-heaving
Violet sea,
At sunset nearing   205
The Happy Islands.

These things, Ulysses,
The wise bards also
Behold and sing.
But oh, what labour!   210
O prince, what pain!

They too can see
Tiresias;—but the Gods,
Who give them vision,
Added this law: 215
That they should bear too
His groping blindness,
His dark foreboding,
His scorn'd white hairs;
Bear Hera's anger   220
Through a life lengthen'd
To seven ages.

They see the Centaurs
On Pelion;—then they feel,
They too, the maddening wine   225
Swell their large veins to bursting; in wild pain
They feel the biting spears
Of the grim Lapithæ, and Theseus, drive,
Drive crashing through their bones; they feel
High on a jutting rock in the red stream   230
Alcmena's dreadful son

214 *1869*: gave them

Ply his bow;—such a price
The Gods exact for song:
To become what we sing.

They see the Indian   235
On his mountain lake; but squalls
Make their skiff reel, and worms
In the unkind spring have gnawn
Their melon-harvest to the heart.—They see
The Scythian; but long frosts   240
Parch them in winter-time on the bare stepp,
Till they too fade like grass; they crawl
Like shadows forth in spring.

They see the merchants
On the Oxus stream;—but care   245
Must visit first them too, and make them pale.
Whether, through whirling sand,
A cloud of desert robber-horse have burst
Upon their caravan; or greedy kings,
In the wall'd cities the way passes through,   250
Crush'd them with tolls; or fever-airs,
On some great river's marge,
Mown them down, far from home.

They see the Heroes
Near harbour;—but they share   255
Their lives, and former violent toil in Thebes,
Seven-gated Thebes, or Troy;
Or where the echoing oars
Of Argo first
Startled the unknown sea.   260

The old Silenus
Came, lolling in the sunshine,
From the dewy forest-coverts,
This way, at noon.

238 *1849*: I' the unkind spring   238 *1849–69*: have gnaw'd
245 *1849–69*: Oxus' stream   248 *1849–57*: has burst

Sitting by me, while his Fauns   265
Down at the water-side
Sprinkled and smoothed
His drooping garland,
He told me these things.

But I, Ulysses,   270
Sitting on the warm steps,
Looking over the valley,
All day long, have seen,
Without pain, without labour,
Sometimes a wild-hair'd Mænad—   275
Sometimes a Faun with torches—
And sometimes, for a moment,
Passing through the dark stems
Flowing-robed, the beloved,
The desired, the divine,   280
Beloved Iacchus.

Ah, cool night-wind, tremulous stars!
Ah, glimmering water,
Fitful earth-murmur,
Dreaming woods!   285
Ah, golden-hair'd, strangely smiling Goddess,
And thou, proved, much enduring,
Wave-toss'd Wanderer!
Who can stand still?
Ye fade, ye swim, ye waver before me—   290
The cup again!

Faster, faster,
O Circe, Goddess,
Let the wild, thronging train,
The bright procession
Of eddying forms,   295
Sweep through my soul!

FRAGMENT OF AN 'ANTIGONE'

[*First published 1849. Reprinted 1855, '69, and thereafter*]

The Chorus

WELL hath he done who hath seized happiness!
For little do the all-containing hours,
    Though opulent, freely give.
    Who, weighing that life well
    Fortune presents unpray'd,   5
Declines her ministry, and carves his own;
    And, justice not infringed,
Makes his own welfare his unswerved-from law.

He does well too, who keeps that clue the mild
Birth-Goddess and the austere Fates first gave.   10
    For from the day when these
    Bring him, a weeping child,
    First to the light, and mark
A country for him, kinsfolk, and a home,
    Unguided he remains,   15
Till the Fates come again, this time with death.

    In little companies,
    And, our own place once left,
Ignorant where to stand, or whom to avoid,
By city and household group'd, we live; and many shocks   20
    Our order heaven-ordain'd
    Must every day endure:
Voyages, exiles, hates, dissensions, wars.
    Besides what waste *he* makes,
    The all-hated, order-breaking,   25
    Without friend, city, or home,
    Death, who dissevers all.

16 *1849–69*: alone, with death.   24 *1849–55*: waste He makes

Him then I praise, who dares
To self-selected good
Prefer obedience to the primal law, 30
Which consecrates the ties of blood; for these, indeed,
Are to the Gods a care;
That touches but himself.
For every day man may be link'd and loosed
With strangers; but the bond 35
Original, deep-inwound,
Of blood, can he not bind,
Nor, if Fate binds, not bear.

But hush! Hæmon, whom Antigone,
Robbing herself of life in burying, 40
Against Creon's law, Polynices,
Robs of a loved bride—pale, imploring,
Waiting her passage,
Forth from the palace hitherward comes.

Hæmon

No, no, old men, Creon I curse not! 45
I weep, Thebans,
One than Creon crueller far!
For he, he, at least, by slaying her,
August laws doth mightily vindicate;
But thou, too-bold, headstrong, pitiless! 50
Ah me!—honourest more than thy lover,
O Antigone!
A dead, ignorant, thankless corpse.

The Chorus

Nor was the love untrue
Which the Dawn-Goddess bore 55
To that fair youth she erst,
Leaving the salt sea-beds
And coming flush'd over the stormy frith
Of loud Euripus, saw—
Saw and snatch'd, wild with love, 60

From the pine-dotted spurs
Of Parnes, where thy waves,
Asopus! gleam rock-hemm'd—
The Hunter of the Tanagræan Field.[14]

But him, in his sweet prime,   65
By severance immature,
By Artemis' soft shafts,
She, though a Goddess born,
Saw in the rocky isle of Delos die.
Such end o'ertook that love.   70
For she desired to make
Immortal mortal man,
And blend his happy life,
Far from the Gods, with hers;
To him postponing an eternal law.   75

Hæmon

But like me, she, wroth, complaining,
Succumb'd to the envy of unkind Gods;
And, her beautiful arms unclasping,
Her fair youth unwillingly gave.

The Chorus

Nor, though enthroned too high   80
To fear assault of envious Gods,
His beloved Argive seer would Zeus retain
From his appointed end

In this our Thebes; but when
His flying steeds came near   85
To cross the steep Ismenian glen,
The broad earth open'd, and whelm'd them and him;
And through the void air sang
At large his enemy's spear.

And fain would Zeus have saved his tired son 90
Beholding him where the Two Pillars stand
    O'er the sun-redden'd western straits,[15]
Or at his work in that dim lower world.
    Fain would he have recall'd
    The fraudulent oath which bound 95
To a much feebler wight the heroic man.

But he preferr'd Fate to his strong desire.
Nor did there need less than the burning pile
    Under the towering Trachis crags,
And the Spercheios vale, shaken with groans, 100
    And the roused Maliac gulph,
    And scared Œtæan snows,
To achieve his son's deliverance, O my child!

FRAGMENT OF CHORUS OF A 'DEJANEIRA'

[*First published 1867. Reprinted 1868 and thereafter*]

O FRIVOLOUS mind of man,
Light ignorance, and hurrying, unsure thoughts!
Though man bewails you not,
How *I* bewail you!

Little in your prosperity 5
Do you seek counsel of the Gods.
Proud, ignorant, self-adored, you live alone.
In profound silence stern,
Among their savage gorges and cold springs,
Unvisited remain 10
The great oracular shrines.

Thither in your adversity
Do you betake yourselves for light,
But strangely misinterpret all you hear.
For you will not put on 15
New hearts with the enquirer's holy robe,
And purged, considerate minds.

FRAGMENT OF CHORUS OF A 'DEJANEIRA'. 4 *1867, 1868: no italic.*

And him on whom, at the end
Of toil and dolour untold,
The Gods have said that repose   20
At last shall descend undisturb'd—
Him you expect to behold
In an easy old age, in a happy home;
No end but this you praise.

But him, on whom, in the prime   25
Of life, with vigour undimm'd,
With unspent mind, and a soul
Unworn, undebased, undecay'd,
Mournfully grating, the gates
Of the city of death have for ever closed—   30
Him, I count *him*, well-starr'd.

EARLY DEATH AND FAME

[First published 1867. Reprinted 1868 and thereafter]

For him who must see many years,
I praise the life which slips away
Out of the light and mutely; which avoids
Fame, and her less fair followers, envy, strife,
Stupid detraction, jealousy, cabal,   5
Insincere praises; which descends
The quiet mossy track to age.

But, when immature death
Beckons too early the guest
From the half-tried banquet of life,   10
Young, in the bloom of his days;
Leaves no leisure to press,
Slow and surely, the sweets
Of a tranquil life in the shade—

EARLY DEATH AND FAME. *First published in* Fraser's Magazine, *May 1855, as lines 121–36 of* Haworth Churchyard; *first printed separately in 1867.*
1 *Fraser 1855*: must live   2 *Fraser 1855*: That life is best which
7 *Fraser 1855*: The mossy quiet   13 *Fraser 1855*: the sweet

Fuller for him be the hours!   15
Give him emotion, though pain!
Let him live, let him feel: *I have lived.*
Heap up his moments with life!
Triple his pulses with fame!

PHILOMELA

[First published 1853. Reprinted 1854, '57, '69, and thereafter]

HARK! ah, the nightingale—
The tawny-throated!
Hark, from that moonlit cedar what a burst!
What triumph! hark!—what pain!

O wanderer from a Grecian shore,   5
Still, after many years, in distant lands,
Still nourishing in thy bewilder'd brain
That wild, unquench'd, deep-sunken, old-world pain—
Say, will it never heal?
And can this fragrant lawn   10
With its cool trees, and night,
And the sweet, tranquil Thames,
And moonshine, and the dew,
To thy rack'd heart and brain
Afford no balm?   15

17 *Fraser 1855*: have liv'd.   19 *Fraser 1855*: Quicken his pulses
    PHILOMELA. 2 *MS.*: inken throated   3–13 *not in MS.; instead*:
                        Hast thou not yet, poor bird
                        Been help'd by slipping years
                        At least to half forgetfulness
                            Of that old pain.
                        Can change of scene, and night,
                        And moonlight, & the dew,
                                    blanch'd song-stirr'd
                        And these frail acacia boughs
                                        light
                        Thro whose frail leaves, & showers
                        Of blossom'd clusters pale,
                                    by
                        Thy voice in gushes comes,
14 *MS.*: torn heart *originally.*

Dost thou to-night behold,
Here, through the moonlight on this English grass,
The unfriendly palace in the Thracian wild?
Dost thou again peruse
With hot cheeks and sear'd eyes   20
The too clear web, and thy dumb sister's shame?
Dost thou once more assay
Thy flight, and feel come over thee,
Poor fugitive, the feathery change
Once more, and once more seem to make resound 25
With love and hate, triumph and agony,
Lone Daulis, and the high Cephissian vale?
Listen, Eugenia—
How thick the bursts come crowding through the leaves!
Again—thou hearest?   30
Eternal passion!
Eternal pain!

URANIA

[*First published 1852. Reprinted 1855, '69, and thereafter*]

I TOO have suffer'd; yet I know
She is not cold, though she seems so;
She is not cold, she is not light;
But our ignoble souls lack might.

16 *MS.*: thou still behold 17 *Not in MS.* 18 *MS.*: On this
fair western lawn 19 *MS.*: still peruse *Between 19 and 20, MS. inserts*:
    In the white acacia flowers
Between 21 and 22, MS. inserts:
    Dost thou still reach
  Thy husband, weak avenger, thro thyself?
28 *MS.*: Hark, hark, Eugenia! 30 *MS.*: *over* Again *is inserted* Once
more
  URANIA. *Title 1852, 1855*: Excuse. 1–4 *The first stanza omitted,
1869 to 1881; in 1885 restored to original position.* 1 *MS. alteration
1881*: but [*cancelled*] I know

She smiles and smiles, and will not sigh,   5
While we for hopeless passion die;
Yet she could love, those eyes declare,
Were but men nobler than they are.

Eagerly once her gracious ken
Was turn'd upon the sons of men;   10
But light the serious visage grew—
She look'd, and smiled, and saw them through.

Our petty souls, our strutting wits,
Our labour'd, puny passion-fits—
Ah, may she scorn them still, till we   15
Scorn them as bitterly as she!

Yet show her once, ye heavenly Powers,
One of some worthier race than ours!
One for whose sake she once might prove
How deeply she who scorns can love.   20

His eyes be like the starry lights—
His voice like sounds of summer nights—
In all his lovely mien let pierce
The magic of the universe!

And she to him will reach her hand,   25
And gazing in his eyes will stand,
And know her friend, and weep for glee,
And cry: *Long, long I've look'd for thee.*

Then will she weep; with smiles, till then,
Coldly she mocks the sons of men.   30
Till then, her lovely eyes maintain
Their pure, unwavering, deep disdain.

17 *1852, 1855*: Yet oh, that Fate would let her see   18 *1852*: One
of some better race than we;   *1855*: One of some worthier race than we;
32 *1852, 1855*: gay, unwavering

EUPHROSYNE

[*First published 1852. Reprinted 1855, '69, and thereafter*]

I MUST not say that thou wast true,
Yet let me say that thou wast fair;
And they, that lovely face who view,
Why should they ask if truth be there?

Truth—what is truth? Two bleeding hearts,   5
Wounded by men, by fortune tried,
Outwearied with their lonely parts,
Vow to beat henceforth side by side.

The world to them was stern and drear
Their lot was but to weep and moan.   10
Ah, let them keep their faith sincere,
For neither could subsist alone!

But souls whom some benignant breath
Hath charm'd at birth from gloom and care,
These ask no love, these plight no faith,   15
For they are happy as they are.

The world to them may nomage make,
And garlands for their forehead weave;
And what the world can give, they take—
But they bring more than they receive.   20

They shine upon the world! Their ears
To one demand alone are coy;
They will not give us love and tears,
They bring us light and warmth and joy.

Title 1852, 1855: Indifference.   **1** *1852–5*: wert true,   *1869*
(*only*): I will not say   *1877–81*: that she was true,   **2** *1852–5*:
wert fair.   *1877–81*: she was fair.   **4** *1852–5*: They will
not ask if truth be there.   *1869–81*: They should not ask if truth be
there.   **14** *1852–77*: Has charm'd   **21** *1852–69*: They smile

It was not love which heaved thy breast,   25
Fair child!—it was the bliss within.
Adieu! and say that one, at least,
Was just to what he did not win.

CALAIS SANDS

[First published 1867. Reprinted 1868 and thereafter]

A THOUSAND knights have rein'd their steeds
To watch this line of sand-hills run,
Along the never-silent Strait,
To Calais glittering in the sun;

To look tow'rd Ardres' Golden Field   5
Across this wide aërial plain,
Which glows as if the Middle Age
Were gorgeous upon earth again.

Oh, that to share this famous scene,
I saw, upon the open sand,   10
Thy lovely presence at my side,
Thy shawl, thy look, thy smile, thy hand!

25 *1852–5*: love that   25 *From 1869 to 1881 the last stanza read*:
On one she smiled, and he was blest!
She smiles elsewhere—we make a din!
But 'twas not love which heaved her breast,
Fair child!—it was the bliss within.

CALAIS SANDS. *Title MS.*: By the seaside near Calais. August. 1850.
2 *MS.*: To see   3 *MS.*: never-silent beach   4 *MS.*: sparkling in
the sun   5 *MS.*: To see   *1867–81*: toward Ardres'   6 *MS.*:
Spread wide away the luminous plain,   9–12 *MS.*:
Oh wert thou here! That I might turn
And see upon the lovely sand
That slight sweet figure at my side—
That shawl,—that step—that look—that hand!

How exquisite thy voice would come,
My darling, on this lonely air!
How sweetly would the fresh sea-breeze   15
Shake loose some band of soft brown hair!

Yet now my glance but once hath roved
O'er Calais and its famous plain;
To England's cliffs my gaze is turn'd,
On the blue strait mine eyes I strain.   20

Thou comest! Yes! the vessel's cloud
Hangs dark upon the rolling sea.
Oh, that yon sea-bird's wings were mine,
To win one instant's glimpse of thee!

I must not spring to grasp thy hand,   25
To woo thy smile, to seek thine eye;
But I may stand far off, and gaze,
And watch thee pass unconscious by,

And spell thy looks, and guess thy thoughts,
Mixt with the idlers on the pier.—   30
Ah, might I always rest unseen,
So I might have thee always near!

To-morrow hurry through the fields
Of Flanders to the storied Rhine!
To-night those soft-fringed eyes shall close   35
Beneath one roof, my queen! with mine.

14 *MS.*: quiet air!   15 *MS.*: fresh sea-wind   16 *MS.*: Shake back
thy bands   16 *1867–9*: some lock   17 *MS.*: Not once to day
these eyes have stay'd   17 *1867–9*: But now   18 *MS.*: On Calais
and its shining plain   19 *MS.*: my look   20 *MS.*: On the blue
sea my gaze I strain   20 *1867–81*: O'er the blue strait   23 *MS.*:
that sea-bird's   25 *MS.*: to touch   26 *MS.*: To catch thy smile
28 *MS.*: see thee pass   29 *MS.*: And watch thy air, and guess   31
MS.: Oh might   34 *MS.*: ancient Rhine   35 *MS.*: soft-veiled eyes

FADED LEAVES

1. THE RIVER

[*First published 1852. Reprinted 1855, '69, and thereafter*]

STILL glides the stream, slow drops the boat
Under the rustling poplars' shade;
Silent the swans beside us float—
None speaks, none heeds; ah, turn thy head!

Let those arch eyes now softly shine,   5
That mocking mouth grow sweetly bland;
Ah, let them rest, those eyes, on mine!
On mine let rest that lovely hand!

My pent-up tears oppress my brain,
My heart is swoln with love unsaid.   10
Ah, let me weep, and tell my pain,
And on thy shoulder rest my head!

Before I die—before the soul,
Which now is mine, must re-attain
Immunity from my control,   15
And wander round the world again;

Before this teased o'erlabour'd heart
For ever leaves its vain employ,
Dead to its deep habitual smart,
And dead to hopes of future joy.   20

2. TOO LATE

[*First published 1852. Reprinted 1855, '69, and thereafter*]

EACH on his own strict line we move,
And some find death ere they find love;
So far apart their lives are thrown
From the twin soul which halves their own.

FADED LEAVES. **1.** *The River. Title 1852*: The River. *Made first poem in* Faded Leaves *group in 1855.*

2. *Too Late. Title 1852*: Too Late. *Made second poem in* Faded Leaves *group in 1855.* **4** *MS., 1852–81*: that halves

And sometimes, by still harder fate,   5
The lovers meet, but meet too late.
—Thy heart is mine!—*True, true! ah, true!*
—Then, love, thy hand!—*Ah no! adieu!*

3. SEPARATION

[First published 1855. Reprinted 1869 and thereafter]

STOP!—not to me, at this bitter departing,
  Speak of the sure consolations of time!
Fresh be the wound, still-renew'd be its smarting,
  So but thy image endure in its prime.

But, if the stedfast commandment of Nature   5
  Wills that remembrance should always decay—
If the loved form and the deep-cherish'd feature
  Must, when unseen, from the soul fade away—

Me let no half-effaced memories cumber!
  Fled, fled at once, be all vestige of thee!   10
Deep be the darkness and still be the slumber—
  Dead be the past and its phantoms to me!

Then, when we meet, and thy look strays toward me,
  Scanning my face and the changes wrought there:
Who, let me say, *is this stranger regards me,*   15
  With the grey eyes, and the lovely brown hair?

4. ON THE RHINE

[First published 1852. Reprinted 1855, '69, and thereafter]

VAIN is the effort to forget.
Some day I shall be cold, I know,
As is the eternal moonlit snow
Of the high Alps, to which I go—
But ah, not yet, not yet!   5

3. *Separation.* 13 *1855–69*: towards
4. *On the Rhine. Title 1852*: On the Rhine. *Made fourth poem in* Faded
Leaves *group in 1855.*

Vain is the agony of grief.
'Tis true, indeed, an iron knot
Ties straitly up from mine thy lot,
And were it snapt—thou lov'st me not!
But is despair relief?   10

Awhile let me with thought have done.
And as this brimm'd unwrinkled Rhine,
And that far purple mountain-line,
Lie sweetly in the look divine
Of the slow-sinking sun;   15

So let me lie, and, calm as they,
Let beam upon my inward view
Those eyes of deep, soft, lucent hue—
Eyes too expressive to be blue,
Too lovely to be grey.   20

Ah, Quiet, all things feel thy balm!
Those blue hills too, this river's flow,
Were restless once, but long ago.
Tamed is their turbulent youthful glow;
Their joy is in their calm.   25

5. LONGING

[First published 1852. Reprinted 1855, '69, and thereafter]

COME to me in my dreams, and then
By day I shall be well again!
For then the night will more than pay
The hopeless longing of the day.

Come, as thou cam'st a thousand times,   5
A messenger from radiant climes,
And smile on thy new world, and be
As kind to others as to me!

5. *Longing. Title 1852*: Longing. *Made fifth poem in* Faded Leaves *group
in 1855.*   3, 15 *1869*: For so the night   8 *1852*: to all the rest
as me.

Or, as thou never cam'st in sooth,
Come now, and let me dream it truth;   10
And part my hair, and kiss my brow,
And say: *My love! why sufferest thou?*

Come to me in my dreams, and then
By day I shall be well again!
For then the night will more than pay   15
The hopeless longing of the day.

DESPONDENCY

[*First published 1852. Reprinted 1855, '69, and thereafter*]

THE thoughts that rain their steady glow
Like stars on life's cold sea,
Which others know, or say they know—
They never shone for me.

Thoughts light, like gleams, my spirit's sky,   5
But they will not remain.
They light me once, they hurry by;
And never come again.

SELF-DECEPTION

[*First published 1852. Reprinted 1855, '69, and thereafter*]

SAY, what blinds us, that we claim the glory
Of possessing powers not our share?
—Since man woke on earth, he knows his story,
But, before we woke on earth, we were.

Long, long since, undower'd yet, our spirit   5
Roam'd, ere birth, the treasuries of God;
Saw the gifts, the powers it might inherit,
Ask'd an outfit for its earthly road.

10 *MS.* deem it   12. *MS.* My friend,

Then, as now, this tremulous, eager being
Strain'd and long'd and grasp'd each gift it saw; 10
Then, as now, a Power beyond our seeing
Staved us back, and gave our choice the law.

Ah, whose hand that day through Heaven guided
Man's new spirit, since it was not we?
Ah, who sway'd our choice, and who decided 15
What our gifts, and what our wants should be?

For, alas! he left us each retaining
Shreds of gifts which he refused in full.
Still these waste us with their hopeless straining,
Still the attempt to use them proves them null. 20

And on earth we wander, groping, reeling;
Powers stir in us, stir and disappear.
Ah! and he, who placed our master-feeling,
Fail'd to place that master-feeling clear.

We but dream we have our wish'd-for powers, 25
Ends we seek we never shall attain.
Ah! *some* power exists there, which is ours?
Some end is there, we indeed may gain?

DOVER BEACH

[First published 1867. Reprinted 1868 and thereafter]

THE sea is calm to-night.
The tide is full, the moon lies fair
Upon the straits;—on the French coast the light
Gleams and is gone; the cliffs of England stand,
Glimmering and vast, out in the tranquil bay. 5
Come to the window, sweet is the night-air!

SELF-DECEPTION. 14 *1855*: blank spirit   16 *1852*: What the parts, and what the whole should be?   24 *1855*: our master-feeling
DOVER BEACH. 4 *MS.*: Shines & is gone: the cliffs of England
6 *MS.*: hush'd is *with* sweet is *as alternative.*

Only, from the long line of spray
Where the sea meets the moon-blanch'd land,
Listen! you hear the grating roar
Of pebbles which the waves draw back, and fling,   10
At their return, up the high strand,
Begin, and cease, and then again begin,
With tremulous cadence slow, and bring
The eternal note of sadness in.

Sophocles long ago   15
Heard it on the Ægæan, and it brought
Into his mind the turbid ebb and flow
Of human misery; we
Find also in the sound a thought,
Hearing it by this distant northern sea.   20

The Sea of Faith
Was once, too, at the full, and round earth's shore
Lay like the folds of a bright girdle furl'd.
But now I only hear
Its melancholy, long, withdrawing roar,   25
Retreating, to the breath
Of the night-wind, down the vast edges drear
And naked shingles of the world.

Ah, love, let us be true
To one another! for the world, which seems   30
To lie before us like a land of dreams,
So various, so beautiful, so new,
Hath really neither joy, nor love, nor light,

8 *1867–77*: Where the ebb meets the moon-blanch'd sand,   *1878–81*:
Where the sea meets the moon-blanch'd sand,   *1880*: Where the sea
meets the moon-blanch'd land, (*as in present reading*).   10 *MS.*: *1867*:
suck back   11 *MS.*: steep strand *with* barr'd strand *as alternative.*
12 *MS.*: Cease and begin   13 *MS.*: regular cadence *with* mournful
cadence *as alternative.*   17 *MS.*: troubled ebb *with* turbid ebb *as alternative.*   21–8 *Written at side of MS.*   23 *MS.*: garment furl'd
with girdle furl'd *as alternative.*   24 *MS.*: we only *with* I only *as
alternative.*   28 *MS.*: And naked shingles of the world. Ah love *&c.*

Nor certitude, nor peace, nor help for pain;
And we are here as on a darkling plain   35
Swept with confused alarms of struggle and flight,
Where ignorant armies clash by night.

GROWING OLD

[First published 1867. Reprinted 1868 and thereafter]

WHAT is it to grow old?
Is it to lose the glory of the form,
The lustre of the eye?
Is it for beauty to forego her wreath?
—Yes, but not this alone.   5

Is it to feel our strength—
Not our bloom only, but our strength—decay?
Is it to feel each limb
Grow stiffer, every function less exact,
Each nerve more loosely strung?   10

Yes, this, and more; but not
Ah, 'tis not what in youth we dream'd 'twould be!
'Tis not to have our life
Mellow'd and soften'd as with sunset-glow,
A golden day's decline.   15

'Tis not to see the world
As from a height, with rapt prophetic eyes,
And heart profoundly stirr'd;
And weep, and feel the fulness of the past,
The years that are no more.   20

It is to spend long days
And not once feel that we were ever young;
It is to add, immured
In the hot prison of the present, month
To month with weary pain.   25

36 *1869, 1877*: and fight [*sic*]
   GROWING OLD. 10 *1867–77*: weakly strung?

It is to suffer this,
And feel but half, and feebly, what we feel.
Deep in our hidden heart
Festers the dull remembrance of a change,
But no emotion—none.   30

It is—last stage of all—
When we are frozen up within, and quite
The phantom of ourselves,
To hear the world applaud the hollow ghost
Which blamed the living man.   35

THE PROGRESS OF POESY

A VARIATION

[First published 1867. Reprinted 1868 and thereafter]

YOUTH rambles on life's arid mount,
And strikes the rock, and finds the vein,
And brings the water from the fount,
The fount which shall not flow again.

The man mature with labour chops   5
For the bright stream a channel grand,
And sees not that the sacred drops
Ran off and vanish'd out of hand.

And then the old man totters nigh,
And feebly rakes among the stones.   10
The mount is mute, the channel dry;
And down he lays his weary bones.

NEW ROME

LINES WRITTEN FOR MISS STORY'S ALBUM

[*First published in the* CORNHILL MAGAZINE, *June 1873. Reprinted 1881 and thereafter*]

THE armless Vatican Cupid
   Hangs down his beautiful head;
For the priests have got him in prison,
   And Psyche long has been dead.

But see, his shaven oppressors   5
   Begin to quake and disband!
And *The Times*, that bright Apollo,
   Proclaims salvation at hand.

'And what,' cries Cupid, 'will save us?'
   Says Apollo: '*Modernise Rome!*   10
What inns! Your streets, too, how narrow!
   Too much of palace and dome!

'O learn of London, whose paupers
   Are not pushed out by the swells!
Wide streets with fine double trottoirs;   15
   And then—the London hotels!'

The armless Vatican Cupid
   Hangs down his head as before.
Through centuries past it has hung so,
   And will through centuries more.   20

5 *MS.*: black-coated gaolers *with* shaven oppressors *as alternative.*
8 *MS.*: Proclaims *with* Instills *as alternative.*   9 *MS.*: asks Cupid,
is coming? *with* will save us? *as alternative.*   10 *MS.*: Modernised
with 'd' *cancelled.*   11 *MS.*: Your streets [are *cancelled*] how ancient
and narrow—   13-14 *MS.*:
       Become like glorious London,
          Where poor have place like the swells;
with, as alternative:
       Be made like London, where paupers
          Are not pushed out by the swells;
15 *MS.*: New streets *with* Wide streets *as alternative.*   19 *MS.*: All
the centuries past *with* Through *written at side.*   20 *MS.*: for centuries

PIS-ALLER

[*First published 1867. Reprinted 1868 and thereafter*]

'MAN is blind because of sin,
Revelation makes him sure;
Without that, who looks within,
Looks in vain, for all's obscure.'

Nay, look closer into man!　　　　　　5
Tell me, can you find indeed
Nothing sure, no moral plan
Clear prescribed, without your creed?

'No, I nothing can perceive!
Without that, all's dark for men.　　　10
That, or nothing, I believe.'—
For God's sake, believe it then!

THE LAST WORD

[*First published 1867. Reprinted 1868 and thereafter*]

CREEP into thy narrow bed,
Creep, and let no more be said!
Vain thy onset! all stands fast.
Thou thyself must break at last.

Let the long contention cease!　　　　5
Geese are swans, and swans are geese.
Let them have it how they will!
Thou art tired; best be still.

They out-talk'd thee, hiss'd thee, tore thee?
Better men fared thus before thee;　　10
Fired their ringing shot and pass'd,
Hotly charged—and sank at last.

Charge once more, then, and be dumb!
Let the victors, when they come,
When the forts of folly fall,　　　　15
Find thy body by the wall!

THE LAST WORD. 12 *1867–9*: and broke

THE LORD'S MESSENGERS

[First published in the CORNHILL MAGAZINE, *July 1860. Reprinted 1881 and thereafter]*

THUS saith the Lord to his own:—
'See ye the trouble below?
Warfare of man from his birth!
Too long let we them groan;
Haste, arise ye, and go,
Carry my peace upon earth!'   5

Gladly they rise at his call,
Gladly obey his command,
Gladly descend to the plain.
—Ah! How few of them all,   10
Those willing servants, shall stand
In the Master's presence again!

Some in the tumult are lost;
Baffled, bewilder'd, they stray.
Some, as prisoners, draw breath.   15
Some, unconquer'd, are cross'd
(Not yet half through the day)
By a pitiless arrow of Death.

Title Cornhill Magazine, *July 1860*: Men of Genius. *In 1860 the poem opened as follows*:

Silent, the Lord of the world
Eyes from the heavenly height,
Girt by his far-shining train,
Us, who with banners unfurl'd
Fight life's many-chanc'd fight
Madly below, in the plain.

1 *1860*: Then saith   **2** *1860*: the battle   **3** *1860*: Turmoil of
death and of birth!   **8** *1860*: Gladly they take   **10** *1860*: Alas! How
few   **12** *1860*: their Master's   **16–18** *1860*:
Others—the bravest—are cross'd,
On the height of their bold-follow'd way,
By the swift-rushing missile of Death.

Hardly, hardly shall one
  Come, with countenance bright,   **20**
    At the close of day, from the plain;
His Master's errand well done,
  Safe through the smoke of the fight,
    Back to his Master again.

A NAMELESS EPITAPH

[*First published 1867. Reprinted 1868 and thereafter*]

Ask not my name, O friend!
That Being only, which hath known each man
From the beginning, can
Remember each unto the end.

BACCHANALIA;

OR,

THE NEW AGE

[*First published 1867. Reprinted 1868 and thereafter*]

I

The evening comes, the fields are still.
The tinkle of the thirsty rill,
Unheard all day, ascends again;
Deserted is the half-mown plain,
Silent the swaths! the ringing wain,   **5**

21 *1860*: O'er the cloud-wrapt, perilous plain:
  A Nameless Epitaph. *In 1867 and 1868 the title* A Nameless Epitaph *was
applied to these lines, discarded in 1869*:
        This sentence have I left behind:
        An aching body, and a mind
        Not wholly clear, nor wholly blind,
        Too keen to rest, too weak to find,
        That travails sore, and brings forth wind,
        Are God's worst portion to mankind.
1–4 *1867, 1868*: *followed the six lines above, entitled* Another.
  Bacchanalia; or, the New Age. 1 *1867–9*: field is still.   **4 *1867*:**
the new-reap'd grain,   **5 *1867*:** Silent the sheaves!

The mower's cry, the dog's alarms,
All housed within the sleeping farms!
The business of the day is done,
The last-left haymaker is gone.
And from the thyme upon the height,   10
And from the elder-blossom white
And pale dog-roses in the hedge,
And from the mint-plant in the sedge,
In puffs of balm the night-air blows
The perfume which the day forgoes.   15
And on the pure horizon far,
See, pulsing with the first-born star,
The liquid sky above the hill!
The evening comes, the fields are still.

> Loitering and leaping,   20
> With saunter, with bounds—
> Flickering and circling
> In files and in rounds—
> Gaily their pine-staff green
> Tossing in air,   25
> Loose o'er their shoulders white
> Showering their hair—
> See! the wild Mænads
> Break from the wood,
> Youth and Iacchus   30
> Maddening their blood.
> See! through the quiet land
> Rioting they pass—
> Fling the fresh heaps about,
> Trample the grass.   35
> Tear from the rifled hedge
> Garlands, their prize;
> Fill with their sports the field,
> Fill with their cries.

6 *1867*: The reaper's cry, the dogs' alarms,   9 *1867*: The last belated gleaner gone.   19 *1867–9*: field is still.   32 *1867*: quiet corn 34 *1867*: piled sheaves about,

Shepherd, what ails thee, then?   40
Shepherd, why mute?
Forth with thy joyous song!
Forth with thy flute!
Tempts not the revel blithe?
Lure not their cries?   45
Glow not their shoulders smooth?
Melt not their eyes?
Is not, on cheeks like those,
Lovely the flush?
—Ah, so the quiet was!   50
So was the hush!

II

The epoch ends, the world is still.
The age has talk'd and work'd its fill—
The famous orators have shone,
The famous poets sung and gone,
The famous men of war have fought,   5
The famous speculators thought,
The famous players, sculptors, wrought,
The famous painters fill'd their wall,
The famous critics judged it all.
The combatants are parted now—   10
Uphung the spear, unbent the bow,
The puissant crown'd, the weak laid low.
And in the after-silence sweet,
Now strifes are hush'd, our ears doth meet,
Ascending pure, the bell-like fame   15
Of this or that down-trodden name,
Delicate spirits, push'd away
In the hot press of the noon-day.
And o'er the plain, where the dead age
Did its now silent warfare wage—   20

3 *1867*: have done,   14 *1867–9*: strife is hush'd,

O'er that wide plain, now wrapt in gloom,
Where many a splendour finds its tomb,
Many spent fames and fallen mights—
The one or two immortal lights
Rise slowly up into the sky   25
To shine there everlastingly,
Like stars over the bounding hill.
The epoch ends, the world is still.

    Thundering and bursting
    In torrents, in waves—
    Carolling and shouting   30
    Over tombs, amid graves—
    See! on the cumber'd plain
    Clearing a stage,
    Scattering the past about,   35
    Comes the new age.
    Bards make new poems,
    Thinkers new schools,
    Statesmen new systems,
    Critics new rules.   40
    All things begin again;
    Life is their prize;
    Earth with their deeds they fill,
    Fill with their cries.

    Poet, what ails thee, then?   45
    Say, why so mute?
    Forth with thy praising voice!
    Forth with thy flute!
    Loiterer! why sittest thou
    Sunk in thy dream?   50
    Tempts not the bright new age?
    Shines not its stream?
    Look, ah, what genius,
    Art, science, wit!
    Soldiers like Cæsar,   55
    Statesmen like Pitt!

Sculptors like Phidias,
Raphaels in shoals,
Poets like Shakespeare—
Beautiful souls! 60
See, on their glowing cheeks
Heavenly the flush!
—*Ah, so the silence was!*
So was the hush!

The world but feels the present's spell, 65
The poet feels the past as well;
Whatever men have done, might do,
Whatever thought, might think it too.

EPILOGUE
TO LESSING'S LAOCOÖN

[First published 1867. Reprinted 1868 and thereafter]

ONE morn as through Hyde Park we walk'd,
My friend and I, by chance we talk'd
Of Lessing's famed Laocoön;
And after we awhile had gone
In Lessing's track, and tried to see 5
What painting is, what poetry—
Diverging to another thought,
'Ah,' cries my friend, 'but who hath taught
Why music and the other arts
Oftener perform aright their parts 10
Than poetry? why she, than they,
Fewer fine successes can display?

'For 'tis so, surely! Even in Greece,
Where best the poet framed his piece,
Even in that Phœbus-guarded ground 15
Pausanias on his travels found
Good poems, if he look'd, more rare
(Though many) than good statues were—

For these, in truth, were everywhere.
Of bards full many a stroke divine   20
In Dante's, Petrarch's, Tasso's line,
The land of Ariosto show'd;
And yet, e'en there, the canvas glow'd
With triumphs, a yet ampler brood,
Of Raphael and his brotherhood.   25
And nobly perfect, in our day
Of haste, half-work, and disarray,
Profound yet touching, sweet yet strong,
Hath risen Goethe's, Wordsworth's song;
Yet even I (and none will bow   30
Deeper to these) must needs allow,
They yield us not, to soothe our pains,
Such multitude of heavenly strains
As from the kings of sound are blown,
Mozart, Beethoven, Mendelssohn.'   35

While thus my friend discoursed, we pass
Out of the path, and take the grass.
The grass had still the green of May,
And still the unblacken'd elms were gay;
The kine were resting in the shade,   40
The flies a summer-murmur made.
Bright was the morn and south the air;
The soft-couch'd cattle were as fair
As those which pastured by the sea,
That old-world morn, in Sicily,   45
When on the beach the Cyclops lay,
And Galatea from the bay
Mock'd her poor lovelorn giant's lay.
'Behold,' I said, 'the painter's sphere!
The limits of his art appear.   50
The passing group, the summer-morn,
The grass, the elms, that blossom'd thorn—
Those cattle couch'd, or, as they rise,

44 *1867, 1868*: those that

Their shining flanks, their liquid eyes—
These, or much greater things, but caught   55
Like these, and in one aspect brought!
In outward semblance he must give
A moment's life of things that live;
Then let him choose his moment well,
With power divine its story tell.'   60

Still we walk'd on, in thoughtful mood,
And now upon the bridge we stood.
Full of sweet breathings was the air,
Of sudden stirs and pauses fair.
Down o'er the stately bridge the breeze   65
Came rustling from the garden-trees
And on the sparkling waters play'd;
Light-plashing waves an answer made,
And mimic boats their haven near'd.
Beyond, the Abbey-towers appear'd,   70
By mist and chimneys unconfined,
Free to the sweep of light and wind;
While through their earth-moor'd nave below
Another breath of wind doth blow,
Sound as of wandering breeze—but sound   75
In laws by human artists bound.
'The world of music!' I exclaim'd:—
'This breeze that rustles by, that famed
Abbey recall it! what a sphere
Large and profound, hath genius here!   80
The inspired musician what a range,
What power of passion, wealth of change!
Some source of feeling he must choose
And its lock'd fount of beauty use,
And through the stream of music tell   85
Its else unutterable spell;
To choose it rightly is his part,

73 *1867*: the earth-moor'd   81 *1867*: Th' inspired   83 *1867*:
pulse of feeling

And press into its inmost heart.

'*Miserere, Domine!*
The words are utter'd, and they flee.   90
Deep is their penitential moan,
Mighty their pathos, but 'tis gone.
They have declared the spirit's sore
Sore load, and words can do no more.
Beethoven takes them then—those two   95
Poor, bounded words—and makes them new;
Infinite makes them, makes them young;
Transplants them to another tongue,
Where they can now, without constraint,
Pour all the soul of their complaint,   100
And roll adown a channel large
The wealth divine they have in charge.
Page after page of music turn,
And still they live and still they burn,
Eternal, passion-fraught, and free—   105
Miserere, Domine!'

Onward we moved, and reach'd the Ride
Where gaily flows the human tide.
Afar, in rest the cattle lay;
We heard, afar, faint music play;   110
But agitated, brisk, and near,
Men, with their stream of life, were here.
Some hang upon the rails, and some
On foot behind them go and come.
This through the Ride upon his steed   115
Goes slowly by, and this at speed.
The young, the happy, and the fair,
The old, the sad, the worn, were there;
Some vacant, and some musing went,
And some in talk and merriment.   120
Nods, smiles, and greetings, and farewells!
And now and then, perhaps, there swells

105 *1869–77*: Perennial, passion-fraught,

A sigh, a tear—but in the throng
All changes fast, and hies along.
Hies, ah, from whence, what native ground?   125
And to what goal, what ending, bound?
'Behold, at last the poet's sphere!
But who,' I said, 'suffices here?

'For, ah! so much he has to do;
Be painter and musician too!   130
The aspect of the moment show,
The feeling of the moment know!
The aspect not, I grant, express
Clear as the painter's art can dress;
The feeling not, I grant, explore   135
So deep as the musician's lore—
But clear as words can make revealing,
And deep as words can follow feeling.
But, ah! then comes his sorest spell
Of toil—he must life's *movement* tell!   140
The thread which binds it all in one,
And not its separate parts alone.
The *movement* he must tell of life,
Its pain and pleasure, rest and strife;
His eye must travel down, at full,   145
The long, unpausing spectacle;
With faithful unrelaxing force
Attend it from its primal source,
From change to change and year to year
Attend it of its mid career,   150
Attend it to the last repose
And solemn silence of its close.

'The cattle rising from the grass
His thought must follow where they pass;
The penitent with anguish bow'd   155
His thought must follow through the crowd.

143 *1867*: movement (*in roman type*)

Yes! all this eddying, motley throng
That sparkles in the sun along,
Girl, statesman, merchant, soldier bold,
Master and servant, young and old,   160
Grave, gay, child, parent, husband, wife,
He follows home, and lives their life.

'And many, many are the souls
Life's movement fascinates, controls;
It draws them on, they cannot save   165
Their feet from its alluring wave;
They cannot leave it, they must go
With its unconquerable flow.
But ah! how few, of all that try
This mighty march, do aught but die!   170
For ill-endow'd for such a way,
Ill-stored in strength, in wits, are they.
They faint, they stagger to and fro,
And wandering from the stream they go;
In pain, in terror, in distress,   175
They see, all round, a wilderness.
Sometimes a momentary gleam
They catch of the mysterious stream;
Sometimes, a second's space, their ear
The murmur of its waves doth hear.   180
That transient glimpse in song they say,
But not as painter can pourtray—
That transient sound in song they tell,
But not, as the musician, well.
And when at last their snatches cease,   185
And they are silent and at peace,
The stream of life's majestic whole
Hath ne'er been mirror'd on their soul.

'Only a few the life-stream's shore
With safe unwandering feet explore;   190

171 *1867*: For ill prepared 172 *1867*: Ill found in strength,
185 *1867*: these snatches

Untired its movement bright attend,
Follow its windings to the end.
Then from its brimming waves their eye
Drinks up delighted ecstasy,
And its deep-toned, melodious voice   195
For ever makes their ear rejoice.
They speak! the happiness divine
They feel, runs o'er in every line;
Its spell is round them like a shower—
It gives them pathos, gives them power.   200
No painter yet hath such a way,
Nor no musician made, as they,
And gather'd on immortal knolls
Such lovely flowers for cheering souls.
Beethoven, Raphael, cannot reach   205
The charm which Homer, Shakespeare, teach.
To these, to these, their thankful race
Gives, then, the first, the fairest place;
And brightest is their glory's sheen,
For greatest hath their labour been.'   210

PERSISTENCY OF POETRY

[First published 1867. Reprinted 1868 and thereafter]

THOUGH the Muse be gone away,
Though she move not earth to-day,
Souls, erewhile who caught her word,
Ah! still harp on what they heard.

210 *1867–9*: has their labour
PERSISTENCY OF POETRY. *This stanza, without title, was prefatory to the volumes of 1867–69.*   2 *MS.*: she rule *with* move *as alternative*

A CAUTION TO POETS

[*First published 1867. Reprinted 1868 and thereafter*]

WHAT poets feel not, when they make,
    A pleasure in creating,
The world, in *its* turn, will not take
    Pleasure in contemplating.

THE YOUTH OF NATURE

[*First published 1852. Reprinted 1855, '69, and thereafter*]

RAISED are the dripping oars,
Silent the boat! the lake,
Lovely and soft as a dream,
Swims in the sheen of the moon.
The mountains stand at its head   5
Clear in the pure June-night,
But the valleys are flooded with haze.
Rydal and Fairfield are there;
In the shadow Wordsworth lies dead.
So it is, so it will be for aye.   10
Nature is fresh as of old,
Is lovely; a mortal is dead.

The spots which recall him survive,
For he lent a new life to these hills.
The Pillar still broods o'er the fields   15
Which border Ennerdale Lake,
And Egremont sleeps by the sea.
The gleam of The Evening Star
Twinkles on Grasmere no more,
But ruin'd and solemn and grey   20
The sheepfold of Michael survives;
And, far to the south, the heath

A CAUTION TO POETS. *This stanza, without title, was prefatory to the volume
of 1869 only; otherwise printed regularly with title.*
THE YOUTH OF NATURE. 16 *1852*: That border

Still blows in the Quantock coombs,
By the favourite waters of Ruth.
These survive!—yet not without pain,   25
Pain and dejection to-night,
Can I feel that their poet is gone.

He grew old in an age he condemn'd.
He look'd on the rushing decay
Of the times which had shelter'd his youth;   30
Felt the dissolving throes
Of a social order he loved;
Outlived his brethren, his peers,
And, like the Theban seer,
Died in his enemies' day.   35

Cold bubbled the spring of Tilphusa,
Copais lay bright in the moon,
Helicon glass'd in the lake
Its firs, and afar rose the peaks
Of Parnassus, snowily clear;   40
Thebes was behind him in flames,
And the clang of arms in his ear,
When his awe-struck captors led
The Theban seer to the spring.
Tiresias drank and died.   45
Nor did reviving Thebes
See such a prophet again.

Well may we mourn, when the head
Of a sacred poet lies low
In an age which can rear them no more!   50
The complaining millions of men
Darken in labour and pain;
But he was a priest to us all
Of the wonder and bloom of the world,
Which we saw with his eyes, and were glad.   55
He is dead, and the fruit-bearing day
Of his race is past on the earth;
And darkness returns to our eyes.

For, oh! is it you, is it you,
Moonlight, and shadow, and lake,   60
And mountains, that fill us with joy,
Or the poet who sings you so well?
Is it you, O beauty, O grace,
O charm, O romance, that we feel,
Or the voice which reveals what you are?   65
Are ye, like daylight and sun,
Shared and rejoiced in by all?
Or are ye immersed in the mass
Of matter, and hard to extract,
Or sunk at the core of the world   70
Too deep for the most to discern?
Like stars in the deep of the sky,
Which arise on the glass of the sage,
But are lost when their watcher is gone.

'They are here'—I heard, as men heard   75
In Mysian Ida the voice
Of the Mighty Mother, or Crete,
The murmur of Nature reply—
'Loveliness, magic, and grace,
They are here! they are set in the world,   80
They abide; and the finest of souls
Hath not been thrill'd by them all,
Nor the dullest been dead to them quite.
The poet who sings them may die,
But they are immortal and live,   85
For they are the life of the world.
Will ye not learn it, and know,
When ye mourn that a poet is dead,
That the singer was less than his themes,
Life, and emotion, and I?   90

'More than the singer are these.
Weak is the tremor of pain

79 *1881*: Loveliness, magic, grace,   82 *1852–77*: Has not been

230

That thrills in his mournfullest chord
To that which once ran through his soul.
Cold the elation of joy   95
In his gladdest, airiest song,
To that which of old in his youth
Fill'd him and made him divine.
Hardly his voice at its best
Gives us a sense of the awe,   100
The vastness, the grandeur, the gloom
Of the unlit gulph of himself.

'Ye know not yourselves; and your bards—
The clearest, the best, who have read
Most in themselves—have beheld   105
Less than they left unreveal'd.
Ye express not yourselves;—can you make
With marble, with colour, with word,
What charm'd you in others re-live?
Can thy pencil, O artist! restore   110
The figure, the bloom of thy love,
As she was in her morning of spring?
Canst thou paint the ineffable smile
Of her eyes as they rested on thine?
Can the image of life have the glow,   115
The motion of life itself?

'Yourselves and your fellows ye know not; and me,
The mateless, the one, will ye know?
Will ye scan me, and read me, and tell
Of the thoughts that ferment in my breast,   120
My longing, my sadness, my joy?
Will ye claim for your great ones the gift
To have render'd the gleam of my skies,
To have echoed the moan of my seas,
Utter'd the voice of my hills?   125
When your great ones depart, will ye say:

102 *1852 (only)*: gulf   107 *1852–81*: Can ye make

231

All things have suffer'd a loss,
Nature is hid in their grave?

'Race after race, man after man,
Have thought that my secret was theirs,   130
Have dream'd that I lived but for them,
That they were my glory and joy.
—They are dust, they are changed, they are gone!
I remain.'

THE YOUTH OF MAN

[First published 1852. Two fragments, entitled 'Richmond Hill' and 'Power of
Youth', 1853. Reprinted, in complete form, 1855, '69, and thereafter.]

WE, O Nature, depart,
Thou survivest us! this,
This, I know, is the law.
Yes! but more than this,
Thou who seest us die   5
Seest us change while we live;
Seest our dreams, one by one,
Seest our errors depart;
Watchest us, Nature! throughout,
Mild and inscrutably calm.   10

Well for us that we change!
Well for us that the power
Which in our morning-prime
Saw the mistakes of our youth,
Sweet, and forgiving, and good,   15
Sees the contrition of age!

Behold, O Nature, this pair!
See them to-night where they stand,
Not with the halo of youth
Crowning their brows with its light,   20

130 *1852, 1855*: dream'd that my secret   131 *1852, 1855*: thought
that I lived

232

Not with the sunshine of hope,
Not with the rapture of spring,
Which they had of old, when they stood
Years ago at my side
In this self-same garden, and said: 25
'We are young, and the world is ours;
Man, man is the king of the world!
Fools that these mystics are
Who prate of Nature! for she
Hath neither beauty, nor warmth,   30
Nor life, nor emotion, nor power.
But man has a thousand gifts,
And the generous dreamer invests
The senseless world with them all.
Nature is nothing; her charm   35
Lives in our eyes which can paint,
Lives in our hearts which can feel.'

Thou, O Nature, wast mute,
Mute as of old! days flew,
Days and years; and Time   40
With the ceaseless stroke of his wings
Brush'd off the bloom from their soul.
Clouded and dim grew their eye,
Languid their heart—for youth
Quicken'd its pulses no more.   45
Slowly, within the walls
Of an ever-narrowing world,
They droop'd, they grew blind, they grew old.
Thee and their youth in thee,
Nature! they saw no more.   50

Murmur of living,
Stir of existence,
Soul of the world!

27 *1852–69*: For man is   29 *1852–81*: but she   30 *1852,*
1855: Has neither   38 *1852, 1855*: wert mute,   51–60 *1853*:
printed separately as Richmond Hill.

Make, oh, make yourselves felt
To the dying spirit of youth!   55
Come, like the breath of the spring!
Leave not a human soul
To grow old in darkness and pain!
Only the living can feel you,
But leave us not while we live!   60

Here they stand to-night—
Here, where this grey balustrade
Crowns the still valley; behind
Is the castled house, with its woods,
Which shelter'd their childhood—the sun   65
On its ivied windows; a scent
From the grey-wall'd gardens, a breath
Of the fragrant stock and the pink,
Perfumes the evening air.
Their children play on the lawns.   70
They stand and listen; they hear
The children's shouts, and at times,
Faintly, the bark of a dog
From a distant farm in the hills.
Nothing besides! in front   75
The wide, wide valley outspreads
To the dim horizon, reposed
In the twilight, and bathed in dew,
Corn-field and hamlet and copse
Darkening fast; but a light,   80
Far off, a glory of day,
Still plays on the city spires;
And there in the dusk by the walls,
With the grey mist marking its course
Through the silent, flowery land,   85
On, to the plains, to the sea,
Floats the imperial stream.

64 *1877*, *1881*: In the castled

Well I know what they feel!
They gaze, and the evening wind
Plays on their faces; they gaze—   90
Airs from the Eden of youth
Awake and stir in their soul;
The past returns—they feel
What they are, alas! what they were.
They, not Nature, are changed.   95
Well I know what they feel!

Hush, for tears
Begin to steal to their eyes!
Hush, for fruit
Grows from such sorrow as theirs!   100

And they remember,
With piercing, untold anguish,
The proud boasting of their youth.
And they feel how Nature was fair.
And the mists of delusion,   105
And the scales of habit,
Fall away from their eyes;
And they see, for a moment,
Stretching out, like the desert
In its weary, unprofitable length,   110
Their faded, ignoble lives.

While the locks are yet brown on thy head,
While the soul still looks through thine eyes,
While the heart still pours
The mantling blood to thy cheek,   115
Sink, O youth, in thy soul!
Yearn to the greatness of Nature;
Rally the good in the depths of thyself!

112–18 *1853: printed separately as* Power of Youth.

PALLADIUM

[*First published 1867. Reprinted 1869 and thereafter*]

SET where the upper streams of Simois flow
Was the Palladium, high 'mid rock and wood;
And Hector was in Ilium, far below,
And fought, and saw it not—but there it stood!

It stood, and sun and moonshine rain'd their light   5
On the pure columns of its glen-built hall.
Backward and forward roll'd the waves of fight
Round Troy—but while this stood, Troy could not fall.

So, in its lovely moonlight, lives the soul.
Mountains surround it, and sweet virgin air;   10
Cold plashing, past it, crystal waters roll;
We visit it by moments, ah, too rare!

We shall renew the battle in the plain
To-morrow;—red with blood will Xanthus be;
Hector and Ajax will be there again,   15
Helen will come upon the wall to see.

Then we shall rust in shade, or shine in strife,
And fluctuate 'twixt blind hopes and blind despairs,
And fancy that we put forth all our life,
And never know how with the soul it fares.   20

Still doth the soul, from its lone fastness high,
Upon our life a ruling effluence send.
And when it fails, fight as we will, we die;
And while it lasts, we cannot wholly end.

13 *1867–81*: Men will renew

PROGRESS

[*First published 1852. Reprinted 1867 and thereafter*]

THE Master stood upon the mount, and taught.
He saw a fire in his disciples' eyes;
'The old law,' they cried, 'is wholly come to nought,
    Behold the new world rise!'

'Was it,' the Lord then said, 'with scorn ye saw   5
The old law observed by Scribes and Pharisees?
I say unto you, see *ye* keep that law
    More faithfully than these!

'Too hasty heads for ordering worlds, alas!
Think not that I to annul the law have will'd;   10
No jot, no tittle from the law shall pass,
    Till all have been fulfill'd.'

So Christ said eighteen hundred years ago.
And what then shall be said to those to-day,
Who cry aloud to lay the old world low   15
    To clear the new world's way?

'Religious fervours! ardour misapplied!
Hence, hence,' they cry, 'ye do but keep man blind!
But keep him self-immersed, preoccupied,
    And lame the active mind!'   20

Ah! from the old world let some one answer give:
'Scorn ye this world, their tears, their inward cares?
I say unto you, see that *your* souls live
    A deeper life than theirs!

'Say ye: "The spirit of man has found new roads,   25
And we must leave the old faiths, and walk therein"?—
Leave then the Cross as ye have left carved gods,
    But guard the fire within!

3 *1852–81*: they said,   12 *1852*: shall be fulfill'd.   *1867–9*:
hath been fulfill'd.   27–8 *1852*:
    Quench then the altar fires of your old Gods!
        Quench not the fire within!

'Bright else and fast the stream of life may roll,
And no man may the other's hurt behold;   30
Yet each will have one anguish—his own soul
    Which perishes of cold.'

Here let that voice make end; then, let a strain,
From a far lonelier distance, like the wind
Be heard, floating through heaven, and fill again   35
    These men's profoundest mind:

'Children of men! the unseen Power, whose eye
For ever doth accompany mankind,
Hath look'd on no religion scornfully
    That men did ever find.   40

'Which has not taught weak wills how much they can?
Which has not fall'n on the dry heart like rain?
Which has not cried to sunk, self-weary man:
    Thou must be born again!

'Children of men! not that your age excel   45
In pride of life the ages of your sires,
But that ye think clear, feel deep, bear fruit well,
    The Friend of man desires.'

37–40 *1852*: 'Children of men! the unseen Power, whose eye
           Ever accompanies the march of man,
           Hath without pain seen *no* religion die,
              Since first the world began.
Between 40 *and* 41 *1852 reads*:
           'That man must still to some new worship press
           Hath in his eye ever but serv'd to show
           The depth of that consuming restlessness
              Which makes man's greatest woe.
40 *1867*: That man   47 *1852*: But that you too feel deeply,   *1867*:
But that *you* think clear, feel deep,   *1868, 1869*: But that you think
1877–81: But that *ye* think

REVOLUTIONS

[*First published 1852. Reprinted 1855, '69, and thereafter*]

BEFORE man parted for this earthly strand,
While yet upon the verge of heaven he stood,
God put a heap of letters in his hand,
And bade him make with them what word he could.

And man has turn'd them many times; made Greece,   5
Rome, England, France;—yes, nor in vain essay'd
Way after way, changes that never cease!
The letters have combined, something was made.

But ah! an inextinguishable sense
Haunts him that he has not made what he should;   10
That he has still, though old, to recommence,
Since he has not yet found the word God would.

And empire after empire, at their height
Of sway, have felt this boding sense come on;
Have felt their huge frames not constructed right,   15
And droop'd, and slowly died upon their throne.

One day, thou say'st, there will at last appear
The word, the order, which God meant should be.
—Ah! we shall know *that* well when it comes near;
The band will quit man's heart, he will breathe free.   20

SELF-DEPENDENCE

[*First published 1852. Reprinted 1853, '54, '57, '69, and thereafter*]

WEARY of myself, and sick of asking
What I am, and what I ought to be,
At this vessel's prow I stand, which bears me
Forwards, forwards, o'er the starlit sea.

REVOLUTIONS. 14 *1877*: have left [*sic*]   SELF-DEPENDENCE. 3 *1852–69*:
the vessel's

And a look of passionate desire   5
O'er the sea and to the stars I send:
'Ye who from my childhood up have calm'd me,
Calm me, ah, compose me to the end!

'Ah, once more,' I cried, 'ye stars, ye waters,
On my heart your mighty charm renew;   10
Still, still let me, as I gaze upon you,
Feel my soul becoming vast like you!'

From the intense, clear, star-sown vault of heaven,
Over the lit sea's unquiet way,
In the rustling night-air came the answer: 15
'Wouldst thou *be* as these are? *Live* as they.

'Unaffrighted by the silence round them,
Undistracted by the sights they see,
These demand not that the things without them
Yield them love, amusement, sympathy.   20

'And with joy the stars perform their shining,
And the sea its long moon-silver'd roll;
For self-poised they live, nor pine with noting
All the fever of some differing soul.

'Bounded by themselves, and unregardful   25
In what state God's other works may be,
In their own tasks all their powers pouring,
These attain the mighty life you see.'

O air-born voice! long since, severely clear,
A cry like thine in mine own heart I hear: 30
'Resolve to be thyself; and know that he,
Who finds himself, loses his misery!'

23 *1852–7*: alone they live,   *1869 (only)*: Why?—self-poised
25 *1852–7*: and unobservant   29 *From 1854 to 1881 the last stanza was
set off from the rest by printer's rule, a row of asterisks, or extra spacing.*
30 *1852–7*: my own

MORALITY

[*First published 1852. Reprinted 1853, '54, '57, '69, and thereafter*]

WE cannot kindle when we will
The fire which in the heart resides;
The spirit bloweth and is still,
In mystery our soul abides.
   But tasks in hours of insight will'd   5
   Can be through hours of gloom fulfill'd.

With aching hands and bleeding feet
We dig and heap, lay stone on stone;
We bear the burden and the heat
Of the long day, and wish 'twere done.   10
   Not till the hours of light return,
   All we have built do we discern.

Then, when the clouds are off the soul,
When thou dost bask in Nature's eye,
Ask, how *she* view'd thy self-control,   15
Thy struggling, task'd morality—
   Nature, whose free, light, cheerful air,
   Oft made thee, in thy gloom, despair.

And she, whose censure thou dost dread,
Whose eye thou wast afraid to seek,   20
See, on her face a glow is spread,
A strong emotion on her cheek!
   'Ah, child!' she cries, 'that strife divine,
   Whence was it, for it is not mine?

'There is no effort on *my* brow—   25
I do not strive, I do not weep;
I rush with the swift spheres and glow
In joy, and when I will, I sleep.
   Yet that severe, that earnest air,
   I saw, I felt it once—but where?   30

2 *1852–7*: fire that   20 *1852–7*: thou wert

'I knew not yet the gauge of time,
Nor wore the manacles of space;
I felt it in some other clime,
I saw it in some other place.
    'Twas when the heavenly house I trod,   35
    And lay upon the breast of God.'

A SUMMER NIGHT

[First published 1852. Reprinted 1855, '69, and thereafter]

In the deserted, moon-blanch'd street,
How lonely rings the echo of my feet!
Those windows, which I gaze at, frown,
Silent and white, unopening down,
Repellent as the world;—but see,   5
A break between the housetops shows
The moon! and, lost behind her, fading dim
Into the dewy dark obscurity
Down at the far horizon's rim,
Doth a whole tract of heaven disclose!   10

And to my mind the thought
Is on a sudden brought
Of a past night, and a far different scene.
Headlands stood out into the moonlit deep
As clearly as at noon;   15
The spring-tide's brimming flow
Heaved dazzlingly between;
Houses, with long white sweep,
Girdled the glistening bay;
Behind, through the soft air,   20
The blue haze-cradled mountains spread away,
That night was far more fair—
But the same restless pacings to and fro,
And the same vainly throbbing heart was there,
And the same bright, calm moon.   25

A SUMMER NIGHT. **22** *1890 (only)*: The night   **24** *1852*: And the
same agitated heart

And the calm moonlight seems to say:
Hast thou then still the old unquiet breast,
Which neither deadens into rest,
Nor ever feels the fiery glow
That whirls the spirit from itself away,   30
But fluctuates to and fro,
Never by passion quite possess'd
And never quite benumb'd by the world's sway?—
And I, I know not if to pray
Still to be what I am, or yield and be   35
Like all the other men I see.

For most men in a brazen prison live,
Where, in the sun's hot eye,
With heads bent o'er their toil, they languidly
Their lives to some unmeaning taskwork give,   40
Dreaming of nought beyond their prison-wall.
And as, year after year,
Fresh products of their barren labour fall
From their tired hands, and rest
Never yet comes more near,   45
Gloom settles slowly down over their breast;
And while they try to stem
The waves of mournful thought by which they are prest,
Death in their prison reaches them,
Unfreed, having seen nothing, still unblest.   50

And the rest, a few,
Escape their prison and depart
On the wide ocean of life anew.
There the freed prisoner, where'er his heart
Listeth, will sail;   55
Nor doth he know how there prevail,
Despotic on that sea,
Trade-winds which cross it from eternity.

28 *1852, 1855*: That neither deadens   *1869 (only)*: *Which never*
deadens   27–33 *1852 quoted in roman*   56 *1852–5*: Nor does he
57 *1852–5*: on life's sea,   58 *1852–5*: Trade-winds that

Awhile he holds some false way, undebarr'd
By thwarting signs, and braves 60
The freshening wind and blackening waves.
And then the tempest strikes him; and between
The lightning-bursts is seen
Only a driving wreck,
And the pale master on his spar-strewn deck 65
With anguish'd face and flying hair
Grasping the rudder hard,
Still bent to make some port he knows not where,
Still standing for some false, impossible shore.
And sterner comes the roar 70
Of sea and wind, and through the deepening gloom
Fainter and fainter wreck and helmsman loom,
And he too disappears, and comes no more.

Is there no life, but these alone?
Madman or slave, must man be one? 75

Plainness and clearness without shadow of stain!
Clearness divine!
Ye heavens, whose pure dark regions have no sign
Of languor, though so calm, and, though so great,
Are yet untroubled and unpassionate; 80
Who, though so noble, share in the world's toil,
And, though so task'd, keep free from dust and soil!
I will not say that your mild deeps retain
A tinge, it may be, of their silent pain
Who have long'd deeply once, and long'd in vain— 85
But I will rather say that you remain
A world above man's head, to let him see
How boundless might his soul's horizons be,
How vast, yet of what clear transparency!
How it were good to abide there, and breathe free; 90
How fair a lot to fill
Is left to each man still!

80 *1881*: And yet [*sic*] 90 *1852, 1855*: to sink there,
1869–81: to live there, 91 *1852*: high a lot

THE BURIED LIFE

[*First published 1852. Reprinted 1855, '69, and thereafter*]

LIGHT flows our war of mocking words, and yet,
Behold, with tears mine eyes are wet!
I feel a nameless sadness o'er me roll.
Yes, yes, we know that we can jest,
We know, we know that we can smile!   5
But there's a something in this breast,
To which thy light words bring no rest,
And thy gay smiles no anodyne.
Give me thy hand, and hush awhile,
And turn those limpid eyes on mine,   10
And let me read there, love! thy inmost soul.

Alas! is even love too weak
To unlock the heart, and let it speak?
Are even lovers powerless to reveal
To one another what indeed they feel?   15
I knew the mass of men conceal'd
Their thoughts, for fear that if reveal'd
They would by other men be met
With blank indifference, or with blame reproved;
I knew they lived and moved   20
Trick'd in disguises, alien to the rest
Of men, and alien to themselves—and yet
The same heart beats in every human breast!

But we, my love!—doth a like spell benumb
Our hearts, our voices?—must we too be dumb?   25

Ah! well for us, if even we,
Even for a moment, can get free
Our heart, and have our lips unchain'd;
For that which seals them hath been deep-ordain'd!

2 *1852–5*: my eyes   23 *1852* (*only*): There beats one heart
24 *1852–5*: does a like

Fate, which foresaw   30
How frivolous a baby man would be—
By what distractions he would be possess'd,
How he would pour himself in every strife,
And well-nigh change his own identity—
That it might keep from his capricious play   35
His genuine self, and force him to obey
Even in his own despite his being's law,
Bade through the deep recesses of our breast
The unregarded river of our life
Pursue with indiscernible flow its way;   40
And that we should not see
The buried stream, and seem to be
Eddying at large in blind uncertainty,
Though driving on with it eternally.

But often, in the world's most crowded streets,   45
But often, in the din of strife,
There rises an unspeakable desire
After the knowledge of our buried life;
A thirst to spend our fire and restless force
In tracking out our true, original course;   50
A longing to inquire
Into the mystery of this heart which beats
So wild, so deep in us—to know
Whence our lives come and where they go.
And many a man in his own breast then delves,   55
But deep enough, alas! none ever mines.
And we have been on many thousand lines,
And we have shown, on each, spirit and power;
But hardly have we, for one little hour,
Been on our own line, have we been ourselves—   60
Hardly had skill to utter one of all
The nameless feelings that course through our breast,
But they course on for ever unexpress'd.

43 *1852–5*: Eddying about   52 *1852–5*: that beats   54 *1852–*
77: our thoughts come   58 *1852–5*: talent and power,

And long we try in vain to speak and act
Our hidden self, and what we say and do   65
Is eloquent, is well—but 'tis not true!
And then we will no more be rack'd
With inward striving, and demand
Of all the thousand nothings of the hour
Their stupefying power;   70
Ah yes, and they benumb us at our call!
Yet still, from time to time, vague and forlorn,
From the soul's subterranean depth upborne
As from an infinitely distant land,
Come airs, and floating echoes, and convey   75
A melancholy into all our day.

Only—but this is rare—
When a belovéd hand is laid in ours,
When, jaded with the rush and glare
Of the interminable hours,   80
Our eyes can in another's eyes read clear,
When our world-deafen'd ear
Is by the tones of a loved voice caress'd—
A bolt is shot back somewhere in our breast,
And a lost pulse of feeling stirs again.   85
The eye sinks inward, and the heart lies plain,
And what we mean, we say, and what we would, we know.
A man becomes aware of his life's flow,
And hears its winding murmur; and he sees
The meadows where it glides, the sun, the breeze. 90

And there arrives a lull in the hot race
Wherein he doth for ever chase
That flying and elusive shadow, rest.
An air of coolness plays upon his face,
And an unwonted calm pervades his breast.   95
And then he thinks he knows
The hills where his life rose,
And the sea where it goes.

70 *1852–5*: stupifying

LINES

WRITTEN IN KENSINGTON GARDENS

[*First published 1852. Reprinted 1867 and thereafter*]

In this lone, open glade I lie,
Screen'd by deep boughs on either hand;
And at its end, to stay the eye,
Those black-crown'd, red-boled pine-trees stand!

Birds here make song, each bird has his,   5
Across the girdling city's hum.
How green under the boughs it is!
How thick the tremulous sheep-cries come!

Sometimes a child will cross the glade
To take his nurse his broken toy;   10
Sometimes a thrush flit overhead
Deep in her unknown day's employ.

Here at my feet what wonders pass,
What endless, active life is here!
What blowing daisies, fragrant grass!   15
An air-stirr'd forest, fresh and clear.

Scarce fresher is the mountain-sod
Where the tired angler lies, stretch'd out,
And, eased of basket and of rod,
Counts his day's spoil, the spotted trout.   20

2 *1852*: dark trees on   3 *MS.*: *as above.*   *1852–68*: at its head,
1869 (only): Where ends the glade,   *1877*: *the MS. reading restored.*
4 *1852 (only)*: black-topp'd,   *Between 4 and 5 1852 (only) reads*
(*as in the MS.*):

> The clouded sky is still and grey,
> Through silken rifts soft peers the sun.
> Light the green-foliag'd chestnuts play,
> The darker elms stand grave and dun.

5 *1852 (only)*: The birds sing sweetly in these trees

In the huge world, which roars hard by,
Be others happy if they can!
But in my helpless cradle I
Was breathed on by the rural Pan.

I, on men's impious uproar hurl'd,   25
Think often, as I hear them rave,
That peace has left the upper world
And now keeps only in the grave.

Yet here is peace for ever new!
When I who watch them am away,   30
Still all things in this glade go through
The changes of their quiet day.

Then to their happy rest they pass!
The flowers upclose, the birds are fed,
The night comes down upon the grass,   35
The child sleeps warmly in his bed.

Calm soul of all things! make it mine
To feel, amid the city's jar,
That there abides a peace of thine,
Man did not make, and cannot mar.   40

The will to neither strive nor cry,
The power to feel with others give!
Calm, calm me more! nor let me die
Before I have begun to live.

A WISH

[*First published 1867. Reprinted 1868 and thereafter*]

I ASK not that my bed of death
From bands of greedy heirs be free;
For these besiege the latest breath
Of fortune's favour'd sons, not me.

21–4 *First inserted in 1867.*   26 *1852 (only):* Think sometimes
34 *1852, 1867:* The flowers close,

A WISH

I ask not each kind soul to keep   5
Tearless, when of my death he hears.
Let those who will, if any, weep!
There are worse plagues on earth than tears.

I ask but that my death may find
The freedom to my life denied;   10
Ask but the folly of mankind
Then, then at last, to quit my side.

Spare me the whispering, crowded room,
The friends who come, and gape, and go;
The ceremonious air of gloom—   15
All, which makes death a hideous show!

Nor bring, to see me cease to live,
Some doctor full of phrase and fame,
To shake his sapient head, and give
The ill he cannot cure a name.   20

Nor fetch, to take the accustom'd toll
Of the poor sinner bound for death,
His brother-doctor of the soul,
To canvass with official breath

The future and its viewless things—   25
That undiscover'd mystery
Which one who feels death's winnowing wings
Must needs read clearer, sure, than he!

Bring none of these; but let me be,
While all around in silence lies,   30
Moved to the window near, and see
Once more, before my dying eyes,

Bathed in the sacred dews of morn
The wide aerial landscape spread—
The world which was ere I was born,   35
The world which lasts when I am dead;

16 *1867–9*: All, that

Which never was the friend of *one*,
Nor promised love it could not give,
But lit for all its generous sun,
And lived itself, and made us live.   40

There let me gaze, till I become
In soul, with what I gaze on, wed!
To feel the universe my home;
To have before my mind—instead

Of the sick room, the mortal strife,   45
The turmoil for a little breath—
The pure eternal course of life,
Not human combatings with death!

Thus feeling, gazing, might I grow
Composed, refresh'd, ennobled, clear;   50
Then willing let my spirit go
To work or wait elsewhere or here!

THE FUTURE

[*First published 1852. Reprinted 1853, '54, '57, '69, and thereafter*]

A WANDERER is man from his birth.
He was born in a ship
On the breast of the river of Time;
Brimming with wonder and joy
He spreads out his arms to the light,   5
Rivets his gaze on the banks of the stream.

45–6 *1869* (*only*):
       Of a sick room, a mortal strife,
       A turmoil
49 *1867–77*: let me grow
THE FUTURE. *1853, '54: these lines printed as a motto to the poem*:
       For Nature hath long kept this inn, the Earth,
       And many a guest hath she therein receiv'd—

As what he sees is, so have his thoughts been.
Whether he wakes,
Where the snowy mountainous pass,
Echoing the screams of the eagles,   10
Hems in its gorges the bed
Of the new-born clear-flowing stream;
Whether he first sees light
Where the river in gleaming rings
Sluggishly winds through the plain;   15
Whether in sound of the swallowing sea—
As is the world on the banks,
So is the mind of the man.

Vainly does each, as he glides,
Fable and dream   20
Of the lands which the river of Time
Had left ere he woke on its breast,
Or shall reach when his eyes have been closed.
Only the tract where he sails
He wots of; only the thoughts,   25
Raised by the objects he passes, are his.

Who can see the green earth any more
As she was by the sources of Time?
Who imagines her fields as they lay
In the sunshine, unworn by the plough?   30
Who thinks as they thought,
The tribes who then roam'd on her breast,
Her vigorous, primitive sons?

What girl
Now reads in her bosom as clear   35
As Rebekah read, when she sate
At eve by the palm-shaded well?
Who guards in her breast
As deep, as pellucid a spring
Of feeling, as tranquil, as sure?   40

32 *1852–4*: liv'd on her breast,

THE FUTURE

What bard,
At the height of his vision, can deem
Of God, of the world, of the soul,
With a plainness as near,
As flashing as Moses felt   45
When he lay in the night by his flock
On the starlit Arabian waste?
Can rise and obey
The beck of the Spirit like him?

This tract which the river of Time   50
Now flows through with us, is the plain.
Gone is the calm of its earlier shore.
Border'd by cities and hoarse
With a thousand cries is its stream.
And we on its breast, our minds   55
Are confused as the cries which we hear,
Changing and shot as the sights which we see.

And we say that repose has fled
For ever the course of the river of Time.
That cities will crowd to its edge   60
In a blacker, incessanter line;
That the din will be more on its banks,
Denser the trade on its stream,
Flatter the plain where it flows,
Fiercer the sun overhead.   65
That never will those on its breast
See an ennobling sight,
Drink of the feeling of quiet again.

But what was before us we know not,
And we know not what shall succeed.   70

Haply, the river of Time—
As it grows, as the towns on its marge
Fling their wavering lights
On a wider, statelier stream—

May acquire, if not the calm 75
Of its early mountainous shore,
Yet a solemn peace of its own.

And the width of the waters, the hush
Of the grey expanse where he floats,
Freshening its current and spotted with foam 80
As it draws to the Ocean, may strike
Peace to the soul of the man on its breast—
As the pale waste widens around him,
As the banks fade dimmer away,
As the stars come out, and the night-wind 85
Brings up the stream
Murmurs and scents of the infinite sea.

ELEGIAC POEMS

THE SCHOLAR-GIPSY[16]

[First published 1853. Reprinted 1854, '57, '69, and thereafter]

Go, for they call you, shepherd, from the hill;
  Go, shepherd, and untie the wattled cotes!
    No longer leave thy wistful flock unfed,
  Nor let thy bawling fellows rack their throats,
    Nor the cropp'd herbage shoot another head.   5
      But when the fields are still,
  And the tired men and dogs all gone to rest,
    And only the white sheep are sometimes seen
    Cross and recross the strips of moon-blanch'd green,
  Come, shepherd, and again begin the quest!   10

Here, where the reaper was at work of late—
  In this high field's dark corner, where he leaves
    His coat, his basket, and his earthen cruse,
  And in the sun all morning binds the sheaves,
    Then here, at noon, comes back his stores to use—   15
      Here will I sit and wait,
  While to my ear from uplands far away
    The bleating of the folded flocks is borne,
    With distant cries of reapers in the corn—
  All the live murmur of a summer's day.   20

Screen'd is this nook o'er the high, half-reap'd field,
  And here till sun-down, shepherd! will I be.
    Through the thick corn the scarlet poppies peep,
  And round green roots and yellowing stalks I see
    Pale pink convolvulus in tendrils creep;   25
      And air-swept lindens yield

5 *1853–81*: cropp'd grasses   10 *1853–7 and 1877–81*: renew the quest. *In 1869 the present reading first appeared, but was not used again till 1885.*   21 *1854–7*: Screen'd in   25 *1853–81*: Pale blue convolvulus

Their scent, and rustle down their perfumed showers
    Of bloom on the bent grass where I am laid,
    And bower me from the August sun with shade;
And the eye travels down to Oxford's towers.   30

And near me on the grass lies Glanvil's book—
    Come, let me read the oft-read tale again!
    The story of the Oxford scholar poor,
Of pregnant parts and quick inventive brain,
      Who, tired of knocking at preferment's door,   35
        One summer-morn forsook
His friends, and went to learn the gipsy-lore,
    And roam'd the world with that wild brotherhood,
    And came, as most men deem'd, to little good,
But came to Oxford and his friends no more.   40

But once, years after, in the country-lanes,
    Two scholars, whom at college erst he knew,
    Met him, and of his way of life enquired;
Whereat he answer'd, that the gipsy-crew,
      His mates, had arts to rule as they desired   45
        The workings of men's brains,
And they can bind them to what thoughts they will.
    'And I,' he said, 'the secret of their art,
    When fully learn'd, will to the world impart;
But it needs heaven-sent moments for this skill.'   50

This said, he left them, and return'd no more.—
    But rumours hung about the country-side,
    That the lost Scholar long was seen to stray,
Seen by rare glimpses, pensive and tongue-tied,
      In hat of antique shape, and cloak of grey,   55
        The same the gipsies wore.
Shepherds had met him on the Hurst in spring;
    At some lone alehouse in the Berkshire moors,
    On the warm ingle-bench, the smock-frock'd boors
Had found him seated at their entering,   60

33 *1853–81*: that Oxford scholar   34 *1869–78, 1881*: shining parts
1880: pregnant parts   50 *1853 (only)*: happy moments

But, 'mid their drink and clatter, he would fly.
  And I myself seem half to know thy looks,
    And put the shepherds, wanderer! on thy trace;
  And boys who in lone wheatfields scare the rooks
    I ask if thou hast pass'd their quiet place;   65
        Or in my boat I lie
  Moor'd to the cool bank in the summer-heats,
    'Mid wide grass meadows which the sunshine fills,
    And watch the warm, green-muffled Cumner hills,
  And wonder if thou haunt'st their shy retreats.   70

For most, I know, thou lov'st retired ground!
  Thee at the ferry Oxford riders blithe,
    Returning home on summer-nights, have met
  Crossing the stripling Thames at Bab-lock-hithe,
    Trailing in the cool stream thy fingers wet,   75
        As the punt's rope chops round;
  And leaning backward in a pensive dream,
    And fostering in thy lap a heap of flowers
    Pluck'd in shy fields and distant Wychwood bowers,
  And thine eyes resting on the moonlit stream.   80

And then they land, and thou art seen no more!—
  Maidens, who from the distant hamlets come
    To dance around the Fyfield elm in May,
  Oft through the darkening fields have seen thee roam,
    Or cross a stile into the public way.   85
        Oft thou hast given them store
  Of flowers—the frail-leaf'd, white anemony,
    Dark bluebells drench'd with dews of summer eves,
    And purple orchises with spotted leaves—
  But none hath words she can report of thee.   90

And, above Godstow Bridge, when hay-time's here
  In June, and many a scythe in sunshine flames,
    Men who through those wide fields of breezy grass
  Where black-wing'd swallows haunt the glittering Thames,

76 *1853–7*: As the slow punt swings round: 77 *1853–7*: backwards
79 *1853–4*: distant woodland bowers,   90 *1853–69*: has words

To bathe in the abandon'd lasher pass,   95
   Have often pass'd thee near
Sitting upon the river bank o'ergrown;
   Mark'd thine outlandish garb, thy figure spare,
   Thy dark vague eyes, and soft abstracted air—
But, when they came from bathing, thou wast gone!   100

At some lone homestead in the Cumner hills,
   Where at her open door the housewife darns,
   Thou hast been seen, or hanging on a gate
To watch the threshers in the mossy barns.
   Children, who early range these slopes and late   105
      For cresses from the rills,
Have known thee eying, all an April-day,
   The springing pastures and the feeding kine;
   And mark'd thee, when the stars come out and shine,
Through the long dewy grass move slow away.   110

In autumn, on the skirts of Bagley Wood—
   Where most the gipsies by the turf-edged way
   Pitch their smoked tents, and every bush you see
With scarlet patches tagg'd and shreds of grey,
   Above the forest-ground called Thessaly—   115
      The blackbird, picking food,
Sees thee, nor stops his meal, nor fears at all;
   So often has he known thee past him stray,
   Rapt, twirling in thy hand a wither'd spray,
And waiting for the spark from heaven to fall.   120

And once, in winter, on the causeway chill
   Where home through flooded fields foot-travellers go,
   Have I not pass'd thee on the wooden bridge,
Wrapt in thy cloak and battling with the snow,
   Thy face tow'rd Hinksey and its wintry ridge?   125
      And thou hast climb'd the hill,

98 *1853–7*: thy outlandish   100 *1853–69*: wert gone   107 *1853–7*: thee watching   *1869*: thee haunting,   125 *1853–7*: towards Hinksey   *1869–81*: toward Hinksey

And gain'd the white brow of the Cumner range;
  Turn'd once to watch, while thick the snowflakes fall.
    The line of festal light in Christ-Church hall—
  Then sought thy straw in some sequester'd grange.   130

But what—I dream! Two hundred years are flown
  Since first thy story ran through Oxford halls,
    And the grave Glanvil did the tale inscribe
  That thou wert wander'd from the studious walls
    To learn strange arts, and join a gipsy-tribe;   135
      And thou from earth art gone
  Long since, and in some quiet churchyard laid—
    Some country-nook, where o'er thy unknown grave
    Tall grasses and white flowering nettles wave,
  Under a dark, red-fruited yew-tree's shade.   140

—No, no, thou hast not felt the lapse of hours!
  For what wears out the life of mortal men?
    'Tis that from change to change their being rolls;
  'Tis that repeated shocks, again, again,
    Exhaust the energy of strongest souls   145
      And numb the elastic powers.
  Till having used our nerves with bliss and teen,
    And tired upon a thousand schemes our wit,
    To the just-pausing Genius we remit
  Our worn-out life, and are—what we have been.   150

Thou hast not lived, why should'st thou perish, so?
  Thou hadst *one* aim, *one* business, *one* desire;
    Else wert thou long since number'd with the dead!
  Else hadst thou spent, like other men, thy fire!
    The generations of thy peers are fled,   155
      And we ourselves shall go;
  But thou possessest an immortal lot,
    And we imagine thee exempt from age
    And living as thou liv'st on Glanvil's page,
  Because thou hadst—what we, alas! have not.   160

150 *1869-81*: well-worn life

For early didst thou leave the world, with powers
   Fresh, undiverted to the world without,
      Firm to their mark, not spent on other things;
   Free from the sick fatigue, the languid doubt,
      Which much to have tried, in much been baffled, brings.
         O life unlike to ours!   166
   Who fluctuate idly without term or scope,
Of whom each strives, nor knows for what he strives,
      And each half lives a hundred different lives;
   Who wait like thee, but not, like thee, in hope.   170

Thou waitest for the spark from heaven! and we,
   Light half-believers of our casual creeds,
      Who never deeply felt, nor clearly will'd,
   Whose insight never has borne fruit in deeds,
      Whose vague resolves never have been fulfill'd;   175
         For whom each year we see
   Breeds new beginnings, disappointments new;
      Who hesitate and falter life away,
      And lose to-morrow the ground won to-day—
   Ah! do not we, wanderer! await it too?   180

Yes, we await it!—but it still delays,
   And then we suffer! and amongst us one,
      Who most has suffer'd, takes dejectedly
   His seat upon the intellectual throne;
      And all his store of sad experience he   185
         Lays bare of wretched days;
   Tells us his misery's birth and growth and signs,
      And how the dying spark of hope was fed,
      And how the breast was soothed, and how the head,
   And all his hourly varied anodynes.   190

This for our wisest! and we others pine,
   And wish the long unhappy dream would end,
      And waive all claim to bliss, and try to bear;
   With close-lipp'd patience for our only friend,

172 *1857*: Vague half-believers   175 *1857*: weak resolves

Sad patience, too near neighbour to despair— 195
    But none has hope like thine!
Thou through the fields and through the woods dost stray,
    Roaming the country-side, a truant boy,
    Nursing thy project in unclouded joy,
And every doubt long blown by time away. 200

O born in days when wits were fresh and clear,
    And life ran gaily as the sparkling Thames;
    Before this strange disease of modern life,
    With its sick hurry, its divided aims,
    Its heads o'ertax'd, its palsied hearts, was rife— 205
        Fly hence, our contact fear!
    Still fly, plunge deeper in the bowering wood!
    Averse, as Dido did with gesture stern
    From her false friend's approach in Hades turn,
Wave us away, and keep thy solitude! 210

Still nursing the unconquerable hope,
    Still clutching the inviolable shade,
    With a free, onward impulse brushing through,
    By night, the silver'd branches of the glade—
    Far on the forest-skirts, where none pursue. 215
        On some mild pastoral slope
    Emerge, and resting on the moonlit pales
    Freshen thy flowers as in former years
    With dew, or listen with enchanted ears,
From the dark dingles, to the nightingales! 220

But fly our paths, our feverish contact fly!
    For strong the infection of our mental strife,
    Which, though it gives no bliss, yet spoils for rest;
    And we should win thee from thy own fair life,
    Like us distracted, and like us unblest. 225
        Soon, soon thy cheer would die,
    Thy hopes grow timorous, and unfix'd thy powers,
    And thy clear aims be cross and shifting made;
    And then thy glad perennial youth would fade,
Fade, and grow old at last, and die like ours. 230

THE SCHOLAR-GIPSY

Then fly our greetings, fly our speech and smiles!
 —As some grave Tyrian trader, from the sea,
  Descried at sunrise an emerging prow
 Lifting the cool-hair'd creepers stealthily,
  The fringes of a southward-facing brow   235
   Among the Ægæan isles;
 And saw the merry Grecian coaster come,
  Freighted with amber grapes, and Chian wine,
  Green, bursting figs, and tunnies steep'd in brine—
 And knew the intruders on his ancient home,   240

The young light-hearted masters of the waves—
 And snatch'd his rudder, and shook out more sail;
  And day and night held on indignantly
 O'er the blue Midland waters with the gale,
  Betwixt the Syrtes and soft Sicily,   245
   To where the Atlantic raves
 Outside the western straits; and unbent sails
  There, where down cloudy cliffs, through sheets of foam,
  Shy traffickers, the dark Iberians come;
 And on the beach undid his corded bales.   250

THYRSIS[17]

A MONODY, *to commemorate the author's friend,*
ARTHUR HUGH CLOUGH, *who died at Florence,* 1861

[*First published in* MACMILLAN'S MAGAZINE, *April 1866. Reprinted 1867
and thereafter*]

How changed is here each spot man makes or fills!
 In the two Hinkseys nothing keeps the same;
  The village street its haunted mansion lacks,
 And from the sign is gone Sibylla's name,

THYRSIS. *1867, 1868: as a prefatory quotation*:
    Thus yesterday, to-day, to-morrow come,
    They hustle one another and they pass;
    But all our hustling morrows only make
    The smooth to-day of God.
       —*From* Lucretius, *an unpublished Tragedy.*

And from the roofs the twisted chimney-stacks— 5
   Are ye too changed, ye hills?
See, 'tis no foot of unfamiliar men
   To-night from Oxford up your pathway strays!
   Here came I often, often, in old days—
Thyrsis and I; we still had Thyrsis then. 10

Runs it not here, the track by Childsworth Farm,
   Past the high wood, to where the elm-tree crowns
   The hill behind whose ridge the sunset flames?
   The signal-elm, that looks on Ilsley Downs,
   The Vale, the three lone weirs, the youthful Thames?—
      This winter-eve is warm, 16
   Humid the air! leafless, yet soft as spring,
   The tender purple spray on copse and briers!
   And that sweet city with her dreaming spires,
She needs not June for beauty's heightening, 20

Lovely all times she lies, lovely to-night!—
   Only, methinks, some loss of habit's power
   Befalls me wandering through this upland dim.
   Once pass'd I blindfold here, at any hour;
   Now seldom come I, since I came with him. 25
      That single elm-tree bright
   Against the west—I miss it! is it gone?
   We prized it dearly; while it stood, we said,
   Our friend, the Gipsy-Scholar, was not dead;
While the tree lived, he in these fields lived on. 30

Too rare, too rare, grow now my visits here,
   But once I knew each field, each flower, each stick;
   And with the country-folk acquaintance made
   By barn in threshing-time, by new-built rick.
   Here, too, our shepherd-pipes we first assay'd. 35
      Ah me! this many a year

12 *1866* (*Macmillan's Magazine*), *1867*, *1868*: Up past the wood
29 *1866–9*: Our friend, the Scholar-Gipsy

My pipe is lost, my shepherd's holiday!
  Needs must I lose them, needs with heavy heart
  Into the world and wave of men depart;
But Thyrsis of his own will went away.   40

It irk'd him to be here, he could not rest.
  He loved each simple joy the country yields,
    He loved his mates; but yet he could not keep,
  For that a shadow lour'd on the fields,
    Here with the shepherds and the silly sheep.   45
      Some life of men unblest
He knew, which made him droop, and fill'd his head.
  He went; his piping took a troubled sound
  Of storms that rage outside our happy ground;
He could not wait their passing, he is dead.   50

So, some tempestuous morn in early June,
  When the year's primal burst of bloom is o'er,
    Before the roses and the longest day—
  When garden-walks and all the grassy floor
    With blossoms red and white of fallen May   55
      And chestnut-flowers are strewn—
So have I heard the cuckoo's parting cry,
  From the wet field, through the vext garden-trees,
  Come with the volleying rain and tossing breeze:
The bloom is gone, and with the bloom go I!   60

Too quick despairer, wherefore wilt thou go?
  Soon will the high Midsummer pomps come on,
    Soon will the musk carnations break and swell,
  Soon shall we have gold-dusted snapdragon,
    Sweet-William with his homely cottage-smell,   65
      And stocks in fragrant blow;
Roses that down the alleys shine afar,
  And open, jasmine-muffled lattices,
  And groups under the dreaming garden-trees,
And the full moon, and the white evening-star.   70

44 *1866–81*: lower'd   65 *1867*: its   66 *1868*: fragant blow [*sic*]

He hearkens not! light comer, he is flown!
  What matters it? next year he will return,
    And we shall have him in the sweet spring-days,
  With whitening hedges, and uncrumpling fern,
    And blue-bells trembling by the forest-ways,   75
      And scent of hay new-mown.
  But Thyrsis never more we swains shall see;
    See him come back, and cut a smoother reed,
    And blow a strain the world at last shall heed—
For Time, not Corydon, hath conquer'd thee!   80

Alack, for Corydon no rival now!—
  But when Sicilian shepherds lost a mate,
    Some good survivor with his flute would go,
  Piping a ditty sad for Bion's fate;
    And cross the unpermitted ferry's flow,   85
      And relax Pluto's brow,
  And make leap up with joy the beauteous head
    Of Proserpine, among whose crowned hair
    Are flowers first open'd on Sicilian air,
And flute his friend, like Orpheus, from the dead.   90

O easy access to the hearer's grace
  When Dorian shepherds sang to Proserpine!
    For she herself had trod Sicilian fields,
  She knew the Dorian water's gush divine,
    She knew each lily white which Enna yields,   95
      Each rose with blushing face;
  She loved the Dorian pipe, the Dorian strain.
    But ah, of our poor Thames she never heard!
    Her foot the Cumner cowslips never stirr'd;
And we should tease her with our plaint in vain!   100

Well! wind-dispersed and vain the words will be,
  Yet, Thyrsis, let me give my grief its hour
    In the old haunt, and find our tree-topp'd hill!
  Who, if not I, for questing here hath power?

71 *1866*: is gone!   86 *1866*: unbend Pluto's brow,   99 *1867–68*:
Cumnor

I know the wood which hides the daffodil,   105
  I know the Fyfield tree,
I know what white, what purple fritillaries
  The grassy harvest of the river-fields,
  Above by Ensham, down by Sandford, yields,
And what sedged brooks are Thames's tributaries;   110

I know these slopes; who knows them if not I?—
  But many a dingle on the loved hill-side,
  With thorns once studded, old, white-blossom'd trees,
Where thick the cowslips grew, and far descried
  High tower'd the spikes of purple orchises,   115
    Hath since our day put by
The coronals of that forgotten time;
  Down each green bank hath gone the ploughboy's team,
  And only in the hidden brookside gleam
Primroses, orphans of the flowery prime.   120

Where is the girl, who by the boatman's door,
  Above the locks, above the boating throng,
  Unmoor'd our skiff when through the Wytham flats,
Red loosestrife and blond meadow-sweet among
  And darting swallows and light water-gnats,   125
    We track'd the shy Thames shore?
Where are the mowers, who, as the tiny swell
  Of our boat passing heaved the river-grass,
  Stood with suspended scythe to see us pass?—
They all are gone, and thou art gone as well!   130

Yes, thou art gone! and round me too the night
  In ever-nearing circle weaves her shade.
  I see her veil draw soft across the day,
I feel her slowly chilling breath invade
  The cheek grown thin, the brown hair sprent with grey;
    I feel her finger light   136
Laid pausefully upon life's headlong train;—
  The foot less prompt to meet the morning dew,
  The heart less bounding at emotion new,
And hope, once crush'd, less quick to spring again.   140

And long the way appears, which seem'd so short
  To the less practised eye of sanguine youth;
    And high the mountain-tops, in cloudy air,
  The mountain-tops where is the throne of Truth,
    Tops in life's morning-sun so bright and bare!   145
      Unbreachable the fort
  Of the long-batter'd world uplifts its wall;
    And strange and vain the earthly turmoil grows,
    And near and real the charm of thy repose,
  And night as welcome as a friend would fall.   150

But hush! the upland hath a sudden loss
  Of quiet!—Look, adown the dusk hill-side,
    A troop of Oxford hunters going home,
  As in old days, jovial and talking, ride!
    From hunting with the Berkshire hounds they come. 155
      Quick! let me fly, and cross
  Into yon farther field!—'Tis done; and see,
    Back'd by the sunset, which doth glorify
    The orange and pale violet evening-sky,
  Bare on its lonely ridge, the Tree! the Tree!   160

I take the omen! Eve lets down her veil,
  The white fog creeps from bush to bush about,
    The west unflushes, the high stars grow bright,
  And in the scatter'd farms the lights come out.
    I cannot reach the signal-tree to-night,   165
      Yet, happy omen, hail!
  Hear it from thy broad lucent Arno-vale
    (For there thine earth-forgetting eyelids keep
    The morningless and unawakening sleep
  Under the flowery oleanders pale),   170

Hear it, O Thyrsis, still our tree is there!—
  Ah, vain! These English fields, this upland dim,
    These brambles pale with mist engarlanded,
  That lone, sky-pointing tree, are not for him;

142 *1866–8*: the unprastised eye   157 *1866–9*: further

To a boon southern country he is fled,   175
   And now in happier air,
Wandering with the great Mother's train divine
   (And purer or more subtle soul than thee,
   I trow, the mighty Mother doth not see)
Within a folding of the Apennine,   180

Thou hearest the immortal chants of old!—
   Putting his sickle to the perilous grain
    In the hot cornfield of the Phrygian king,
For thee the Lityerses-song again
    Young Daphnis with his silver voice doth sing;[18] 185
     Sings his Sicilian fold,
His sheep, his hapless love, his blinded eyes—
   And how a call celestial round him rang,
   And heavenward from the fountain-brink he sprang,
And all the marvel of the golden skies.   190

There thou art gone, and me thou leavest here
   Sole in these fields! yet will I not despair.
    Despair I will not, while I yet descry
   'Neath the mild canopy of English air
    That lonely tree against the western sky.   195
     Still, still these slopes, 'tis clear,
Our Gipsy-Scholar haunts, outliving thee!
   Fields where soft sheep from cages pull the hay,
   Woods with anemonies in flower till May,
Know him a wanderer still; then why not me?   200

A fugitive and gracious light he seeks,
   Shy to illumine; and I seek it too.
    This does not come with houses or with gold,
   With place, with honour, and a flattering crew;
    'Tis not in the world's market bought and sold— 205
     But the smooth-slipping weeks
Drop by, and leave its seeker still untired;

181 *1866, 1867*: immortal strains   194 *1866–78, 1881*: soft canopy
1880: mild canopy (*as in present reading*).   198 *1866*: where the sheep

Out of the heed of mortals he is gone,
He wends unfollow'd, he must house alone;
Yet on he fares, by his own heart inspired.   210

Thou too, O Thyrsis, on like quest wast bound;
Thou wanderedst with me for a little hour!
Men gave thee nothing; but this happy quest,
If men esteem'd thee feeble, gave thee power,
If men procured thee trouble, gave thee rest.   215
And this rude Cumner ground,
Its fir-topped Hurst, its farms, its quiet fields,
Here cam'st thou in thy jocund youthful time,
Here was thine height of strength, thy golden prime!
And still the haunt beloved a virtue yields.   220

What though the music of thy rustic flute
Kept not for long its happy, country tone;
Lost it too soon, and learnt a stormy note
Of men contention-tost, of men who groan,
Which task'd thy pipe too sore, and tired thy throat—
It fail'd, and thou wast mute!   226
Yet hadst thou alway visions of our light,
And long with men of care thou couldst not stay,
And soon thy foot resumed its wandering way,
Left human haunt, and on alone till night.   230

Too rare, too rare, grow now my visits here!
'Mid city-noise, not, as with thee of yore,
Thyrsis! in reach of sheep-bells is my home.
—Then through the great town's harsh, heart-wearying
roar,
Let in thy voice a whisper often come,   235
To chase fatigue and fear:
Why faintest thou? I wander'd till I died.
Roam on! The light we sought is shining still.
Dost thou ask proof? Our tree yet crowns the hill,
Our Scholar travels yet the loved hill-side.   240

208 *1866*: is he gone,   211 *1866–8*: wert bound   216 *1867–8*: Cumnor
226 *1866*: wert mute

MEMORIAL VERSES

APRIL, 1850

[*First published in* FRASER'S MAGAZINE, *June 1850. Reprinted 1852,*
'55, '69, and thereafter]

GOETHE in Weimar sleeps, and Greece,
Long since, saw Byron's struggle cease.
But one such death remain'd to come;
The last poetic voice is dumb—
We stand to-day by Wordsworth's tomb.   5

When Byron's eyes were shut in death,
We bow'd our head and held our breath.
He taught us little; but our soul
Had *felt* him like the thunder's roll.
With shivering heart the strife we saw   10
Of passion with eternal law;
And yet with reverential awe
We watch'd the fount of fiery life
Which served for that Titanic strife.

   When Goethe's death was told, we said: 15
Sunk, then, is Europe's sagest head.
Physician of the iron age,
Goethe has done his pilgrimage.
He took the suffering human race,
He read each wound, each weakness clear;   20
And struck his finger on the place,
And said: *Thou ailest here, and here!*
He look'd on Europe's dying hour
Of fitful dream and feverish power;
His eye plunged down the weltering strife,   25

Date, Both MS. and Fraser give the date in full, April 27th, 1850.
5 *MS., Fraser*: We stand to-day at   *1852, 1855*: What shall be said o'er
Wordsworth's tomb?   6 *1877*: where shut [*sic*]   7 *MS., Fraser*:
bow'd our heads   14 *MS.*: Suffic'd for that Titanic strife   *Fraser*:
Which flow'd for that Titanic strife.   15 *MS., Fraser*: When Goethe
pass'd away,   16–18 *1855*: italics   20 *Fraser*: He scann'd each
wound, each weakness near,   *The reading of the MS. was restored in 1852.*
25 *MS., Fraser*: seething strife,

The turmoil of expiring life—
He said: *The end is everywhere,*
Art still has truth, take refuge there!
And he was happy, if to know
Causes of things, and far below   30
His feet to see the lurid flow
Of terror, and insane distress,
And headlong fate, be happiness.

And Wordsworth!—Ah, pale ghosts, rejoice!
For never has such soothing voice   35
Been to your shadowy world convey'd,
Since erst, at morn, some wandering shade
Heard the clear song of Orpheus come
Through Hades, and the mournful gloom.
Wordsworth has gone from us—and ye,   40
Ah, may ye feel his voice as we!
He too upon a wintry clime
Had fallen—on this iron time
Of doubts, disputes, distractions, fears.
He found us when the age had bound   45
Our souls in its benumbing round;
He spoke, and loosed our heart in tears.
He laid us as we lay at birth
On the cool flowery lap of earth,
Smiles broke from us and we had ease;   50
The hills were round us, and the breeze
Went o'er the sun-lit fields again;
Our foreheads felt the wind and rain.
Our youth return'd; for there was shed

40 *MS., Fraser, 1852*: is gone   43 *MS., Fraser*: Was fallen, on the
iron time.   44 *First inserted in 1852.*   46 *MS., Fraser*: Our spirits
in a brazen round: *Between 47 and 48 these lines appear in MS. and
in Fraser*:   He tore us from the prison-cell
                      Of festering thoughts and personal fears,
                      Where we had long been doom'd to dwell.
48 *MS.*: Once more as we lay as erst at birth,   54 *MS., Fraser*: youth
came back

271

On spirits that had long been dead,   55
Spirits dried up and closely furl'd,
The freshness of the early world.

Ah! since dark days still bring to light
Man's prudence and man's fiery might,
Time may restore us in his course   60
Goethe's sage mind and Byron's force;
But where will Europe's latter hour
Again find Wordsworth's healing power?
Others will teach us how to dare,
And against fear our breast to steel;   65
Others will strengthen us to bear—
But who, ah! who, will make us feel?
The cloud of mortal destiny,
Others will front it fearlessly—
But who, like him, will put it by?   70

Keep fresh the grass upon his grave
O Rotha, with thy living wave!
Sing him thy best! for few or none
Hears thy voice right, now he is gone.

STANZAS

IN MEMORY OF EDWARD QUILLINAN

[First published 1853. Reprinted 1854, '57, '69, and thereafter]

I saw him sensitive in frame,
   I knew his spirits low;
And wish'd him health, success, and fame—
   I do not wish it now.

56 *MS., Fraser*: Spirits deep-crushed   60 *Fraser (only)*: in its course
62 *MS., Fraser*: where shall

STANZAS IN MEMORY OF EDWARD QUILLINAN. *Title, 1853–69*: Stanzas In memory of the late Edward Quillinan, Esq.

For these are all their own reward,   5
   And leave no good behind;
They try us, oftenest make us hard,
   Less modest, pure, and kind.

Alas! yet to the suffering man,
   In this his mortal state,   10
Friends could not give what fortune can—
   Health, ease, a heart elate.

But he is now by fortune foil'd
   No more; and we retain
The memory of a man unspoil'd,   15
   Sweet, generous, and humane—

With all the fortunate have not,
   With gentle voice and brow.
—Alive, we would have changed his lot,
   We would not change it now.   20

STANZAS FROM CARNAC

[*First published 1867. Reprinted 1868 and thereafter*]

FAR on its rocky knoll descried
Saint Michael's chapel cuts the sky.
I climb'd;—beneath me, bright and wide,
Lay the lone coast of Brittany.

Bright in the sunset, weird and still,   5
It lay beside the Atlantic wave,
As though the wizard Merlin's will
Yet charm'd it from his forest-grave.

6 *Rotha Quillinan's MS. Album, (dated December 27, 1851)*: leave no trace
10 *MS. album*: living state   15 *MS. album*: image of a Man
   STANZAS FROM CARNAC. Title, *1867-9*: Stanzas composed at Carnac,
May 6, 1859.   7 *MS., 1867*: As if

Behind me on their grassy sweep,
Bearded with lichen, scrawl'd and grey,⠀⠀⠀⠀10
The giant stones of Carnac sleep,
In the mild evening of the May.

No priestly stern procession now
Moves through their rows of pillars old;
No victims bleed, no Druids bow—⠀⠀⠀⠀15
Sheep make the daisied aisles their fold.

From bush to bush the cuckoo flies,
The orchis red gleams everywhere;
Gold furze with broom in blossom vies,
The blue-bells perfume all the air.⠀⠀⠀⠀20

And o'er the glistening, lonely land,
Rise up, all round, the Christian spires;
The church of Carnac, by the strand,
Catches the westering sun's last fires.

And there, across the watery way,⠀⠀⠀⠀25
See, low above the tide at flood,
The sickle-sweep of Quiberon Bay,
Whose beach once ran with loyal blood!

And beyond that, the Atlantic wide!—
All round, no soul, no boat, no hail;⠀⠀⠀⠀30
But, on the horizon's verge descried,
Hangs, touch'd with light, one snowy sail!

Ah! where is he, who should have come[19]
Where that far sail is passing now,
Past the Loire's mouth, and by the foam⠀⠀⠀⠀35
Of Finistère's unquiet brow,

10 *MS.*: old and grey⠀⠀⠀⠀⠀⠀14 *MS.*, *1867–81*: Streams through
16 *MS.*, *1867*: furze-grown aisles⠀⠀19 *MS.*, *1867*: Gold broom with furze
20 *1868–77*: The furze-scent perfumes all the air.⠀⠀⠀⠀32 *MS.*: distant
sail.

Home, round into the English wave?
—He tarries where the Rock of Spain
Mediterranean waters lave;
He enters not the Atlantic main.   40

Oh, could he once have reach'd this air
Freshen'd by plunging tides, by showers!
Have felt this breath he loved, of fair
Cool northern fields, and grass, and flowers!

He long'd for it—press'd on.—In vain!   45
At the Straits fail'd that spirit brave.
The south was parent of his pain,
The south is mistress of his grave.

A SOUTHERN NIGHT

[*First published in* VICTORIA REGIA, *1861. Reprinted 1867 and hereafter*]

THE sandy spits, the shore-lock'd lakes,
    Melt into open, moonlit sea;
The soft Mediterranean breaks
        At my feet, free.

Dotting the fields of corn and vine,   5
    Like ghosts the huge, gnarl'd olives stand
Behind, that lovely mountain-line!
        While, by the strand,

Cette, with its glistening houses white,
    Curves with the curving beach away   10
To where the lighthouse beacons bright
        Far in the bay.

Ah! such a night, so soft, so lone,
    So moonlit, saw me once of yore[20]
Wander unquiet, and my own   15
        Vext heart deplore.

38 *MS.*: He lingers   45 *MS.*: He long'd it, he press'd on—

But now that trouble is forgot;
   Thy memory, thy pain, to-night,
My brother! and thine early lot,[21]
     Possess me quite.   20

The murmur of this Midland deep
   Is heard to-night around thy grave,
There, where Gibraltar's cannon'd steep
     O'erfrowns the wave.

For there, with bodily anguish keen,   25
   With Indian heats at last fordone,
With public toil and private teen—
     Thou sank'st, alone.

Slow to a stop, at morning grey,
   I see the smoke-crown'd vessel come;   30
Slow round her paddles dies away
     The seething foam.

A boat is lower'd from her side;
   Ah, gently place him on the bench!
That spirit—if all have not yet died—   35
     A breath might quench.

Is this the eye, the footstep fast,
   The mien of youth we used to see,
Poor, gallant boy!—for such thou wast,
     Still art, to me.   40

The limbs their wonted tasks refuse;
   The eyes are glazed, thou canst not speak;
And whiter than thy white burnous
     That wasted cheek!

Enough! The boat, with quiet shock,   45
   Unto its haven coming nigh,
Touches, and on Gibraltar's rock
     Lands thee to die.

26 *1861 (Victoria Regia)*: suns   37 *1861*: the eye, the form alert,
39 *1861*: thou wert,

Ah me! Gibraltar's strand is far,
    But farther yet across the brine   50
Thy dear wife's ashes buried are,
        Remote from thine.

For there, where morning's sacred fount
    Its golden rain on earth confers,
The snowy Himalayan Mount   55
        O'ershadows hers.

Strange irony of fate, alas,
    Which, for two jaded English, saves,
When from their dusty life they pass,
        Such peaceful graves!   60

In cities should we English lie,
    Where cries are rising ever new,
And men's incessant stream goes by—
        We who pursue

Our business with unslackening stride,   65
    Traverse in troops, with care-fill'd breast,
The soft Mediterranean side,
        The Nile, the East,

And see all sights from pole to pole,
    And glance, and nod, and bustle by,   70
And never once possess our soul
        Before we die.

Not by those hoary Indian hills,
    Not by this gracious Midland sea
Whose floor to-night sweet moonshine fills,   75
        Should our graves be.

Some sage, to whom the world was dead,
    And men were specks, and life a play;
Who made the roots of trees his bed,
        And once a day   80

With staff and gourd his way did bend
  To villages and homes of man,
For food to keep him till he end
    His mortal span

And the pure goal of being reach;   85
  Hoar-headed, wrinkled, clad in white,
Without companion, without speech,
    By day and night

Pondering God's mysteries untold,
  And tranquil as the glacier-snows   90
He by those Indian mountains old
    Might well repose.

Some grey crusading knight austere,
  Who bore Saint Louis company,
And came home hurt to death, and here   95
    Landed to die;

Some youthful troubadour, whose tongue
  Fill'd Europe once with his love-pain,
Who here outworn had sunk, and sung
    His dying strain;   100

Some girl, who here from castle-bower,
  With furtive step and cheek of flame,
'Twixt myrtle-hedges all in flower
    By moonlight came

To meet her pirate-lover's ship;   105
  And from the wave-kiss'd marble stair
Beckon'd him on, with quivering lip
    And floating hair;

82 *1861*: haunts of man.   86 *1861–81*: Grey-headed   96 *1861*:
Touch'd shore to die;   99 *1861–9*: here outwearied sunk
100 *1861*: A dying strain;   101 *1861*: palace-bower   108 *1867 (only)*:
unbound hair;

And lived some moons in happy trance,
   Then learnt his death and pined away—   110
Such by these waters of romance
      'Twas meet to lay.

But you—a grave for knight or sage,
   Romantic, solitary, still,
O spent ones of a work-day age!   115
      Befits you ill.

So sang I; but the midnight breeze,
   Down to the brimm'd, moon-charmed main,
Comes softly through the olive-trees,
      And checks my strain.   120

I think of her, whose gentle tongue
   All plaint in her own cause controll'd;
Of thee I think, my brother! young
      In heart, high-soul'd—

That comely face, that cluster'd brow,   125
   That cordial hand, that bearing free,
I see them still, I see them now,
      Shall always see!

And what but gentleness untired,
   And what but noble feeling warm,   130
Wherever shown, howe'er inspired,
      Is grace, is charm?

What else is all these waters are,
   What else is steep'd in lucid sheen,
What else is bright, what else is fair,   135
      What else serene?

Mild o'er her grave, ye mountains, shine!
   Gently by his, ye waters, glide!
To that in you which is divine
      They were allied.   140

113 *1861*: a grave for Girl or Sage,   131 *1861, 1867*: howe'er attir'd,

HAWORTH CHURCHYARD

APRIL, 1855

[First published in FRASER'S MAGAZINE, *May 1855. Reprinted 1877 and thereafter. Extracted lines, entitled 'Early Death and Fame', reprinted separately 1867 and thereafter]*

WHERE, under Loughrigg, the stream
Of Rotha sparkles through fields
Vested for ever with green,
Four years since, in the house
Of a gentle spirit, now dead—   5
Wordsworth's son-in-law, friend—
I saw the meeting of two
Gifted women.[22] The one,
Brilliant with recent renown,
Young, unpractised, had told   10
With a master's accent her feign'd
Story of passionate life;
The other, maturer in fame,
Earning, she too, her praise
First in fiction, had since   15
Widen'd her sweep, and survey'd
History, politics, mind.

The two held converse; they wrote
In a book which of world-famous souls

1–8 *This opening passage in Fraser 1855, read as follows:*
> Where, under Loughrigg, the stream
> Of Rotha sparkles, the fields
> Are green, in the house of one
> Friendly and gentle, now dead,
> Wordsworth's son-in-law, friend—
> Four years since, on a mark'd
> Evening, a meeting I saw.
>   Two friends met there, two fam'd
> Gifted women. The one,

12 *Fraser 1855:* History of   18 *Fraser 1855:* They met, held
19 *Fraser 1855:* glorious souls

Kept the memorial;—bard,   20
Warrior, statesman, had sign'd
Their names; chief glory of all,
Scott had bestow'd there his last
Breathings of song, with a pen
Tottering, a death-stricken hand.   25

Hope at that meeting smiled fair.
Years in number, it seem'd,
Lay before both, and a fame
Heighten'd, and multiplied power.—
Behold! The elder, to-day,   30
Lies expecting from death,
In mortal weakness, a last
Summons! the younger is dead!

First to the living we pay
Mournful homage;—the Muse   35
Gains not an earth-deafen'd ear.

Hail to the steadfast soul,
Which, unflinching and keen,
Wrought to erase from its depth
Mist and illusion and fear!   40
Hail to the spirit which dared
Trust its own thoughts, before yet
Echoed her back by the crowd!
Hail to the courage which gave
Voice to its creed, ere the creed   45
Won consecration from time!

20 *Fraser 1855*: Held memorial: Bard,   21 *Fraser 1855*: had left
22 *Fraser 1855*: chief treasure   23 *Fraser 1855*: had consign'd
26 *Took place of two lines in Fraser 1855*:
    I beheld; the obscure
    Saw the famous. Alas!
After line 46 *these lines appear in Fraser 1855*:
    Turn, O Death, on the vile,
    Turn on the foolish the stroke
    Hanging now o'er a head
    Active, beneficent, pure!

Turn we next to the dead.
—How shall we honour the young,
The ardent, the gifted? how mourn?
Console we cannot, her ear   50
Is deaf. Far northward from here,
In a churchyard high 'mid the moors
Of Yorkshire, a little earth
Stops it for ever to praise.

Where, behind Keighley, the road   55
Up to the heart of the moors
Between heath-clad showery hills
Runs, and colliers' carts
Poach the deep ways coming down,

But, if the prayer be in vain—
But, if the stroke *must* fall—
Her, whom we cannot save,
What might we say to console?

She will not see her country lose
Its greatness, nor the reign of fools prolong'd.
She will behold no more
This ignominious spectacle,
Power dropping from the hand
Of paralytic factions, and no soul
To snatch and wield it: will not see
Her fellow-people sit
Helplessly gazing on their own decline.

Myrtle and rose fit the young,
Laurel and oak the mature.
Private affections, for these,
Have run their circle, and left
Space for things far from themselves,
Thoughts of the general weal,
Country, and public cares:
Public cares, which move
Seldom and faintly the depth
Of younger passionate souls
Plung'd in themselves, who demand
Only to live by the heart,
Only to love and be lov'd.

47 *Added in 1877.*

And a rough, grimed race have their homes— 60
There on its slope is built
The moorland town. But the church
Stands on the crest of the hill,
Lonely and bleak;—at its side
The parsonage-house and the graves. 65

Strew with laurel the grave
Of the early-dying! Alas,
Early she goes on the path
To the silent country, and leaves
Half her laurels unwon, 70
Dying too soon!—yet green
Laurels she had, and a course
Short, but redoubled by fame.

62 *1877 (only)*: moorland place. *After line* 65 *these lines appear in*
Fraser 1855:

> See! in the desolate house
> The childless father! Alas—
> Age, whom the most of us chide,
> Chide, and put back, and delay—
> Come, unupbraided for once!
> Lay thy benumbing hand,
> Gratefully cold, on this brow!
> Shut out the grief, the despair!
> Weaken the sense of his loss!
> Deaden the infinite pain!
>
> Another grief I see,
> Younger: but this the Muse,
> In pity and silent awe
> Revering what she cannot soothe,
> With veil'd face and bow'd head,
> Salutes, and passes by.

66 *Fraser 1855*: with roses   73 *Fraser 1855*: yet redoubled   *After*
line 73 these lines appeared in Fraser 1855:

> For him who must live many years
> That life is best which slips away
> Out of the light, and mutely; which avoids
> Fame, and her less-fair followers, Envy, Strife,
> Stupid Detraction, Jealousy, Cabal,
> Insincere Praises:—which descends
> The mossy quiet track to Age.

And not friendless, and not
Only with strangers to meet,   75
Faces ungreeting and cold,
Thou, O mourn'd one, to-day
Enterest the house of the grave!
Those of thy blood, whom thou lov'dst,
Have preceded thee—young,   80
Loving, a sisterly band;
Some in art, some in gift
Inferior—all in fame.
They, like friends, shall receive
This comer, greet her with joy;   85
Welcome the sister, the friend;
Hear with delight of thy fame!

Round thee they lie—the grass
Blows from their graves to thy own!
She, whose genius, though not   90
Puissant like thine, was yet
Sweet and graceful;—and she
(How shall I sing her?) whose soul
Knew no fellow for might,
Passion, vehemence, grief,   95
Daring, since Byron died,

But, when immature Death
Beckons too early the guest
From the half-tried Banquet of Life,
Young, in the bloom of his days;
Leaves no leisure to press,
Slow and surely, the sweet
Of a tranquil life in the shade—
Fuller for him be the hours!
Give him emotion, though pain!
Let him live, let him feel, *I have liv'd.*
Heap up his moments with life!
Quicken his pulses with Fame!

These lines were published separately, in New Poems, *1867, and in the edition
of 1869, under the title* 'Early Death and Fame'. *See p. 199 f. for alterations made.*
74 *Fraser 1855:* friendless, nor yet   82 *Fraser 1855:* Some in gift,
some in art   89 *Fraser 1855:* graves toward thine.

That world-famed son of fire—she, who sank
Baffled, unknown, self-consumed;
Whose too bold dying song[23]
Stirr'd, like a clarion-blast, my soul.   100

Of one, too, I have heard,
A brother—sleeps he here?
Of all that gifted race
Not the least gifted; young,
Unhappy, eloquent—the child   105
Of many hopes, of many tears.
O boy, if here thou sleep'st, sleep well!
On thee too did the Muse
Bright in thy cradle smile;
But some dark shadow came   110
(I know not what) and interposed.

Sleep, O cluster of friends,
Sleep!—or only when May,
Brought by the west-wind, returns
Back to your native heaths,   115
And the plover is heard on the moors,
Yearly awake to behold
The opening summer, the sky,
The shining moorland—to hear
The drowsy bee, as of old,   120
Hum o'er the thyme, the grouse
Call from the heather in bloom!
Sleep, or only for this
Break your united repose!

EPILOGUE

So I sang; but the Muse,   125
Shaking her head, took the harp—
Stern interrupted my strain,
Angrily smote on the chords.

100 *1877–81*: Shook, like a clarion-blast,   103 *Fraser 1855*: his gifted
105 *Fraser 1855*: Unhappy, beautiful; the cause   125–38 *The* Epilogue
added in 1877.

April showers
Rush o'er the Yorkshire moors.   130
Stormy, through driving mist,
Loom the blurr'd hills; the rain
Lashes the newly-made grave.

Unquiet souls!
—In the dark fermentation of earth,   135
In the never idle workshop of nature,
In the eternal movement,
Ye shall find yourselves again!

RUGBY CHAPEL

NOVEMBER 1857

[*First published 1867. Reprinted 1868 and thereafter*]

COLDLY, sadly descends
The autumn-evening. The field
Strewn with its dank yellow drifts
Of wither'd leaves, and the elms,
Fade into dimness apace,   5
Silent;—hardly a shout
From a few boys late at their play!
The lights come out in the street,
In the school-room windows;—but cold,
Solemn, unlighted, austere,   10
Through the gathering darkness, arise
The chapel-walls, in whose bound
Thou, my father! art laid.

There thou dost lie, in the gloom
Of the autumn evening. But ah!   15
That word, *gloom*, to my mind
Brings thee back, in the light
Of thy radiant vigour, again;
In the gloom of November we pass'd

Days not dark at thy side;   20
Seasons impair'd not the ray
Of thy buoyant cheerfulness clear.
Such thou wast! and I stand
In the autumn evening, and think
Of bygone autumns with thee.   25

Fifteen years have gone round
Since thou arosest to tread,
In the summer-morning, the road
Of death, at a call unforeseen,
Sudden. For fifteen years,   30
We who till then in thy shade
Rested as under the boughs
Of a mighty oak, have endured
Sunshine and rain as we might,
Bare, unshaded, alone,   35
Lacking the shelter of thee.

O strong soul, by what shore
Tarriest thou now? For that force,
Surely, has not been left vain!
Somewhere, surely, afar,   40
In the sounding labour-house vast
Of being, is practised that strength,
Zealous, beneficent, firm!

Yes, in some far-shining sphere,
Conscious or not of the past,   45
Still thou performest the word
Of the Spirit in whom thou dost live—
Prompt, unwearied, as here!
Still thou upraisest with zeal
The humble good from the ground,   50
Sternly repressest the bad!
Still, like a trumpet, dost rouse

20 *MS.*, *1867–9*: Days not of gloom   22 *MS.*, *1867–77*: thine even
cheerfulness

Those who with half-open eyes
Tread the border-land dim
'Twixt vice and virtue; reviv'st,⠀⠀⠀⠀⠀⠀⠀55
Succourest!—this was thy work,
This was thy life upon earth.

What is the course of the life
Of mortal men on the earth?—
Most men eddy about⠀⠀⠀⠀⠀⠀⠀60
Here and there—eat and drink,
Chatter and love and hate,
Gather and squander, are raised
Aloft, are hurl'd in the dust,
Striving blindly, achieving⠀⠀⠀⠀⠀⠀⠀65
Nothing; and then they die—
Perish;—and no one asks
Who or what they have been,
More than he asks what waves,
In the moonlit solitudes mild⠀⠀⠀⠀⠀⠀⠀70
Of the midmost Ocean, have swell'd,
Foam'd for a moment, and gone.

And there are some, whom a thirst
Ardent, unquenchable, fires,
Not with the crowd to be spent,⠀⠀⠀⠀⠀⠀⠀75
Not without aim to go round
In an eddy of purposeless dust,
Effort unmeaning and vain.
Ah yes! some of us strive
Not without action to die⠀⠀⠀⠀⠀⠀⠀80
Fruitless, but something to snatch
From dull oblivion, nor all
Glut the devouring grave!
We, we have chosen our path—
Path to a clear-purposed goal,⠀⠀⠀⠀⠀⠀⠀85
Path of advance!—but it leads
A long, steep journey, through sunk

64 *1881*: art hurl'd [*sic*]

Gorges, o'er mountains in snow.
Cheerful, with friends, we set forth—
Then, on the height, comes the storm.   90
Thunder crashes from rock
To rock, the cataracts reply,
Lightnings dazzle our eyes.
Roaring torrents have breach'd
The track, the stream-bed descends   95
In the place where the wayfarer once
Planted his footstep—the spray
Boils o'er its borders! aloft
The unseen snow-beds dislodge
Their hanging ruin; alas,   100
Havoc is made in our train!
Friends, who set forth at our side,
Falter, are lost in the storm.
We, we only are left!
With frowning foreheads, with lips   105
Sternly compress'd, we strain on,
On—and at nightfall at last
Come to the end of our way,
To the lonely inn 'mid the rocks;
Where the gaunt and taciturn host   110
Stands on the threshold, the wind
Shaking his thin white hairs—
Holds his lantern to scan
Our storm-beat figures, and asks:
Whom in our party we bring?   115
Whom we have left in the snow?

Sadly we answer: We bring
Only ourselves! we lost
Sight of the rest in the storm.
Hardly ourselves we fought through,   120
Stripp'd, without friends, as we are.
Friends, companions, and train,
The avalanche swept from our side.

But thou would'st not *alone*
Be saved, my father! *alone*   125
Conquer and come to thy goal,
Leaving the rest in the wild.
We were weary, and we
Fearful, and we in our march
Fain to drop down and to die.   130
Still thou turnedst, and still
Beckonedst the trembler, and still
Gavest the weary thy hand.

If, in the paths of the world,
Stones might have wounded thy feet,   135
Toil or dejection have tried
Thy spirit, of that we saw
Nothing—to us thou wast still
Cheerful, and helpful, and firm!
Therefore to thee it was given   140
Many to save with thyself;
And, at the end of thy day,
O faithful shepherd! to come,
Bringing thy sheep in thy hand.

And through thee I believe   145
In the noble and great who are gone;
Pure souls honour'd and blest
By former ages, who else—
Such, so soulless, so poor,
Is the race of men whom I see—   150
Seem'd but a dream of the heart,
Seem'd but a cry of desire.
Yes! I believe that there lived
Others like thee in the past,
Not like the men of the crowd   155
Who all round me to-day
Bluster or cringe, and make life
Hideous, and arid, and vile;

    138 *MS., 1867–9:* wert still

But souls temper'd with fire,
Fervent, heroic, and good,   160
Helpers and friends of mankind.

Servants of God!—or sons
Shall I not call you? because
Not as servants ye knew
Your Father's innermost mind,   165
His, who unwillingly sees
One of his little ones lost—
Yours is the praise, if mankind
Hath not as yet in its march
Fainted, and fallen, and died!   170

See! In the rocks of the world
Marches the host of mankind,
A feeble, wavering line.
Where are they tending?—A God
Marshall'd them, gave them their goal.   175
Ah, but the way is so long!
Years they have been in the wild!
Sore thirst plagues them, the rocks,
Rising all round, overawe;
Factions divide them, their host   180
Threatens to break, to dissolve.
—Ah, keep, keep them combined!
Else, of the myriads who fill
That army, not one shall arrive;
Sole they shall stray; in the rocks   185
Stagger for ever in vain,
Die one by one in the waste.

Then, in such hour of need
Of your fainting, dispirited race,
Ye, like angels, appear,   190
Radiant with ardour divine!

185 _1877–81_: on the rocks   186 _MS._, _1867–9_: Labour for ever in
vain,   _1877–81_: Batter for ever in vain,   _1881 MS. alteration_:
Labour for ever [_not adopted_]

Beacons of hope, ye appear!
Languor is not in your heart,
Weakness is not in your word,
Weariness not on your brow.   195
Ye alight in our van! at your voice,
Panic, despair, flee away.
Ye move through the ranks, recall
The stragglers, refresh the outworn,
Praise, re-inspire the brave!   200
Order, courage, return.
Eyes rekindling, and prayers,
Follow your steps as ye go.
Ye fill up the gaps in our files,
Strengthen the wavering line,   205
Stablish, continue our march,
On, to the bound of the waste,
On, to the City of God.

HEINE'S GRAVE

[*First published 1867. Reprinted 1868 and thereafter*]

'HENRI HEINE'——'tis here!
That black tombstone, the name
Carved there—no more! and the smooth,
Swarded alleys, the limes
Touch'd with yellow by hot   5
Summer, but under them still,
In September's bright afternoon,
Shadow, and verdure, and cool.
Trim Montmartre! the faint
Murmur of Paris outside;   10
Crisp everlasting-flowers,
Yellow and black, on the graves.

Half blind, palsied, in pain,
Hither to come, from the streets'

HEINE'S GRAVE. 2 *1867–81*: The black tombstone

Uproar, surely not loath   15
Wast thou, Heine!—to lie
Quiet, to ask for closed
Shutters, and darken'd room,
And cool drinks, and an eased
Posture, and opium, no more;   20
Hither to come, and to sleep
Under the wings of Renown.

Ah! not little, when pain
Is most quelling, and man
Easily quell'd, and the fine   25
Temper of genius so soon
Thrills at each smart, is the praise,
Not to have yielded to pain!
No small boast, for a weak
Son of mankind, to the earth   30
Pinn'd by the thunder, to rear
His bolt-scathed front to the stars;
And, undaunted, retort
'Gainst thick-crashing, insane,
Tyrannous tempests of bale,   35
Arrowy lightnings of soul.

Hark! through the alley resounds
Mocking laughter! A film
Creeps o'er the sunshine; a breeze
Ruffles the warm afternoon,   40
Saddens my soul with its chill.
Gibing of spirits in scorn
Shakes every leaf of the grove,
Mars the benignant repose
Of this amiable home of the dead.   45

Bitter spirits, ye claim
Heine?—Alas, he is yours!

25–7 *1867–9:*   and the fine
                        Temper of genius alive
                        Quickest to ill,

Only a moment I long'd
Here in the quiet to snatch
From such mates the outworn   50
Poet, and steep him in calm.
Only a moment! I knew
Whose he was who is here
Buried—I knew he was yours!
Ah, I knew that I saw   55
Here no sepulchre built
In the laurell'd rock, o'er the blue
Naples bay, for a sweet
Tender Virgil! no tomb
On Ravenna sands, in the shade   60
Of Ravenna pines, for a high
Austere Dante! no grave
By the Avon side, in the bright
Stratford meadows, for thee,
Shakespeare! loveliest of souls,   65
Peerless in radiance, in joy.

What, then, so harsh and malign,
Heine! distils from thy life?
Poisons the peace of thy grave?

I chide with thee not, that thy sharp   70
Upbraidings often assail'd
England, my country—for we,
Heavy and sad, for her sons,
Long since, deep in our hearts,
Echo the blame of her foes.   75
We, too, sigh that she flags;
We, too, say that she now—
Scarce comprehending the voice
Of her greatest, golden-mouth'd sons
Of a former age any more—   80
Stupidly travels her round

67 *1867–9*: What so harsh and malign,   73 *1867, 1868*: Fearful and
sad,   *1869*: Troublous and sad,

Of mechanic business, and lets
Slow die out of her life
Glory, and genius, and joy.

So thou arraign'st her, her foe;   85
So we arraign her, her sons.

  Yes, we arraign her! but she,
The weary Titan, with deaf
Ears, and labour-dimm'd eyes,
Regarding neither to right   90
Nor left, goes passively by,
Staggering on to her goal;
Bearing on shoulders immense,
Atlanteän, the load,
Wellnigh not to be borne,   95
Of the too vast orb of her fate.

But was it thou—I think
Surely it was!—that bard
Unnamed, who, Goethe said,
Had every other gift, but wanted love;   100
Love, without which the tongue
Even of angels sounds amiss?

Charm is the glory which makes
Song of the poet divine,
Love is the fountain of charm.   105
How without charm wilt thou draw,
Poet! the world to thy way?
Not by the lightnings of wit—
Not by the thunder of scorn!
These to the world, too, are given;   110
Wit it possesses, and scorn—
Charm is the poet's alone.
Hollow and dull are the great,
And artists envious, and the mob profane.
We know all this, we know!   115
Cam'st thou from heaven, O child

Of light! but this to declare?
Alas, to help us forget
Such barren knowledge awhile,
God gave the poet his song!   120

Therefore a secret unrest
Tortured thee, brilliant and bold!
Therefore triumph itself
Tasted amiss to thy soul.
Therefore, with blood of thy foes,   125
Trickled in silence thine own.
Therefore the victor's heart
Broke on the field of his fame.

Ah! as of old, from the pomp
Of Italian Milan, the fair   130
Flower of marble of white
Southern palaces—steps
Border'd by statues, and walks
Terraced, and orange-bowers
Heavy with fragrance—the blond   135
German Kaiser full oft
Long'd himself back to the fields,
Rivers, and high-roof'd towns
Of his native Germany; so,
So, how often! from hot   140
Paris drawing-rooms, and lamps
Blazing, and brilliant crowds,
Starr'd and jewell'd, of men
Famous, of women the queens
Of dazzling converse—from fumes   145
Of praise, hot, heady fumes, to the poor brain
That mount, that madden—how oft
Heine's spirit outworn
Long'd itself out of the din,
Back to the tranquil, the cool   150
Far German home of his youth!

145 *1867–9*: and fumes

See! in the May-afternoon,
O'er the fresh, short turf of the Hartz,
A youth, with the foot of youth,
Heine! thou climbest again!   155
Up, through the tall dark firs
Warming their heads in the sun,
Chequering the grass with their shade—
Up, by the stream, with its huge
Moss-hung boulders, and thin   160
Musical water half-hid—
Up, o'er the rock-strewn slope,
With the sinking sun, and the air
Chill, and the shadows now
Long on the grey hill-side—   165
To the stone-roof'd hut at the top!

Or, yet later, in watch
On the roof of the Brocken-tower
Thou standest, gazing!—to see
The broad red sun, over field,   170
Forest, and city, and spire,
And mist-track'd stream of the wide,
Wide, German land, going down
In a bank of vapours——again
Standest, at nightfall, alone!   175

Or, next morning, with limbs
Rested by slumber, and heart
Freshen'd and light with the May,
O'er the gracious spurs coming down
Of the Lower Hartz, among oaks,   180
And beechen coverts, and copse
Of hazels green in whose depth
Ilse, the fairy transform'd,
In a thousand water-breaks light
Pours her petulant youth—   185
Climbing the rock which juts
O'er the valley, the dizzily perch'd

Rock—to its iron cross
Once more thou cling'st; to the Cross
Clingest! with smiles, with a sigh!   190

Goethe, too, had been there.[24]
In the long-past winter he came
To the frozen Hartz, with his soul
Passionate, eager—his youth
All in ferment!—but he   195
Destined to work and to live
Left it, and thou, alas!
Only to laugh and to die.

But something prompts me: Not thus
Take leave of Heine! not thus   200
Speak the last word at his grave!
Not in pity, and not
With half censure—with awe
Hail, as it passes from earth
Scattering lightnings, that soul!   205

The Spirit of the world,
Beholding the absurdity of men—
Their vaunts, their feats—let a sardonic smile,
For one short moment, wander o'er his lips.
That smile was Heine!—for its earthly hour   210
The strange guest sparkled; now 'tis pass'd away.

That was Heine! and we,
Myriads who live, who have lived,
What are we all, but a mood,
A single mood, of the life   215
Of the Spirit in whom we exist,
Who alone is all things in one?

Spirit, who fillest us all!
Spirit, who utterest in each
New-coming son of mankind   220

216 *1867-9*: the Being

Such of thy thoughts as thou wilt!
O thou, one of whose moods,
Bitter and strange, was the life
Of Heine—his strange, alas,
His bitter life!—may a life   225
Other and milder be mine!
May'st thou a mood more serene,
Happier, have utter'd in mine!
May'st thou the rapture of peace
Deep have embreathed at its core;   230
Made it a ray of thy thought,
Made it a beat of thy joy!

STANZAS FROM THE GRANDE CHARTREUSE

[*First published in* FRASER'S MAGAZINE, *April 1855. Reprinted 1867 and thereafter*]

THROUGH Alpine meadows soft-suffused
With rain, where thick the crocus blows,
Past the dark forges long disused,
The mule-track from Saint Laurent goes.
The bridge is cross'd, and slow we ride,   5
Through forest, up the mountain-side.

The autumnal evening darkens round,
The wind is up, and drives the rain;
While, hark! far down, with strangled sound
Doth the Dead Guier's stream complain,   10
Where that wet smoke, among the woods,
Over his boiling cauldron broods.

Swift rush the spectral vapours white
Past limestone scars with ragged pines,
Showing—then blotting from our sight!—   15
Halt—through the cloud-drift something shines!
High in the valley, wet and drear,
The huts of Courrerie appear.

STANZAS FROM THE GRANDE CHARTREUSE. **12** *Fraser 1855*: cauldrons
13 *Fraser 1855*: Fast rush

Strike leftward! cries our guide; and higher
Mounts up the stony forest-way.   20
At last the encircling trees retire;
Look! through the showery twilight grey
What pointed roofs are these advance?—
A palace of the Kings of France?

Approach, for what we seek is here!   25
Alight, and sparely sup, and wait
For rest in this outbuilding near;
Then cross the sward and reach that gate.
Knock; pass the wicket! Thou art come
To the Carthusians' world-famed home.   30

The silent courts, where night and day
Into their stone-carved basins cold
The splashing icy fountains play—
The humid corridors behold!
Where, ghostlike in the deepening night,   35
Cowl'd forms brush by in gleaming white.

The chapel, where no organ's peal
Invests the stern and naked prayer—
With penitential cries they kneel
And wrestle; rising then, with bare   40
And white uplifted faces stand,
Passing the Host from hand to hand;

Each takes, and then his visage wan
Is buried in his cowl once more.
The cells!—the suffering Son of Man   45
Upon the wall—the knee-worn floor—
And where they sleep, that wooden bed,
Which shall their coffin be, when dead!

The library, where tract and tome
Not to feed priestly pride are there,   50
To hymn the conquering march of Rome,
Nor yet to amuse, as ours are!

52 *1869 (only)*: as worldlings' are.

They paint of souls the inner strife,
Their drops of blood, their death in life.

The garden, overgrown—yet mild,   55
See, fragrant herbs are flowering there!
Strong children of the Alpine wild
Whose culture is the brethren's care;
Of human tasks their only one,
And cheerful works beneath the sun.   60

Those halls, too, destined to contain
Each its own pilgrim-host of old,
From England, Germany, or Spain—
All are before me! I behold
The House, the Brotherhood austere!   65
—And what am I, that I am here?

For rigorous teachers seized my youth,
And purged its faith, and trimm'd its fire,
Show'd me the high, white star of Truth,
There bade me gaze, and there aspire.   70
Even now their whispers pierce the gloom:
What dost thou in this living tomb?

Forgive me, masters of the mind!
At whose behest I long ago
So much unlearnt, so much resign'd—   75
I come not here to be your foe!
I seek these anchorites, not in ruth,
To curse and to deny your truth;

Not as their friend, or child, I speak!
But as, on some far northern strand,   80
Thinking of his own Gods, a Greek
In pity and mournful awe might stand
Before some fallen Runic stone—
For both were faiths, and both are gone.

56 *Fraser 1855–77*: Those fragrant herbs   68 *Fraser 1855*: prun'd
its faith and quench'd its fire.   69 *Fraser 1855*: the pale cold star

Wandering between two worlds, one dead,   85
The other powerless to be born,
With nowhere yet to rest my head,
Like these, on earth I wait forlorn.
Their faith, my tears, the world deride—
I come to shed them at their side.   90

Oh, hide me in your gloom profound,
Ye solemn seats of holy pain!
Take me, cowl'd forms, and fence me round,
Till I possess my soul again;
Till free my thoughts before me roll,   95
Not chafed by hourly false control!

For the world cries your faith is now
But a dead time's exploded dream;
My melancholy, sciolists say,
Is a pass'd mode, an outworn theme—   100
As if the world had ever had
A faith, or sciolists been sad!

Ah, if it *be* pass'd, take away,
At least, the restlessness, the pain;
Be man henceforth no more a prey   105
To these out-dated stings again!
The nobleness of grief is gone—
Ah, leave us not the fret alone!

But—if you cannot give us ease—
Last of the race of them who grieve   110
Here leave us to die out with these
Last of the people who believe!
Silent, while years engrave the brow;
Silent—the best are silent now.

---

93 *Fraser 1855*: Invest me, steep me, fold me round   96 *Fraser 1855*:
controul   99 *All editions during author's lifetime, the rhyme notwithstanding,
read* sciolists say,   101 *Fraser 1855: ever* (italics)   108 *Fraser 1855*:
pang alone.

Achilles ponders in his tent,   115
The kings of modern thought are dumb;
Silent they are, though not content,
And wait to see the future come.
They have the grief men had of yore,
But they contend and cry no more.   120

Our fathers water'd with their tears
This sea of time whereon we sail,
Their voices were in all men's ears
Who pass'd within their puissant hail.
Still the same ocean round us raves,   125
But we stand mute, and watch the waves.

For what avail'd it, all the noise
And outcry of the former men?—
Say, have their sons achieved more joys,
Say, is life lighter now than then?   130
The sufferers died, they left their pain—
The pangs which tortured them remain.

What helps it now, that Byron bore,
With haughty scorn which mock'd the smart,
Through Europe to the Ætolian shore   135
The pageant of his bleeding heart?
That thousands counted every groan,
And Europe made his woe her own?

What boots it, Shelley! that the breeze
Carried thy lovely wail away,   140
Musical through Italian trees
Which fringe thy soft blue Spezzian bay?
Inheritors of thy distress
Have restless hearts one throb the less?

121 *Fraser 1855*: Their fathers   126 *Fraser 1855*: they stand
129 *1867–9*: sons obtain'd   142 *Fraser 1855–68*: That fringe   *Fraser*
1855: thy dark blue

Or are we easier, to have read,   145
O Obermann! the sad, stern page,
Which tells us how thou hidd'st thy head
From the fierce tempest of thine age
In the lone brakes of Fontainebleau,
Or chalets near the Alpine snow?   150

Ye slumber in your silent grave!—
The world, which for an idle day
Grace to your mood of sadness gave,
Long since hath flung her weeds away.
The eternal trifler breaks your spell;   155
But we—we learnt your lore too well!

Years hence, perhaps, may dawn an age,
More fortunate, alas! than we,
Which without hardness will be sage,
And gay without frivolity.   160
Sons of the world, oh, speed those years;
But, while we wait, allow our tears!

Allow them! We admire with awe
The exulting thunder of your race;
You give the universe your law,   165
You triumph over time and space!
Your pride of life, your tireless powers,
We laud them, but they are not ours.

We are like children rear'd in shade
Beneath some old-world abbey wall,   170
Forgotten in a forest-glade,

151 *Fraser 1855*: They slumber in their silent grave.   153 *Fraser
1855*: to their mood   154 *Fraser 1855*: hath thrown
155 *Fraser 1855*: breaks their spell: 156 *Fraser 1855*: their lore
157 *Fraser 1855–68*: There may, perhaps, yet dawn an age,   *1869*: There
yet, perhaps, may dawn an age,   161 *Fraser 1855–69*: oh, haste those
years: 162 *Fraser 1855–69*: But, till they rise,   168 *Fraser
1855*: They awe us, but they   *1867–9*: We mark them, but they
1877–81: We praise them, but they

And secret from the eyes of all.
Deep, deep the greenwood round them waves,
Their abbey, and its close of graves!

But, where the road runs near the stream,   175
Oft through the trees they catch a glance
Of passing troops in the sun's beam—
Pennon, and plume, and flashing lance!
Forth to the world those soldiers fare,
To life, to cities, and to war!   180

And through the wood, another way,
Faint bugle-notes from far are borne,
Where hunters gather, staghounds bay,
Round some fair forest-lodge at morn.
Gay dames are there, in sylvan green;   185
Laughter and cries—those notes between!

The banners flashing through the trees
Make their blood dance and chain their eyes;
That bugle-music on the breeze
Arrests them with a charm'd surprise.   190
Banner by turns and bugle woo:
Ye shy recluses, follow too!

O children, what do ye reply?—
'Action and pleasure, will ye roam
Through these secluded dells to cry   195
And call us?—but too late ye come!
Too late for us your call ye blow,
Whose bent was taken long ago.

'Long since we pace this shadow'd nave;
We watch those yellow tapers shine,   200
Emblems of hope over the grave,

179 *Fraser 1855*: to the mighty world they fare,   181 *Fraser*
1855–81: the woods,   184 *Fraser 1855–81*: old forest-lodge
194–210 *Fraser 1855*: italics   201 *Fraser 1855*: *light above the grave,*

In the high altar's depth divine;
The organ carries to our ear
Its accents of another sphere.

'Fenced early in this cloistral round   205
Of reverie, of shade, of prayer,
How should we grow in other ground?
How can we flower in foreign air?
—Pass, banners, pass, and bugles, cease;
And leave our desert to its peace!'   210

STANZAS IN MEMORY OF THE AUTHOR OF 'OBERMANN'[25]

NOVEMBER, 1849

[First published 1852. Reprinted 1855, '69, and thereafter]

In front the awful Alpine track
Crawls up its rocky stair;
The autumn storm-winds drive the rack,
Close o'er it, in the air.

Behind are the abandon'd baths[26]   5
Mute in their meadows lone;
The leaves are on the valley-paths,
The mists are on the Rhone—

The white mists rolling like a sea!
I hear the torrents roar.   10
—Yes, Obermann, all speaks of thee;
I feel thee near once more!

I turn thy leaves! I feel their breath
Once more upon me roll;
That air of languor, cold, and death,   15
Which brooded o'er thy soul.

208 *Fraser 1855–69: should we*   210 *Fraser 1855: leave our forest*
to its peace.

STANZAS IN MEMORY OF THE AUTHOR OF 'OBERMANN'. *Title 1855 (only):*
Obermann. *Date added in 1877.*

Fly hence, poor wretch, whoe'er thou art,
Condemn'd to cast about,
All shipwreck in thy own weak heart,
For comfort from without!   20

A fever in these pages burns
Beneath the calm they feign;
A wounded human spirit turns,
Here, on its bed of pain.

Yes, though the virgin mountain-air   25
Fresh through these pages blows;
Though to these leaves the glaciers spare
The soul of their white snows;

Though here a mountain-murmur swells
Of many a dark-bough'd pine;   30
Though, as you read, you hear the bells
Of the high-pasturing kine—

Yet, through the hum of torrent lone,
And brooding mountain-bee,
There sobs I know not what ground-tone   35
Of human agony.

Is it for this, because the sound
Is fraught too deep with pain,
That, Obermann! the world around
So little loves thy strain?   40

Some secrets may the poet tell,
For the world loves new ways;
To tell too deep ones is not well—
It knows not what he says.

Yet, of the spirits who have reign'd   45
In this our troubled day,
I know but two, who have attain'd,
Save thee, to see their way.

28 *1852, 1881*: mute snows

307

By England's lakes, in grey old age,
His quiet home one keeps;   50
And one, the strong much-toiling sage,
In German Weimar sleeps.

But Wordsworth's eyes avert their ken
From half of human fate;
And Goethe's course few sons of men   55
May think to emulate.

For he pursued a lonely road,
His eyes on Nature's plan;
Neither made man too much a God,
Nor God too much a man.   60

Strong was he, with a spirit free
From mists, and sane, and clear;
Clearer, how much! than ours—yet we
Have a worse course to steer.

For though his manhood bore the blast   65
Of a tremendous time,
Yet in a tranquil world was pass'd
His tenderer youthful prime.

But we, brought forth and rear'd in hours
Of change, alarm, surprise—   70
What shelter to grow ripe is ours?
What leisure to grow wise?

Like children bathing on the shore,
Buried a wave beneath,
The second wave succeeds, before   75
We have had time to breathe.

Too fast we live, too much are tried,
Too harass'd, to attain
Wordsworth's sweet calm, or Goethe's wide
And luminous view to gain.   80

66 *1855* (*only*): Of Europe's stormiest time,

And then we turn, thou sadder sage,
To thee! we feel thy spell!
—The hopeless tangle of our age,
Thou too hast scann'd it well!

Immoveable thou sittest, still   85
As death, composed to bear!
Thy head is clear, thy feeling chill,
And icy thy despair.

Yes, as the son of Thetis said,
I hear thee saying now: 90
Greater by far than thou are dead;
Strive not! die also thou!

Ah! two desires toss about
The poet's feverish blood.
One drives him to the world without,   95
And one to solitude.

The glow, he cries, *the thrill of life*,
Where, where do these abound?—
Not in the world, not in the strife
Of men, shall they be found.   100

He who hath watch'd, not shared, the strife,
Knows how the day hath gone.
He only lives with the world's life,
Who hath renounced his own.

To thee we come, then! Clouds are roll'd   105
Where thou, O seer! art set;
Thy realm of thought is drear and cold—
The world is colder yet!

And thou hast pleasures, too, to share
With those who come to thee—   110
Balms floating on thy mountain-air,
And healing sights to see.

90 *1852–77*: One hears thee   91 *1885–90: than thou art dead* [sic]
97 *1852*: The glow of thought, the thrill of life   97–8 *1852: not italicized.*

How often, where the slopes are green
On Jaman, hast thou sate
By some high chalet-door, and seen   115
The summer-day grow late;

And darkness steal o'er the wet grass
With the pale crocus starr'd,
And reach that glimmering sheet of glass
Beneath the piny sward,   120

Lake Leman's waters, far below!
And watch'd the rosy light
Fade from the distant peaks of snow;
And on the air of night

Heard accents of the eternal tongue   125
Through the pine branches play—
Listen'd, and felt thyself grow young!
Listen'd and wept——Away!

Away the dreams that but deceive
And thou, sad guide, adieu!   130
I go, fate drives me; but I leave
Half of my life with you.

We, in some unknown Power's employ,
Move on a rigorous line;
Can neither, when we will, enjoy,   135
Nor, when we will, resign.

I in the world must live; but thou,
Thou melancholy shade!
Wilt not, if thou canst see me now,
Condemn me, nor upbraid.   140

For thou art gone away from earth,
And place with those dost claim,
The Children of the Second Birth,
Whom the world could not tame;

And with that small, transfigured band,   145
Whom many a different way
Conducted to their common land,
Thou learn'st to think as they.

Christian and pagan, king and slave,
Soldier and anchorite,   150
Distinctions we esteem so grave,
Are nothing in their sight.

They do not ask, who pined unseen,
Who was on action hurl'd,
Whose one bond is, that all have been   155
Unspotted by the world.

There without anger thou wilt see
Him who obeys thy spell
No more, so he but rest, like thee,
Unsoil'd!—and so, farewell.   160

Farewell!—Whether thou now liest near
That much-loved inland sea,
The ripples of whose blue waves cheer
Vevey and Meillerie:

And in that gracious region bland,   165
Where with clear-rustling wave
The scented pines of Switzerland
Stand dark round thy green grave,

Between the dusty vineyard-walls
Issuing on that green place   170
The early peasant still recalls
The pensive stranger's face,

And stoops to clear thy moss-grown date
Ere he plods on again;—
Or whether, by maligner fate,   175
Among the swarms of men,

Where between granite terraces
The blue Seine rolls her wave,
The Capital of Pleasure sees
The hardly-heard-of grave;—   180

Farewell! Under the sky we part,
In this stern Alpine dell.
O unstrung will! O broken heart!
A last, a last farewell!

OBERMANN ONCE MORE

(COMPOSED MANY YEARS AFTER THE PRECEDING)

[*First published 1867. Reprinted 1868 and thereafter*]

Savez-vous quelque bien qui console du regret d'un monde? OBERMANN.

GLION?——Ah, twenty years, it cuts[27]
All meaning from a name!
White houses prank where once were huts.
Glion, but not the same!

And yet I know not! All unchanged   5
The turf, the pines, the sky!
The hills in their old order ranged;
The lake, with Chillon by!

And, 'neath those chestnut-trees, where stiff
And stony mounts the way,   10
The crackling husk-heaps burn, as if
I left them yesterday!

Across the valley, on that slope,
The huts of Avant shine!
Its pines, under their branches, ope   15
Ways for the pasturing kine.

178 *1852*: The Seine conducts her wave,   180 *1852–77*: Thy hardly
heard of grave—
    OBERMANN ONCE MORE. *Second line of title added in 1869.*   11 *1867–*
9: Their crackling   16 *1867–9*: tinkling kine

Full-foaming milk-pails, Alpine fare,
Sweet heaps of fresh-cut grass,
Invite to rest the traveller there
Before he climb the pass—   20

The gentian-flower'd pass, its crown
With yellow spires aflame;[28]
Whence drops the path to Allière down,
And walls where Byron came,[29]

By their green river, who doth change   25
His birth-name just below;
Orchard, and croft, and full-stored grange
Nursed by his pastoral flow.

But stop!—to fetch back thoughts that stray
Beyond this gracious bound,   30
The cone of Jaman, pale and grey,
See, in the blue profound!

Ah, Jaman! delicately tall
Above his sun-warm'd firs—
What thoughts to me his rocks recall,   35
What memories he stirs!

And who but thou must be, in truth,
Obermann! with me here?
Thou master of my wandering youth,
But left this many a year!   40

Yes, I forget the world's work wrought,
Its warfare waged with pain;
An eremite with thee, in thought
Once more I slip my chain,

And to thy mountain-chalet come,   45
And lie beside its door,
And hear the wild bee's Alpine hum,
And thy sad, tranquil lore!

Again I feel the words inspire
Their mournful calm; serene,   50
Yet tinged with infinite desire
For all that *might* have been—

The harmony from which man swerved
Made his life's rule once more!
The universal order served,   55
Earth happier than before!

—While thus I mused, night gently ran
Down over hill and wood.
Then, still and sudden, Obermann
On the grass near me stood.   60

Those pensive features well I knew,
On my mind, years before,
Imaged so oft! imaged so true!
—A shepherd's garb he wore,

A mountain-flower was in his hand,   65
A book was in his breast.
Bent on my face, with gaze which scann'd
My soul, his eyes did rest.

'And is it thou,' he cried, 'so long
Held by the world which we   70
Loved not, who turnest from the throng
Back to thy youth and me?

'And from thy world, with heart opprest,
Choosest thou *now* to turn?—
Ah me! we anchorites read things best,   75
Clearest their course discern!

49 *1867-9*: its words 67 *1867-8*: that scann'd 75, 76 *1867-9*:
          we anchorites knew it best!
          Best can its course discern!

'Thou fledst me when the ungenial earth,
Man's work-place, lay in gloom.
Return'st thou in her hour of birth,
Of hopes and hearts in bloom?   80

'Perceiv'st thou not the change of day?
    Ah! Carry back thy ken,
What, some two thousand years! Survey
The world as it was then!

'Like ours it look'd in outward air.   85
Its head was clear and true,
Sumptuous its clothing, rich its fare,
No pause its action knew;

'Stout was its arm, each thew and bone
Seem'd puissant and alive—   90
But, ah! its heart, its heart was stone,
And so it could not thrive!

'On that hard Pagan world disgust
And secret loathing fell.
Deep weariness and sated lust   95
Made human life a hell.

'In his cool hall, with haggard eyes,
The Roman noble lay;
He drove abroad, in furious guise,
Along the Appian way.   100

77 *1867–77*: fledd'st
77, 78 *1867–9*:   when the ungenial earth
                      Thou soughtest,
81–4 *1867–9*:   Wellnigh two thousand years have brought
                      Their load, and gone away,
                      Since last on earth there lived and wrought
                      A world like ours to-day.
after 84 *1868, 1869 insert*: Like ours it look'd in outward air—
                      But of that inward prize,
                      Soul, that than they we take more care,
                      Ah, there our future lies.
In 1869 the third line of this stanza was changed to read: *Soul,* that we take more
count and care,   89 *1867, 1868*: pulse and bone

'He made a feast, drank fierce and fast,
And crown'd his hair with flowers—
No easier nor no quicker pass'd
The impracticable hours.

'The brooding East with awe beheld   105
Her impious younger world.
The Roman tempest swell'd and swell'd,
And on her head was hurl'd.

'The East bow'd low before the blast
In patient, deep disdain;   110
She let the legions thunder past,
And plunged in thought again.

'So well she mused, a morning broke
Across her spirit grey;
A conquering, new-born joy awoke,   115
And fill'd her life with day.

' "Poor world," she cried, "so deep accurst,
That runn'st from pole to pole
To seek a draught to slake thy thirst—
Go, seek it in thy soul!"   120

'She heard it, the victorious West,
In crown and sword array'd!
She felt the void which mined her breast,
She shiver'd and obey'd.

'She veil'd her eagles, snapp'd her sword,   125
And laid her sceptre down;
Her stately purple she abhorr'd,
And her imperial crown.

'She broke her flutes, she stopp'd her sports,
Her artists could not please;   130
She tore her books, she shut her courts,
She fled her palaces;

'Lust of the eye and pride of life
She left it all behind,
And hurried, torn with inward strife, 135
The wilderness to find.

'Tears wash'd the trouble from her face!
She changed into a child!
'Mid weeds and wrecks she stood—a place
Of ruin—but she smiled! 140

'Oh, had I lived in that great day,
How had its glory new
Fill'd earth and heaven, and caught away
My ravish'd spirit too!

'No thoughts that to the world belong 145
Had stood against the wave
Of love which set so deep and strong
From Christ's then open grave.

'No cloister-floor of humid stone
Had been too cold for me. 150
For me no Eastern desert lone
Had been too far to flee.

'No lonely life had pass'd too slow,
When I could hourly scan
Upon his Cross, with head sunk low, 155
That nail'd, thorn-crowned Man!

'Could see the Mother with her Child
Whose tender winning arts
Have to his little arms beguiled
So many wounded hearts! 160

145-8 *1867-9: follow lines* 149-52. 153-6 *From 1867 to 1869 this
stanza read as follows:*
  No lonely life had pass'd too slow
  When I could hourly see
  That wan, nail'd Form, with head droop'd low,
  Upon the bitter tree;
157 *1867-81:* the Child

'And centuries came and ran their course,
And unspent all that time
Still, still went forth that Child's dear force,
And still was at its prime.

'Ay, ages long endured his span   165
Of life—'tis true received—
That gracious Child, that thorn-crown'd Man!
—He lived while we believed.

'While we believed, on earth he went,
And open stood his grave.   170
Men call'd from chamber, church, and tent;
And Christ was by to save.

'Now he is dead! Far hence he lies
In the lorn Syrian town;
And on his grave, with shining eyes,   175
The Syrian stars look down.

'In vain men still, with hoping new,
Regard his death-place dumb,
And say the stone is not yet to,
And wait for words to come.   180

'Ah, o'er that silent sacred land,
Of sun, and arid stone,
And crumbling wall, and sultry sand,
Sounds now one word alone!

181 *1867–81*: 'Ah, from   184 *1867–81*: Comes now   *After* 184
from 1867 to 1881 appeared:
        'From David's lips this word did roll,
        'Tis true and living yet:
        No man can save his brother's soul,
        Nor pay his brother's debt.
In 1877 and 1881 the first line of the quatrain read:
        From David's lips that word did roll.

'Unduped of fancy, henceforth man 185
Must labour!—must resign
His all too human creeds, and scan
Simply the way divine!

'But slow that tide of common thought,
Which bathed our life, retired; 190
Slow, slow the old world wore to nought,
And pulse by pulse expired.

'Its frame yet stood without a breach
When blood and warmth were fled;
And still it spake its wonted speech— 195
But every word was dead.

'And oh, we cried, that on this corse
Might fall a freshening storm!
Rive its dry bones, and with new force
A new-sprung world inform! 200

'—Down came the storm! O'er France it pass'd
In sheets of scathing fire;
All Europe felt that fiery blast,
And shook as it rush'd by her.

'Down came the storm! In ruins fell 205
The worn-out world we knew.
It pass'd, that elemental swell!
Again appear'd the blue;

'The sun shone in the new-wash'd sky,
And what from heaven saw he? 210
Blocks of the past, like icebergs high,
Float on a rolling sea!

185 *1867–81*: Alone, self-poised, henceforward man   *This reading*
survived until the final revision of the text, when, for the first time, the stanza was
italicized, as constituting the 'word' which sounds over Syria.
185 *1881* MS. alterations [*cancelled*]:
          Unled of fancy, henceforth man
          Self-poised, clear-minded, henceforth man
201–4 *Added in 1868.*   205 *1867*: In ruin   206 *1867–9*: outworn world   212 *1867*: Float in

'Upon them plies the race of man
All it before endeavour'd;
"Ye live," I cried, "ye work and plan,   215
And know not ye are sever'd!

' "Poor fragments of a broken world
Whereon men pitch their tent!
Why were ye too to death not hurl'd
When your world's day was spent?   220

' "That glow of central fire is done
Which with its fusing flame
Knit all your parts, and kept you one—
But ye, ye are the same!

' "The past, its mask of union on,   225
Had ceased to live and thrive.
The past, its mask of union gone,
Say, is it more alive?

' "Your creeds are dead, your rites are dead,
Your social order too!   230
Where tarries he, the Power who said:
See, I make all things new?

' "The millions suffer still, and grieve,
And what can helpers heal
With old-world cures men half believe   235
For woes they wholly feel?

' "And yet men have such need of joy!
But joy whose grounds are true;
And joy that should all hearts employ
As when the past was new.   240

213–16 *1867–9*:
        Upon them ply the race of man
        All they before endeavour'd;
        They come and go, they work and plan,
        And know not they are sever'd.
218 *1867–9*: we pitch our tent!   221 *1867, 1868*: The glow
237 *1867–9*: yet they have   238 *1867–9*: And joy

'"Ah, not the emotion of that past,
Its common hope, were vain!
Some new such hope must dawn at last,
Or man must toss in pain.

'"But now the old is out of date,   245
The new is not yet born,
And who can be *alone* elate,
While the world lies forlorn?"

'Then to the wilderness I fled.—
There among Alpine snows   250
And pastoral huts I hid my head,
And sought and found repose.

'It was not yet the appointed hour.
Sad, patient, and resign'd,
I watch'd the crocus fade and flower,   255
I felt the sun and wind.

'The day I lived in was not mine,
Man gets no second day.
In dreams I saw the future shine—
But ah! I could not stay!   260

'Action I had not, followers, fame;
I pass'd obscure, alone.
The after-world forgets my name,
Nor do I wish it known.

'Composed to bear, I lived and died,   265
And knew my life was vain,
With fate I murmur not, nor chide,
At Sèvres by the Seine

'(If Paris that brief flight allow)
My humble tomb explore!   270
It bears: *Eternity, be thou
My refuge!* and no more.

243 *1867–9*: A new   245 *1867–9*: the past   246 *1867–9*: The
future not yet born—   265 *1867–9*: 'Gloom-wrapped within, I lived
and died,

M   *321*

'But thou, whom fellowship of mood
Did make from haunts of strife
Come to my mountain-solitude,   275
And learn my frustrate life;

'O thou, who, ere thy flying span
Was past of cheerful youth,
Didst find the solitary man
And love his cheerless truth—   280

'Despair not thou as I despair'd,
Nor be cold gloom thy prison!
Forward the gracious hours have fared,
And see! the sun is risen!

'He breaks the winter of the past;   285
A green, new earth appears.
Millions, whose life in ice lay fast,
Have thoughts, and smiles, and tears.

'What though there still need effort, strife?
Though much be still unwon?   290
Yet warm it mounts, the hour of life!
Death's frozen hour is done!

'The world's great order dawns in sheen,
After long darkness rude,
Divinelier imaged, clearer seen,   295
With happier zeal pursued.

'With hope extinct and brow composed
I mark'd the present die;
Its term of life was nearly closed,
Yet it had more than I.   300

'But thou, though to the world's new hour
Thou come with aspect marr'd,
Shorn of the joy, the bloom, the power
Which best befits its bard—

279 *1867–9*: Didst seek 285 *1867–9*: 'He melts the icebergs of the
past, 289–92 *Added in 1877*. 304 *1867–9*: best beseem

'Though more than half thy years be past,   305
And spent thy youthful prime;
Though, round thy firmer manhood cast,
Hang weeds of our sad time

'Whereof thy youth felt all the spell,
And traversed all the shade—   310
Though late, though dimm'd, though weak, yet tell
Hope to a world new-made!

'Help it to fill that deep desire,
The want which rack'd our brain,
Consumed our heart with thirst like fire,   315
Immedicable pain;

'Which to the wilderness drove out
Our life, to Alpine snow,
And palsied all our word with doubt,
And all our work with woe—   320

'What still of strength is left, employ
That end to help attain:
One common wave of thought and joy
Lifting mankind again!'

—The vision ended. I awoke   325
As out of sleep, and no
Voice moved;—only the torrent broke
The silence, far below.

Soft darkness on the turf did lie.
Solemn, o'er hut and wood,   330
In the yet star-sown nightly sky,
The peak of Jaman stood.

312 *1869*: world re-made!   313 *1867–9*: reach our deep desire,
314 *1867–9*: dream which fill'd our brain,   *1877–81*: want which crazed
our brain,   *1881 MS. alterations* [*cancelled*]: want which wore our brain,
315 *1867–9*: Fix'd in our soul a thirst   *1877–81*: Consum'd our soul
with thirst   319 *1867–9*: our deed   320 *1867–9*: our word
322 *1867–9*: That end to help men gain: *1877–81*: This end to help
attain: **323** *1867–9*: *mighty wave*   324 *1867–9*: *mankind*
amain!

Still in my soul the voice I heard
Of Obermann!——away
I turned; by some vague impulse stirr'd,   335
Along the rocks of Naye

Past Sonchaud's piny flanks I gaze
And the blanch'd summit bare
Of Malatrait, to where in haze
The Valais opens fair,   340

And the domed Velan, with his snows,
Behind the upcrowding hills,
Doth all the heavenly opening close
Which the Rhone's murmur fills;—

And glorious there, without a sound,   345
Across the glimmering lake,
High in the Valais-depth profound,
I saw the morning break.

337 *1867–9*: And Sonchaud's

DRAMATIC POEMS

MEROPE

A TRAGEDY

[First published 1858. Reprinted 1885 and thereafter]

STORY OF THE DRAMA

Apollodorus says:—'Cresphontes had not reigned long in Messenia when he was murdered, together with two of his sons. And Polyphontes reigned in his stead, he, too, being of the family of Hercules; and he had for his wife, against her will, Merope, the widow of the murdered king. But Merope had borne to Cresphontes a third son, 5 called Æpytus; him she gave to her own father to bring up. He, when he came to man's estate, returned secretly to Messenia, and slew Polyphontes and the other murderers of his father.'

Hyginus says:—'Merope sent away and concealed her infant son. Polyphontes sought for him everywhere in vain. He, when he grew up, 10 laid a plan to avenge the murder of his father and brothers. In pursuance of this plan he came to king Polyphontes and reported the death of the son of Cresphontes and Merope. The king ordered him to be hospitably entertained, intending to inquire further of him. He, being very tired, went to sleep, and an old man, who was the channel through 15 whom the mother and son used to communicate, arrives at this moment in tears, bringing word to Merope that her son had disappeared from his protector's house, and was slain. Merope, believing that the sleeping stranger is the murderer of her son, comes into the guest-chamber with an axe, not knowing that he whom she would slay was her son; 20

MEROPE. STORY OF THE DRAMA. *In 1858 this is called an* 'Historical Introduction', *following the* Preface *to that edition. The* Introduction *opens:*

In the foregoing Preface [*note refers to* Page xiii *of the Preface*] the story of Merope is detailed: what is here added may serve to explain allusions which occur in the course of the tragedy, and to illustrate the situation of its chief personages at the moment when it commences.

On pp. xiii and xiv of 1858 occur the passages from Apollodorus and Hyginus, with these differences:

Hyginus:

10 *1858*: for him everywhere, and promised gold to whoever should slay him.
12 *1858*: and asked for the promised gold, saying that he had slain the son
18 and was slain *first inserted in 1885.*

325

the old man recognised him, and withheld Merope from slaying him. The king, Polyphontes, rejoicing at the supposed death of Æpytus, celebrated a sacrifice; his guest, pretending to strike the sacrificial victim, slew the king, and so got back his father's kingdom.'

25 The events on which the action of the drama turns belong to the period of transition from the heroic and fabulous to the human and historic age of Greece. The doings of the hero Hercules, the ancestor of the Messenian Æpytus, belong to fable; but the invasion of Peloponnesus by the Dorians under chiefs claiming to be descended from
30 Hercules, and their settlement in Argos, Lacedæmon, and Messenia, belong to history. Æpytus is descended on the father's side from Hercules, Perseus, and the kings of Argos; on the mother's side from Pelasgus, and the aboriginal kings of Arcadia. Callisto, the daughter of the wicked Lycaon, and the mother, by Zeus, of Arcas, from whom the
35 Arcadians took their name, was the granddaughter of Pelasgus. The birth of Arcas brought upon Callisto the anger of the virgin-goddess Artemis, whose service she followed: she was changed into a she-bear, and in this form was chased by her own son, grown to manhood. Zeus interposed, and the mother and son were removed from the earth, and
40 placed among the stars. Callisto became the famous constellation of the Great Bear; her son became Arcturus, Arctophylax, or Boötes. From this son of Callisto were descended Cypselus, the maternal grandfather of Æpytus, and the children of Cypselus, Laias and Merope.

The story of the life of Hercules, the paternal ancestor of Æpytus, is
45 so well known that there is no need to record it. The reader will remember that, although entitled to the throne of Argos by right of descent from Perseus and Danaus, and to the thrones of Sparta and Messenia by right of conquest, Hercules yet passed his life in labours and wanderings, subjected by the decree of fate to the commands of
50 his kinsman, the feeble and malignant Eurystheus. At his death he

21 *After sentence ending* from slaying him, *1858 has*: After the recognition had taken place, Merope, to prepare the way for her vengeance, affected to be reconciled with Polyphontes.   22 *1858*: king, overjoyed, celebrated a sacrifice: 25 of the drama *first inserted in 1885*.   27 doings of the *first inserted in 1885*.   38 *1858*: At the critical moment Zeus interposed,   42 *1858*: From him, Cypselus   43 *1858*: and Merope, were lineally descended.   44 *1858*: The events of the life . . . are so
45 *1858*: that it is hardly necessary to record them.   45 *1858*: It is sufficient to remind the reader, that   48 *1858*: he yet passed   49
1858: of his far inferior kinsman,   50 *After sentence ending* malignant
Eurystheus, *1858 has*: Hercules, who is represented with the violence as well

bequeathed to his offspring, the Heracleidæ, his own claims to the
kingdoms of Peloponnesus, and to the persecution of Eurystheus. They
at first sought shelter with Ceyx, king of Trachis; he was too weak to
protect them, and they then took refuge at Athens. The Athenians
refused to deliver them up at the demand of Eurystheus; he invaded 55
Attica, and a battle was fought near Marathon, in which, after Macaria,
a daughter of Hercules, had devoted herself for the preservation of her
house, Eurystheus fell, and the Heracleidæ and their Athenian protectors were victorious. The memory of Macaria's self-sacrifice was per-
petuated by the name of a spring of water on the plain of Marathon, 60
the spring Macaria. The Heracleidæ then endeavoured to effect their
return to Peloponnesus. Hyllus, the eldest of them, inquired of the
oracle at Delphi respecting their return; he was told to return by the
narrow passage and in the *third harvest.* Accordingly, in the third year
from that time Hyllus led an army to the Isthmus of Corinth; but there 65
he was encountered by an army of Achaians and Arcadians, and fell
in single combat with Echemus, king of Tegea. Upon this defeat the
Heracleidæ retired to northern Greece; there, after much wandering,
they finally took refuge with Ægimius, king of the Dorians, who appears
to have been the fastest friend of their house, and whose Dorian warriors 70
formed the army which at last achieved their return. But, for a hundred
years from the date of their first attempt, the Heracleidæ were defeated

as the virtues of an adventurous ever-warring hero, attacked and slew
Eurytus, an Euboean king, with whom he had a quarrel, and carried off the
daughter of Eurytus, the beautiful Iole. The wife of Hercules, Deianeira,
seized with jealous anxiety, remembered that long ago the centaur Nessus,
dying by the poisoned arrows of Hercules, had assured her that the blood
flowing from his mortal wound would prove an infallible love-charm to win
back the affections of her husband, if she should ever lose them. With this
philtre Deianeira now anointed a robe of triumph, which she sent to her
victorious husband: he received it when about to offer public sacrifice, and
immediately put it on: but the sun's rays called into activity the poisoned
blood with which the robe was smeared: it clung to the flesh of the hero and
consumed it. In dreadful agonies Hercules caused himself to be transported
from Euboea to Mount Œta: there, under the crags of Trachis, an immense
funeral pile was constructed. Recognizing the divine will in the fate which
had overtaken him, the hero ascended the pile, and called on his children
and followers to set it on fire. They refused; but the office was performed
by Poeas, the father of Philoctetes, who, passing near, was attracted by the
concourse round the pile, and who received the bow and arrows of Hercules
for his reward. The flames arose, and the apotheosis of Hercules was con-
summated.   *1858 does not have* At his death

in their successive invasions of Peloponnesus. Cleolaus and Aristomachus, the son and grandson of Hyllus, fell in unsuccessful expedi-
75 tions. At length the sons of Aristomachus, Temenus, Cresphontes,
and Aristodemus, when grown up, repaired to Delphi and taxed the
oracle with the non-fulfilment of the promise made to their ancestor
Hyllus. But Apollo replied that his oracle had been misunderstood; for
that by the *third harvest* he had meant the third generation, and by the
80 *narrow passage* he had meant the straits of the Corinthian Gulf. After
this explanation the sons of Aristomachus built a fleet at Naupactus;
and finally, in the hundredth year from the death of Hyllus and the
eightieth from the fall of Troy, the invasion was again attempted and
was this time successful. The son of Orestes, Tisamenus, who ruled
85 both Argos and Lacedæmon, fell in battle; many of his vanquished
subjects left their homes and took refuge in Achaia.

The spoil was now to be divided among the conquerors. Aristodemus, the youngest of the sons of Aristomachus, did not survive to
enjoy his share. He was slain at Delphi by the sons of Pylades and
90 Electra, the kinsmen, through their mother, of the house of Agamemnon, that house which the Heracleidæ with their Dorian army had
dispossessed. The claims of Aristodemus descended to his two sons,
Procles and Eurysthenes, children under the guardianship of their
maternal uncle, Theras. Temenus, the eldest of the sons of Aristo-
95 machus, took the kingdom of Argos. For the two remaining kingdoms,
that of Sparta and that of Messenia, his two nephews, who were to rule
jointly, and their uncle Cresphontes, had to cast lots. Cresphontes
wished to have the fertile Messenia, and induced his brother to acquiesce
in a trick which secured it to him. The lot of Cresphontes and that of
100 his two nephews were to be placed in a water-jar, and thrown out.
Messenia was to belong to him whose lot came out first. With the
connivance of Temenus, Cresphontes marked as his own lot a pellet
composed of baked clay, as the lot of his nephews, a pellet of unbaked
clay; the unbaked pellet was of course dissolved in the water, while the
105 brick pellet fell out alone. Messenia, therefore, was assigned to
Cresphontes.

Messenia was at this time ruled by Melanthus, a descendant of Neleus.
This ancestor, a prince of the great house of Æolus, had come from
Thessaly and succeeded to the Messenian throne on the failure of the

86 *1858*: and retired to Achaia.   90–1 *1858*: the kinsmen of the
house of Agamemnon—   91 had *first inserted in 1885.*   97 *1858*:
were to cast

328

previous dynasty. Melanthus and his race were thus foreigners in 110
Messenia and were unpopular. His subjects offered little or no opposi-
tion to the invading Dorians; Melanthus abandoned his kingdom to
Cresphontes, and retired to Athens.

Cresphontes married Merope, whose native country, Arcadia, was
not affected by the Dorian invasion. This marriage, the issue of which 115
was three sons, connected him with the native population of Peloponnesus. He built a new capital of Messenia, Stenyclaros, and transferred
thither, from Pylos, the seat of government; he proposed, moreover,
says Pausanias, to divide Messenia into five states, and to confer on the
native Messenians equal privileges with their Dorian conquerors. The 120
Dorians complained that his administration unduly favoured the vanquished people; his chief magnates, headed by Polyphontes, himself a
descendant of Hercules, formed a cabal against him, and he was slain
with his two eldest sons. The youngest son of Cresphontes, Æpytus,
then an infant, was saved by his mother, who sent him to her father, 125
Cypselus, the king of Arcadia, under whose protection he was
brought up.

The drama begins at the moment when Æpytus, grown to manhood,
returns secretly to Messenia to take vengeance on his father's murderers.
At this period Temenus was no longer reigning at Argos; he had been 130
murdered by his sons, jealous of their brother-in-law, Deiphontes. The
sons of Aristodemus, Procles and Eurysthenes, at variance with their
uncle and ex-guardian, Theras, were reigning at Sparta.

PERSONS OF THE DRAMA.

LAIAS, *uncle of* ÆPYTUS, *brother of* MEROPE.
ÆPYTUS, *son of* MEROPE *and* CRESPHONTES.
POLYPHONTES, *king of* MESSENIA.
MEROPE, *widow of* CRESPHONTES, *the murdered king of* MESSENIA.
THE CHORUS, *of* MESSENIAN *maidens.*
ARCAS, *an old man of* MEROPE'S *household.*
MESSENGER.
GUARDS, ATTENDANTS, &c.

The Scene is before the royal palace in STENYCLAROS, *the capital of* MESSENIA.
In the foreground is the tomb of CRESPHONTES. *The action commences at day-
break.*

118–19 *1858*: he at first proposed, it is said by Pausanias,   133 *1858*:
guardian, were reigning

MEROPE

Laias

Son of Cresphontes, we have reach'd the goal
Of our night-journey, and thou see'st thy home.
Behold thy heritage, thy father's realm!
This is that fruitful, famed Messenian land,
Wealthy in corn and flocks, which, when at last   5
The late-relenting Gods with victory brought
The Heracleidæ back to Pelops' isle,
Fell to thy father's lot, the second prize.
Before thy feet this recent city spreads
Of Stenyclaros, which he built, and made   10
Of his fresh-conquer'd realm the royal seat,
Degrading Pylos from its ancient rule.
There stands the temple of thine ancestor,
Great Heracles; and, in that public place,
Zeus hath his altar, where thy father fell.   15
Southward and west, behold those snowy peaks,
Taygetus, Laconia's border-wall;
And, on this side, those confluent streams which make
Pamisus watering the Messenian plain;
Then to the north, Lycæus and the hills   20
Of pastoral Arcadia, where, a babe
Snatch'd from the slaughter of thy father's house,
Thy mother's kin received thee, and rear'd up.—
Our journey is well made, the work remains
Which to perform we made it; means for that   25
Let us consult, before this palace sends
Its inmates on their daily tasks abroad.
Haste and advise, for day comes on apace.

Æpytus

O brother of my mother, guardian true,

14 *and throughout*: *1858*: Hercules   16 *1858*: Thence to the south,
behold

330

And second father from that hour when first   30
My mother's faithful servant laid me down,
An infant, at the hearth of Cypselus,
My grandfather, the good Arcadian king—
Thy part it were to advise, and mine to obey.
But let us keep that purpose, which, at home,   35
We judged the best; chance finds no better way.
Go thou into the city, and seek out
Whate'er in the Messenian people stirs
Of faithful fondness for their former king
Or hatred to their present; in this last   40
Will lie, my grandsire said, our fairest chance.
For tyrants make man good beyond himself;
Hate to their rule, which else would die away,
Their daily-practised chafings keep alive.
Seek this! revive, unite it, give it hope;   45
Bid it rise boldly at the signal given.
Meanwhile within my father's palace I,
An unknown guest, will enter, bringing word
Of my own death—but, Laias, well I hope
Through that pretended death to live and reign.   50
[THE CHORUS *comes forth.*

Softly, stand back!—see, to these palace gates
What black procession slowly makes approach?—
Sad-chanting maidens clad in mourning robes,
With pitchers in their hands, and fresh-pull'd flowers—
Doubtless, they bear them to my father's tomb.   55
[MEROPE *comes forth.*

And look, to meet them, that one, grief-plunged Form,
Severer, paler, statelier than they all,
A golden circlet on her queenly brow!
O Laias, Laias, let the heart speak here—
Shall I not greet her? shall I not leap forth?   60
[POLYPHONTES *comes forth, following* MEROPE

38 *1858*: Messenian city   39 *1858*: towards their   51 *1858*:
tow'rd the palace   56 *1858*: And see

Laias

Not so! thy heart would pay its moment's speech
By silence ever after, for, behold!
The King (I know him, even through many years)
Follows the approaching Queen, who stops, as call'd.
No lingering now! straight to the city I;   65
Do thou, till for thine entrance to this house
The happy moment comes, lurk here unseen
Behind the shelter of thy father's tomb;
Remove yet further off, if aught comes near.
But, here while harbouring, on its margin lay,   70
Sole offering that thou hast, locks from thy head;
And fill thy leisure with an earnest prayer
To his avenging Shade, and to the Gods
Who under earth watch guilty deeds of men,
To guide our vengeance to a prosperous close.   75

> [LAIAS *goes out.* POLYPHONTES, MEROPE, *and* THE
> CHORUS *come forward. As they advance,* ÆPYTUS,
> *who at first conceals himself behind the tomb, moves off
> the stage.*

Polyphontes (*To* THE CHORUS)

Set down your pitchers, maidens, and fall back!
Suspend your melancholy rites awhile;
Shortly ye shall resume them with your Queen.—

(*To* MEROPE)

I sought thee, Merope; I find thee thus,
As I have ever found thee; bent to keep,   80
By sad observances and public grief,
A mournful feud alive, which else would die.
I blame thee not, I do thy heart no wrong!
Thy deep seclusion, thine unyielding gloom,
Thine attitude of cold, estranged reproach,   85
These punctual funeral honours, year by year

64 *1858*: issuing Queen   75 *1858*: our effort

Repeated, are in thee, I well believe,
Courageous, faithful actions, nobly dared.
But, Merope, the eyes of other men
Read in these actions, innocent in thee, 90
Perpetual promptings to rebellious hope,
War-cries to faction, year by year renew'd,
Beacons of vengeance, not to be let die.
And me, believe it, wise men gravely blame,
And ignorant men despise me, that I stand 95
Passive, permitting thee what course thou wilt.
Yes, the crowd mutters that remorseful fear
And paralysing conscience stop my arm,
When it should pluck thee from thy hostile way.
All this I bear, for, what I seek, I know: 100
Peace, peace is what I seek, and public calm;
Endless extinction of unhappy hates,
Union cemented for this nation's weal.
And even now, if to behold me here,
This day, amid these rites, this black-robed train, 105
Wakens, O Queen! remembrance in thy heart
Too wide at variance with the peace I seek—
I will not violate thy noble grief,
The prayer I came to urge I will defer.

Merope

This day, to-morrow, yesterday, alike 110
I am, I shall be, have been, in my mind
Tow'rd thee; toward thy silence as thy speech.
Speak, therefore, or keep silence, which thou wilt.

Polyphontes

Hear me, then, speak; and let this mournful day,
The twentieth anniversary of strife, 115
Henceforth be honour'd as the date of peace.
Yes, twenty years ago this day beheld
The king Cresphontes, thy great husband, fall;

112 *1858*: Tow'rds thee; towards thy

It needs no yearly offerings at his tomb
To keep alive that memory in my heart—   120
It lives, and, while I see the light, will live.
For we were kinsmen—more than kinsmen—friends;
Together we had grown, together lived;
Together to this isle of Pelops came
To take the inheritance of Heracles,   125
Together won this fair Messenian land—
Alas, that, how to rule it, was our broil!
He had his counsel, party, friends—I mine;
He stood by what he wish'd for—I the same;
I smote him, when our wishes clash'd in arms—   130
He had smit me, had he been swift as I.
But while I smote him, Queen, I honour'd him;
Me, too, had he prevail'd, he had not scorn'd.
Enough of this! Since that, I have maintain'd
The sceptre—not remissly let it fall—   135
And I am seated on a prosperous throne;
Yet still, for I conceal it not, ferments
In the Messenian people what remains
Of thy dead husband's faction—vigorous once,
Now crush'd but not quite lifeless by his fall.   140
And these men look to thee, and from thy grief—
Something too studiously, forgive me, shown—
Infer thee their accomplice; and they say
That thou in secret nurturest up thy son,
Him whom thou hiddest when thy husband fell,   145
To avenge that fall, and bring them back to power.
Such are their hopes—I ask not if by thee
Willingly fed or no—their most vain hopes;
For I have kept conspiracy fast-chain'd
Till now, and I have strength to chain it still.   150
But, Merope, the years advance;—I stand
Upon the threshold of old age, alone,
Always in arms, always in face of foes.
The long repressive attitude of rule

123 *1858*: had sprung   134 *1858*: Since then,

334

Leaves me austerer, sterner, than I would;   155
Old age is more suspicious than the free
And valiant heart of youth, or manhood's firm
Unclouded reason; I would not decline
Into a jealous tyrant, scourged with fears,
Closing in blood and gloom his sullen reign.   160
The cares which might in me with time, I feel,
Beget a cruel temper, help me quell!
The breach between our parties help me close!
Assist me to rule mildly; let us join
Our hands in solemn union, making friends   165
Our factions with the friendship of their chiefs.
Let us in marriage, King and Queen, unite
Claims ever hostile else, and set thy son—
No more an exile fed on empty hopes,
And to an unsubstantial title heir,   170
But prince adopted by the will of power,
And future king—before this people's eyes.
Consider him! consider not old hates!
Consider, too, this people, who were dear
To their dead king, thy husband—yea, too dear,   175
For that destroy'd him. Give them peace! thou can'st.
O Merope, how many noble thoughts,
How many precious feelings of man's heart,
How many loves, how many gratitudes,
Do twenty years wear out, and see expire!   180
Shall they not wear one hatred out as well?

Merope

Thou hast forgot, then, who I am who hear,
And who thou art who speakest to me? I
Am Merope, thy murder'd master's wife;
And thou art Polyphontes, first his friend,   185
And then . . . his murderer. These offending tears
That murder moves; this breach that thou would'st close
Was by that murder open'd; that one child

187 *1858*: murder draws;

(If still, indeed, he lives) whom thou would'st seat
Upon a throne not thine to give, is heir,   190
Because thou slew'st his brothers with their father.
Who can patch union here? What can there be
But everlasting horror 'twixt us two,
Gulfs of estranging blood? Across that chasm
Who can extend their hands? . . . Maidens, take back   195
These offerings home! our rites are spoil'd to-day.

Polyphontes

Not so; let these Messenian maidens mark
The fear'd and blacken'd ruler of their race,
Albeit with lips unapt to self-excuse,
Blow off the spot of murder from his name.—   200
Murder!—but what *is* murder? When a wretch
For private gain or hatred takes a life,
We call it murder, crush him, brand his name.
But when, for some great public cause, an arm
Is, without love or hate, austerely raised   205
Against a power exempt from common checks,
Dangerous to all, to be but thus annull'd—
Ranks any man with murder such an act?
With grievous deeds, perhaps; with murder, no!
Find then such cause, the charge of murder falls—   210
Be judge thyself if it abound not here.
All know how weak the eagle, Heracles,
Soaring from his death-pile on Œta, left
His puny, callow eaglets; and what trials—
Infirm protectors, dubious oracles   215
Construed awry, misplann'd invasions—wore
Three generations of his offspring out;
Hardly the fourth, with grievous loss, regain'd
Their father's realm, this isle, from Pelops named.
Who made that triumph, though deferr'd, secure?   220
Who, but the kinsmen of the royal brood

216 *1858*: invasions—us'd   217 *1858*: Two generations of his
offspring up;   218 *1858*: the third

Of Heracles, scarce Heracleidæ less
Than they? these, and the Dorian lords, whose king
Ægimius gave our outcast house a home
When Thebes, when Athens dared not; who in arms   225
Thrice issued with us from their pastoral vales,
And shed their blood like water in our cause?
Such were the dispossessors; of what stamp
Were they we dispossessed?—of us I speak,
Who to Messenia with thy husband came;   230
I speak not now of Argos, where his brother,
Not now of Sparta, where his nephews reign'd.—
What we found here were tribes of fame obscure,
Much turbulence, and little constancy,
Precariously ruled by foreign lords   235
From the Æolian stock of Neleus sprung,
A house once great, now dwindling in its sons.
Such were the conquer'd, such the conquerors; who
Had most thy husband's confidence? Consult
His acts! the wife he chose was—full of virtues—   240
But an Arcadian princess, more akin
To his new subjects than to us; his friends
Were the Messenian chiefs; the laws he framed
Were aim'd at their promotion, our decline.
And, finally, this land, then half-subdued,   245
Which from one central city's guarded seat
As from a fastness in the rocks our scant
Handful of Dorian conquerors might have curb'd,
He parcell'd out in five confederate states,
Sowing his victors thinly through them all,   250
Mere prisoners, meant or not, among our foes.
If this was fear of them, it shamed the king;
If jealousy of us, it shamed the man.
Long we refrain'd ourselves, submitted long,
Construed his acts indulgently, revered,   255
Though found perverse, the blood of Heracles;
Reluctantly the rest—but, against all,
One voice preach'd patience, and that voice was mine!

At last it reach'd us, that he, still mistrustful,
Deeming, as tyrants deem, our silence hate,   260
Unadulating grief conspiracy,
Had to this city, Stenyclaros, call'd
A general assemblage of the realm,
With compact in that concourse to deliver,
For death, his ancient to his new-made friends,   265
Patience was thenceforth self destruction. I,
I his chief kinsman, I his pioneer
And champion to the throne, I honouring most
Of men the line of Heracles, preferr'd
The many of that lineage to the one;   270
What his foes dared not, I, his lover, dared;
I at that altar, where mid shouting crowds
He sacrificed, our ruin in his heart,
To Zeus, before he struck his blow, struck mine—
Struck once, and awed his mob, and saved this realm.   275
Murder let others call this, if they will;
I, self-defence and righteous execution.

Merope

Alas, how fair a colour can his tongue,
Who self-exculpates, lend to foulest deeds!
Thy trusting lord didst thou, his servant, slay;   280
Kinsman, thou slew'st thy kinsman; friend, thy friend—
This were enough; but let me tell thee, too,
Thou hadst no cause, as feign'd, in his misrule.
For ask at Argos, ask in Lacedæmon,
Whose people, when the Heracleidæ came,   285
Were hunted out, and to Achaia fled,
Whether is better, to abide alone,
A wolfish band, in a dispeopled realm,
Or conquerors with conquer'd to unite
Into one puissant folk, as he design'd?   290
These sturdy and unworn Messenian tribes,
Who shook the fierce Neleidæ on their throne,
Who to the invading Dorians stretch'd a hand,

And half bestow'd, half yielded up their soil—
He would not let his savage chiefs alight,   295
A cloud of vultures, on this vigorous race,
Ravin a little while in spoil and blood,
Then, gorged and helpless, be assail'd and slain.
He would have saved you from your furious selves.
Not in abhorr'd estrangement let you stand;   300
He would have mix'd you with your friendly foes,
Foes dazzled with your prowess, well inclined
To reverence your lineage, more, to obey;
So would have built you, in a few short years,
A just, therefore a safe, supremacy.   305
For well he knew, what you, his chiefs, did not—
How of all human rules the over-tense
Are apt to snap; the easy-stretch'd endure.
O gentle wisdom, little understood!
O arts above the vulgar tyrant's reach!   310
O policy too subtle far for sense
Of heady, masterful, injurious men!
This good he meant you, and for this he died!
Yet not for this—else might thy crime in part
Be error deem'd—but that pretence is vain.   315
For, if ye slew him for supposed misrule,
Injustice to his kin and Dorian friends,
Why with the offending father did ye slay
Two unoffending babes, his innocent sons?
Why not on them have placed the forfeit crown,   320
Ruled in their name, and train'd them to your will?
Had *they* misruled? had *they* forgot their friends,
Forsworn their blood? ungratefully had *they*
Preferr'd Messenian serfs to Dorian lords?
No! but to thy ambition their poor lives   325
Were bar—and this, too, was their father's crime.
That thou might'st reign he died, not for his fault
Even fancied; and his death thou wroughtest chief!
For, if the other lords desired his fall
Hotlier than thou, and were by thee kept back,   330

Why dost thou only profit by his death?
Thy crown condemns thee, while thy tongue absolves.
And now to me thou tenderest friendly league,
And to my son reversion to thy throne!
Short answer is sufficient; league with thee,   335
For me I deem such impious; and for him
Exile abroad more safe than heirship here.

Polyphontes

I ask thee not to approve thy husband's death,
No, nor expect thee to admit the grounds,
In reason good, which justified my deed.   340
With women the heart argues, not the mind.
But, for thy children's death, I stand assoil'd—
I saved them, meant them honour; but thy friends
Rose, and with fire and sword assailed my house
By night; in that blind tumult they were slain.   345
To chance impute their deaths, then, not to me.

Merope

Such chance as kill'd the father, kill'd the sons.

Polyphontes

One son at least I spared, for still he lives.

Merope

Tyrants think him they murder not they spare.

Polyphontes

Not much a tyrant thy free speech displays me.   350

Merope

Thy shame secures my freedom, not thy will.

Polyphontes

Shame rarely checks the genuine tyrant's will.

Merope

One merit, then, thou hast; exult in that.

Polyphontes

Thou standest out, I see, repellest peace.

Merope

Thy sword repell'd it long ago, not I.   355

Polyphontes

Doubtless thou reckonest on the help of friends.

Merope

Not help of men, although, perhaps, of Gods.

Polyphontes

What Gods? the Gods of concord, civil weal?

Merope

No! the avenging Gods, who punish crime.

Polyphontes

Beware! from thee upbraidings I receive   360
With pity, nay, with reverence; yet, beware!
I know, I know how hard it is to think
That right, that conscience pointed to a deed,
Where interest seems to have enjoin'd it too.
Most men are led by interest; and the few   365
Who are not, expiate the general sin,
Involved in one suspicion with the base.
Dizzy the path and perilous the way
Which in a deed like mine a just man treads,
But it is sometimes trodden, oh! believe it.   370
Yet how *canst* thou believe it? therefore thou
Hast all impunity. Yet, lest thy friends,
Embolden'd by my lenience, think it fear,

356 *1858*: the hope

And count on like impunity, and rise,
And have to thank thee for a fall, beware!　　375
To rule this kingdom I intend; with sway
Clement, if may be, but to rule it—there
Expect no wavering, no retreat, no change.
And now I leave thee to these rites, esteem'd
Pious, but impious, surely, if their scope　　380
Be to foment old memories of wrath.
Pray, as thou pour'st libations on this tomb,
To be deliver'd from thy foster'd hate,
Unjust suspicion, and erroneous fear.

[POLYPHONTES *goes into the palace*. THE CHORUS *and*
MEROPE *approach the tomb with their offerings.*

The Chorus

Draw, draw near to the tomb!　　　　　*strophe.*　385
Lay honey-cakes on its marge,
Pour the libation of milk,
Deck it with garlands of flowers.
Tears fall thickly the while!
Behold, O King from the dark　　　　　390
House of the grave, what we do!

O Arcadian hills,　　　　　　　　　*antistrophe.*
Send us the Youth whom ye hide,
Girt with his coat for the chase,
With the low broad hat of the tann'd　　395
Hunter o'ershadowing his brow;
Grasping firm, in his hand
Advanced, two javelins, not now
Dangerous alone to the deer!

Merope

What shall I bear, O lost　　　　　*str.* 1.　400
Husband and King, to thy grave?—
Pure libations, and fresh
Flowers? But thou, in the gloom,

Discontented, perhaps,
Demandest vengeance, not grief?   405
Sternly requirest a man,
Light to spring up to thy house?

The Chorus

Vengeance, O Queen, is his due,   *str.* 2.
His most just prayer; yet his house—
If that might soothe him below—   410
Prosperous, mighty, came back
In the third generation, the way
Order'd by Fate, to their home;
And now, glorious, secure,
Fill the wealth-giving thrones   415
Of their heritage, Pelops' isle.

Merope

Suffering sent them, Death   *ant.* 1.
March'd with them, Hatred and Strife
Met them entering their halls.
For from the day when the first   420
Heracleidæ received
That Delphic hest to return,
What hath involved them, but blind
Error on error, and blood?

The Chorus

Truly I hear of a Maid   *ant.* 2.   425
Of that stock born, who bestow'd
Her blood that so she might make
Victory sure to her race,
When the fight hung in doubt! but she now,
Honour'd and sung of by all,   430
Far on Marathon plain,
Gives her name to the spring
Macaria, blessed Child.

407 *1858*: thy race?   409 *1858*: yet his race—

Merope

She led the way of death. *str.* 3.
And the plain of Tegea, 435
And the grave of Orestes—
Where, in secret seclusion
Of his unreveal'd tomb,
Sleeps Agamemnon's unhappy,
Matricidal, world-famed, 440
Seven-cubit-statured son—
Sent forth Echemus, the victor, the king,
By whose hand, at the Isthmus,
At the fate-denied straits,
Fell the eldest of the sons of Heracles, 445
Hyllus, the chief of his house.
Brother follow'd sister
The all-wept way.

The Chorus

Yes; but his seed still, wiser-counsell'd,
Sail'd by the fate-meant Gulf to their conquest— 450
Slew their enemies' king, Tisamenus.
Wherefore accept that happier omen!
Yet shall restorer appear to the race.

Merope

Three brothers won the field, *ant.* 3.
And to two did Destiny 455
Give the thrones that they conquer'd,
But the third, what delays him
From his unattain'd crown? ...
Ah Pylades and Electra,
Ever faithful, untired, 460
Jealous, blood-exacting friends!
Your sons leap upon the foe of your kin,
In the passes of Delphi,

449 *1858*: his son's seed, wiser-counsell'd,   453 *1858*: shall restorers
462 *1858*: Ye lie watching for the foe

In the temple-built gorge!
There the youngest of the band of conquerors   465
Perish'd, in sight of the goal.
Thrice son follow'd sire
The all-wept way.

The Chorus

Thou tellest the fate of the last   *str. 4.*
Of the three Heracleidæ.   470
Not of him, of Cresphontes thou shared'st the lot!
A king, a king was he while he lived,
Swaying the sceptre with predestined hand;
And now, minister loved,
Holds rule.

Merope

Ah me ... Ah ...   475

The Chorus

For the awful Monarchs below.

Merope

Thou touchest the worst of my ills.   *str. 5.*
Oh had he fallen of old
At the Isthmus, in fight with his foes,
By Achaian, Arcadian spear!   480
Then had his sepulchre risen
On the high sea-bank, in the sight
Of either Gulf, and remain'd
All-regarded afar,
Noble memorial of worth   485
Of a valiant Chief, to his own.

The Chorus

There rose up a cry in the streets   *ant. 4.*
From the terrified people.

467 *1858*: Grandson follow'd sire

From the altar of Zeus, from the crowd, came a wail.
A blow, a blow was struck, and he fell,   490
Sullying his garment with dark-streaming blood;
While stood o'er him a Form—
Some Form

Merope

Ah me ... Ah ...

The Chorus

Of a dreadful Presence of fear.

Merope

More piercing the second cry rang,   *ant.* 5.   495
Wail'd from the palace within,
From the Children. . . . The Fury to them,
Fresh from their father, draws near.
Ah bloody axe! dizzy blows!
In these ears, they thunder, they ring,   500
These poor ears, still! and these eyes
Night and day see them fall,
Fiery phantoms of death,
On the fair, curl'd heads of my sons.

The Chorus

Not to thee only hath come   *str.* 6.   505
Sorrow, O Queen, of mankind.
Had not Electra to haunt
A palace defiled by a death unavenged,
For years, in silence, devouring her heart?
But her nursling, her hope, came at last.   510
Thou, too, rearest in hope,
Far 'mid Arcadian hills,
Somewhere, for vengeance, a champion, a light.

511 *1858*: in joy   513 *1858*: in safety, a nursling, a light.

Soon, soon shall Zeus bring him home!
Soon shall he dawn on this land! 515

Merope

Him in secret, in tears, *str.* 7.
Month after month, I await
Vainly. For he, in the glens
Of Lycæus afar,
A gladsome hunter of deer, 520
Basks in his morning of youth,
Spares not a thought to his home.

The Chorus

Give not thy heart to despair. *ant.* 6.
No lamentation can loose
Prisoners of death from the grave; 525
But Zeus, who accounteth thy quarrel his own,
Still rules, still watches, and numb'reth the hours
Till the sinner, the vengeance, be ripe.
Still, by Acheron stream,
Terrible Deities throned 530
Sit, and eye grimly the victim unscourged.
Still, still the Dorian boy,
Exiled, remembers his home.

Merope

Him if high-ruling Zeus *ant.* 7.

514 *1858*: Yet, yet shall   515 *1858*: Yet shall   *For* 517–22 *1858*:
      Month after month, through the slow-dragging year,
      Longing, listening, I wait, I implore.
      But he comes not. What dell,
      O Erymanthus! from sight
      Of his mother, which of thy glades,
      O Lycæus! conceals
      The happy hunter? He basks
      In youth's pure morning, nor thinks
      On the blood-stain'd home of his birth.
527 *1858*: and numbers   531 *1858*: Sit, and make ready the serpent,
the scourge.

Bring to me safe, let the rest 535
Go as it will! But if this
Clash with justice, the Gods
Forgive my folly, and work
Vengeance on sinner and sin—
Only to me give my child! 540

The Chorus

Hear us and help us, Shade of our King!   *str.* 8.

Merope

A return, O Father! give to thy boy!   *str.* 9.

The Chorus

Send an avenger, Gods of the dead!   *ant.* 8.

Merope

An avenger I ask not—send me my son!   *ant.* 9.

The Chorus

O Queen, for an avenger to appear, 545
Thinking that so I pray'd aright, I pray'd;
If I pray'd wrongly, I revoke the prayer.

Merope

Forgive me, maidens, if I seem too slack
In calling vengeance on a murderer's head.
Impious I deem the alliance which he asks, 550

For 535–40 *1858:*
>Bring to his mother, the rest I commit,
>Willing, patient, to Zeus, to his care.
>Blood I ask not. Enough
>Sated, and more than enough,
>Are mine eyes with blood. But if this,
>O my comforters! strays
>Amiss from Justice, the Gods
>Forgive my folly, and work
>What they will!—but to me give my son!

Requite him words severe for seeming kind,
And righteous, if he falls, I count his fall.
With this, to those unbribed inquisitors
Who in man's inmost bosom sit and judge,
The true avengers these, I leave his deed,   555
By him shown fair, but, I believe, most foul.
If these condemn him, let them pass his doom!
That doom obtain effect, from Gods or men!
So be it; yet will that more solace bring
To the chafed heart of Justice than to mine.   560
To hear another tumult in these streets,
To have another murder in these halls,
To see another mighty victim bleed—
Small comfort offers for a woman there!
A woman, O my friends, has one desire: 565
To see secure, to live with, those she loves.
Can vengeance give me back the murdered? no!
Can it bring home my child? Ah, if it can,
I pray the Furies' ever-restless band,
And pray the Gods, and pray the all-seeing sun: 570
'Sun, who careerest through the height of Heaven,
When o'er the Arcadian forests thou art come,
And see'st my stripling hunter there afield,
Put tightness in thy gold-embossed rein,
And check thy fiery steeds, and, leaning back,   575
Throw him a pealing word of summons down,
To come, a late avenger, to the aid
Of this poor soul who bare him, and his sire.'
If this will bring him back, be this my prayer!
But Vengeance travels in a dangerous way,   580
Double of issue, full of pits and snares
For all who pass, pursuers and pursued—
That way is dubious for a mother's prayer.
Rather on thee I call, Husband beloved—
May Hermes, herald of the dead, convey   585

564 *1858*: There is small comfort for a woman here.   578 *1858*: who bore

My words below to thee, and make thee hear—
Bring back our son! if may be, without blood!
Install him in thy throne, still without blood!
Grant him to reign there wise and just like thee,
More fortunate than thee, more fairly judged!   590
This for our son; and for myself I pray,
Soon, having once beheld him, to descend
Into the quiet gloom, where thou art now.
These words to thine indulgent ear, thy wife,
I send, and these libations pour the while.   595

> [*They make their offerings at the tomb.* MEROPE *then turns to go towards the palace.*

The Chorus

The dead hath now his offerings duly paid.
But whither go'st thou hence, O Queen, away?

Merope

To receive Arcas, who to-day should come,
Bringing me of my boy the annual news.

The Chorus

No certain news if like the rest it run.   600

Merope

Certain in this, that 'tis uncertain still.

The Chorus

What keeps him in Arcadia from return?

Merope

His grandsire and his uncles fear the risk.

The Chorus

Of what? it lies with them to make risk none.

After 595 1858: stage direction, second sentence, reads: MEROPE *then goes towards the palace.*

Merope

Discovery of a visit made by stealth.   605

The Chorus

With arms then they should send him, not by stealth.

Merope

With arms they dare not, and by stealth they fear.

The Chorus

I doubt their caution little suits their ward.

Merope

The heart of youth I know; that most I fear.

The Chorus

I augur thou wilt hear some bold resolve.   610

Merope

I dare not wish it; but, at least, to hear
That my son still survives, in health, in bloom;
To hear that still he loves, still longs for, me,
Yet, with a light uncareworn spirit, turns
Quick from distressful thought, and floats in joy—   615
Thus much from Arcas, my old servant true,
Who saved him from these murderous halls a babe.
And since has fondly watch'd him night and day
Save for this annual charge, I hope to hear.
If this be all, I know not; but I know,   620
These many years I live for this alone.

[MEROPE *goes in.*

The Chorus

Much is there which the sea   *str.* 1.
Conceals from man, who cannot plumb its depths.
Air to his unwing'd form denies a way,
And keeps its liquid solitudes unscaled.   625

Even earth, whereon he treads,
So feeble is his march, so slow,
Holds countless tracts untrod.

But more than all unplumb'd, *ant.* 1.
Unscaled, untrodden, is the heart of man. 630
More than all secrets hid, the way it keeps.
Nor any of our organs so obtuse,
Inaccurate, and frail,
As those wherewith we try to test
Feelings and motives there. 635

Yea, and not only have we not explored *str.* 2.
That wide and various world, the heart of others,
But even our own heart, that narrow world
Bounded in our own breast, we hardly know,
Of our own actions dimly trace the causes. 640
Whether a natural obscureness, hiding
That region in perpetual cloud,
Or our own want of effort, be the bar.

Therefore—while acts are from their motives judged, *ant.* 2.
And to one act many most unlike motives, 645
This pure, that guilty, may have each impell'd—
Power fails us to try clearly if that cause
Assign'd us by the actor be the true one;
Power fails the man himself to fix distinctly
The cause which drew him to his deed, 650
And stamp himself, thereafter, bad or good.

The most are bad, wise men have said. *str.* 3.
Let the best rule, they say again.
The best, then, to dominion hath the right.
Rights unconceded and denied, 655
Surely, if rights, may be by force asserted—
May be, nay should, if for the general weal.
The best, then, to the throne may carve his way,
And strike opposers down,

634 *1858*: those with which   654 *1858*: have the right
659 *1858*: And hew

352

Free from all guilt of lawlessness,   660
Or selfish lust of personal power;
Bent only to serve virtue,
Bent to diminish wrong.

And truly, in this ill-ruled world,   *ant.* 3.
Well sometimes may the good desire   665
To give to virtue her dominion due!
Well may he long to interrupt
The reign of folly, usurpation ever,
Though fenced by sanction of a thousand years!
Well thirst to drag the wrongful ruler down;   670
Well purpose to pen back
Into the narrow path of right
The ignorant, headlong multitude,
Who blindly follow, ever,
Blind leaders, to their bane!   675

But who can say, without a fear: *str.* 4.
That best, who ought to rule, am I;
The mob, who ought to obey, are these;
I the one righteous, they the many bad?
Who, without check of conscience, can aver   680
That he to power makes way by arms,
Sheds blood, imprisons, banishes, attaints,
Commits all deeds the guilty oftenest do,
Without a single guilty thought,
Arm'd for right only, and the general good?   685

Therefore, with censure unallay'd,   *ant.* 4.
Therefore, with unexcepting ban,
Zeus and pure-thoughted Justice brand
Imperious self-asserting violence;
Sternly condemn the too bold man, who dares   690
Elect himself Heaven's destined arm;
And, knowing well man's inmost heart infirm,
However noble the committer be,

667 *1858*: they long

His grounds however specious shown,
Turn with averted eyes from deeds of blood.   695

Thus, though a woman, I was school'd   *epode.*
By those whom I revere.
Whether I learnt their lessons well,
Or, having learnt them, well apply
To what hath in this house befall'n,   700
If in the event be any proof,
The event will quickly show.

[Æpytus *comes in.*

Æpytus

Maidens, assure me if they told me true
Who told me that the royal house was here.

The Chorus

Rightly they told thee, and thou art arrived.   705

Æpytus

Here, then, it is, where Polyphontes dwells?

The Chorus

He doth; thou hast both house and master right.

Æpytus

Might some one straight inform him he is sought?

The Chorus

Inform him that thyself, for here he comes.

[POLYPHONTES *comes forth, with* ATTENDANTS *and*
GUARDS.

Æpytus

O King, all hail! I come with weighty news;   710
Most likely, grateful; but, in all case, sure.

Polyphontes

Speak them, that I may judge their kind myself.

Æpytus

Accept them in one word, for good or bad:
Æpytus, the Messenian prince, is dead!

Polyphontes

Dead!—and when died he? where? and by what hand?   715
And who art thou, who bringest me such news?

Æpytus

He perish'd in Arcadia, where he dwelt
With Cypselus; and two days since he died.
One of the train of Cypselus am I.

Polyphontes

Instruct me of the manner of his death.   720

Æpytus

That will I do, and to this end I came.
For, being of like age, of birth not mean,
The son of an Arcadian noble, I
Was chosen his companion from a boy;
And on the hunting-rambles which his heart,   725
Unquiet, drove him ever to pursue
Through all the lordships of the Arcadian dales,
From chief to chief, I wander'd at his side,
The captain of his squires, and his guard.
On such a hunting-journey, three morns since,   730
With beaters, hounds, and huntsmen, he and I
Set forth from Tegea, the royal town.
The prince at start seem'd sad, but his regard
Clear'd with blithe travel and the morning air.
We rode from Tegea, through the woods of oaks,   735
Past Arnê spring, where Rhea gave the babe
Poseidon to the shepherd-boys to hide
From Saturn's search among the new-yean'd lambs,
To Mantineia, with its unbaked walls;

717 *1858*: where he liv'd   739 *1858*: To Mantinea

Thence, by the Sea-God's Sanctuary and the tomb   740
Whither from wintry Mænalus were brought
The bones of Arcas, whence our race is named,
On, to the marshy Orchomenian plain,
And the Stone Coffins;—then, by Caphyæ Cliffs,
To Pheneos with its craggy citadel.   745
There, with the chief of that hill-town, we lodged
One night; and the next day at dawn fared on
By the Three Fountains and the Adder's Hill
To the Stymphalian Lake, our journey's end,
To draw the coverts on Cyllenê's side.   750
There, on a high green spur which bathes its point
Far in the liquid lake, we sate, and drew
Cates from our hunters' pouch, Arcadian fare,
Sweet chestnuts, barley-cakes, and boar's-flesh dried;
And as we ate, and rested there, we talk'd   755
Of places we had pass'd, sport we had had,
Of beasts of chase that haunt the Arcadian hills,
Wild hog, and bear, and mountain-deer, and roe;
Last, of our quarters with the Arcadian chiefs.
For courteous entertainment, welcome warm,   760
Sad, reverential homage, had our prince
From all, for his great lineage and his woes;
All which he own'd, and praised with grateful mind.
But still over his speech a gloom there hung,
As of one shadow'd by impending death;   765
And strangely, as we talk'd, he would apply
The story of spots mention'd to his own;
Telling us, Arnê minded him, he too
Was saved a babe, but to a life obscure,
Which he, the seed of Heracles, dragg'd on   770
Inglorious, and should drop at last unknown,
Even as those dead unepitaph'd, who lie
In the stone coffins at Orchomenus.
And, then, he bade remember how we pass'd

751 *1858*: There, on a grassy spur which bathes its root

The Mantineän Sanctuary, forbid
To foot of mortal, where his ancestor,   775
Named Æpytus like him, having gone in,
Was blinded by the outgushing springs of brine.
Then, turning westward to the Adder's Hill—
Another ancestor, named, too, like me,   780
Died of a snake-bite, said he, *on that brow;*
Still at his mountain-tomb men marvel, built
Where, as life ebb'd, his bearers laid him down.
So he play'd on; then ended, with a smile:
This region is not happy for my race.   785
We cheer'd him; but, that moment, from the copse
By the lake-edge, broke the sharp cry of hounds;
The prickers shouted that the stag was gone.
We sprang upon our feet, we snatch'd our spears,
We bounded down the swarded slope, we plunged   790
Through the dense ilex-thickets to the dogs.
Far in the woods ahead their music rang;
And many times that morn we coursed in ring
The forests round that belt Cyllenê's side;
Till I, thrown out and tired, came to halt   795
On that same spur where we had sate at morn.
And resting there to breathe, I watch'd the chase—
Rare, straggling hunters, foil'd by brake and crag,
And the prince, single, pressing on the rear
Of that unflagging quarry and the hounds.   800
Now in the woods far down I saw them cross
An open glade; now he was high aloft
On some tall scar fringed with dark feathery pines,
Peering to spy a goat-track down the cliff,
Cheering with hand, and voice, and horn his dogs.   805
At last the cry drew to the water's edge—
And through the brushwood, to the pebbly strand,
Broke, black with sweat, the antler'd mountain-stag,
And took the lake. Two hounds alone pursued,

775 *1858*: Mantinean   794 *1858*: which belt   796 *1858*: the same
797 *1858*: I saw below

Then came the prince; he shouted and plunged in.   810
—There is a chasm rifted in the base
Of that unfooted precipice, whose rock
Walls on one side the deep Stymphalian Lake;
There the lake-waters, which in ages gone
Wash'd, as the marks upon the hills still show,   815
All the Stymphalian plain, are now suck'd down.
A headland, with one aged plane-tree crown'd,
Parts from this cave-pierced cliff the shelving bay
Where first the chase plunged in; the bay is smooth,
But round the headland's point a current sets,   820
Strong, black, tempestuous, to the cavern-mouth,
Stoutly, under the headland's lee, they swam;
But when they came abreast the point, the race
Caught them as wind takes feathers, whirl'd them round
Struggling in vain to cross it, swept them on,   825
Stag, dogs, and hunter, to the yawning gulph.
All this, O King, not piecemeal, as to thee
Now told, but in one flashing instant pass'd.
While from the turf whereon I lay I sprang
And took three strides, quarry and dogs were gone;   830
A moment more—I saw the prince turn round
Once in the black and arrowy race, and cast
An arm aloft for help; then sweep beneath
The low-brow'd cavern-arch, and disappear.
And what I could, I did—to call by cries   835
Some straggling hunters to my aid, to rouse
Fishers who live on the lake-side, to launch
Boats, and approach, near as we dared, the chasm.
But of the prince nothing remain'd, save this,
His boar-spear's broken shaft, back on the lake   840
Cast by the rumbling subterranean stream;
And this, at landing spied by us and saved,
His broad-brimm'd hunter's hat, which, in the bay,
Where first the stag took water, floated still.
And I across the mountains brought with haste   845

818 *1858*: the cave-pierc'd   833 *1858*: One arm

To Cypselus, at Basilis, this news—
Basilis, his new city, which he now
Near Lycosura builds, Lycaon's town,
First city founded on the earth by men.
He to thee sends me on, in one thing glad,   850
While all else grieves him, that his grandchild's death
Extinguishes distrust 'twixt him and thee.
But I from our deplored mischance learn this:
The man who to untimely death is doom'd,
Vainly you hedge him from the assault of harm;   855
He bears the seed of ruin in himself.

The Chorus

So dies the last shoot of our royal tree!
Who shall tell Merope this heavy news?

Polyphontes

Stranger, this news thou bringest is too great
For instant comment, having many sides   860
Of import, and in silence best received,
Whether it turn at last to joy or woe.
But thou, the zealous bearer, hast no part
In what it hath of painful, whether now,
First heard, or in its future issue shown.   865
Thou for thy labour hast deserved our best
Refreshment, needed by thee, as I judge,
With mountain-travel and night-watching spent.—
To the guest-chamber lead him, some one! give
All entertainment which a traveller needs,   870
And such as fits a royal house to show;
To friends, still more, and labourers in our cause.

[ATTENDANTS *conduct* ÆPYTUS *within the palace.*

The Chorus

The youth is gone within; alas! he bears
A presence sad for some one through those doors.

859 *1858*: the news   864 *1858*: it has

Polyphontes

Admire then, maidens, how in one short hour 875
The schemes, pursued in vain for twenty years,
Are—by a stroke, though undesired, complete—
Crown'd with success, not in my way, but Heaven's!
This at a moment, too, when I had urged
A last, long-cherish'd project, in my aim 880
Of peace, and been repulsed with hate and scorn.
Fair terms of reconcilement, equal rule,
I offer'd to my foes, and they refused;
Worse terms than mine they have obtain'd from Heaven.
Dire is this blow for Merope; and I 885
Wish'd, truly wish'd, solution to our broil
Other than by this death; but it hath come!
I speak no word of boast, but this I say:
A private loss here founds a nation's peace.

[POLYPHONTES *goes out.*

The Chorus

Peace, who tarriest too long; *str.* 890
Peace, with delight in thy train;
Come, come back to our prayer!
Then shall the revel again
Visit our streets, and the sound
Of the harp be heard with the pipe, 895
When the flashing torches appear
In the marriage-train coming on,
With dancing maidens and boys—
While the matrons come to the doors,
And the old men rise from their bench, 900
When the youths bring home the bride.

Not condemn'd by my voice *ant.*
He who restores thee shall be,
Not unfavour'd by Heaven.

881 *1858*: Of concord, and been baffled with disdain. 902 *1858*: Not
decried

Surely no sinner the man,   905
Dread though his acts, to whose hand
Such a boon to bring hath been given.
Let her come, fair Peace! let her come!
But the demons long nourish'd here,
Murder, Discord, and Hate,   910
In the stormy desolate waves
Of the Thracian Sea let her leave,
Or the howling outermost main!

[MEROPE *comes forth.*

Merope

A whisper through the palace flies of one
Arrived from Tegea with weighty news;   915
And I came, thinking to find Arcas here.
Ye have not left this gate, which he must pass;
Tell me—hath one not come? or, worse mischance,
Come, but been intercepted by the King?

The Chorus

A messenger, sent from Arcadia here,   920
Arrived, and of the King had speech but now.

Merope

Ah me! the wrong expectant got his news.

The Chorus

The message brought was for the King design'd.

Merope

How so? was Arcas not the messenger?

The Chorus

A younger man, and of a different name.   925

Merope

And what Arcadian news had he to tell?

MEROPE

The Chorus

Learn that from other lips, O Queen, than mine.

Merope

He kept his tale, then, for the King alone?

The Chorus

His tale was meeter for that ear than thine.

Merope

Why dost thou falter, and make half reply?   930

The Chorus

O thrice unhappy, how I groan thy fate!

Merope

Thou frightenest and confound'st me by thy words.
O were but Arcas come, all would be well!

The Chorus

If so, all's well: for look, the old man speeds
Up from the city tow'rd this gated hill.   935

[ARCAS *comes in.*

Merope

Not with the failing breath and foot of age
My faithful follower comes. Welcome, old friend!

Arcas

Faithful, not welcome, when my tale is told.
O that my over-speed and bursting grief
Had on the journey choked my labouring breath,   940
And lock'd my speech for ever in my breast!
Yet then another man would bring this news,
Wherewith from end to end Arcadia rings.—
O honour'd Queen, thy son, my charge, is gone.

935 *1858*: tow'rds this   943 *First inserted in 1885.*

MEROPE

The Chorus

Too suddenly thou tellest such a loss.   945
Look up, O Queen! look up, O mistress dear!
Look up, and see thy friends who comfort thee.

Merope

Ah ... Ah ... Ah me!

The Chorus

              And I, too, say, ah me!

Arcas

Forgive, forgive the bringer of such news!

Merope

Better from thine than from an enemy's tongue.   950

The Chorus

And yet no enemy did this, O Queen:
But the wit-baffling will and hand of Heaven.

Arcas

No enemy! and what hast thou, then, heard?
Swift as I came, hath falsehood been before?

The Chorus

A youth arrived but now—the son, he said,   955
Of an Arcadian lord—our prince's friend—
Jaded with travel, clad in hunter's garb.
He brought report that his own eyes had seen
The prince, in chase after a swimming stag,
Swept down a chasm rifted in the cliff   960
Which hangs o'er the Stymphalian Lake, and drown'd.

Arcas

Ah me! with what a foot doth treason post,
While loyalty, with all her speed, is slow!

960 *1858*: chasm broken

Another tale, I trow, thy messenger
For the King's private ear reserves, like this   965
In one thing only, that the prince is dead.

The Chorus

And how then runs this true and private tale?

Arcas

As much to the King's wish, more to his shame,
This young Arcadian noble, guard and mate
To Æpytus, the king seduced with gold,   970
And had him at the prince's side in leash,
Ready to slip on his unconscious prey.
He on a hunting party two days since,
Among the forests on Cyllenê's side,
Perform'd good service for his bloody wage;   975
Our prince, and the good Laias, whom his ward
Had in a father's place, he basely murder'd.
'Tis so, 'tis so, alas, for see the proof:
Uncle and nephew disappear; their death
Is charged against this stripling; agents, fee'd   980
To ply 'twixt the Messenian king and him,
Come forth, denounce the traffic and the traitor.
Seized, he escapes—and next I find him here.
Take this for true, the other tale for feign'd.

973 *1858*: three days   976 *1858*: The prince, his uncle Laias, whom
978–80 *First inserted in 1885.*   981–3 *Altered from part of 1858 text
otherwise omitted in 1885 (see below, after line 985).*   *Between 984 and 986
1858:*

The Chorus
And this perfidious murder who reveal'd?

Arcas
The faithless murderer's own, no other tongue.

The Chorus
Did conscience goad him to denounce himself?

Arcas
To Cypselus at Basilis he brought
This strange unlikely tale, the prince was drown'd.

The Chorus
But not a word appears of murder here.

The Chorus

The youth, thou say'st, we saw and heard but now—   985

Arcas

He comes to tell his prompter he hath sped.

The Chorus

Still he repeats the drowning story here.

Arcas

To thee—that needs no Œdipus to explain.

The Chorus

Interpret, then; for we, it seems, are dull.

Arcas

Your King desired the profit of his death,   990
Not the black credit of his murderer.
That stern word '*murder*' had too dread a sound
For the Messenian hearts, who loved the prince.

The Chorus

Suspicion grave I see, but no firm proof.

Merope

Peace! peace! all's clear.—The wicked watch and work   995

Arcas
Examin'd close, he own'd this story false.
Then evidence came—his comrades of the hunt,
Who saw the prince and Laias last with him,
Never again in life—next, agents, fee'd
To ply 'twixt the Messenian king and him,
Spoke, and reveal'd that traffic, and the traitor.
So charg'd, he stood dumb-founder'd: Cypselus,
On this suspicion, cast him into chains.
Thence he escap'd—and next I find him here.
The Chorus
His presence with the King, thou mean'st, implies—

985 *First inserted in 1885.*   994 *1858*: clear proof.

While the good sleep; the workers have the day.
Yes! yes! now I conceive the liberal grace
Of this far-scheming tyrant and his boon
Of heirship to his kingdom for my son:
He had his murderer ready, and the sword   1000
Lifted, and that unwish'd-for heirship void—
A tale, meanwhile, forged for his subjects' ears—
And me, henceforth sole rival with himself
In their allegiance, me, in my son's death-hour,
When all turn'd tow'rds me, me he would have shown   1005
To my Messenians, duped, disarm'd, despised,
The willing sharer of his guilty rule,
All claim to succour forfeit, to myself
Hateful, by each Messenian heart abhorr'd.
His offers I repell'd—but what of that?   1010
If with no rage, no fire of righteous hate,
Such as ere now hath spurr'd to fearful deeds
Weak women with a thousandth part my wrongs,
But calm, but unresentful, I endured
His offers, coldly heard them, cold repell'd?   1015
How much men think me abject, void of heart,
While all this time I bear to linger on
In this blood-deluged palace, in whose halls
Either a vengeful Fury I should stalk,
Or else not live at all!—but here I haunt,   1020
A pale, unmeaning ghost, powerless to fright
Or harm, and nurse my longing for my son,
A helpless one, I know it—but the Gods
Have temper'd me e'en thus, and, in some souls,
Misery, which rouses others, breaks the spring.   1025
And even now, my son, ah me! my son,
Fain would I fade away, as I have lived,

Between 996 and 997 1858:

> He who was sent hath sped, and now comes back,
> To chuckle with his sender o'er the game
> Which foolish innocence plays with subtle guilt.

997 *1858*: Ah! now I comprehend the liberal grace   1016 *First inserted in 1885*.

Without a cry, a struggle, or a blow,
All vengeance unattempted, and descend
To the invisible plains, to roam with thee,   1030
Fit denizen, the lampless under-world——
But with what eyes should I encounter there
My husband, wandering with his stern compeers,
Amphiaraos, or Mycenæ's king,
Who led the Greeks to Ilium, Agamemnon,   1035
Betray'd like him, but, not like him, avenged?
Or with what voice shall I the questions meet
Of my two elder sons, slain long ago,
Who sadly ask me, what, if not revenge,
Kept me, their mother, from their side so long?   1040
Or how reply to thee, my child last-born,
Last-murder'd, who reproachfully wilt say:
Mother, I well believed thou lived'st on
In the detested palace of thy foe,
With patience on thy face, death in thy heart,   1045
Counting, till I grew up, the laggard years,
That our joint hands might then together pay
To our unhappy house the debt we owe.
My death makes my debt void, and doubles thine—
But down thou fleest here, and leav'st our scourge   1050
Triumphant, and condemnest all our race
To lie in gloom for ever unappeased.
What shall I have to answer to such words?—
No, something must be dared; and, great as erst
Our dastard patience, be our daring now!   1055
Come, ye swift Furies, who to him ye haunt
Permit no peace till your behests are done;
Come Hermes, who dost friend the unjustly kill'd,
And can'st teach simple ones to plot and feign;
Come, lightning Passion, that with foot of fire   1060
Advancest to the middle of a deed
Almost before 'tis plann'd; come, glowing Hate;
Come, baneful Mischief, from thy murky den

1048 *1858*: To one unhappy   1058 *1858*: dost watch

Under the dripping black Tartarean cliff
Which Styx's awful waters trickle down—   1065
Inspire this coward heart, this flagging arm!
How say ye, maidens, do ye know these prayers?
Are these words Merope's—is this voice mine?
Old man, old man, thou had'st my boy in charge,
And he is lost, and thou hast that to atone!   1070
Fly, find me on the instant where confer
The murderer and his impious setter-on—
And ye, keep faithful silence, friends, and mark
What one weak woman can achieve alone.

Arcas

O mistress, by the Gods, do nothing rash!   1075

Merope

Unfaithful servant, dost thou, too, desert me?

Arcas

I go! I go!—The King holds council—there
Will I seek tidings. Take, the while, this word:
Attempting deeds beyond thy power to do,
Thou nothing profitest thy friends, but mak'st   1080
Our misery more, and thine own ruin sure.

[ARCAS *goes out.*

The Chorus

I have heard, O Queen, how a prince,   *str.* 1.
Agamemnon's son, in Mycenæ,
Orestes, died but in name,
Lived for the death of his foes.   1085

Merope

Peace!

The Chorus

What is it?

1077–8 *In 1858 one line only*: I go! I go!—yet, Queen, take this one word:

Merope

Alas,

Thou destroyest me!

The Chorus

How?

Merope

Whispering hope of a life
Which no stranger unknown,
But the faithful servant and nurse,   **1090**
Whose tears warrant his truth,
Bears sad witness is lost.

The Chorus

Wheresoe'er men are, there is grief.   *ant.* **1.**
In a thousand countries, a thousand
Homes, e'en now is there wail;   **1095**
Mothers lamenting their sons.

Merope

Yes——

The Chorus

Thou knowest it?

Merope

This,

Who lives, witnesses.

The Chorus

True.

Merope

But is it only a fate
Sure, all-common, to lose   **1100**
In a land of friends, by a friend,
One last, murder-saved child?

1090 *1858*: and guard,

MEROPE

The Chorus

Merope

Thou confessest the prize
In the rushing, thundering, mad,   **1105**
Cloud-enveloped, obscure,
Unapplauded, unsung
Race of calamity, mine?

The Chorus

None can truly claim that
Mournful preëminence, not   **1110**
Thou.

Merope

Fate *gives* it, ah me!

The Chorus

Not, above all, in the doubts,
Double and clashing, that hang——

Merope

What then?   *ant.* 2.
Seems it lighter, my loss,   **1115**
If, perhaps, unpierced by the sword,
My child lies in his jagg'd
Sunless prison of rock,
On the black wave borne to and fro?

The Chorus

Worse, far worse, if his friend,   **1120**
If the Arcadian within,
If——

Merope (with a start)

How say'st thou? within? . . .

1117 *1858*: in a jagg'd   **1118** *1858*: of rocks

The Chorus

He in the guest-chamber now,
Faithlessly murder'd his friend.

Merope

Ye, too, ye, too, join to betray, then   1125
Your Queen!

The Chorus
What is this?

Merope
Ye knew,

O false friends! into what
Haven the murderer had dropp'd?
Ye kept silence?

The Chorus
In fear,
O loved mistress! in fear,   1130
Dreading thine over-wrought mood,
What I knew, I conceal'd.

Merope

Swear by the Gods henceforth to obey me!

The Chorus

Unhappy one, what deed
Purposes thy despair?   1135
I promise; but I fear.

Merope

From the altar, the unavenged tomb,
Fetch me the sacrifice-axe!——

    [THE CHORUS *goes towards the tomb of* CRESPHONTES,
      and their leader brings back the axe.

O Husband, O clothed
With the grave's everlasting,   1140

All-covering darkness! O King,
Well-mourn'd, but ill-avenged!
Approv'st thou thy wife now?——
The axe!—who brings it?

The Chorus

'Tis here!
But thy gesture, thy look,   1145
Appals me, shakes me with awe.

Merope

Thrust back now the bolt of that door!

The Chorus

Alas! alas!—
Behold the fastenings withdrawn
Of the guest-chamber door!—   1150
Ah! I beseech thee—with tears—

Merope

Throw the door open!

The Chorus

'Tis done! . . .

[*The door of the house is thrown open: the interior of the
guest-chamber is discovered, with* ÆPYTUS *asleep on
a couch.*

Merope

He sleeps—sleeps calm. O ye all-seeing Gods!
Thus peacefully do ye let sinners sleep,
While troubled innocents toss, and lie awake?   1155
What sweeter sleep than this could I desire
For thee, my child, if thou wert yet alive?
How often have I dream'd of thee like this,
With thy soil'd hunting-coat, and sandals torn,
Asleep in the Arcadian glens at noon,   1160

Thy head droop'd softly, and the golden curls
Clustering o'er thy white forehead, like a girl's;
The short proud lip showing thy race, thy cheeks
Brown'd with thine open-air, free, hunter's life.
Ah me!   1165
And where dost thou sleep now, my innocent boy?—
In some dark fir-tree's shadow, amid rocks
Untrodden, on Cyllenê's desolate side;
Where travellers never pass, where only come
Wild beasts, and vultures sailing overhead.   1170
There, there thou liest now, my hapless child!
Stretch'd among briars and stones, the slow, black gore
Oozing through thy soak'd hunting-shirt, with limbs
Yet stark from the death-struggle, tight-clench'd hands,
And eyeballs staring for revenge in vain.   1175
Ah miserable!
And thou, thou fair-skinn'd Serpent! thou art laid
In a rich chamber, on a happy bed,
In a king's house, thy victim's heritage;
And drink'st untroubled slumber, to sleep off   1180
The toils of thy foul service, till thou wake
Refresh'd, and claim thy master's thanks and gold.—
Wake up in hell from thine unhallow'd sleep,
Thou smiling Fiend, and claim thy guerdon there!
Wake amid gloom, and howling, and the noise   1185
Of sinners pinion'd on the torturing wheel,
And the stanch Furies' never-silent scourge.
And bid the chief tormentors there provide
For a grand culprit shortly coming down.
Go thou the first, and usher in thy lord!   1190
A more just stroke than that thou gav'st my son
Take——

> [MEROPE *advances towards the sleeping* ÆPYTUS, *with the*
> *axe uplifted. At the same moment* ARCAS *re-enters.*

Interrupting line 1192 *1858: stage direction, second sentence reads*: *At the same*
moment ARCAS *returns*

Arcas (to the Chorus)

     Not with him to council did the King
Carry his messenger, but left him here.

                   [*Sees* MEROPE *and* ÆPYTUS.

O Gods! . . .

Merope

          Foolish old man, thou spoil'st my blow!

Arcas

What do I see? . . .

Merope

          A murderer at death's door.   1195
Therefore no words!

Arcas

        A murderer? . . .

Merope

               And a captive
To the dear next-of-kin of him he murder'd.
Stand, and let vengeance pass!

Arcas

         Hold, O Queen, hold!
Thou know'st not whom thou strik'st . . .

Merope

               I know his crime.

Arcas

Unhappy one! thou strik'st——

Merope

            A most just blow.   1200

Arcas

No, by the Gods, thou slay'st——

Merope

Stand off!

Arcas

Thy son!

Merope

Ah!...

[*She lets the axe drop, and falls insensible.*

Æpytus (*awaking*)

Who are these? What shrill, ear-piercing scream
Wakes me thus kindly from the perilous sleep
Wherewith fatigue and youth had bound mine eyes,
Even in the deadly palace of my foe?—   1205
Arcas! Thou here?

Arcas (*embracing him*)

O my dear master! O
My child, my charge beloved, welcome to life!
As dead we held thee, mourn'd for thee as dead.

Æpytus

In word I died, that I in deed might live.
But who are these?

Arcas

Messenian maidens, friends.   1210

Æpytus

And, Arcas!—but I tremble!

Arcas

Boldly ask.

Æpytus

That black-robed, swooning figure? ...

Arcas

Merope.

Æpytus

O mother! mother!

Merope

Who upbraids me? Ah! ...

[*seeing the axe.*

Æpytus

Upbraids thee? no one.

Merope

Thou dost well: but take ...

Æpytus

What wav'st thou off?

Merope

That murderous axe away!   1215

Æpytus

Thy son is here.

Merope

One said so, sure, but now.

Æpytus

Here, here thou hast him!

Merope

Slaughter'd by this hand! ...

Æpytus

No, by the Gods, alive and like to live!

Merope

What, thou?—I dream——

Æpytus

May'st thou dream ever so!

Merope (advancing towards him)

My child? unhurt? . . .

Æpytus

Only by over joy.   1220

Merope

Art thou, then, come? . . .

Æpytus

Never to part again.

[*They fall into one another's arms.   Then* MEROPE, *holding* ÆPYTUS *by the hand, turns to* THE CHORUS.

Merope

O kind Messenian maidens, O my friends,
Bear witness, see, mark well, on what a head
My first stroke of revenge had nearly fallen!

The Chorus

We see, dear mistress: and we say, the Gods,   1225
As hitherto they kept him, keep him now.

Merope

O my son!   *str.*
I have, I have thee . . . the years
Fly back, my child! and thou seem'st
Ne'er to have gone from these eyes,   1230
Never been torn from this breast.

377

Æpytus

Mother, my heart runs over; but the time
Presses me, chides me, will not let me weep.

Merope

Fearest thou now?

Æpytus

I fear not, but I think on my design. 1235

Merope

At the undried fount of this breast,
A babe, thou smilest again.
Thy brothers play at my feet,
Early-slain innocents! near,
Thy kind-speaking father stands. 1240

Æpytus

Remember, to revenge his death I come!

Merope

Ah . . . revenge! *ant.*
That word! it kills me! I see
Once more roll back on my house,
Never to ebb, the accurst 1245
All-flooding ocean of blood.

Æpytus

Mother, sometimes the justice of the Gods
Appoints the way to peace through shedding blood.

Merope

Sorrowful peace!

Æpytus

And yet the only peace to us allow'd. 1250

Merope

From the first-wrought vengeance is born
A long succession of crimes.
Fresh blood flows, calling for blood.
Fathers, sons, grandsons, are all
One death-dealing vengeful train.   1255

Æpytus

Mother, thy fears are idle; for I come
To close an old wound, not to open new.
In all else willing to be taught, in this
Instruct me not; I have my lesson clear.—
Arcas, seek out my uncle Laias, now   1260
Conferring in the city with our friends;
Here bring him, ere the king come back from council.
That, how to accomplish what the Gods enjoin,
And the slow-ripening time at last prepares,
We two with thee, my mother, may consult;   1265
For whose help dare I count on, if not thine?

Merope

Approves my brother Laias this intent?

Æpytus

Yes, and alone is with me here to share.

Merope

And what of thine Arcadian mate, who bears
Suspicion from thy grandsire of thy death,   1270
For whom, as I suppose, thou passest here?

Æpytus

Sworn to our plot he is; if false surmise
Fix him the author of my death, I know not.

1261 *1858*: Concerting in   1267 *1858*: this design?   1272 *1858*:
but, that surmise   1273 *1858*: Fix'd him the author of my death, I
knew not.

Merope

Proof, not surmise, shows him in commerce close——

Æpytus

With this Messenian tyrant—that I know.   1275

Merope

And entertain'st thou, child, such dangerous friends?

Æpytus

This commerce for my best behoof he plies.

Merope

That thou may'st read thine enemy's counsel plain?

Æpytus

Too dear his secret wiles have cost our house.

Merope

And of his unsure agent what demands he?   1280

Æpytus

News of my business, pastime, temper, friends.

Merope

His messages, then, point not to thy murder?

Æpytus

Not yet, though such, no doubt, his final aim.

Merope

And what Arcadian helpers bring'st thou here?

Æpytus

Laias alone; no errand mine for crowds.   1285

Merope

On what relying, to crush such a foe?

Æpytus

One sudden stroke, and the Messenians' love.

Merope

O thou long-lost, long seen in dreams alone,
But now seen face to face, my only child!
Why wilt thou fly to lose as soon as found   1290
My new-won treasure, thy belovéd life?
Or how expectest not to lose, who com'st
With such slight means to cope with such a foe?
Thine enemy thou know'st not, nor his strength.
The stroke thou purposest is desperate, rash—
Yet grant that it succeeds—thou hast behind   1295
The stricken king a second enemy
Scarce dangerous less than him, the Dorian lords.
These are not now the savage band who erst
Follow'd thy father from their northern hills,   1300
Mere ruthless and uncounsell'd wolves of war,
Good to obey, without a leader nought.
Their chief hath train'd them, made them like himself,
Sagacious, men of iron, watchful, firm,
Against surprise and sudden panic proof.   1305
Their master fall'n, these will not flinch, but band
To keep their master's power; thou wilt find
Behind his corpse their hedge of serried spears.
But, to match these, thou hast the people's love?
On what a reed, my child, thou leanest there!   1310
Knowest thou not how timorous, how unsure,
How useless an ally a people is
Against the one and certain arm of power?
Thy father perish'd in this people's cause,
Perish'd before their eyes, yet no man stirr'd!   1315
For years, his widow, in their sight I stand,
A never-changing index to revenge—
What help, what vengeance, at their hands have I?—
At least, if thou wilt trust them, try them first.

1301 *1858*: tools of war

Against the King himself array the host   1320
Thou countest on to back thee 'gainst his lords;
First rally the Messenians to thy cause,
Give them cohesion, purpose, and resolve,
Marshal them to an army—then advance,
Then try the issue; and not, rushing on   1325
Single and friendless, give to certain death
That dear-beloved, that young, that gracious head.
Be guided, O my son! spurn counsel not!
For know thou this, a violent heart hath been
Fatal to all the race of Heracles.   1330

The Chorus

With sage experience she speaks; and thou,
O Æpytus, weigh well her counsel given.

Æpytus

Ill counsel, in my judgment, gives she here,
Maidens, and reads experience much amiss;
Discrediting the succour which our cause   1335
Might from the people draw, if rightly used;
Advising us a course which would, indeed,
If follow'd, make their succour slack and null.
A people is no army, train'd to fight,
A passive engine, at their general's will;   1340
And, if so used, proves, as thou say'st, unsure.
A people, like a common man, is dull,
Is lifeless, while its heart remains untouch'd;
A fool can drive it, and a fly may scare.
When it admires and loves, its heart awakes: 1345
Then irresistibly it lives, it works;
A people, then, is an ally indeed—
It is ten thousand fiery wills in one.
Now I, if I invite them to run risk
Of life for my advantage, and myself,   1350
Who chiefly profit, run no more than they—
How shall I rouse their love, their ardour so?

1326 *1858*: throw to

382

But, if some signal, unassisted stroke,
Dealt at my own sole risk, before their eyes,
Announces me their rightful prince return'd——   1355
The undegenerate blood of Heracles——
The daring claimant of a perilous throne——
How might not such a sight as this revive
Their loyal passion tow'rd my father's house,
Kindle their hearts, make them no more a mob,   1360
A craven mob, but a devouring fire?
Then might I use them, then, for one who thus
Spares not himself, themselves they will not spare.
Haply, had but one daring soul stood forth
To rally them and lead them to revenge,   1365
When my great father fell, they had replied!
Alas! our foe alone stood forward then.
And thou, my mother, hadst thou made a sign——
Hadst thou, from thy forlorn and captive state
Of widowhood in these polluted halls,   1370
Thy prison-house, raised one imploring cry——
Who knows but that avengers thou hadst found?
But mute thou sat'st, and each Messenian heart
In thy despondency desponded too.
Enough of this!—Though not a finger stir   1375
To succour me in my extremest need;
Though all free spirits in this land were dead,
And only slaves and tyrants left alive;
Yet for me, mother, I had liefer die
On native ground, than drag the tedious hours   1380
Of a protected exile any more.
Hate, duty, interest, passion call one way;
Here stand I now, and the attempt shall be.

The Chorus

Prudence is on the other side; but deeds
Condemn'd by prudence have sometimes gone well.   1385

1360 *1858*: Electrify their hearts? make them no more   1377 *1858*:
be dead,

Merope

Not till the ways of prudence all are tried,
And tried in vain, the turn of rashness comes.
Thou leapest to thy deed, and hast not ask'd
Thy kinsfolk and thy father's friends for aid.

Æpytus

And to what friends should I for aid apply?　　　　1390

Merope

The royal race of Temenus, in Argos——

Æpytus

That house, like ours, intestine murder maims.

Merope

Thy Spartan cousins, Procles and his brother——

Æpytus

Love a won cause, but not a cause to win.

Merope

My father, then, and his Arcadian chiefs——　　　　1395

Æpytus

Mean still to keep aloof from Dorian broil.

Merope

Wait, then, until sufficient help appears.

Æpytus

Orestes in Mycenæ had no more.

Merope

He to fulfil an order raised his hand.

Æpytus

What order more precise had he than I?　　　　1400

Merope

Apollo peal'd it from his Delphian cave.

Æpytus

A mother's murder needed hest divine.

Merope

He had a hest, at least, and thou hast none.

Æpytus

The Gods command not where the heart speaks clear.

Merope

Thou wilt destroy, I see, thyself and us.   1405

Æpytus

O suffering! O calamity! how ten,
How twentyfold worse are ye, when your blows
Not only wound the sense, but kill the soul,
The noble thought, which is alone the man!
That I, to-day returning, find myself   1410
Orphan'd of both my parents—by his foes
My father, by your strokes my mother slain!
For this is not my mother, who dissuades,
At the dread altar of her husband's tomb,
His son from vengeance on his murderer;   1415
And not alone dissuades him, but compares
His just revenge to an unnatural deed,
A deed so awful, that the general tongue
Fluent of horrors, falters to relate it—
Of darkness so tremendous, that its author,   1420
Though to his act empower'd, nay, impell'd,
By the oracular sentence of the Gods,
Fled, for years after, o'er the face of earth,
A frenzied wanderer, a God-driven man,
And hardly yet, some say, hath found a grave—   1425
With such a deed as *this* thou matchest mine,

o   *385*

Which Nature sanctions, which the innocent blood
Clamours to find fulfill'd, which good men praise,
And only bad men joy to see undone!
O honour'd father! hide thee in thy grave   1430
Deep as thou canst, for hence no succour comes;
Since from thy faithful subjects what revenge
Canst thou expect, when thus thy widow fails?
Alas! an adamantine strength indeed,
Past expectation, hath thy murderer built;   1435
For this is the true strength of guilty kings,
When they corrupt the souls of those they rule.

The Chorus

Zeal makes him most unjust; but, in good time,
Here, as I guess, the noble Laias comes.

Laias

Break off, break off your talking, and depart   1440
Each to his post, where the occasion calls;
Lest from the council-chamber presently
The King return, and find you prating here.
A time will come for greetings; but to-day
The hour for words is gone, is come for deeds.   1445

Æpytus

O princely Laias! to what purpose calls
The occasion, if our chief confederate fails?
My mother stands aloof, and blames our deed.

Laias

My royal sister? . . . but, without some cause,
I know, she honours not the dead so ill.   1450

Merope

Brother, it seems thy sister must present,
At this first meeting after absence long,
Not welcome, exculpation to her kin;

Yet exculpation needs it, if I seek,
A woman and a mother, to avert   1455
Risk from my new-restored, my only son?—
Sometimes, when he was gone, I wish'd him back,
Risk what he might; now that I have him here,
Now that I feed mine eyes on that young face,
Hear that fresh voice, and clasp that gold-lock'd head, 1460
I shudder, Laias, to commit my child
To murder's dread arena, where I saw
His father and his ill-starr'd brethren fall!
I loathe for him the slippery way of blood;
I ask if bloodless means may gain his end.   1465
In me the fever of revengeful hate,
Passion's first furious longing to imbrue
Our own right hand in the detested blood
Of enemies, and count their dying groans—
If in this feeble bosom such a fire   1470
Did ever burn—is long by time allay'd,
And I would now have Justice strike, not me.
Besides—for from my brother and my son
I hide not even this—the reverence deep,
Remorseful, tow'rd my hostile solitude,   1475
By Polyphontes never fail'd-in once
Through twenty years; his mournful anxious zeal
To efface in me the memory of his crime—
Though it efface not that, yet makes me wish
His death a public, not a personal act,   1480
Treacherously plotted 'twixt my son and me;
To whom this day he came to proffer peace,
Treaty, and to this kingdom for my son
Heirship, with fair intent, as I believe.—
For that he plots thy death, account it false;   1485
                                          [*to* ÆPYTUS.

Number it with the thousand rumours vain,
Figments of plots, wherewith intriguers fill
The enforcéd leisure of an exile's ear.
Immersed in serious state-craft is the King,

Bent above all to pacify, to ruie, 1490
Rigidly, yet in settled calm, this realm;
Not prone, all say, averse to bloodshed now.—
So much is due to truth, even tow'rds our foe.

[*to* LAIAS.

Do I, then, give to usurpation grace,
And from his natural rights my son debar? 1495
Not so! let him—and none shall be more prompt
Than I to help—raise his Messenian friends;
Let him fetch succours from Arcadia, gain
His Argive or his Spartan cousins' aid;
Let him do this, do aught but recommence 1500
Murder's uncertain, secret, perilous game—
And I, when to his righteous standard down
Flies Victory wing'd, and Justice raises *then*
Her sword, will be the first to bid it fall.
If, haply, at this moment, such attempt 1505
Promise not fair, let him a little while
Have faith, and trust the future and the Gods.
He may; for never did the Gods allow
Fast permanence to an ill-gotten throne.—
These are but woman's words—yet, Laias, thou 1510
Despise them not! for, brother, thou and I
Were not among the feuds of warrior-chiefs,
Each sovereign for his dear-bought hour, born;
But in the pastoral Arcadia rear'd,
With Cypselus our father, where we saw 1515
The simple patriarchal state of kings,
Where sire to son transmits the unquestion'd crown,
Unhack'd, unsmirch'd, unbloodied, and have learnt
That spotless hands unshaken sceptres hold.
Having learnt this, then, use thy knowledge now. 1520

The Chorus

Which way to lean I know not: bloody strokes
Are never free from doubt, though sometimes due.

1492 *1858*: to useless bloodshed   1511 *1858*: thou, like me,
1512 *1858*: Wert not   1518 *1858*: hast learnt

388

Laias

O Merope, the common heart of man
Agrees to deem some deeds so dark in guilt,
That neither gratitude, nor tie of race, 1525
Womanly pity, nor maternal fear,
Nor any pleader else, shall be indulged
To breathe a syllable to bar revenge.
All this, no doubt, thou to thyself hast urged—
Time presses, so that theme forbear I now; 1530
Direct to thy dissuasions I reply.
Blood-founded thrones, thou say'st, are insecure;
Our father's kingdom, because pure, is safe.
True; but what cause to our Arcadia gives
Its privileged immunity from blood, 1535
But that, since first the black and fruitful Earth
In the primeval mountain-forests bore
Pelasgus, our forefather and mankind's,
Legitimately sire to son, with us,
Bequeaths the allegiance of our shepherd-tribes, 1540
More loyal, as our line continues more?—
How can your Heracleidan chiefs inspire
This awe which guards our earth-sprung, lineal kings?
What permanence, what stability like ours,
Whether blood flows or no, can yet invest 1545
The broken order of your Dorian thrones,
Fix'd yesterday, and ten times changed since then?—
Two brothers, and their orphan nephews, strove
For the three conquer'd kingdoms of this isle;
The eldest, mightiest brother, Temenus, took 1550
Argos; a juggle to Cresphontes gave
Messenia; to those helpless Boys, the lot
Worst of the three, the stony Sparta, fell.
August, indeed, was the foundation here!
What follow'd?—His most trusted kinsman slew 1555
Cresphontes in Messenia; Temenus
Perish'd in Argos by his jealous sons;

1524 *1858*: so horrible

The Spartan Brothers with their guardian strive.
Can houses thus ill-seated, thus embroil'd,
Thus little founded in their subjects' love,   1560
Practise the indulgent, bloodless policy
Of dynasties long-fix'd, and honour'd long?
No! Vigour and severity must chain
Popular reverence to these recent lines.
Be their first-founded order strict maintain'd—   1565
Their murder'd rulers terribly avenged—
Ruthlessly their rebellious subjects crush'd!
Since policy bids thus, what fouler death
Than thine illustrious husband's to avenge
Shall we select? than Polyphontes, what   1570
More daring and more grand offender find?
Justice, my sister, long demands this blow,
And Wisdom, now thou see'st, demands it too.
To strike it, then, dissuade thy son no more;
For to live disobedient to these two,   1575
Justice and Wisdom, is no life at all.

The Chorus

The Gods, O mistress dear! the hard-soul'd man,
Who spared not others, bid not us to spare.

Merope

Alas! against my brother, son, and friends,
One, and a woman, how can I prevail?—   1580
O brother, thou hast conquer'd; yet, I fear!
Son! with a doubting heart thy mother yields;
May it turn happier than my doubts portend!

Laias

Meantime on thee the task of silence only
Shall be imposed; to us shall be the deed.   1585
Now, not another word, but to our act!
Nephew! thy friends are sounded, and prove true.

1565 *1858*: If their first-founded order be maintain'd

Thy father's murderer, in the public place,
Performs, this noon, a solemn sacrifice;
Be with him—choose the moment—strike thy blow!   1590
If prudence counsels thee to go unarm'd,
The sacrificer's axe will serve thy turn.
To me and the Messenians leave the rest,
With the Gods' aid—and, if they give but aid
As our just cause deserves, I do not fear.   1595

    [ÆPYTUS, LAIAS, *and* ARCAS *go out.*

The Chorus

O Son and Mother,   *str.* I.
Whom the Gods o'ershadow
In dangerous trial,
With certainty of favour!
As erst they shadow'd   1600
Your race's founders
From irretrievable woe;
When the seed of Lycaon
Lay forlorn, lay outcast,
Callisto and her Boy.   1605

What deep-grass'd meadow   *ant.* I.
At the meeting valleys—
Where clear-flowing Ladon,
Most beautiful of waters,
Receives the river   1610
Whose trout are vocal,
The Aroanian stream—
Without home, without mother:
Hid the babe, hid Arcas,
The nursling of the dells?   1615

But the sweet-smelling myrtle,   *str.* 2.
And the pink-flower'd oleander,
And the green agnus-castus,
To the west-wind's murmur,

    1590 *1858*: Go with

Rustled round his cradle;   1620
And Maia rear'd him.
Then, a boy, he startled,
In the snow-fill'd hollows
Of high Cyllenê,
The white mountain-birds;   1625
Or surprised, in the glens,
The basking tortoises,
Whose striped shell founded
In the hand of Hermes
The glory of the lyre.   1630

But his mother, Callisto,   *ant.* 2.
In her hiding-place of the thickets
Of the lentisk and ilex
In her rough form, fearing
The hunter on the outlook,   1635
Poor changeling! trembled.
Or the children, plucking
In the thorn-choked gullies
Wild gooseberries, scared her,
The shy mountain-bear!   1640
Or the shepherds, on slopes
With pale-spiked lavender
And crisp thyme tufted,
Came upon her, stealing
At day-break through the dew.   1645

Once, 'mid those gorges,   *str.* 3.
Spray-drizzled, lonely,
Unclimb'd of man—
O'er whose cliffs the townsmen
Of crag-perch'd Nonacris   1650
Behold in summer
The slender torrent
Of Styx come dancing,
A wind-blown thread—

1646 *1858*: the gorges 1648 *1858*: by man—

By the precipices of Khelmos,   1655
The fleet, desperate hunter,
The youthful Arcas, born of Zeus,
His fleeing mother,
Transform'd Callisto,
Unwitting follow'd—   1660
And raised his spear.

Turning, with piteous,   *ant.* 3.
Distressful longing,
Sad, eager eyes,
Mutely she regarded   1665
Her well-known enemy.
Low moans half utter'd
What speech refused her;
Tears coursed, tears human,
Down those disfigured,   1670
Once human cheeks.
With unutterable foreboding
Her son, heart-stricken, eyed her.
The Gods had pity, made them Stars.
Stars now they sparkle   1675
In the northern Heaven—
The guard Arcturus,
The guard-watch'd Bear.

So, o'er thee and thy child,   *epode.*
Some God, Merope, now,   1680
In dangerous hour, stretches his hand.
So, like a star, dawns thy son,
Radiant with fortune and joy.

[POLYPHONTES *comes in.*

Polyphontes

O Merope, the trouble on thy face
Tells me enough thou know'st the news which all   1685
Messenia speaks! the prince, thy son, is dead.
Not from my lips should consolation fall;

To offer that, I come not; but to urge,
Even after news of this sad death, our league.
Yes, once again I come; I will not take   1690
This morning's angry answer for thy last.
To the Messenian kingdom thou and I
Are the sole claimants left; what cause of strife
Lay in thy son is buried in his grave.
Most honourably I meant, I call the Gods   1695
To witness, offering him return and power;
Yet, had he lived, suspicion, jealousy,
Inevitably had surged up, perhaps,
'Twixt thee and me—suspicion, that I nursed
Some ill design against him; jealousy,   1700
That he enjoy'd but part, being heir to all.
And he himself, with the impetuous heart
Of youth, 'tis like, had never quite forgone
The thought of vengeance on me, never quite
Unclosed his itching fingers from his sword.   1705
But thou, O Merope, though deeply wrong'd,
Though injured past forgiveness, as men deem,
Yet hast been long at school with thoughtful time,
And from that teacher may'st have learn'd, like me,
That all may be endured, and all forgiv'n—   1710
Have learn'd, that we must sacrifice the bent
Of personal feeling to the public weal—
Have learn'd, that there are guilty deeds, which leave
The hand that does them guiltless; in a word,
That kings live for their peoples, not themselves.   1715
This having known, let us a union found
(For the last time I ask, ask earnestly)
Based on pure public welfare; let us be
Not Merope and Polyphontes, foes
Blood-sever'd, but Messenia's King and Queen!   1720
Let us forget ourselves for those we rule!
Speak! I go hence to offer sacrifice

1688 *1858*: I came   1711 *1858*: the thirst   1712 *1858*: personal
vengeance   1716 *1858*: having learn'd,

To the Preserver Zeus; let me return
Thanks to him for our amity as well.

Merope

Oh had'st thou, Polyphontes, still but kept   1725
The silence thou hast kept for twenty years!

Polyphontes

Henceforth, if what I urge displease, I may.
But fair proposal merits fair reply.

Merope

And thou shalt have it! Yes, because thou *hast*
For twenty years forborne to interrupt   1730
The solitude of her whom thou hast wrong'd—
That scanty grace shall earn thee this reply.—
First, for our union. Trust me, 'twixt us two
The brazen-footed Fury ever stalks,
Waving her hundred hands, a torch in each,   1735
Aglow with angry fire, to keep us twain.
Now, for thyself. Thou com'st with well-cloak'd joy,
To announce the ruin of my husband's house,
To sound thy triumph in his widow's ears,
To bid her share thine unendanger'd throne.   1740
To this thou would'st have answer. Take it: Fly! . . .
Cut short thy triumph, seeming at its height;
Fling off thy crown, supposed at last secure;
Forsake this ample, proud Messenian realm;
To some small, humble, and unnoted strand,   1745
Some rock more lonely than that Lemnian isle
Where Philoctetes pined, take ship and flee!
Some solitude more inaccessible
Than the ice-bastion'd Caucasian Mount
Chosen a prison for Prometheus, climb!   1750
There in unvoiced oblivion sink thy name,
And bid the sun, thine only visitant,

1751 *1858*: hide thy

Divulge not to the far-off world of men
What once-famed wretch he there did espy hid.
There nurse a late remorse, and thank the Gods,   1755
And thank thy bitterest foe, that, having lost
All things but life, thou lose not life as well.

Polyphontes

What mad bewilderment of grief is this?

Merope

Thou art bewilder'd; the sane head is mine.

Polyphontes

I pity thee, and wish thee calmer mind.   1760

Merope

Pity thyself; none needs compassion more.

Polyphontes

Yet, oh! could'st thou but act as reason bids!

Merope

And in my turn I wish the same for thee.

Polyphontes

All I could do to soothe thee has been tried.

Merope

For that, in this my warning, thou art paid.   1765

Polyphontes

Know'st thou then aught, that thus thou sound'st the alarm?

Merope

Thy crime! that were enough to make one fear.

Polyphontes

My deed is of old date, and long atoned.

1754 *1858*: he hath seen lurking there.

396

Merope

Atoned this very day, perhaps, it is.

Polyphontes

My final victory proves the Gods appeased.   1770

Merope

O victor, victor, trip not at the goal!

Polyphontes

Hatred and passionate envy blind thine eyes.

Merope

O Heaven-abandon'd wretch, that envies thee!

Polyphontes

Thou hold'st so cheap, then, the Messenian crown?

Merope

I think on what the future hath in store.   1775

Polyphontes

To-day I reign; the rest I leave to Fate.

Merope

For Fate thou wait'st not long; since, in this hour——

Polyphontes

What? for so far Fate hath not proved my foe—

Merope

Fate seals my lips, and drags to ruin thee.

Polyphontes

Enough! enough! I will no longer hear   1780
The ill-boding note which frantic hatred sounds

1778 *1858*: she hath   1781 *1858*: Envy sounds

To affright a fortune which the Gods secure.
Once more my friendship thou rejectest; well!
More for this land's sake grieve I, than mine own.
I chafe not with thee, that thy hate endures,   1785
Nor bend myself too low, to make it yield.
What I have done is done; by my own deed,
Neither exulting nor ashamed, I stand.
Why should this heart of mine set mighty store
By the construction and report of men?   1790
Not men's good word hath made me what I am.
Alone I master'd power; and alone,
Since so thou wilt, I dare maintain it still.

                    [POLYPHONTES *goes out.*

The Chorus

Did I then waver   *str.* 1.
(O woman's judgment!)   1795
Misled by seeming
Success of crime?
And ask, if sometimes
The Gods, perhaps, allow'd you,
O lawless daring of the strong,   1800
O self-will recklessly indulged?

Not time, not lightning,   *ant.* 1.
Not rain, not thunder,
Efface the endless
Decrees of Heaven—   1805
Make Justice alter,
Revoke, assuage her sentence,
Which dooms dread ends to dreadful deeds,
And violent deaths to violent men.

But the signal example   *str.* 2.   1810
Of invariableness of justice
Our glorious founder
Heracles gave us,
Son loved of Zeus his father—for he sinn'd,

    1793 *1858*: will maintain   1814 *1858*: he err'd,

And the strand of Eubœa, *ant. 2.* 1815
And the promontory of Cenæum,
His painful, solemn
Punishment witness'd,
Beheld his expiation—for he died.

O villages of Œta *str. 3.* 1820
With hedges of the wild rose!
O pastures of the mountain,
Of short grass, beaded with dew,
Between the pine-woods and the cliffs!
O cliffs, left by the eagles, 1825
On that morn, when the smoke-cloud
From the oak-built, fiercely-burning pyre,
Up the precipices of Trachis,
Drove them screaming from their eyries!
A willing, a willing sacrifice on that day 1830
Ye witness'd, ye mountain lawns,
When the shirt-wrapt, poison-blister'd Hero
Ascended, with undaunted heart,
Living, his own funeral-pile,
And stood, shouting for a fiery torch; 1835
And the kind, chance-arrived Wanderer,[30]
The inheritor of the bow,
Coming swiftly through the sad Trachinians,
Put the torch to the pile.
That the flame tower'd on high to the Heaven; 1840
Bearing with it, to Olympus,
To the side of Hebe,
To immortal delight,
The labour-released Hero.

O heritage of Neleus, *ant. 3.* 1845
Ill-kept by his infirm heirs!
O kingdom of Messenê,
Of rich soil, chosen by craft,
Possess'd in hatred, lost in blood!
O town, high Stenyclaros, 1850

With new walls, which the victors
From the four-town'd, mountain-shadow'd Doris,
For their Heracles-issued princes
Built in strength against the vanquish'd!
Another, another sacrifice on this day   1855
Ye witness, ye new-built towers!
When the white-robed, garland-crowned Monarch
Approaches, with undoubting heart,
Living, his own sacrifice-block,
And stands, shouting for a slaughterous axe;   1860
And the stern, destiny-brought Stranger,
The inheritor of the realm,
Coming swiftly through the jocund Dorians,
Drives the axe to its goal.
That the blood rushes in streams to the dust;   1865
Bearing with it, to Erinnys,
To the Gods of Hades,
To the dead unavenged,
The fiercely-required Victim.

Knowing he did it, unknowing pays for it.   [*epode.*
Unknowing, unknowing,   1871
Thinking atoned-for
Deeds unatonable,
Thinking appeased
Gods unappeasable,   1875
Lo, the ill-fated one,
Standing for harbour
Right at the harbour-mouth
Strikes with all sail set
Full on the sharp-pointed   1880
Needle of ruin!

[*A* MESSENGER *comes in.*

Messenger

O honour'd Queen, O faithful followers
Of your dead master's line, I bring you news

400

To make the gates of this long-mournful house
Leap, and fly open of themselves for joy!   1885

[noise and shouting heard.

Hark how the shouting crowds tramp hitherward
With glad acclaim! Ere they forestall my news,
Accept it:—Polyphontes is no more.

Merope

Is my son safe? that question bounds my care.

Messenger

He is, and by the people hail'd for king.   1890

Merope

The rest to me is little; yet, since that
Must from some mouth be heard, relate it thou.

Messenger

Not little, if thou saw'st what love, what zeal,
At thy dead husband's name the people show.
For when this morning in the public square   1895
I took my stand, and saw the unarm'd crowds
Of citizens in holiday attire,
Women and children intermix'd; and then,
Group'd around Zeus's altar, all in arms,
Serried and grim, the ring of Dorian lords—   1900
I trembled for our prince and his attempt.
Silence and expectation held us all;
Till presently the King came forth, in robe
Of sacrifice, his guards clearing the way
Before him—at his side, the prince, thy son,   1905
Unarm'd and travel-soil'd, just as he was.
With him conferring the King slowly reach'd
The altar in the middle of the square,
Where, by the sacrificing minister,
The flower-dress'd victim stood—a milk-white bull,   1910
Swaying from side to side his massy head

With short impatient lowings. There he stopp'd,
And seem'd to muse awhile, then raised his eyes
To heaven, and laid his hand upon the steer,
And cried: *O Zeus, let what blood-guiltiness*   1915
Yet stains our land be by this blood wash'd out,
And grant henceforth to the Messenians peace!
That moment, while with upturn'd eyes he pray'd,
The prince snatch'd from the sacrificer's hand
The axe, and on the forehead of the King,   1920
Where twines the chaplet, dealt a mighty blow
Which fell'd him to the earth, and o'er him stood,
And shouted: *Since by thee defilement came,*
What blood so meet as thine to wash it out?
What hand to strike thee meet as mine, the hand   1925
Of Æpytus, thy murder'd master's son?—
But, gazing at him from the ground, the King . . .
Is it, then, thou? he murmur'd; and with that,
He bow'd his head, and deeply groan'd, and died.
Till then we all seem'd stone, but then a cry   1930
Broke from the Dorian lords; forward they rush'd
To circle the prince round—when suddenly
Laias in arms sprang to his nephew's side,
Crying: *O ye Messenians, will ye leave*
The son to perish as ye left the sire?   1935
And from that moment I saw nothing clear;
For from all sides a deluge, as it seem'd
Burst o'er the altar and the Dorian lords,
Of holiday-clad citizens transform'd
To armed warriors;—I heard vengeful cries,   1940
I heard the clash of weapons; then I saw
The Dorians lying dead, thy son hail'd king.
And, truly, one who sees, what seem'd so strong,
The power of this tyrant and his lords,
Melt like a passing smoke, a nightly dream,   1945
At one bold word, one enterprising blow—
Might ask, why we endured their yoke so long;
But that we know how every perilous feat

Of daring, easy as it seems when done,
Is easy at no moment but the right.   1950

The Chorus

Thou speakest well; but here, to give our eyes
Authentic proof of what thou tell'st our ears,
The conquerors, with the King's dead body, come.

[ÆPYTUS, LAIAS, *and* ARCAS *come in with the dead body
of* POLYPHONTES, *followed by a crowd of the* MES-
SENIANS.

Laias

Sister, from this day forth thou art no more
The widow of a husband unavenged,   1955
The anxious mother of an exiled son.
Thine enemy is slain, thy son is king!
Rejoice with us! and trust me, he who wish'd
Welfare to the Messenian state, and calm,
Could find no way to found them sure as this.   1960

Æpytus

Mother, all these approve me; but if thou
Approve not too, I have but half my joy.

Merope

O Æpytus, my son, behold, behold
This iron man, my enemy and thine,
This politic sovereign, lying at our feet,   1965
With blood-bespatter'd robes, and chaplet shorn!
Inscrutable as ever, see, it keeps
Its sombre aspect of majestic care,
Of solitary thought, unshared resolve,
Even in death, that countenance austere!   1970
So look'd he, when to Stenyclaros first,
A new-made wife, I from Arcadia came,
And found him at my husband's side, his friend,
His kinsman, his right hand in peace and war,

Unsparing in his service of his toil,   1975
His blood—to me, for I confess it, kind;
So look'd he in that dreadful day of death;
So, when he pleaded for our league but now.
What meantest thou, O Polyphontes, what
Desired'st thou, what truly spurr'd thee on?   1980
Was policy of state, the ascendency
Of the Heracleidan conquerors, as thou said'st,
Indeed thy lifelong passion and sole aim?
Or did'st thou but, as cautious schemers use,
Cloak thine ambition with these specious words?   1985
I know not; just, in either case, the stroke
Which laid thee low, for blood requires blood;
But yet, not knowing this, I triumph not
Over thy corpse—triumph not, neither mourn,—
For I find worth in thee, and badness too.   1990
What mood of spirit, therefore, shall we call
The true one of a man—what way of life
His fix'd condition and perpetual walk?
None, since a twofold colour reigns in all.
But thou, my son, study to make prevail   1995
One colour in thy life, the hue of truth;
That justice, that sage order, not alone
Natural vengeance, may maintain thine act,
And make it stand indeed the will of Heaven.
Thy father's passion was this people's ease,   2000
This people's anarchy, thy foe's pretence.
As the chiefs rule, my son, the people are.
Unhappy people, where the chiefs themselves
Are, like the mob, vicious and ignorant!
So rule! that even thine enemies may fail   2005
To find in thee a fault whereon to found,
Of tyrannous harshness, or remissness weak—
So rule, that as thy father thou be loved!
So rule, that as his foe thou be obey'd!
Take these, my son, over thine enemy's corpse   2010

2002 *1858*: rule, indeed, the   2009 *1858*: thy foe

Thy mother's prayers! and this prayer last of all:
That even in thy victory thou show,
Mortal, the moderation of a man.

Æpytus

O mother, my best diligence shall be
In all by thy experience to be ruled   2015
Where my own youth falls short! But, Laias, now,
First work after such victory, let us go
To render to my true Messenians thanks,
To the Gods grateful sacrifice; and then,
Assume the ensigns of my father's power.   2020

The Chorus

Son of Cresphontes, past what perils
Com'st thou, guided safe, to thy home!
What things daring! what enduring!
And all this by the will of the Gods.

EMPEDOCLES ON ETNA

A DRAMATIC POEM

[*First published 1852. Fragments reprinted 1853, '54, '55, '57. Reprinted entire 1867 and thereafter*]

PERSONS

EMPEDOCLES.
PAUSANIAS, *a Physician.*
CALLICLES, *a young Harp-player.*

The Scene of the Poem is on Mount Etna; at first in the forest region, afterwards on the summit of the mountain.

ACT I. SCENE I.

Morning. A Pass in the forest region of Etna.

CALLICLES.
(*Alone, resting on a rock by the path.*)

THE mules, I think, will not be here this hour;
They feel the cool wet turf under their feet
By the stream-side, after the dusty lanes
In which they have toil'd all night from Catana,
And scarcely will they budge a yard. O Pan,   5
How gracious is the mountain at this hour!
A thousand times have I been here alone,
Or with the revellers from the mountain-towns,
But never on so fair a morn;—the sun
Is shining on the brilliant mountain-crests,   10
And on the highest pines; but farther down,
Here in the valley, is in shade; the sward
Is dark, and on the stream the mist still hangs;
One sees one's footprints crush'd in the wet grass,
One's breath curls in the air; and on these pines   15
That climb from the stream's edge, the long grey tufts,

1852–77: after First Act: First Scene *A Pass in the forest region of Etna. Morning.*   11 *1852–68:* further

Which the goats love, are jewell'd thick with dew.
Here will I stay till the slow litter comes.
I have my harp too—that is well.—Apollo!
What mortal could be sick or sorry here?   20
I know not in what mind Empedocles,
Whose mules I follow'd, may be coming up,
But if, as most men say, he is half mad
With exile, and with brooding on his wrongs,
Pausanias, his sage friend, who mounts with him,   25
Could scarce have lighted on a lovelier cure.
The mules must be below, far down. I hear
Their tinkling bells, mix'd with the song of birds,
Rise faintly to me—now it stops!—Who's here?
Pausanias! and on foot? alone?

Pausanias

                       And thou, then?   30
I left thee supping with Peisianax,
With thy head full of wine, and thy hair crown'd,
Touching thy harp as the whim came on thee,
And praised and spoil'd by master and by guests
Almost as much as the new dancing-girl.   35
Why hast thou follow'd us?

Callicles

                      The night was hot,
And the feast past its prime; so we slipp'd out,
Some of us, to the portico to breathe;—
Peisianax, thou know'st, drinks late;—and then,
As I was lifting my soil'd garland off,   40
I saw the mules and litter in the court,
And in the litter sate Empedocles;
Thou, too, wast with him. Straightway I sped home;
I saddled my white mule, and all night long
Through the cool lovely country follow'd you,   45

31 *1852*: Pisianax, *and so throughout.*   43 *1852–68*: wert with him.

Pass'd you a little since as morning dawn'd,
And have this hour sate by the torrent here,
Till the slow mules should climb in sight again.
And now?

Pausanias

        And now, back to the town with speed!
Crouch in the wood first, till the mules have pass'd;   50
They do but halt, they will be here anon.
Thou must be viewless to Empedocles;
Save mine, he must not meet a human eye.
One of his moods is on him that thou know'st;
I think, thou wouldst not vex him.

Callicles

               No—and yet   55
I would fain stay, and help thee tend him. Once
He knew me well, and would oft notice me;
And still, I know not how, he draws me to him,
And I could watch him with his proud sad face,
His flowing locks and gold-encircled brow   60
And kingly gait, for ever; such a spell
In his severe looks, such a majesty
As drew of old the people after him,
In Agrigentum and Olympia,
When his star reign'd, before his banishment,   65
Is potent still on me in his decline.
But oh! Pausanias, he is changed of late;
There is a settled trouble in his air
Admits no momentary brightening now,
And when he comes among his friends at feasts,   70
'Tis as an orphan among prosperous boys.
Thou know'st of old he loved this harp of mine,
When first he sojourn'd with Peisianax;
He is now always moody, and I fear him;
But I would serve him, soothe him, if I could,   75
Dared one but try.

Pausanias

Thou wast a kind child ever!
He loves thee, but he must not see thee now.
Thou hast indeed a rare touch on thy harp,
He loves that in thee, too;—there was a time
(But that is pass'd), he would have paid thy strain   80
With music to have drawn the stars from heaven.
He hath his harp and laurel with him still,
But he has laid the use of music by,
And all which might relax his settled gloom.
Yet thou may'st try thy playing, if thou wilt—   85
But thou must keep unseen; follow us on,
But at a distance! in these solitudes,
In this clear mountain-air, a voice will rise,
Though from afar, distinctly; it may soothe him.
Play when we halt, and, when the evening comes   90
And I must leave him (for his pleasure is
To be left musing these soft nights alone
In the high unfrequented mountain-spots),
Then watch him, for he ranges swift and far,
Sometimes to Etna's top, and to the cone;   95
But hide thee in the rocks a great way down,
And try thy noblest strains, my Callicles,
With the sweet night to help thy harmony!
Thou wilt earn my thanks sure, and perhaps his.

Callicles

More than a day and night, Pausanias,   100
Of this fair summer-weather, on these hills,
Would I bestow to help Empedocles.
That needs no thanks; one is far better here
Than in the broiling city in these heats.
But tell me, how hast thou persuaded him   105
In this his present fierce, man-hating mood,
To bring thee out with him alone on Etna?

76 *1852, 1867*: wert   82 *1852–81*: He has his harp

Pausanias

Thou hast heard all men speaking of Pantheia
The woman who at Agrigentum lay
Thirty long days in a cold trance of death,   110
And whom Empedocles call'd back to life.
Thou art too young to note it, but his power
Swells with the swelling evil of this time,
And holds men mute to see where it will rise.
He could stay swift diseases in old days,   115
Chain madmen by the music of his lyre,
Cleanse to sweet airs the breath of poisonous streams,
And in the mountain-chinks inter the winds.
This he could do of old; but now, since all
Clouds and grows daily worse in Sicily,   120
Since broils tear us in twain, since this new swarm
Of sophists has got empire in our schools
Where he was paramount, since he is banish'd
And lives a lonely man in triple gloom—
He grasps the very reins of life and death.   125
I ask'd him of Pantheia yesterday,
When we were gather'd with Peisianax,
And he made answer, I should come at night
On Etna here, and be alone with him,
And he would tell me, as his old, tried friend,   130
Who still was faithful, what might profit me;
That is, the secret of this miracle.

Callicles

Bah! Thou a doctor! Thou art superstitious.
Simple Pausanias, 'twas no miracle!
Pantheia, for I know her kinsmen well,   135
Was subject to these trances from a girl.
Empedocles would say so, did he deign;
But he still lets the people, whom he scorns,
Gape and cry *wizard* at him, if they list.

108 *1852*: Panthea, *and so throughout.*   139 *1852–69*: cry wizard

But thou, thou art no company for him!   140
Thou art as cross, as sour'd as himself!
Thou hast some wrong from thine own citizens,
And then thy friend is banish'd, and on that,
Straightway thou fallest to arraign the times,
As if the sky was impious not to fall.   145
The sophists are no enemies of his;
I hear, Gorgias, their chief, speaks nobly of him,
As of his gifted master, and once friend.
He is too scornful, too high-wrought, too bitter.
'Tis not the times, 'tis not the sophists vex him;   150
There is some root of suffering in himself,
Some secret and unfollow'd vein of woe,
Which makes the time look black and sad to him.
Pester him not in this his sombre mood
With questionings about an idle tale,   155
But lead him through the lovely mountain-paths,
And keep his mind from preying on itself,
And talk to him of things at hand and common,
Not miracles! thou art a learned man,
But credulous of fables as a girl.   160

Pausanias

And thou, a boy whose tongue outruns his knowledge,
And on whose lightness blame is thrown away.
Enough of this! I see the litter wind
Up by the torrent-side, under the pines.
I must rejoin Empedocles. Do thou   165
Crouch in the brushwood till the mules have pass'd;
Then play thy kind part well. Farewell till night!

153 *1852*: the times

EMPEDOCLES ON ETNA

SCENE II

Noon. A Glen on the highest skirts of the woody region of Etna.

EMPEDOCLES—PAUSANIAS

Pausanias

The noon is hot. When we have cross'd the stream,
We shall have left the woody tract, and come
Upon the open shoulder of the hill.
See how the giant spires of yellow bloom
Of the sun-loving gentian, in the heat,   5
Are shining on those naked slopes like flame!
Let us rest here; and now, Empedocles,
Pantheia's history!

> [*A harp-note below is heard.*

Empedocles

   Hark! what sound was that
Rose from below? If it were possible,
And we were not so far from human haunt,   10
I should have said that some one touch'd a harp.
Hark! there again!

Pausanias

   'Tis the boy Callicles,
The sweetest harp-player in Catana.
He is for ever coming on these hills,
In summer, to all country-festivals,   15
With a gay revelling band; he breaks from them
Sometimes, and wanders far among the glens.
But heed him not, he will not mount to us;
I spoke with him this morning. Once more, therefore,
Instruct me of Pantheia's story, Master,   20
As I have pray'd thee.

Empedocles

   That? and to what end?

Pausanias

It is enough that all men speak of it.
But I will also say, that when the Gods
Visit us as they do with sign and plague,
To know those spells of thine which stay their hand   25
Were to live free from terror.

Empedocles

                    Spells? Mistrust them!
Mind is the spell which governs earth and heaven.
Man has a mind with which to plan his safety;
Know that, and help thyself!

Pausanias

                    But thine own words?
'The wit and counsel of man was never clear,   30
Troubles confound the little wit he has.'
Mind is a light which the Gods mock us with,
To lead those false who trust it.

                              [*The harp sounds again.*

Empedocles

                    Hist! once more!
Listen, Pausanias!—Ay, 'tis Callicles;
I know these notes among a thousand. Hark!   35

Callicles

(*Sings unseen, from below*)

The track winds down to the clear stream,
To cross the sparkling shallows; there
The cattle love to gather, on their way
To the high mountain-pastures, and to stay,
Till the rough cow-herds drive them past,   40
Knee-deep in the cool ford; for 'tis the last

25 *1852–67*: of time that stay   *1868, 1869*: of thine that stay
26 *1852*: free'd from terror.   29 *1852–77*: thy own   31 *1852–*
69: Troubles confuse   35 *1852–81*: those notes   36–76 *1855*:
printed separately as The Harp-player on Etna. I. The Last Glen.

Of all the woody, high, well-water'd dells
On Etna; and the beam
Of noon is broken there by chestnut-boughs
Down its steep verdant sides; the air   45
Is freshen'd by the leaping stream, which throws
Eternal showers of spray on the moss'd roots
Of trees, and veins of turf, and long dark shoots
Of ivy-plants, and fragrant hanging bells
Of hyacinths, and on late anemonies,   50
That muffle its wet banks; but glade,
And stream, and sward, and chestnut-trees,
End here; Etna beyond, in the broad glare
Of the hot noon, without a shade,
Slope behind slope, up to the peak, lies bare;   55
The peak, round which the white clouds play.

In such a glen, on such a day,
On Pelion, on the grassy ground,
Chiron, the aged Centaur lay,
The young Achilles standing by.   60
The Centaur taught him to explore
The mountains; where the glens are dry
And the tired Centaurs come to rest,
And where the soaking springs abound
And the straight ashes grow for spears,   65
And where the hill-goats come to feed,
And the sea-eagles build their nest.
He show'd him Phthia far away,
And said: O boy, I taught this lore
To Peleus, in long distant years!   70
He told him of the Gods, the stars,
The tides;—and then of mortal wars,
And of the life which heroes lead
Before they reach the Elysian place
And rest in the immortal mead;   75
And all the wisdom of his race.

The music below ceases, and EMPEDOCLES *speaks, accompanying himself in a solemn manner on his harp.*

The out-spread world to span
A cord the Gods first slung,
And then the soul of man
There, like a mirror, hung,   80
And bade the winds through space impel the gusty toy.

Hither and thither spins
The wind-borne, mirroring soul,
A thousand glimpses wins,
And never sees a whole;   85
Looks once, and drives elsewhere, and leaves its last employ.

The Gods laugh in their sleeve
To watch man doubt and fear,
Who knows not what to believe
Since he sees nothing clear,   90
And dares stamp nothing false where he finds nothing sure.

Is this, Pausanias, so?
And can our souls not strive,
But with the winds must go,
And hurry where they drive?   95
Is fate indeed so strong, man's strength indeed so poor?

I will not judge. That man,
Howbeit, I judge as lost,
Whose mind allows a plan,
Which would degrade it most;   100
And he treats doubt the best who tries to see least ill.

Be not, then, fear's blind slave!
Thou art my friend; to thee,
All knowledge that I have,
All skill I wield, are free.   105
Ask not the latest news of the last miracle,

77 *1852*: The howling void to span   90 *1852*: Where he sees

Ask not what days and nights
In trance Pantheia lay,
But ask how thou such sights
May'st see without dismay;   110
Ask what most helps when known, thou son of Anchitus!

What? hate, and awe, and shame
Fill thee to see our time;
Thou feelest thy soul's frame
Shaken and out of chime?   115
What? life and chance go hard with thee too, as with us;

Thy citizens, 'tis said,
Envy thee and oppress,
Thy goodness no men aid,
All strive to make it less;   120
Tyranny, pride, and lust, fill Sicily's abodes;

Heaven is with earth at strife,
Signs make thy soul afraid,
The dead return to life,
Rivers are dried, winds stay'd;   125
Scarce can one think in calm, so threatening are the Gods;

And we feel, day and night,
The burden of ourselves—
Well, then, the wiser wight
In his own bosom delves,   130
And asks what ails him so, and gets what cure he can.

The sophist sneers: Fool, take
Thy pleasure, right or wrong.
The pious wail: Forsake
A world these sophists throng.   135
Be neither saint nor sophist-led, but be a man!

113 *1852*: to see our day *1867-77*: to see our world 115 *1852*:
Shaken and in dismay: *1867-77*: Shaken and rudely hurl'd.
116 *1852-77*: life and time go hard

These hundred doctors try
To preach thee to their school.
We have the truth! they cry;
And yet their oracle,   140
Trumpet it as they will, is but the same as thine.

Once read thy own breast right,
And thou hast done with fears;
Man gets no other light,
Search he a thousand years.   145
Sink in thyself! there ask what ails thee, at that shrine!

What makes thee struggle and rave?
Why are men ill at ease?—
'Tis that the lot they have
Fails their own will to please;   150
For man would make no murmuring, were his will obey'd.

And why is it, that still
Man with his lot thus fights?—
'Tis that he makes this *will*
The measure of his *rights*,   155
And believes Nature outraged if his will's gainsaid.

Couldst thou, Pausanias, learn
How deep a fault is this;
Couldst thou but once discern
Thou hast no *right* to bliss,   160
No title from the Gods to welfare and repose;

Then thou wouldst look less mazed
Whene'er of bliss debarr'd,
Nor think the Gods were crazed
When thy own lot went hard.   165
But we are all the same—the fools of our own woes!

163 *1852, 1867*: from bliss

P   417

For, from the first faint morn
Of life, the thirst for bliss
Deep in man's heart is born;
And, sceptic as he is,   170
He fails not to judge clear if this be quench'd or no.

Nor is the thirst to blame.
Man errs not that he deems
His welfare his true aim,
He errs because he dreams   175
The world does but exist that welfare to bestow.

We mortals are no kings
For each of whom to sway
A new-made world up-springs,
Meant merely for his play;   180
No, we are strangers here; the world is from of old.

In vain our pent wills fret,
And would the world subdue.
Limits we did not set
Condition all we do;   185
Born into life we are, and life must be our mould.

Born into life!—man grows
Forth from his parents' stem,
And blends their bloods, as those
Of theirs are blent in them;   190
So each new man strikes root into a far fore-time.

Born into life!—we bring
A bias with us here,
And, when here, each new thing
Affects us we come near;   195
To tunes we did not call our being must keep chime.

171 *1852*: if this is   172 *1852–81*: that thirst   187–96 *First*
inserted in 1867.

Born into life!—in vain,
Opinions, those or these,
Unalter'd to retain
The obstinate mind decrees;   200
Experience, like a sea, soaks all-effacing in.

Born into life!—who lists
May what is false hold dear,
And for himself make mists
Through which to see less clear;   205
The world is what it is, for all our dust and din.

Born into life!—'tis we,
And not the world, are new;
Our cry for bliss, our plea,
Others have urged it too—   210
Our wants have all been felt, our errors made before.

No eye could be too sound
To observe a world so vast,
No patience too profound
To sort what's here amass'd;   215
How man may here best live no care too great to explore.

But we—as some rude guest
Would change, where'er he roam,
The manners there profess'd
To those he brings from home—   220
We mark not the world's course, but would have *it* take *ours*.

The world's course proves the terms
On which man wins content;
Reason the proof confirms—
We spurn it, and invent   225
A false course for the world, and for ourselves, false powers.

197–201 *follow* 202–6 *in 1852.*   203 *1852*: false maintain,
205 *1852*: less plain: 221 *1852*: We mark not the world's ways, but
would have *it* learn *ours.*   222 *1852*: The world proclaims the terms
224 *1852*: Reason its voice confirms.   225 *1852*: spurn them
226 *1852*: False weakness in the world, and in ourselves

Riches we wish to get,
Yet remain spendthrifts still;
We would have health, and yet
Still use our bodies ill;   230
Bafflers of our own prayers, from youth to life's last scenes.

We would have inward peace,
Yet will not look within;
We would have misery cease,
Yet will not cease from sin;   235
We want all pleasant ends, but will use no harsh means;

We do not what we ought,
What we ought not, we do,
And lean upon the thought
That chance will bring us through;   240
But our own acts, for good or ill, are mightier powers.

Yet, even when man forsakes
All sin,—is just, is pure,
Abandons all which makes
His welfare insecure,—   245
Other existences there are, that clash with ours.

Like us, the lightning-fires
Love to have scope and play;
The stream, like us, desires
An unimpeded way;   250
Like us, the Libyan wind delights to roam at large.

Streams will not curb their pride
The just man not to entomb,
Nor lightnings go aside
To give his virtues room;   255
Nor is that wind less rough which blows a good man's barge.

244 *1852*: all that makes   246 *1852*: which clash   255 *1852*,
1867: leave his virtues   256 *1852*: the wind less rough that blows

Nature, with equal mind,
Sees all her sons at play;
Sees man control the wind,
The wind sweep man away;   260
Allows the proudly-riding and the foundering bark.

And, lastly, though of ours
No weakness spoil our lot,
Though the non-human powers
Of Nature harm us not,   265
The ill deeds of other men make often *our* life dark.

What were the wise man's plan?—
Through this sharp, toil-set life.
To work as best he can,
And win what's won by strife.—   270
But we an easier way to cheat our pains have found.

Scratch'd by a fall, with moans
As children of weak age
Lend life to the dumb stones
Whereon to vent their rage,   275
And bend their little fists, and rate the senseless ground;

So, loath to suffer mute,
We, peopling the void air,
Make Gods to whom to impute
The ills we ought to bear;   280
With God and Fate to rail at, suffering easily.

Yet grant—as sense long miss'd
Things that are now perceived,
And much may still exist
Which is not yet believed—   285
Grant that the world were full of Gods we cannot see;

261 *1852–69*: the founder'd bark.   269 *1852–81*: To fight

All things the world which fill
Of but one stuff are spun,
That we who rail are still,
With what we rail at, one;   290
One with the o'erlabour'd Power that through the breadth and
      length

Of earth, and air, and sea,
In men, and plants, and stones,
Hath toil perpetually,
And travails, pants, and moans;   295
Fain would do all things well, but sometimes fails in strength.

And patiently exact
This universal God
Alike to any act
Proceeds at any nod,   300
And quietly declaims the cursings of himself.

This is not what man hates,
Yet he can curse but this.
Harsh Gods and hostile Fates
Are dreams! this only *is*—   305
Is everywhere; sustains the wise, the foolish elf.

Nor only, in the intent
To attach blame elsewhere,
Do we at will invent
Stern Powers who make their care   310
To embitter human life, malignant Deities;

But, next, we would reverse
The scheme ourselves have spun,
And what we made to curse
We now would lean upon,   315
And feign kind Gods who perfect what man vainly tries.

287 *1852*: that fill   294 *1852*: Has toil   295 *1852–68*: And
struggles, pants, and moans;   *1869*: And travails, strives, and moans;
297 *1852*: punctually exact   301 *1852*: patiently declaims

Look, the world tempts our eye,
And we would know it all!
We map the starry sky,
We mine this earthen ball,   320
We measure the sea-tides, we number the sea-sands;

We scrutinise the dates
Of long-past human things,
The bounds of effaced states,
The lines of deceased kings;   325
We search out dead men's words, and works of dead men's hands;

We shut our eyes, and muse
How our own minds are made,
What springs of thought they use,
How righten'd, how betray'd—   330
And spend our wit to name what most employ unnamed.

But still, as we proceed
The mass swells more and more
Of volumes yet to read,
Of secrets yet to explore.   335
Our hair grows grey, our eyes are dimm'd, our heat is tamed;

We rest our faculties,
And thus address the Gods:
'True science if there is,
It stays in your abodes!   340
Man's measures cannot mete the immeasurable All.

'You only can take in
The world's immense design.
Our desperate search was sin,
Which henceforth we resign,   345
Sure only that your mind sees all things which befal.'

341 *1852*: cannot span the illimitable   346 *1852–69*: *your* mind

Fools! That in man's brief term
He cannot all things view,
Affords no ground to affirm
That there are Gods who do;   350
Nor does being weary prove that he has where to rest.

Again.—Our youthful blood
Claims rapture as its right;
The world, a rolling flood
Of newness and delight,   355
Draws in the enamour'd gazer to its shining breast;

Pleasure, to our hot grasp,
Gives flowers after flowers;
With passionate warmth we clasp
Hand after hand in ours;   360
Now do we soon perceive how fast our youth is spent.

At once our eyes grow clear!
We see, in blank dismay,
Year posting after year,
Sense after sense decay;   365
Our shivering heart is mined by secret discontent;

Yet still, in spite of truth,
In spite of hopes entomb'd,
That longing of our youth
Burns ever unconsumed,   370
Still hungrier for delight as delights grow more rare.

We pause; we hush our heart,
And thus address the Gods:
'The world hath fail'd to impart
The joy our youth forebodes,   375
Fail'd to fill up the void which in our breasts we bear.

361 *1852–69*: Nor do we   373 *1852–77*: And then address

'Changeful till now, we still
Look'd on to something new;
Let us, with changeless will,
Henceforth look on to you,   380
To find with you the joy we in vain here require!'

Fools! That so often here
Happiness mock'd our prayer,
I think, might make us fear
A like event elsewhere;   385
Make us, not fly to dreams, but moderate desire.

And yet, for those who know
Themselves, who wisely take
Their way through life, and bow
To what they cannot break,   390
Why should I say that life need yield but *moderate* bliss?

Shall we, with temper spoil'd,
Health sapp'd by living ill,
And judgment all embroil'd
By sadness and self-will,   395
Shall *we* judge what for man is not true bliss or is?

Is it so small a thing
To have enjoy'd the sun,
To have lived light in the spring,
To have loved, to have thought, to have done; 400
To have advanced true friends, and beat down baffling foes—

That we must feign a bliss
Of doubtful future date,
And, while we dream on this,
Lose all our present state,   405
And relegate to worlds yet distant our repose?

381 *1852–69*: in vain *here* 392 *1852*: tempers spoil'd, 394 *1852*:
And judgments 396 *1852*: high bliss 401 *MS.*: rais'd faithful
friends, & cut down spiteful foes 402 *MS.*: demand a bliss *with*
must claim some bliss *as alternative reading.* 404 *MS.*: dream of this
406 *MS.*: And clasp conjectured joys, or dread conjectured woes. *with*
(*as alternative reading*): And kiss conjectured joys, or fear conjectured woes.

Not much, I know, you prize
What pleasures may be had,
Who look on life with eyes
Estranged, like mine, and sad;   410
And yet the village-churl feels the truth more than you,

Who's loath to leave this life
Which to him little yields—
His hard-task'd sunburnt wife,
His often-labour'd fields,   415
The boors with whom he talk'd, the country-spots he knew.

But thou, because thou hear'st
Men scoff at Heaven and Fate,
Because the Gods thou fear'st
Fail to make blest thy state,   420
Tremblest, and wilt not dare to trust the joys there are!

I say: Fear not! Life still
Leaves human effort scope.
But, since life teems with ill,
Nurse no extravagant hope;   425
Because thou must not dream, thou need'st not then despair!

*A long pause. At the end of it the notes of a harp below are
again heard, and* CALLICLES *sings:—*

Far, far from here,
The Adriatic breaks in a warm bay
Among the green Illyrian hills; and there
The sunshine in the happy glens is fair,   430
And by the sea, and in the brakes.
The grass is cool, the sea-side air
Buoyant and fresh, the mountain flowers
More virginal and sweet than ours.

407 *MS.*: Not much thou knowst I prize *with* (*as alternative reading*): not
overmuch I prize 409 *MS.*: Who strive to see 410 *MS.*:
Not eager, nor not sad 411 *MS.*: But then I say (*only*)
427–60 *1853, 1854, 1857, 1878, 1880: printed separately as* Cadmus and
Harmonia. 434 *1852, 1867, 1868, 1869:* As virginal and sweet as ours.

And there, they say, two bright and aged snakes,   435
Who once were Cadmus and Harmonia,
Bask in the glens or on the warm sea-shore,
In breathless quiet, after all their ills;
Nor do they see their country, nor the place
Where the Sphinx lived among the frowning hills,   440
Nor the unhappy palace of their race,
Nor Thebes, nor the Ismenus, any more.

   There those two live, far in the Illyrian brakes!
They had stay'd long enough to see,
In Thebes, the billow of calamity   445
Over their own dear children roll'd,
Curse upon curse, pang upon pang,
For years, they sitting helpless in their home,
A grey old man and woman; yet of old
The Gods had to their marriage come,   450
And at the banquet all the Muses sang.

Therefore they did not end their days
In sight of blood; but were rapt, far away,
To where the west-wind plays,
And murmurs of the Adriatic come   455
To those untrodden mountain-lawns; and there
Placed safely in changed forms, the pair
Wholly forget their first sad life, and home,
And all that Theban woe, and stray
For ever through the glens, placid and dumb.   460

Empedocles

That was my harp-player again!—where is he?
Down by the stream?

Pausanias

           Yes, Master, in the wood.

Empedocles

He ever loved the Theban story well!
But the day wears. Go now, Pausanias,

For I must be alone. Leave me one mule; 465
Take down with thee the rest to Catana.
And for young Callicles, thank him from me;
Tell him, I never fail'd to love his lyre—
But he must follow me no more to-night.

Pausanias

Thou wilt return to-morrow to the city? 470

Empedocles

Either to-morrow or some other day,
In the sure revolutions of the world,
Good friend, I shall revisit Catana.
I have seen many cities in my time,
Till mine eyes ache with the long spectacle, 475
And I shall doubtless see them all again;
Thou know'st me for a wanderer from of old.
Meanwhile, stay me not now. Farewell, Pausanias!

He departs on his way up the mountain.

Pausanias (*alone*)

I dare not urge him further—he must go;
But he is strangely wrought!—I will speed back 480
And bring Peisianax to him from the city;
His counsel could once soothe him. But, Apollo!
How his brow lighten'd as the music rose!
Callicles must wait here, and play to him;
I saw him through the chestnuts far below, 485
Just since, down at the stream.—Ho! Callicles!

He descends, calling.

ACT II

Evening. The Summit of Etna.

EMPEDOCLES

Alone!—
On this charr'd, blacken'd, melancholy waste,

475 *1852–69*: my eyes

Crown'd by the awful peak, Etna's great mouth.
Round which the sullen vapour rolls—alone!
Pausanias is far hence, and that is well,   5
For I must henceforth speak no more with man.
He hath his lesson too, and that debt's paid;
And the good, learned, friendly, quiet man
May bravelier front his life, and in himself
Find henceforth energy and heart. But I—   10
The weary man, the banish'd citizen,
Whose banishment is not his greatest ill,
Whose weariness no energy can reach,
And for whose hurt courage is not the cure—
What should I do with life and living more?   15

  No, thou art come too late, Empedocles!
And the world hath the day, and must break thee,
Not thou the world. With men thou canst not live,
Their thoughts, their ways, their wishes, are not thine;
And being lonely thou art miserable,   20
For something has impair'd thy spirit's strength,
And dried its self-sufficing fount of joy.
Thou canst not live with men nor with thyself—
O sage! O sage!—Take then the one way left;
And turn thee to the elements, thy friends,   25
Thy well-tried friends, thy willing ministers,
And say: Ye helpers, hear Empedocles,
Who asks this final service at your hands!
Before the sophist-brood hath overlaid
The last spark of man's consciousness with words—   30
Ere quite the being of man, ere quite the world
Be disarray'd of their divinity—
Before the soul lose all her solemn joys,
And awe be dead, and hope impossible,
And the soul's deep eternal night come on—   35
Receive me, hide me, quench me, take me home!

7 *1852–81*: He has   27 *1852–81*: Ye servants,

He advances to the edge of the crater. Smoke and fire break
forth with a loud noise, and CALLICLES *is heard below*
singing:—

The lyre's voice is lovely everywhere;
In the court of Gods, in the city of men,
And in the lonely rock-strewn mountain-glen,
In the still mountain air.   40

Only to Typho it sounds hatefully;
To Typho only, the rebel o'erthrown,
Through whose heart Etna drives her roots of stone
To imbed them in the sea.

Wherefore dost thou groan so loud?   45
Wherefore do thy nostrils flash,
Through the dark night, suddenly,
Typho, such red jets of flame?—
Is thy tortured heart still proud?
Is thy fire-scathed arm still rash?   50
Still alert thy stone-crush'd frame?
Doth thy fierce soul still deplore
Thine ancient rout by the Cilician hills,
And that curst treachery on the Mount of Gore?[31]
Do thy bloodshot eyes still weep   55
The fight which crown'd thine ills,
Thy last mischance on this Sicilian deep?
Hast thou sworn, in thy sad lair,
Where erst the strong sea-currents suck'd thee down,
Never to cease to writhe, and try to rest,   60
Letting the sea-stream wander through thy hair?
That thy groans, like thunder prest,

37–88 *1855*: *printed separately as* The Harp-player on Etna. II. Typho.
42 *1852–5*: Only to Typho, the rebel o'erthrown,   52 *1852, 1855*
(Harp-player on Etna): Does   53 *1852, 1855*: Thy ancient rout
1867–9: The ancient rout by the Cilician hills,   53 *1855* (Harp-player
on Etna): in the Cilician hills,   55 *1852–68*: still see   *1869*: still
flee   56 *1852–68*: that crown'd thy ills,   57 *1852–69*: Thy last
defeat in this Sicilian sea?   60 *1852–69*: try to sleep,   62 *1852–*
69: like thunder deep,

Begin to roll, and almost drown
The sweet notes whose lulling spell
Gods and the race of mortals love so well,   65
When through thy caves thou hearest music swell?

But an awful pleasure bland
Spreading o'er the Thunderer's face,
When the sound climbs near his seat,
The Olympian council sees;   70
As he lets his lax right hand,
Which the lightnings doth embrace,
Sink upon his mighty knees.
And the eagle, at the beck
Of the appeasing, gracious harmony,   75
Droops all his sheeny, brown, deep-feather'd neck,
Nestling nearer to Jove's feet;
While o'er his sovran eye
The curtains of the blue films slowly meet
And the white Olympus-peaks   80
Rosily brighten, and the soothed Gods smile
At one another from their golden chairs,
And no one round the charmed circle speaks.
Only the loved Hebe bears
The cup about, whose draughts beguile   85
Pain and care, with a dark store
Of fresh-pull'd violets wreathed and nodding o'er;
And her flush'd feet glow on the marble floor.

Empedocles

He fables, yet speaks truth!
The brave, impetuous heart yields everywhere   90
To the subtle, contriving head;
Great qualities are trodden down,
And littleness united
Is become invincible.

These rumblings are not Typho's groans, I know!   95

78 *1852–69*: sovereign eye   90 *1852*: impetuous hand

These angry smoke-bursts
Are not the passionate breath
Of the mountain-crush'd, tortured, intractable Titan king—
But over all the world
What suffering is there not seen   100
Of plainness oppress'd by cunning,
As the well-counsell'd Zeus oppress'd
That self-helping son of earth!
What anguish of greatness,
Rail'd and hunted from the world,   105
Because its simplicity rebukes
This envious, miserable age!

I am weary of it.
—Lie there, ye ensigns
Of my unloved preëminence   110
In an age like this!
Among a people of children,
Who throng'd me in their cities,
Who worshipp'd me in their houses,
And ask'd, not wisdom,   115
But drugs to charm with,
But spells to mutter—
All the fool's-armoury of magic!—Lie there,
My golden circlet,
My purple robe!   120

Callicles (from below).
As the sky-brightening south-wind clears the day,
And makes the mass'd clouds roll,
The music of the lyre blows away
The clouds which wrap the soul.

Oh! that Fate had let me see   125
That triumph of the sweet persuasive lyre,
That famous, final victory,
When jealous Pan with Marsyas did conspire;

103 *1852–68*: The self-helping   121–90 *1855*: *printed separately as*
The Harp-player on Etna. III. Marsyas.   124 *1852–69*: that wrap

432

When, from far Parnassus' side,
Young Apollo, all the pride   130
Of the Phrygian flutes to tame,
To the Phrygian highlands came;
Where the long green reed-beds sway
In the rippled waters grey
Of that solitary lake   135
Where Mæander's springs are born;
Whence the ridged pine-wooded roots
Of Messogis westward break,
Mounting westward, high and higher.
There was held the famous strife;   140
There the Phrygian brought his flutes,
And Apollo brought his lyre;
And, when now the westering sun
Touch'd the hills, the strife was done,
And the attentive Muses said: 145
'Marsyas, thou art vanquished!'
Then Apollo's minister
Hang'd upon a branching fir
Marsyas, that unhappy Faun,
And began to whet his knife.   150
But the Mænads, who were there,
Left their friend, and with robes flowing
In the wind, and loose dark hair
O'er their polish'd bosoms blowing,
Each her ribbon'd tambourine   155
Flinging on the mountain-sod,
With a lovely frighten'd mien
Came about the youthful God.
But he turn'd his beauteous face
Haughtily another way,   160
From the grassy sun-warm'd place
Where in proud repose he lay,

137 *1852*: Where the ridg'd pine-darken'd roots   *1855*: Whence the
ridg'd pine-muffled roots   *1867–81*: Where the ridg'd pine-wooded
roots

With one arm over his head,
Watching how the whetting sped.

But aloof, on the lake-strand,   165
Did the young Olympus stand,
Weeping at his master's end;
For the Faun had been his friend.
For he taught him how to sing,
And he taught him flute-playing.   170
Many a morning had they gone
To the glimmering mountain-lakes,
And had torn up by the roots
The tall crested water-reeds
With long plumes and soft brown seeds,   175
And had carved them into flutes,
Sitting on a tabled stone
Where the shoreward ripple breaks.
And he taught him how to please
The red-snooded Phrygian girls,   180
Whom the summer evening sees
Flashing in the dance's whirls
Underneath the starlit trees
In the mountain-villages.
Therefore now Olympus stands,   185
At his master's piteous cries
Pressing fast with both his hands
His white garment to his eyes,
Not to see Apollo's scorn;—
Ah, poor Faun, poor Faun! ah, poor Faun!   190

Empedocles

And lie thou there,
My laurel bough!
Scornful Apollo's ensign, lie thou there!
Though thou hast been my shade in the world's heat—
Though I have loved thee, lived in honouring thee—   195

193 *First inserted in 1867.*

434

Yet lie thou there,
My laurel bough!

I am weary of thee.
I am weary of the solitude
Where he who bears thee must abide—   200
Of the rocks of Parnassus,
Of the gorge of Delphi,
Of the moonlit peaks, and the caves.
Thou guardest them, Apollo!
Over the grave of the slain Pytho,   205
Though young, intolerably severe!
Thou keepest aloof the profane,
But the solitude oppresses thy votary!
The jars of men reach him not in thy valley—
But can life reach him?   210
Thou fencest him from the multitude—
Who will fence him from himself?
He hears nothing but the cry of the torrents,
And the beating of his own heart.
The air is thin, the veins swell,   215
The temples tighten and throb there—
Air! air!

Take thy bough, set me free from my solitude;
I have been enough alone!

Where shall thy votary fly then? back to men?—   220
But they will gladly welcome him once more,
And help him to unbend his too tense thought,
And rid him of the presence of himself,
And keep their friendly chatter at his ear,
And haunt him, till the absence from himself,   225
That other torment, grow unbearable;
And he will fly to solitude again,
And he will find its air too keen for him,
And so change back; and many thousand times
Be miserably bandied to and fro   230

202 *1890* (*erroneously*): Of the rocks of Delphi,

Like a sea-wave, betwixt the world and thee,
Thou young, implacable God! and only death
Can cut his oscillations short, and so
Bring him to poise. There is no other way.

And yet what days were those, Parmenides!   235
When we were young, when we could number friends
In all the Italian cities like ourselves,
When with elated hearts we join'd your train,
Ye Sun-born Virgins! on the road of truth.[32]
Then we could still enjoy, then neither thought   240
Nor outward things were closed and dead to us;
But we received the shock of mighty thoughts
On simple minds with a pure natural joy;
And if the sacred load oppress'd our brain,
We had the power to feel the pressure eased,   245
The brow unbound, the thoughts flow free again,
In the delightful commerce of the world.
We had not lost our balance then, nor grown
Thought's slaves, and dead to every natural joy.
The smallest thing could give us pleasure then—   250
The sports of the country-people,
A flute-note from the woods,
Sunset over the sea;
Seed-time and harvest,
The reapers in the corn,   255
The vinedresser in his vineyard,
The village-girl at her wheel.

Fulness of life and power of feeling, ye
Are for the happy, for the souls at ease,
Who dwell on a firm basis of content!   260
But he, who has outlived his prosperous days—
But he, whose youth fell on a different world
From that on which his exiled age is thrown—
Whose mind was fed on other food, was train'd
By other rules than are in vogue to-day—   265

233 *1852-81*: Shall cut

Whose habit of thought is fix'd, who will not change,
But, in a world he loves not, must subsist
In ceaseless opposition, be the guard
Of his own breast, fetter'd to what he guards,
That the world win no mastery over him—   270
Who has no friend, no fellow left, not one;
Who has no minute's breathing space allow'd
To nurse his dwindling faculty of joy——
Joy and the outward world must die to him,
As they are dead to me.   275

> *A long pause, during which* EMPEDOCLES *remains motion-*
> *less, plunged in thought. The night deepens. He*
> *moves forward and gazes round him, and proceeds:*—

And you, ye stars,
Who slowly begin to marshal,
As of old, in the fields of heaven,
Your distant, melancholy lines!
Have you, too, survived yourselves?   280
Are you, too, what I fear to become?
You, too, once lived;
You, too, moved joyfully
Among august companions,
In an older world, peopled by Gods,   285
In a mightier order,
The radiant, rejoicing, intelligent Sons of Heaven.
But now, ye kindle
Your lonely, cold-shining lights,
Unwilling lingerers   290
In the heavenly wilderness,
For a younger, ignoble world;
And renew, by necessity,
Night after night your courses,
In echoing, unnear'd silence,   295
Above a race you know not—

276–300 *1855*: *printed separately as* The Philosopher and the Stars.
280 *1867–9*: Have *you*   281 *1867–9*: Are *you*   288 *1852–69*: you
kindle

Uncaring and undelighted,
Without friend and without home;
Weary like us, though not
Weary with our weariness.   300

No, no, ye stars! there is no death with you,
No languor, no decay! languor and death,
They are with me, not you! ye are alive—
Ye, and the pure dark ether where ye ride
Brilliant above me! And thou, fiery world,   305
That sapp'st the vitals of this terrible mount
Upon whose charr'd and quaking crust I stand—
Thou, too, brimmest with life!—the sea of cloud,
That heaves its white and billowy vapours up
To moat this isle of ashes from the world,   310
Lives; and that other fainter sea, far down,
O'er whose lit floor a road of moonbeams leads
To Etna's Liparëan sister-fires
And the long dusky line of Italy—
That mild and luminous floor of waters lives,   315
With held-in joy swelling its heart; I only,
Whose spring of hope is dried, whose spirit has fail'd,
I, who have not, like these, in solitude
Maintain'd courage and force, and in myself
Nursed an immortal vigour—I alone   320
Am dead to life and joy, therefore I read
In all things my own deadness.

                              A long silence. He continues:—

Oh, that I could glow like this mountain!
Oh, that my heart bounded with the swell of the sea!
Oh, that my soul were full of light as the stars!   325
Oh, that it brooded over the world like the air!

But no, this heart will glow no more; thou art
A living man no more, Empedocles!
Nothing but a devouring flame of thought—
But a naked, eternally restless mind!   330

                              After a pause:—

438

To the elements it came from
Everything will return—
Our bodies to earth,
Our blood to water,
Heat to fire,   335
Breath to air.
They were well born, they will be well entomb'd—
But mind? . . .

And we might gladly share the fruitful stir
Down in our mother earth's miraculous womb;   340
Well would it be
With what roll'd of us in the stormy main;
We might have joy, blent with the all-bathing air,
Or with the nimble, radiant life of fire.

But mind, but thought—   345
If these have been the master part of us—
Where will *they* find their parent element?
What will receive *them*, who will call *them* home?
But we shall still be in them, and they in us,
And we shall be the strangers of the world,   350
And they will be our lords, as they are now;
And keep us prisoners of our consciousness,
And never let us clasp and feel the All
But through their forms, and modes, and stifling veils.
And we shall be unsatisfied as now;   355
And we shall feel the agony of thirst,
The ineffable longing for the life of life
Baffled for ever; and still thought and mind
Will hurry us with them on their homeless march,
Over the unallied unopening earth,   360
Over the unrecognising sea; while air
Will blow us fiercely back to sea and earth,
And fire repel us from its living waves.

341 *1867 (only)*: might it be   342 *1852*: stormy deep.
343 *1852, 1868*: should have   344 *1852*: active, radiant life

And then we shall unwillingly return
Back to this meadow of calamity,   365
This uncongenial place, this human life;
And in our individual human state
Go through the sad probation all again,
To see if we will poise our life at last,
To see if we will now at last be true   370
To our own only true, deep-buried selves,
Being one with which we are one with the whole world;
Or whether we will once more fall away
Into some bondage of the flesh or mind,
Some slough of sense, or some fantastic maze   375
Forged by the imperious lonely thinking-power.
And each succeeding age in which we are born
Will have more peril for us than the last;
Will goad our senses with a sharper spur,
Will fret our minds to an intenser play,   380
Will make ourselves harder to be discern'd.
And we shall struggle awhile, gasp and rebel—
And we shall fly for refuge to past times,
Their soul of unworn youth, their breath of greatness;
And the reality will pluck us back,   385
Knead us in its hot hand, and change our nature
And we shall feel our powers of effort flag,
And rally them for one last fight—and fail;
And we shall sink in the impossible strife,
And be astray for ever.

     Slave of sense   390
I have in no wise been;—but slave of thought? . . .
And who can say: I have been always free,
Lived ever in the light of my own soul?—
I cannot; I have lived in wrath and gloom,
Fierce, disputatious, ever at war with man,   395
Far from my own soul, far from warmth and light.
But I have not grown easy in these bonds—
But I have not denied what bonds these were.

Yea, I take myself to witness,
That I have loved no darkness,   400
Sophisticated no truth,
Nursed no delusion,
Allow'd no fear!

And therefore, O ye elements! I know—
Ye know it too—it hath been granted me   405
Not to die wholly, not to be all enslaved.
I feel it in this hour. The numbing cloud
Mounts off my soul; I feel it, I breathe free.

Is it but for a moment?
—Ah, boil up, ye vapours!   410
Leap and roar, thou sea of fire!
My soul glows to meet you.
Ere it flag, ere the mists
Of despondency and gloom
Rush over it again,   415
Receive me, save me!

[He plunges into the crater.

Callicles

(*from below*)

Through the black, rushing smoke-bursts,
Thick breaks the red flame;
All Etna heaves fiercely
Her forest-clothed frame.   420

Not here, O Apollo!
Are haunts meet for thee.
But, where Helicon breaks down
In cliff to the sea,

417–68 *1855*: *printed separately as* The harp-player on Etna. IV. Apollo.
Also separately in Selections *of 1878 and 1880 as* Apollo Musagetes.
418 *1855*: Quick breaks

Where the moon-silver'd inlets   425
Send far their light voice
Up the still vale of Thisbe,
O speed, and rejoice!

On the sward at the cliff-top
Lie strewn the white flocks,   430
On the cliff-side the pigeons
Roost deep in the rocks.

In the moonlight the shepherds,
Soft lull'd by the rills,
Lie wrapt in their blankets   435
Asleep on the hills.

—What forms are these coming
So white through the gloom?
What garments out-glistening
The gold-flower'd broom?   440

What sweet-breathing presence
Out-perfumes the thyme?
What voices enrapture
The night's balmy prime?—

'Tis Apollo comes leading   445
His choir, the Nine.
—The leader is fairest,
But all are divine.

They are lost in the hollows!
They stream up again!   450
What seeks on this mountain
The glorified train?—

They bathe on this mountain,
In the spring by their road;
Then on to Olympus,   455
Their endless abode.

—Whose praise do they mention?
Of what is it told?—
What will be for ever;
What was from of old.   460

First hymn they the Father
Of all things; and then,
The rest of immortals,
The action of men.

The day in his hotness,   465
The strife with the palm;
The night in her silence,
The stars in their calm.

465 *1852, 855*: in its hotness,   467 *1852, 1855*: in its silence,

LATER POEMS

WESTMINSTER ABBEY

JULY 25, 1881.

(The Day of Burial, in the Abbey, of ARTHUR PENRHYN STANLEY, *Dean of Westminster.)*

[*First published in* THE NINETEENTH CENTURY, *January 1882. Reprinted 1885 and thereafter*]

WHAT! for a term so scant
 Our shining visitant
Cheer'd us, and now is pass'd into the night?
  Couldst thou no better keep, O Abbey old,
  The boon thy dedication-sign foretold,[33]   5
The presence of that gracious inmate, light?—
   A child of light appear'd;
Hither he came, late-born and long-desired,
 And to men's hearts this ancient place endear'd;
What, is the happy glow so soon expired?   10

  —Rough was the winter eve;
   Their craft the fishers leave,
And down over the Thames the darkness drew.
  One still lags last, and turns, and eyes the Pile
  Huge in the gloom, across in Thorney Isle,   15
King Sebert's work, the wondrous Minster new.
   —'Tis Lambeth now, where then
They moor'd their boats among the bulrush stems;
 And that new Minster in the matted fen
The world-famed Abbey by the westering Thames.   20

   His mates are gone, and he
   For mist can scarcely see
A strange wayfarer coming to his side—
  Who bade him loose his boat, and fix his oar,
  And row him straightway to the further shore,   25

5 *1882*: The boon to thy foundation-hour   22 *1882*: can hardly

444

And wait while he did there a space abide.
    The fisher awed obeys,
That voice had note so clear of sweet command;
    Through pouring tide he pulls, and drizzling haze,
And sets his freight ashore on Thorney strand.   30

    The Minster's outlined mass
    Rose dim from the morass,
And thitherward the stranger took his way.
    Lo, on a sudden all the Pile is bright!
    Nave, choir and transept glorified with light,   35
While tongues of fire on coign and carving play!
    And heavenly odours fair
Come streaming with the floods of glory in,
    And carols float along the happy air,
As if the reign of joy did now begin.   40

    Then all again is dark;
    And by the fisher's bark
The unknown passenger returning stands.
    O Saxon fisher! thou hast had with thee
    The fisher from the Lake of Galilee—   45
So saith he, blessing him with outspread hands;
    Then fades, but speaks the while:
At dawn thou to King Sebert shalt relate
    How his St. Peter's Church in Thorney Isle
Peter, his friend, with light did consecrate.   50

    Twelve hundred years and more
    Along the holy floor
Pageants have pass'd, and tombs of mighty kings
    Efface the humbler graves of Sebert's line,
    And, as years sped, the minster-aisles divine   55
Grew used to the approach of Glory's wings.
    Arts came, and arms, and law,
And majesty, and sacred form and fear;
    Only that primal guest the fisher saw,
Light, only light, was slow to reappear.   60

The Saviour's happy light,
　　Wherein at first was dight
His boon of life and immortality,
　　In desert ice of subtleties was spent
　　Or drown'd in mists of childish wonderment,　　65
Fond fancies here, there false philosophy!
　　And harsh the temper grew
Of men with mind thus darken'd and astray;
　　And scarce the boon of life could struggle through,
For want of light which should the boon convey.　　70

　　Yet in this latter time
　　The promise of the prime
Seem'd to come true at last, O Abbey old!
　　It seem'd, a child of light did bring the dower
　　Foreshown thee in thy consecration-hour,　　75
And in thy courts his shining freight unroll'd:
　　Bright wits, and instincts sure,
And goodness warm, and truth without alloy,
　　And temper sweet, and love of all things pure,
And joy in light, and power to spread the joy.　　80

　　And on that countenance bright
　　Shone oft so high a light,
That to my mind there came how, long ago,
　　Lay on the hearth, amid a fiery ring,
　　The charm'd babe of the Eleusinian king—[34]　　85
His nurse, the Mighty Mother, will'd it so.
　　Warm in her breast, by day,
He slumber'd, and ambrosia balm'd the child;
　　But all night long amid the flames he lay,
Upon the hearth, and play'd with them, and smiled.　　90

　　But once, at midnight deep,
　　His mother woke from sleep,
And saw her babe amidst the fire, and scream'd.

62 *1882*: Wherewith　　　68 *1882*: men whose minds were darken'd
70 *1882*: lack of light　　　72 *1882*: That promise　　77 *1882*: instinct

446

A sigh the Goddess gave, and with a frown
    Pluck'd from the fire the child, and laid him down;   95
Then raised her face, and glory round her stream'd.
        The mourning-stole no more
Mantled her form, no more her head was bow'd;
    But raiment of celestial sheen she wore,
And beauty fill'd her, and she spake aloud:—   100

      'O ignorant race of man!
      Achieve your good who can,
If your own hands the good begun undo?
    Had human cry not marr'd the work divine,
    Immortal had I made this boy of mine;   105
But now his head to death again is due
      And I have now no power
Unto this pious household to repay
    Their kindness shown me in my wandering hour.'
—She spake, and from the portal pass'd away.   110

      The Boy his nurse forgot,
      And bore a mortal lot.
Long since, his name is heard on earth no more.
    In some chance battle on Cithæron-side
    The nursling of the Mighty Mother died,   115
And went where all his fathers went before.
      —On thee too, in thy day
Of childhood, Arthur! did some check have power,
    That, radiant though thou wert, thou couldst but stay,
Bringer of heavenly light, a human hour?   120

      Therefore our happy guest
      Knew care, and knew unrest,
And weakness warn'd him, and he fear'd decline.
    And in the grave he laid a cherish'd wife,
    And men ignoble harass'd him with strife,   125

96 *1882*: round her beam'd   124 *1882*: to the grave he bore

And deadly airs his strength did undermine.
      Then from his Abbey fades
The sound beloved of his victorious breath;
    And light's fair nursling stupor first invades,
And next the crowning impotence of death.   130

      But hush! This mournful strain,
      Which would of death complain,
The oracle forbade, not ill-inspired.—
    That Pair, whose head did plan, whose hands did forge
    The Temple in the pure Parnassian gorge,[35]   135
Finish'd their work, and then a meed required.
    'Seven days,' the God replied,
'Live happy, then expect your perfect meed!'
    Quiet in sleep, the seventh night, they died.
Death, death was judged the boon supreme indeed.   140

      And truly he who here
      Hath run his bright career,
And served men nobly, and acceptance found,
    And borne to light and right his witness high,
    What could he better wish than then to die,   145
And wait the issue, sleeping underground?
      Why should he pray to range
Down the long age of truth that ripens slow;
    And break his heart with all the baffling change,
And all the tedious tossing to and fro?   150

      For this and that way swings
      The flux of mortal things,
Though moving inly to one far-set goal.—
    What had our Arthur gain'd, to stop and see,
    After light's term, a term of cecity,   155

126 *1882*: his force   127 *1882*: And from   129 *1882*: languor
first invades   130 *1882*: And then   136 *1882*: Had finish'd, and
a meed of price   145 *1882*: What can he better crave   153 *1882*:
one far-off goal.

A Church once large and then grown strait in soul?
    To live, and see arise,
Alternating with wisdom's too short reign,
    Folly revived, re-furbish'd sophistries,
And pullulating rites externe and vain?   160

    Ay me! 'Tis deaf, that ear
    Which joy'd my voice to hear;
Yet would I not disturb thee from thy tomb,
    Thus sleeping in thine Abbey's friendly shade,
    And the rough waves of life for ever laid!   165
I would not break thy rest, nor change thy doom.
    Even as my father, thou—
Even as that loved, that well-recorded friend—
    Hast thy commission done; ye both may now
Wait for the leaven to work, the let to end.   170

    And thou, O Abbey grey!
    Predestined to the ray
By this dear guest over thy precinct shed—
    Fear not but that thy light once more shall burn,
    Once more thine immemorial gleam return,   175
Though sunk be now this bright, this gracious head!
    Let but the light appear
And thy transfigured walls be touch'd with flame—
    Our Arthur will again be present here,
Again from lip to lip will pass his name.   180

GEIST'S GRAVE

[*First published in* THE FORTNIGHTLY REVIEW, *January 1881. Reprinted in collected edition of 1881 and thereafter*]

    FOUR years!—and didst thou stay above
    The ground, which hides thee now, but four?
    And all that life, and all that love,
    Were crowded, Geist! into no more?

164 *1882*: Here sleeping   173 *1882*: this dear soul   175 *1882*:
One day thine   176 *1882*: sunk is now

Only four years those winning ways,   5
Which make me for thy presence yearn,
Call'd us to pet thee or to praise,
Dear little friend! at every turn?

That loving heart, that patient soul,
Had they indeed no longer span,   10
To run their course, and reach their goal,
And read their homily to man?

That liquid, melancholy eye,
From whose pathetic, soul-fed springs
Seem'd surging the Virgilian cry,*   15
The sense of tears in mortal things—

That steadfast, mournful strain, consoled
By spirits gloriously gay,
And temper of heroic mould—
What, was four years their whole short day?   20

Yes, only four!—and not the course
Of all the centuries yet to come,
And not the infinite resource
Of Nature, with her countless sum

Of figures, with her fulness vast   25
Of new creation evermore,
Can ever quite repeat the past,
Or just thy little self restore.

Stern law of every mortal lot!
Which man, proud man, finds hard to bear,   30
And builds himself I know not what
Of second life I know not where.

But thou, when struck thine hour to go,
On us, who stood despondent by,
A meek last glance of love didst throw,   35
And humbly lay thee down to die.

* *Sunt lacrimæ rerum!* [M.A.]
20 *MS.*: stay altered to day

Yet would we keep thee in our heart—
Would fix our favourite on the scene,
Nor let thee utterly depart
And be as if thou ne'er hadst been.   40

And so there rise these lines of verse
On lips that rarely form them now;
While to each other we rehearse:
Such ways, such arts, such looks hadst thou!

We stroke thy broad brown paws again,   45
We bid thee to thy vacant chair,
We greet thee by the window-pane,
We hear thy scuffle on the stair.

We see the flaps of thy large ears
Quick raised to ask which way we go;   50
Crossing the frozen lake, appears
Thy small black figure on the snow!

Nor to us only art thou dear
Who mourn thee in thine English home;
Thou hast thine absent master's tear,   55
Dropt by the far Australian foam.

Thy memory lasts both here and there,
And thou shalt live as long as we.
And after that—thou dost not care!
In us was all the world to thee.   60

Yet, fondly zealous for thy fame,
Even to a date beyond our own
We strive to carry down thy name,
By mounded turf, and graven stone.

We lay thee, close within our reach,   65
Here, where the grass is smooth and warm,
Between the holly and the beech,
Where oft we watch'd thy couchant form,

Asleep, yet lending half an ear
To travellers on the Portsmouth road;—   70
There build we thee, O guardian dear,
Mark'd with a stone, thy last abode!

Then some, who through this garden pass,
When we too, like thyself, are clay,
Shall see thy grave upon the grass,   75
And stop before the stone, and say:

People who lived here long ago
Did by this stone, it seems, intend
To name for future times to know
The dachs-hound, Geist, their little friend.   80

POOR MATTHIAS

[First published in MACMILLAN'S MAGAZINE, *December 1882. Reprinted*
1885 and thereafter]

POOR Matthias!—Found him lying
Fall'n beneath his perch and dying?
Found him stiff, you say, though warm—
All convulsed his little form?
Poor canary! many a year   5
Well he knew his mistress dear;
Now in vain you call his name,
Vainly raise his rigid frame,
Vainly warm him in your breast,
Vainly kiss his golden crest,   10
Smooth his ruffled plumage fine,
Touch his trembling beak with wine.
One more gasp—it is the end!
Dead and mute our tiny friend!
—Songster thou of many a year,   15
Now thy mistress brings thee here,

71 *MS., 1881 (The Fortnightly Review), 1881:* choose we

Says, it fits that I rehearse,
Tribute due to thee, a verse,
Meed for daily song of yore
Silent now for evermore.   20

Poor Matthias! Wouldst thou have
More than pity? claim'st a stave?
—Friends more near us than a bird
We dismiss'd without a word.
Rover, with the good brown head,   25
Great Atossa, they are dead;
Dead, and neither prose nor rhyme
Tells the praises of their prime.
Thou didst know them old and grey,
Know them in their sad decay.   30
Thou hast seen Atossa sage
Sit for hours beside thy cage;
Thou wouldst chirp, thou foolish bird,
Flutter, chirp—she never stirr'd!
What were now these toys to her?   35
Down she sank amid her fur;
Eyed thee with a soul resign'd—
And thou deemedst cats were kind!
—Cruel, but composed and bland,
Dumb, inscrutable and grand,   40
So Tiberius might have sat,
Had Tiberius been a cat.

Rover died—Atossa too.
Less than they to us are you!
Nearer human were their powers,   45
Closer knit their life with ours.
Hands had stroked them, which are cold,
Now for years, in churchyard mould;
Comrades of our past were they,
Of that unreturning day.   50

18 *1882*: ask'd by thee,

Changed and aging, they and we
Dwelt, it seem'd, in sympathy.
Alway from their presence broke
Somewhat which remembrance woke
Of the loved, the lost, the young—   55
Yet they died, and died unsung.

Geist came next, our little friend;
Geist had verse to mourn his end.
Yes, but that enforcement strong
Which compell'd for Geist a song—   60
All that gay courageous cheer,
All that human pathos dear;
Soul-fed eyes with suffering worn,
Pain heroically borne,
Faithful love in depth divine—   65
Poor Matthias, were they thine?

Max and Kaiser we to-day
Greet upon the lawn at play;
Max a dachshound without blot—
Kaiser should be, but is not.   70
Max, with shining yellow coat,
Prinking ears and dewlap throat—
Kaiser, with his collie face,
Penitent for want of race.
—Which may be the first to die,   75
Vain to augur, they or I?
But, as age comes on, I know,
Poet's fire gets faint and low;
If so be that travel they
First the inevitable way,   80
Much I doubt if they shall have
Dirge from me to crown their grave.

Yet, poor bird, thy tiny corse
Moves me, somehow, to remorse;

82 *1882*: Dirge of mine

Something haunts my conscience, brings   85
Sad, compunctious visitings.
Other favourites, dwelling here,
Open lived to us, and near;
Well we knew when they were glad,
Plain we saw if they were sad,   90
Joy'd with them when they were gay,
Soothed them in their last decay;
Sympathy could feel and show
Both in weal of theirs and woe.

  Birds, companions more unknown,   95
Live beside us, but alone;
Finding not, do all they can,
Passage from their souls to man.
Kindness we bestow, and praise,
Laud their plumage, greet their lays;   100
Still, beneath their feather'd breast,
Stirs a history unexpress'd.
Wishes there, and feelings strong,
Incommunicably throng;
What they want, we cannot guess,   105
Fail to track their deep distress—
Dull look on when death is nigh,
Note no change, and let them die.
Poor Matthias! couldst thou speak,
What a tale of thy last week!   110
Every morning did we pay
Stupid salutations gay,
Suited well to health, but how
Mocking, how incongruous now!
Cake we offer'd, sugar, seed,   115
Never doubtful of thy need;
Praised, perhaps, thy courteous eye,
Praised thy golden livery.
Gravely thou the while, poor dear!
Sat'st upon thy perch to hear,   120

Fixing with a mute regard
Us, thy human keepers hard,
Troubling, with our chatter vain,
Ebb of life, and mortal pain—
Us, unable to divine   125
Our companion's dying sign,
Or o'erpass the severing sea
Set betwixt ourselves and thee,
Till the sand thy feathers smirch
Fallen dying off thy perch!   130

Was it, as the Grecian sings,
Birds were born the first of things,
Before the sun, before the wind,
Before the gods, before mankind,
Airy, ante-mundane throng—   135
Witness their unworldly song!
Proof they give, too, primal powers,
Of a prescience more than ours—
Teach us, while they come and go,
When to sail, and when to sow.   140
Cuckoo calling from the hill,
Swallow skimming by the mill,
Swallows trooping in the sedge,
Starlings swirling from the hedge,
Mark the seasons, map our year,   145
As they show and disappear.
But, with all this travail sage
Brought from that anterior age,
Goes an unreversed decree
Whereby strange are they and we,   150
Making want of theirs, and plan,
Indiscernible by man.

No, away with tales like these
Stol'n from Aristophanes![36]

143-4 *Added in 1885.*

Does it, if we miss your mind,   155
Prove us so remote in kind?
Birds! we but repeat on you
What amongst ourselves we do.
Somewhat more or somewhat less.
'Tis the same unskilfulness.   160
What you feel, escapes our ken—
Know we more our fellow men?
Human suffering at our side,
Ah, like yours is undescried!
Human longings, human fears,   165
Miss our eyes and miss our ears.
Little helping, wounding much,
Dull of heart, and hard of touch,
Brother man's despairing sign
Who may trust us to divine?   170
Who assure us, sundering powers
Stand not 'twixt his soul and ours?

   Poor Matthias! See, thy end
What a lesson doth it lend!
For that lesson thou shalt have,   175
Dead canary bird, a stave!
Telling how, one stormy day,
Stress of gale and showers of spray
Drove my daughter small and me
Inland from the rocks and sea.   180
Driv'n inshore, we follow down
Ancient streets of Hastings town—
Slowly thread them—when behold,
French canary-merchant old
Shepherding his flock of gold   185
In a low dim-lighted pen
Scann'd of tramps and fishermen!
There a bird, high-coloured, fat,
Proud of port, though something squat—
Pursy, play'd-out Philistine—   190

Dazzled Nelly's youthful eyne.
But, far in, obscure, there stirr'd
On his perch a sprightlier bird,
Courteous-eyed, erect and slim;
And I whisper'd: 'Fix on *him!*'   195
Home we brought him, young and fair,
Songs to trill in Surrey air.
Here Matthias sang his fill,
Saw the cedars of Pains Hill;
Here he pour'd his little soul,   200
Heard the murmur of the Mole.
Eight in number now the years
He hath pleased our eyes and ears;
Other favourites he hath known
Go, and now himself is gone.   205
—Fare thee well, companion dear!
Fare for ever well, nor fear,
Tiny though thou art, to stray
Down the uncompanion'd way!
We without thee, little friend,   210
Many years have not to spend;
What are left, will hardly be
Better than we spent with thee.

KAISER DEAD

APRIL 6, 1887

[First published in THE FORTNIGHTLY REVIEW, *July 1887. Reprinted in 1890]*

WHAT, Kaiser dead? The heavy news
Post-haste to Cobham calls the Muse,
From where in Farringford she brews
    The ode sublime,
Or with Pen-bryn's bold bard pursues   5
    A rival rhyme.

Kai's bracelet tail, Kai's busy feet,
Were known to all the village-street.
'What, poor Kai dead?' say all I meet;
   'A loss indeed!'   10
O for the croon pathetic, sweet,
    Of Robin's reed!³⁷

Six years ago I brought him down,
A baby dog, from London town;
Round his small throat of black and brown 15
    A ribbon blue,
And vouch'd by glorious renown
    A dachshound true.

His mother, most majestic dame,
Of blood-unmix'd, from Potsdam came;   20
And Kaiser's race we deem'd the same—
    No lineage higher.
And so he bore the imperial name.
    But ah, his sire!

Soon, soon the days conviction bring.   25
The collie hair, the collie swing,
The tail's indomitable ring,
    The eye's unrest—
The case was clear; a mongrel thing
    Kai stood confest.   30

But all those virtues, which commend
The humbler sort who serve and tend,
Were thine in store, thou faithful friend.
    What sense, what cheer!
To us, declining tow'rds our end,   35
    A mate how dear!

For Max, thy brother-dog, began
To flag, and feel his narrowing span.

And cold, besides, his blue blood ran,
        Since, 'gainst the classes,   40
He heard, of late, the Grand Old Man
        Incite the masses.

Yes, Max and we grew slow and sad;
But Kai, a tireless shepherd-lad,
Teeming with plans, alert, and glad   45
        In work or play,
Like sunshine went and came, and bade
        Live out the day!

Still, still I see the figure smart—
Trophy in mouth, agog to start,   50
Then, home return'd, once more depart;
        Or prest together
Against thy mistress, loving heart,
        In winter weather.

I see the tail, like bracelet twirl'd,   55
In moments of disgrace uncurl'd,
Then at a pardoning word re-furl'd,
        A conquering sign;
Crying, 'Come on, and range the world,
        And never pine.'   60

Thine eye was bright, thy coat it shone;
Thou hadst thine errands, off and on;
In joy thy last morn flew; anon,
        A fit! All's over;
And thou art gone where Geist hath gone,   65
        And Toss, and Rover.

Poor Max, with downcast, reverent head,
Regards his brother's form outspread;
Full well Max knows the friend is dead
        Whose cordial talk,   70
And jokes in doggish language said,
        Beguiled his walk.

And Glory, stretch'd at Burwood gate,
Thy passing by doth vainly wait;
And jealous Jock, thy only hate,   75
      The chiel from Skye,
Lets from his shaggy Highland pate
      Thy memory die.

Well, fetch his graven collar fine,
And rub the steel, and make it shine,   80
And leave it round thy neck to twine,
      Kai, in thy grave.
There of thy master keep that sign,
      And this plain stave.

CANCELLED AND UNCOLLECTED POEMS

ALARIC AT ROME

[*A prize poem recited in Rugby School, June 12, 1840. Published at Rugby the same year. Not reprinted by Arnold*]

'Admire, exult, despise, laugh, weep, for here
'There is such matter for all feeling.'
Childe Harold

I

UNWELCOME shroud of the forgotten dead,
Oblivion's dreary fountain, where art thou:
Why speed'st thou not thy deathlike wave to shed
O'er humbled pride, and self-reproaching woe:
Or time's stern hand, why blots it not away   5
The saddening tale that tells of sorrow and decay?

II

There are, whose glory passeth not away—
Even in the grave their fragrance cannot fade:
Others there are as deathless full as they,
Who for themselves a monument have made   10
By their own crimes—a lesson to all eyes—
Of wonder to the fool—of warning to the wise.

III

Yes, there are stories registered on high,
Yes, there are stains time's fingers cannot blot,
Deeds that shall live when they who did them, die;   15
Things that may cease, but never be forgot:
Yet some there are, their very lives would give
To be remembered thus, and yet they cannot live.

IV

But thou, imperial City! that hast stood
In greatness once, in sackcloth now and tears,   20
A mighty name, for evil or for good,
Even in the loneness of thy widowed years:
Thou that hast gazed, as the world hurried by,
Upon its headlong course with sad prophetic eye.

V

Is thine the laurel-crown that greatness wreathes   25
Round the wan temples of the hallowed dead—
Is it the blighting taint dishonour breathes
In fires undying o'er the guilty head,
Or the brief splendour of that meteor light
That for a moment gleams, and all again is night?   30

VI

Fain would we deem that thou hast risen so high
Thy dazzling light an eagle's gaze should tire;
No meteor brightness to be seen and die,
No passing pageant, born but to expire,
But full and deathless as the deep dark hue   35
Of ocean's sleeping face, or heaven's unbroken blue.

VII

Yet stains there are to blot thy brightest page,
And wither half the laurels on thy tomb;
A glorious manhood, yet a dim old age,
And years of crime, and nothingness, and gloom: 40
And then that mightiest crash, that giant fall,
Ambition's boldest dream might sober and appal.

VIII

Thou wondrous chaos, where together dwell
Present and past, the living and the dead,
Thou shattered mass, whose glorious ruins tell   45

The vanisht might of that discrownèd head:
Where all we see, or do, or hear, or say,
Seems strangely echoed back by tones of yesterday:

IX

Thou solemn grave, where every step we tread
Treads on the slumbering dust of other years;   50
The while there sleeps within thy precincts dread
What once had human passions, hopes, and fears;
And memory's gushing tide swells deep and full
And makes thy very ruin fresh and beautiful.

X

Alas, no common sepulchre art thou,   55
No habitation for the nameless dead,
Green turf above, and crumbling dust below,
Perchance some mute memorial at their head,
But one vast fane where all unconscious sleep
Earth's old heroic forms in peaceful slumbers deep.   60

XI

Thy dead are kings, thy dust are palaces,
Relics of nations thy memorial-stones:
And the dim glories of departed days
Fold like a shroud around thy withered bones:
And o'er thy towers the wind's half uttered sigh   65
Whispers, in mournful tones, thy silent elegy.

XII

Yes, in such eloquent silence didst thou lie
When the Goth stooped upon his stricken prey,
And the deep hues of an Italian sky
Flasht on the rude barbarian's wild array: 70
While full and ceaseless as the ocean roll,
Horde after horde streamed up thy frowning Capitol.

XIII

[a]Twice, ere that day of shame, the embattled foe
Had gazed in wonder on that glorious sight;
Twice had the eternal city bowed her low   75
In sullen homage to the invader's might:
Twice had the pageant of that vast array
Swept, from thy walls, O Rome, on its triumphant way.

XIV

Twice, from without thy bulwarks, hath the din
Of Gothic clarion smote thy startled ear;   80
Anger, and strife, and sickness are within,
[b]Famine and sorrow are no strangers here:
Twice hath the cloud hung o'er thee, twice been stayed
Even in the act to burst, twice threatened, twice delayed.

XV

Yet once again, stern Chief, yet once again,   85
Pour forth the foaming vials of thy wrath:
There lies thy goal, to miss or to attain,
Gird thee, and on upon thy fateful path,
The world hath bowed to Rome, oh! cold were he
Who would not burst his bonds, and in his turn be free: 90

XVI

Therefore arise and arm thee! lo, the world
Looks on in fear! and when the seal is set,
The doom pronounced, the battle-flag unfurled,
Scourge of the nations, wouldest thou linger yet?
Arise and arm thee! spread thy banners forth,   95
Pour from a thousand hills thy warriors of the north!

a The sieges of Rome by the Goths under Alaric were three in number.
The first was commenced A.D. 408, and concluded A.D. 409, by Alaric's accept-
ing a ransom. In the second Alaric entered the city in triumph, and appointed
Attalus Emperor. After again degrading this new monarch of his own creation,
he finally captured and sacked the city, A.D. 410.

b 'That unfortunate city gradually experienced the distress of scarcity, and
at length the horrid calamities of famine. The miseries of which were succeeded
and aggravated by the contagion of a pestilential disease.'—*Gibbon.*

XVII

Hast thou not marked on a wild autumn day
When the wind slumbereth in a sudden lull,
What deathlike stillness o'er the landscape lay,
How calmly sad, how sadly beautiful;   100
How each bright tint of tree, and flower, and heath
Were mingling with the sere and withered hues of death.

XVIII

And thus, beneath the clear, calm, vault of heaven
In mournful loveliness that city lay,
And thus, amid the glorious hues of even   105
That city told of languor and decay:
Till what at morning's hour lookt warm and bright
Was cold and sad beneath that breathless, voiceless night.

XIX

Soon was that stillness broken: like the cry
Of the hoarse onset of the surging wave,   110
Or louder rush of whirlwinds sweeping by
Was the wild shout those Gothic myriads gave,
As towered on high, above their moonlit road,
Scenes where a Cæsar triumpht, or a Scipio trod.

XX

^cThink ye it strikes too slow, the sword of fate,   115
Think ye the avenger loiters on his way,
That your own hands must open wide the gate,
And your own voice guide him to his prey;
Alas, it needs not; is it hard to know
Fate's threat'nings are not vain, the spoiler comes not slow.   120

c 'They (the Senate) were unable to guard against the secret conspiracy of
their slaves and domestics.' 'At the hour of midnight the Salarian gate was
silently opened and the inhabitants were awakened by the tremendous sound
of the Gothic trumpet.'—*Gibbon.*

XXI

And were there none, to stand and weep alone,
And as the pageant swept before their eyes
To hear a dim and long forgotten tone
Tell of old times, and holiest memories,
   Till fanciful regret and dreamy woe   125
Peopled night's voiceless shades with forms of long Ago.

XXII

Oh yes! if fancy feels, beyond to day,
Thoughts of the past and of the future time,
How should that mightiest city pass away
And not bethink her of her glorious prime,   130
   Whilst every chord that thrills at thoughts of home
Jarr'd with the bursting shout, 'they come, the Goth, they come'!

XXIII

^dThe trumpet swells yet louder: they are here!
Yea, on your fathers bones the avengers tread,
Not this the time to weep upon the bier   135
That holds the ashes of your hero-dead,
   If wreaths may twine for you, or laurels wave,
They shall not deck your life, but sanctify your grave.

XXIV

Alas! no wreaths are here. Despair may teach
Cowards to conquer and the weak to die;   140
Nor tongue of man, nor fear, nor shame can preach
So stern a lesson as necessity,
   Yet here it speaks not. Yea, though all around
Unhallowed feet are trampling on this haunted ground,

XXV

Though every holiest feeling, every tie   145
That binds the heart of man with mightiest power,
All natural love, all human sympathy

d 'Adest Alaricus, trepidam urbem obsidet, turbat, irrumpit.'—*Orosius Lib. vil. cap.* 39.

Be crusht, and outraged in this bitter hour,
Here is no echo to the sound of home,
No shame that suns should rise to light a conquer'd Rome.   150

XXVI

That troublous night is over: on the brow
Of thy stern hill, thou mighty Capitol,
One form stands gazing: silently below
The morning mists from tower and temple roll,
And lo! the eternal city, as they rise,   155
Bursts, in majestic beauty, on her conqueror's eyes.

XXVII

Yes, there he stood, upon that silent hill,
And there beneath his feet his conquest lay:
Unlike that ocean-city,[e] gazing still
Smilingly forth upon her sunny bay,   160
But o'er her vanisht might and humbled pride
Mourning, as widowed Venice o'er her Adrian tide.

XXVIII

Breathe there not spirits on the peopled air?
Float there not voices on the murmuring wind?
Oh! sound there not some strains of sadness there,   165
To touch with sorrow even a victor's mind,
And wrest one tear from joy! Oh! who shall pen
The thoughts that toucht thy breast, thou lonely conqueror, then?

XXIX

Perchance his wandering heart was far away,
Lost in dim memories of his early home,   170
And his young dreams of conquest; how to-day
Beheld him master of Imperial Rome,
Crowning his wildest hopes: perchance his eyes
As they looked sternly on, beheld new victories,

e Naples. —'Stabiasque, et in otia natam
        Parthenopen.'—*Ovid Metam. Lib. xv. vers.* 711–12.

XXX

New dreams of wide dominion, mightier, higher,   175
Come floating up from the abyss of years;
Perchance that solemn sight might quench the fire
Even of that ardent spirit; hopes and fears
Might well be mingling at that murmured sigh,
Whispering from all around, 'All earthly things must die.'   180

XXXI

Perchance that wondrous city was to him
But as one voiceless blank; a place of graves,
And recollections indistinct and dim,
Whose sons were conquerors once, and now were slaves:
It may be in that desolate sight his eye   185
Saw but another step to climb to victory!

XXXII

Alas! that fiery spirit little knew
The change of life, the nothingness of power,
How both were hastening, as they flowered and grew,
Nearer and nearer to their closing hour: 190
How every birth of time's miraculous womb
Swept off the withered leaves that hide the naked tomb.

XXXIII

^fOne little year; that restless soul shall rest,
That frame of vigour shall be crumbling clay,
And tranquilly, above that troubled breast,   195
The sunny waters^g hold their joyous way:
And gently shall the murmuring ripples flow,
Nor wake the weary soul that slumbers on below.

f Alaric died after a sudden illness, while engaged in attempting the invasion of Sicily, A.D. 410, the very year of the third siege of Rome by his forces.

g For an account of the death and singular burial of the Gothic monarch, see Gibbon, vol. v. p. 329–30. 'By the labour of a captive multitude the course

XXXIV

Alas! far other thoughts might well be ours
And dash our holiest raptures while we gaze: 200
Energies wasted, unimproved hours,
The saddening visions of departed days:
And while they rise here might we stand alone,
And mingle with thy ruins somewhat of our own.

XXXV

Beautiful city! If departed things   205
Ever again put earthly likeness on,
Here should a thousand forms on fancy's wings
Float up to tell of ages that are gone:
Yea though hand touch thee not, nor eye should see,
Still should the spirit hold communion, Rome, with thee!   210

XXXVI

Oh! it is bitter, that each fairest dream
Should fleet before us but to melt away;
That wildest visions still should loveliest seem
And soonest fade in the broad glare of day:
That while we feel the world is dull and low,   215
Gazing on thee, we wake to find it is not so.

XXXVII

A little while, alas, a little while,
And the same world has tongue, and ear, and eye,
The careless glance, the cold unmeaning smile,
The thoughtless word, the lack of sympathy!   220
Who would not turn him from the barren sea
And rest his weary eyes on the green land and thee!

of the Burentinus was forcibly diverted, a small river that washes the walls of
Consentia. The royal sepulchre, adorned with the splendid trophies of Rome
was constructed in the vacant bed, and the waters were then restored to their
natural channel, and the secret spot where the remains of Alaric had been
deposited was for ever concealed by the inhuman massacre of the prisoners
who had been employed to execute the work.'

XXXVIII

So pass we on. But oh! to harp aright
The vanisht glories of thine early day,
There needs a minstrel of diviner might,   225
A holier incense than this feeble lay;
To chant thy requiem with more passionate breath,
And twine with bolder hand thy last memorial wreath!

———

The End.

CROMWELL

[*A prize poem scheduled for recitation in the Sheldonian Theatre, Oxford, June 28, 1843. First published by J. Vincent, Oxford, 1843. Reprinted in* ADDITIONS TO PRIZE POEMS, *Oxford, 1846, and by T. and G. Shrimpton, Oxford, 1863*]

SYNOPSIS

INTRODUCTION—The mountains and the sea the cradles of freedom—contrasted with the birth-place of Cromwell—His childhood and youth—The germs of his future character probably formed during his life of inaction.—Cromwell at the moment of his intended embarkation—Retrospect of his past life and profligate youth—Temptations held out by the prospect of a life of rest in America—How far such rest was allowable—Vision of his future life—Different persons represented in it—Charles the First—Cromwell himself—His victories and maritime glory—Pym—Strafford—Laud—Hampden—Falkland—Milton—Charles the First—Cromwell on his death-bed—His character—Dispersion of the Vision—Conclusion.

CROMWELL

Schrecklich ist es, deiner Wahrheit
Sterbliches Gefäss zu seyn.
SCHILLER.

HIGH fate is their's, ye sleepless waves, whose ear
Learns Freedom's lesson from your voice of fear;
Whose spell-bound sense from childhood's hour hath known

Familiar meanings in your mystic tone:
Sounds of deep import—voices that beguile   5
Age of its tears and childhood of its smile,
To yearn with speechless impulse to the free
And gladsome greetings of the buoyant sea!
ªHigh fate is their's, who where the silent sky
Stoops to the soaring mountains, live and die;   10
Who scale the cloud-capt height, or sink to rest
In the deep stillness of its shelt'ring breast;—
Around whose feet the exulting waves have sung,
The eternal hills their giant shadows flung.

No wonders nurs'd thy childhood; not for thee   15
Did the waves chaunt their song of liberty!
Thine was no mountain home, where Freedom's form
Abides enthron'd amid the mist and storm,
And whispers to the listening winds, that swell
With solemn cadence round her citadel!   20
These had no sound for thee: that cold calm eye
Lit with no rapture as the storm swept by,
To mark with shiver'd crest the reeling wave
Hide his torn head beneath his sunless cave;
Or hear 'mid circling crags, the impatient cry   25
Of the pent winds, that scream in agony!
Yet all high sounds that mountain children hear
Flash'd from thy soul upon thine inward ear;
All Freedom's mystic language—storms that roar
By hill or wave, the mountain or the shore,—   30
All these had stirr'd thy spirit, and thine eye
In common sights read secret sympathy;
Till all bright thoughts that hills or waves can yield,
Deck'd the dull waste, and the familiar field;
Or wondrous sounds from tranquil skies were borne   35

ª This is in allusion to the idea expressed in the twelfth of Mr. Wordsworth's Sonnets to Liberty:—
          'Two voices are there: one is of the sea,' &c.
contrasting it with the fact of Cromwell's birth-place having been the fen
country of Huntingdonshire, where he lived till he was forty years old.

Far o'er the glistening sheets of windy corn:
Skies—that, unbound by clasp of mountain chain,
Slope stately down, and melt into the plain;
Sounds—such as erst the lone wayfaring man
[b]Caught, as he journeyed, from the lips of Pan;   40
[c]Or that mysterious cry, that smote with fear,
Like sounds from other worlds, the Spartan's ear,
While, o'er the dusty plain, the murmurous throng
Of Heaven's embattled myriads swept along.

Say not such dreams are idle: for the man   45
Still toils to perfect what the child began;
And thoughts, that were but outlines, time engraves
Deep on his life; and childhood's baby waves,
Made rough with care, become the changeful sea,
Stemm'd by the strength of manhood fearlessly;   50
And fleeting thoughts, that on the lonely wild
Swept o'er the fancy of that heedless child,
Perchance had quicken'd with a living truth
The cold dull soil of his unfruitful youth;
Till, with his daily life, a life, that threw   55
Its shadows o'er the future, flower'd and grew,
With common cares unmingling, and apart,
Haunting the shrouded chambers of his heart;
Till life, unstirr'd by action, life became
Threaded and lighten'd by a track of flame;   60
An inward light, that, with its streaming ray,
On the dark current of his changeless day
Bound all his being with a silver chain—
Like a swift river thro' a silent plain!

High thoughts were his, when by the gleaming flood,   65
With heart new strung, and stern resolve, he stood;
Where rode the tall dark ships, whose loosen'd sail
All idly flutter'd in the eastern gale;[d]

b *Herod.* vi. 106.

c The vision of Demaratus on the plain of Eleusis.—*Herod.* viii. 65.

d Eight ships, lying in the Thames, and ready to sail, were detained by order of Council.—*Hume*, vi. 309.

High thoughts were his;—but Memory's glance the while
Fell on the cherish'd past with tearful smile;   70
And peaceful joys and gentler thoughts swept by,
Like summer lightnings o'er a darken'd sky.
The peace of childhood, and the thoughts that roam,
Like loving shadows, round that childhood's home;
Joys that had come and vanish'd, half unknown,   75
Then slowly brighten'd, as the days had flown;
Years that were sweet or sad, becalm'd or toss'd
On life's wild waves—the living and the lost.
Youth stain'd with follies: and the thoughts of ill
Crush'd, as they rose, by manhood's sterner will.   80
Repentant prayers, that had been strong to save—
And the first sorrow, which is childhood's grave!
All shapes that haunt remembrance; soft and fair,
Like a green land at sunset, all were there!
Eyes that he knew, old faces, unforgot,   85
Gaz'd sadly down on his unrestful lot,
And Memory's calm clear voice, and mournful eye,
Chill'd every buoyant hope that floated by;
Like frozen winds on southern vales that blow
From a far land—the children of the snow—   90
O'er flowering plain and blossom'd meadow fling
The cold dull shadow of their icy wing.

Then Fancy's roving visions, bold and free,
A moment dispossess'd reality.
All airy hopes that idle hearts can frame,   95
Like dreams between two sorrows, went and came:
Fond hearts that fain would clothe the unwelcome truth
Of toilsome manhood in the dreams of youth,
To bend in rapture at some idol throne,
Some lifeless soulless phantom of their own;   100
Some shadowy vision of a tranquil life,
Of joys unclouded, years unstirr'd by strife;
Of sleep unshadow'd by a dream of woe;
Of many a lawny hill, and streams with silver flow;

Of giant mountains by the western main,   105
The sunless forest, and the sealike plain;
Those lingering hopes of coward hearts, that still
Would play the traitor to the stedfast will,
One moment's space, perchance, might charm his eye
From the stern future, and the years gone by.   110
One moment's space might waft him far away
To western shores—the death-place of the day!
Might paint the calm, sweet peace—the rest of home,
Far o'er the pathless waste of labouring foam—
Peace, that recall'd his childish hours anew,   115
More calm, more deep, than childhood ever knew!
Green happy places—like a flowery lea
Between the barren mountains and the stormy sea.

O pleasant rest, if once the race were run!
O happy slumber, if the day were done!   120
Dreams that were sweet at eve, at morn were sin;
With cares to conquer, and a goal to win!
His were no tranquil years—no languid sleep—
No life of dreams—no home beyond the deep—
No softening ray—no visions false and wild—   125
No glittering hopes on life's grey distance smiled—
Like isles of sunlight on a mountain's brow,
Lit by a wandering gleam, we know not how,
Far on the dim horizon, when the sky
With glooming clouds broods dark and heavily.   130

Then his eye slumber'd, and the chain was broke
That bound his spirit, and his heart awoke;
Then—like a kingly river—swift and strong
The future roll'd its gathering tides along!
The shout of onset and the shriek of fear   135
Smote, like the rush of waters, on his ear;
And his eye kindled with the kindling fray,
The surging battle and the mail'd array!
All wondrous deeds the coming days should see,
And the long Vision of the years to be.   140

Pale phantom hosts, like shadows, faint and far,
Councils, and armies, and the pomp of war!
And one sway'd all, who wore a kingly crown,
Until another rose and smote him down.
A form that tower'd above his brother men;   145
A form he knew—but it was shrouded then!
With stern, slow steps—unseen—yet still the same,
By leaguer'd tower and tented field it came;
By Naseby's hill, o'er Marston's heathy waste,
By Worcester's field, the warrior-vision pass'd!   150
From their deep base, thy beetling cliffs, Dunbar,
Rang, as he trode them, with the voice of war!
The soldier kindled at his words of fire;
The statesman quail'd before his glance of ire!
Worn was his brow with cares no thought could scan;   155
His step was loftier than the steps of man;
[e]And the winds told his glory—and the wave
Sonorous witness to his empire gave!

What forms are these, that with complaining sound,
And slow reluctant steps are gathering round?   160
Forms that with him shall tread life's changing stage,
Cross his lone path, or share his pilgrimage.
There, as he gazed, a wond'rous band—they came,
Pym's look of hate, and Strafford's glance of flame:
There Laud, with noiseless steps and glittering eye,   165
In priestly garb, a frail old man, went by;
His drooping head bowed meekly on his breast;
His hands were folded, like a saint at rest!
[f]There Hampden bent him o'er his saddle bow,
And death's cold dews bedimm'd his earnest brow;   170
Still turn'd to watch the battle—still forgot

e 'It is just to say, that the maritime glory of England may first be traced from the era of the commonwealth in a track of continuous light.'—*Hallam's Const. Hist.* ii.

f 'His head bending down, and his hands resting on his horse's neck, he was seen riding from the field.'—*Lord Nugent's Memorials of Hampden*, ii. 435.

Himself, his sufferings, in his country's lot!
^gThere Falkland ey'd the strife that would not cease,
Shook back his tangled locks, and murmur'd—'Peace!'
With feet that spurn'd the ground, lo! Milton there   175
Stood like a statue; and his face was fair—
Fair beyond human beauty; and his eye,
That knew not earth, soar'd upwards to the sky!
^hHe, too, was there—it was the princely boy,
The child-companion of his childish joy!   180
But oh! how chang'd—those deathlike features wore
Childhood's bright glance and sunny smile no more!
That brow so sad, so pale, so full of care—
What trace of careless childhood linger'd there?
What spring of youth in that majestic mien,   185
So sadly calm, so kingly, so serene?
No—all was chang'd—the monarch wept alone,
Between a ruin'd church and shatter'd throne!
Friendless and hopeless—like a lonely tree,
On some bare headland, straining mournfully,   190
That all night long its weary moan doth make
To the vex'd waters of a mountain lake!
Still, as he gaz'd, the phantom's mournful glance
Shook the deep slumber of his deathlike trance;
Like some forgotten strain that haunts us still,   195
That calm eye follow'd, turn him where he will;
Till the pale monarch, and the long array,
Pass'd, like a morning mist, in tears away!

Then all his dream was troubled, and his soul
Thrill'd with a dread no slumber could control;   200
On that dark form his eyes had gaz'd before,
Nor known it then;—but it was veil'd no more!
^hIn broad clear light the ghastly vision shone,—

^g 'In his clothes and habit, which he had minded before always with more neatness and industry, he was now, not only incurious, but negligent.'—*Clarendon.*
   h Alluding to the stories of Cromwell's childish intimacy with Charles the First.

That form was his,—those features were his own!
The night of terrors, and the day of care,   205
The years of toil, all, all were written there!
Sad faces watch'd around him, and his breath
Came faint and feeble in the embrace of death.
[i]The gathering tempest, with its voice of fear,
[k]His latest loftiest music, smote his ear!   210
[l]That day of boundless hope and promise high,
That day that hail'd his triumphs, saw him die!
Then from those whitening lips, as death drew near,
[m]The imprisoning chains fell off, and all was clear!
Like lowering clouds, that at the close of day,   215
Bath'd in a blaze of sunset, melt away;
And with its clear calm tones, that dying prayer
Cheer'd all the failing hearts that sorrow'd there!

A Life—whose ways no human thought could scan,—
A life—that was not as the life of man;   220
A life—that wrote its purpose with a sword,
Moulding itself in action, not in word!
Rent with tumultuous thoughts, whose conflict rung
Deep thro' his soul, and chok'd his faltering tongue;
A heart that reck'd not of the countless dead,   225
That strew'd the blood-stain'd path where Empire led;
A daring hand, that shrunk not to fulfil
The thought that spurr'd it; and a dauntless will,
Bold action's parent; and a piercing ken
Thro' the dark chambers of the hearts of men,   230
To read each thought, and teach that master mind

---

222 *1863*: into action [*wrongly*]

i Clarendon mentions a great storm which attended the death of Cromwell.

k 'He was a great lover of music, and he entertained the most skilful in that science in his pay and family.'—*Perfect Politician*.

l Cromwell died on his fortunate day, the anniversary of Dunbar and Worcester,—September 3rd.

m There is a remarkable contrast between the perfect clearness of the celebrated prayer Cromwell is recorded to have uttered on his death bed, and the confusedness of the speeches which are attributed to him.

The fears and hopes and passions of mankind;
All these were thine—Oh thought of fear!—and thou
Stretch'd on that bed of death, art nothing now.

Then all his vision faded, and his soul   235
Sprang from its sleep! and lo, the waters roll
Once more beneath him; and the fluttering sail,
Where the dark ships rode proudly, woo'd the gale;
And the wind murmur'd round him, and he stood
Once more alone beside the gleaming flood.   240

THE HAYSWATER BOAT

[Published 1849]

A REGION desolate and wild.
Black, chafing water: and afloat,
And lonely as a truant child
In a waste wood, a single boat:
No mast, no sails are set thereon;   5
It moves, but never moveth on:
And welters like a human thing
Amid the wild waves weltering.

Behind, a buried vale doth sleep,
Far down the torrent cleaves its way: 10
In front the dumb rock rises steep,
A fretted wall of blue and grey;
Of shooting cliff and crumbled stone
With many a wild weed overgrown:
All else, black water: and afloat,   15
One rood from shore, that single boat.

Last night the wind was up and strong;
The grey-streak'd waters labour still:
The strong blast brought a pigmy throng
From that mild hollow in the hill;   20

From those twin brooks, that beached strand
So featly strewn with drifted sand;
From those weird domes of mounded green
That spot the solitary scene.

This boat they found against the shore: 25
The glossy rushes nodded by.
One rood from land they push'd, no more;
Then rested, listening silently.
The loud rains lash'd the mountain's crown,
The grating shingle straggled down: 30
All night they sate; then stole away,
And left it rocking in the bay.

Last night?—I look'd, the sky was clear,
The boat was old, a batter'd boat.
In sooth, it seems a hundred year   35
Since that strange crew did ride afloat.
The boat hath drifted in the bay—
The oars have moulder'd as they lay—
The rudder swings—yet none doth steer.
    What living hand hath brought it here?   40

SONNET TO THE HUNGARIAN NATION

[Published in THE EXAMINER, *July 21, 1849]*

NOT in sunk Spain's prolong'd death agony;
Not in rich England, bent but to make pour
The flood of the world's commerce on her shore;
Not in that madhouse, France, from whence the cry
Afflicts grave Heaven with its long senseless roar;   5
Not in American vulgarity,
Nor wordy German imbecility—
Lies any hope of heroism more.
Hungarians! Save the world! Renew the stories
Of men who against hope repell'd the chain,   10

And make the world's dead spirit leap again!
On land renew that Greek exploit, whose glories
Hallow the Salaminian promontories,
And the Armada flung to the fierce main.

DESTINY

[Published 1852]

WHY each is striving, from of old,
To love more deeply than he can?
Still would be true, yet still grows cold?
—Ask of the Powers that sport with man!

They yok'd in him, for endless strife,   5
A heart of ice, a soul of fire;
And hurl'd him on the Field of Life,
An aimless unallay'd Desire.

COURAGE

[Published 1852]

TRUE, we must tame our rebel will:
True, we must bow to Nature's law:
Must bear in silence many an ill;
Must learn to wait, renounce, withdraw.

Yet now, when boldest wills give place,   5
When Fate and Circumstance are strong,
And in their rush the human race
Are swept, like huddling sheep, along;

Those sterner spirits let me prize,
Who, though the tendence of the whole   10
They less than us might recognize,
Kept, more than us, their strength of soul.

Yes, be the second Cato prais'd!
Not that he took the course to die—
But that, when 'gainst himself he rais'd   15
His arm, he rais'd it dauntlessly.

R   *481*

And, Byron! let us dare admire,
If not thy fierce and turbid song,
Yet that, in anguish, doubt, desire,
Thy fiery courage still was strong.   20

The sun that on thy tossing pain
Did with such cold derision shine,
He crush'd thee not with his disdain—
    He had his glow, and thou hadst thine.

Our bane, disguise it as we may,   25
Is weakness, is a faltering course.
Oh that past times could give our day,
Join'd to its clearness, of their force!

THEKLA'S ANSWER

[*Published 1853*]

(*From Schiller*)

WHERE I am, thou ask'st, and where I wended
    When my fleeting shadow pass'd from thee?—
Am I not concluded now, and ended?
    Have not life and love been granted me?

Ask, where now those nightingales are singing,   5
    Who, of late, on the soft nights of May,
Set thine ears with soul-fraught music ringing—
    Only, while their love liv'd, lasted they.

Find I him, from whom I had to sever?—
    Doubt it not, we met, and we are one.   10
There, where what is join'd, is join'd for ever,
    There, where tears are never more to run.

There thou too shalt live with us together,
    When thou too hast borne the love we bore:
There, from sin deliver'd, dwells my Father,   15
    Track'd by Murder's bloody sword no more.

There he feels, it was no dream deceiving
    Lur'd him starwards to uplift his eye:
God doth match his gifts to man's believing;
    Believe, and thou shalt find the Holy nigh.   20

All thou augurest here of lovely seeming
    There shall find fulfilment in its day:
Dare, O Friend, be wandering, dare be dreaming;
    Lofty thought lies oft in childish play.

'BELOW THE SURFACE-STREAM'

[*These lines first appeared in the second instalment of 'St. Paul and
Protestantism', the* CORNHILL MAGAZINE, *November 1869*]

BELOW the surface-stream, shallow and light,
Of what we *say* we feel—below the stream,
As light, of what we *think* we feel—there flows
With noiseless current strong, obscure and deep,
The central stream of what we feel indeed.

ROME-SICKNESS

[*Published in* IN MEMORIAM: A WREATH OF STRAY LEAVES TO THE MEMORY OF
EMILY BLISS GOULD, *Rome, 1875*]

To daily tasks we set our hand,
    And oft the spirit, pent at home,
Breaks out and longs for Switzerland,
    Longs oftener yet and pines for Rome.

I pass'd to-day o'er Walton Heath—   5
    The coming spring-time's earliest stir
Quickened and moved, a happy breath,
    In moss, and gorse, and shining fir.

Fortunate firs! who never think
    How firs less curst by Fortune's frown   10
O'er Glion fringe the mountain's brink,
    Or dot the slopes to Vevey down.

I cross'd St. George's Hill to-day—
 There in the leaf-strewn copse I found
The tender foxglove-plants display   15
 Their first green muffle on the ground.

They envy not, this tranquil brood,
 The cyclamens whose blossoms fill
With fragrance all Frascati's wood
 Along the gracious Alban Hill!   20

Man only, with eternal bent
 To come and go, to shift and range,
At life and living not content,
 Chafes in his place, and pines for change.

Yet happy,—since his feverish blood   25
 Leaves him no rest, and change he will,—
When restlessness is restless good,
 Still mending, lessening, human ill!

Unwearied, as from land to land
 The incessant wanderer takes his way,   30
To hold the light and reach the hand
 To all who sink, to all who stray!

S.S. 'LUSITANIA'

[*Published in* THE NINETEENTH CENTURY, *January, 1879*]

I READ in Dante how that horned light,
Which hid Ulysses, waved itself and said:
'Following the sun, we set our vessel's head
To the great main; pass'd Seville on the right

'And Ceuta on the left; then southward sped. 5
At last in air, far off, dim rose a Height.
We cheer'd; but from it rush'd a blast of might,
And struck—and o'er us the sea-waters spread.'

I dropp'd the book, and of my child I thought
In his long black ship speeding night and day   10
O'er those same seas; dark Teneriffe rose, fraught

With omen; 'Oh! were that Mount pass'd', I say.
Then the door opens and this card is brought:
'Reach'd Cape Verde Islands, "Lusitania".'

NOTES BY THE AUTHOR

NOTE 1, PAGE 2

Saw The Wide Prospect, and the Asian Fen

The name Europe (*Εὐρώπη, the wide prospect*) probably describes the appearance of the European coast to the Greeks on the coast of Asia Minor opposite. The name Asia, again, comes, it has been thought, from the muddy fens of the rivers of Asia Minor, such as the Cayster or Mæander, which struck the imagination of the Greeks living near them.

[In 1849, '53, '54, and '57 Arnold is content with the simple note: *Εὐρώπη*.
l. 4. fens of the marshy rivers (1869) *becomes* muddy fens of the rivers (1877).]

NOTE 2, PAGE 8

Mycerinus

'After Cephren, Mycerinus, son of Cheops, reigned over Egypt. He abhorred his father's courses, and judged his subjects more justly than any of their kings had done.—To him there came an oracle from the city of Buto, to the effect that he was to live but six years longer, and to die in the seventh year from that time.'—HERODOTUS.

[Note first inserted in 1853. The 1849 edition merely gives the reference 'Herodotus, II. 133' in a footnote.]

NOTE 3, PAGE 38

Stagirius

Stagirius was a young monk to whom St. Chrysostom addressed three books, and of whom those books give an account. They will be found in the first volume of the Benedictine edition of St. Chrysostom's works.

[Note first published in 1877.]

NOTE 4, PAGE 47

Horatian Echo

Written in 1847. Printed by permission of Mr. Arthur Galton, to whom the Poem was given in 1886 for publication in *The Hobby Horse*.
[Publisher's note in edition of 1890.]

NOTES BY THE AUTHOR

NOTE 5, PAGE 53

Those who have been long familiar with the English Lake-Country will find no difficulty in recalling, from the description in the text, the roadside inn at Wythburn on the descent from Dunmail Raise towards Keswick; its sedentary landlord of thirty years ago, and the passage over the Wythburn Fells to Watendlath.

[Note first published in 1869.

l. 2. have (1869) *becomes* find (1877).

l. 4. twenty (1869) *becomes* thirty (1877).]

NOTE 6, PAGE 61

Sohrab and Rustum

The story of Sohrab and Rustum is told in Sir John Malcolm's *History of Persia*, as follows:—

'The young Sohrab was the fruit of one of Rustum's early amours. He had left his mother, and sought fame under the banners of Afrasiab, whose armies he commanded, and soon obtained a renown beyond that of all contemporary heroes but his father. He had carried death and dismay into the ranks of the Persians, and had terrified the boldest warriors of that country, before Rustum encountered him, which at last that hero resolved to do, under a feigned name. They met three times. The first time they parted by mutual consent, though Sohrab had the advantage; the second, the youth obtained a victory, but granted life to his unknown father; the third was fatal to Sohrab, who, when writhing in the pangs of death, warned his conqueror to shun the vengeance that is inspired by parental woes, and bade him dread the rage of the mighty Rustum, who must soon learn that he had slain his son Sohrab. These words, we are told, were as death to the aged hero; and when he recovered from a trance, he called in despair for proofs of what Sohrab had said. The afflicted and dying youth tore open his mail, and showed his father a seal which his mother had placed on his arm when she discovered to him the secret of his birth, and bade him seek his father. The sight of his own signet rendered Rustum quite frantic; he cursed himself, attempting to put an end to his existence, and was only prevented by the efforts of his expiring son. After Sohrab's death, he burnt his tents and all his goods, and carried the corpse to Seistan, where it was interred; the army of Turan was, agreeably to the last request of Sohrab, permitted to cross the Oxus unmolested. To reconcile us to the improbability of this tale, we are informed that Rustum could have no idea his son was in existence. The mother of Sohrab had written to him her child was a daughter, fearing to lose her darling infant if she revealed the truth; and Rustum, as before stated, fought under a feigned name, an usage not uncommon in the chivalrous combats of those days.'

[Note first published in 1854, omitted in 1857, and restored in 1869.]

In 1854, seven lines from the end, this additional sentence: 'It was commanded by Haman: and Zoarrah attended, on the part of Rustum, to see that this engagement was respected by the Persians.'

In 1854 only, the quotation from Malcolm was followed by this further note:

M. Sainte-Beuve, also, that most delightful of critics, in a notice of an edition of Ferdousi's great poem by M. Mohl now in course of publication at Paris, containing the original text and a prose translation, gives an analysis of this episode, with extracts from M. Mohl's translation, which I will quote at length: commencing from the point where Rustum leaves Tehmineh, the future mother of Sohrab, before the birth of her child; having given her an onyx with instructions to let the child wear it in her hair, if a girl, and on his arm, if a boy. Of M. Mohl's book itself I have not been able to obtain sight.

'Là-dessus Roustem part au matin, monté sur son cheval Raksch; il s'en retourne vers l'Iran, et, durant des années, il n'a plus que de vagues nouvelles de la belle Tehmineh et du fils qui lui est né; car c'est un fils et non une fille. Ce fils est beau et au visage brillant; on l'appelle Sohrab. "Quand il eut un mois, il était comme un enfant d'un an; quand il eut trois ans, il s'exerçait au jeu des armes, et à cinq ans il avait le cœur d'un lion. Quand il eut atteint l'âge de dix ans, personne dans son pays n'osait lutter contre lui." Il se distinguait, à première vue, de tous les Turcs d'alentour; il devenait manifeste qu'il était issu d'une autre race. L'enfant, sentant sa force, alla fièrement demander à sa mère le nom de son père, et, quand il le sut, il n'eut plus de cesse qu'il n'eût assemblé une armée pour aller combattre les Iraniens et se faire reconnaître du glorieux Roustem à ses exploits et à sa bravoure.

'Sohrab choisit un cheval assez fort pour le porter, un cheval fort comme un éléphant; il assemble une armée et se met en marche, non pour combattre son père, mais pour combattre et détrôner le souverain dont Roustem est le feudataire, et afin de mettre la race vaillante de Roustem à la place de ce roi déjà fainéant. C'est ici que l'action commence à se nouer avec un art et une habileté qui appartiennent au poëte. La solution fatale est à la fois entrevue et retardée moyennant des gradations qui vont la rendre plus dramatique. Roustem, mandé en toute hâte par le roi effrayé, ne s'empresse point d'accourir. A cette nouvelle d'une armée de Turcs commandée par un jeune homme si vaillant et si héroïque, il a l'idée d'abord que ce pourrait bien être son fils; mais non: ce rejeton de sa race est trop enfant, se dit-il, "et ses lèvres sentent encore le lait". Roustem arrive pourtant; mais, mal accueilli par le roi, il entre dans une colère d'Achille, et il est tout prêt à s'en retourner dans sa tente. On ne le fléchit qu'en lui représentant que s'abstenir en une telle rencontre, ce serait paraître reculer devant le jeune héros. Cependant les armées sont en présence. Roustem, déguisé en Turc, s'introduit dans un château qu'occupe l'ennemi, pour juger de tout par lui-même. Il voit son fils assis à un festin: il l'admire, il le compare, pour la force et la beauté, à sa propre race; on dirait, à un moment, que le sang au-dedans va parler et lui crier: *C'est lui!* Le jeune Sohrab, de son côté, quand vient le matin, en présence de cette armée dont le camp se déploie devant lui, est avide de savoir si son noble père n'en est pas. Monté sur un lieu élevé, il se fait nommer par un prisonnier tous les chefs illustres dont il voit se dérouler les étendards. Le prisonnier les énumère avec complaisance et les lui nomme tous, tous excepté un seul, excepté celui, précisément, qui l'intéresse. Le prisonnier fait semblant de croire que Roustem n'est pas venu, car il craint que ce jeune orgueilleux, dans sa force indomptable, ne veuille se signaler en s'attaquant de préférence à ce chef illustre, et qu'il ne cause un grand malheur. Sohrab insiste et trouve étonnant qu'entre tant de chefs, le vaillant Roustem, le premier de tous, ait manqué cette fois à l'appel; il presse de questions le prisonnier, qui lutte de ruse, et qui s'obstine, sur ce point, à lui cacher la vérité; "Sans doute, réplique celui-ci, le héros sera allé dans le Zaboulistan, car c'est le temps des fêtes dans les jardins de roses." A quoi Sohrab, sentant bouillonner son sang, répond: "Ne parle pas ainsi, car le front de Roustem se tourne toujours vers le combat." Mais Sohrab a beau vouloir forcer le secret, la fatalité l'emporte: "Comment veux-tu gouverner ce monde que gouverne Dieu?" s'écrie le poëte. "C'est le Créateur qui a déterminé d'avance toutes choses. Le sort a écrit autrement que tu n'aurais voulu, et, comme il te mène, il faut que tu suives."

'Sohrab engage le combat; tout plie devant lui. Jamais nos vieux romans de chevalerie n'ont retenti de pareils coups d'épée. Les plus vaillants chefs reculent. Roustem est appelé; il arrive, il se trouve seul en présence de sons fils, et le duel va s'entamer. La pitié, tout à coup, saisit le vieux chef, en voyant ce jeune guerrier si fier, et si beau:

' "O jeune homme si tendre!" lui dit-il, "la terre est sèche et froide, l'air est doux et chaud. Je suis vieux; j'ai vu maint champ de bataille, j'ai détruit mainte armée, et je n'ai jamais été battu. . . . Mais j'ai pitié de toi et ne voudrais pas t'arracher la vie. Ne reste pas avec les Turcs; je ne connais personne dans l'Iran qui ait des épaules et des bras comme toi."

'En entendant ces paroles qui semblent sortir d'une âme amie, le cœur de Sohrab s'élance, il a un pressentiment soudain; il demande ingénument au guerrier s'il n'est pas celui qu'il cherche, s'il n'est pas l'illustre Roustem. Mais le vieux chef, qui ne veut pas donner à ce jouvenceau trop d'orgueil, répond avec ruse qu'il n'est pas Roustem, et le cœur de Sohrab se resserre aussitôt; le nuage qui venait de s'entr'ouvrir se referme, et la destinée se poursuit.

'Le duel commence: il n'est pas sans vicissitudes et sans péripéties singulières; il dure deux jours. Dès le premier choc, les épées des combattants se brisent en éclats sous leurs coups: "Quels coups! on eût dit qu'ils amenaient la Résurrection!" Le combat continue à coups de massue; nous sommes en plein âge héroïque. Le premier jour, le duel n'a pas de résultat. Après une lutte acharnée, les deux chefs s'éloignent, se donnant rendez-vous pour le lendemain. Roustem s'étonne d'avoir rencontré pour la première fois son égal, presque son maître, et de sentir son cœur défaillir sans savoir pourquoi. Le second jour, au moment de reprendre la lutte, Sohrab a un mouvement de tendresse, et la nature, près de succomber, fait en lui comme un suprême effort. En abordant le vieux chef, il s'adresse à lui le sourire sur les lèvres et comme s'ils avaient passé la nuit amicalement ensemble:

' "Comment as-tu dormi?" lui demande-t-il, "comment t'es-tu levé ce matin? Pourquoi as-tu préparé ton cœur pour la lutte? Jette cette massue et cette épée de la vengeance, jette tout cet appareil d'un combat impie. Asseyons-nous tous deux à terre, et adoucissons avec du vin nos regards courroucés. Faisons un traité en invoquant Dieu, et repentons-nous dans notre cœur de cette inimitié. Attends qu'un autre se présente pour le combat, et apprête avec moi une fête. Mon cœur te communiquera son amour, et je ferai couler de tes yeux des larmes de honte. Puisque tu es né d'une noble race, fais-moi connaître ton origine; ne me cache pas ton nom, puisque tu vas me combattre: ne serais-tu pas Roustem?"

'Roustem, par sentiment d'orgueil, et soupçonnant toujours une feinte de la part d'un jeune homme avide de gloire, dissimule une dernière fois, et, dès ce moment, le sort n'a plus de trêve. Toutes les ruses de Roustem (et j'en supprime encore) tournent contre lui; il finit par plonger un poignard dans la poitrine de son fils, et ne le reconnaît que dans l'instant suprême. Le jeune homme meurt avec résignation, avec douceur, en pensant à sa mère, à ses amis, en recommandant qu'on épargne après lui cette armée qu'il a engagée dans une entreprise téméraire:

' "Pendant bien des jours, je leur ai donné de belles paroles, je leur ai donné l'espoir de tout obtenir; car comment pouvais-je savoir, ô héros illustre, que je périrais de la main de mon père? . . . Je voyais les signes que ma mère m'avait indiqués, mais je n'en croyais pas mes yeux. Mon sort était écrit au-dessus de ma tête, et je devais mourir de la main de mon père. Je suis venu comme la foudre, je m'en vais comme le vent; peut-être que je te retrouverai heureux dans le ciel!"

'Ainsi parle en expirant cet autre Hippolyte, immolé ici de la main de Thésée.'

A writer in the *Christian Remembrancer* (of the general tenour of whose remarks I have, assuredly, no right to complain) having made the discovery of this notice by M. Sainte-Beuve, has pointed out the passages in which I have made use of the extracts from M. Mohl's translation which it contains; has observed, apparently with blame, that I 'have not thought fit to offer a single syllable of acknowledgment to an author to whom I have been manifestly very largely indebted'; has complained of being 'under some embarrassment from not being sure how much of the treatment is Mr. Arnold's own'; and, finally, has suggested that 'the whole work of M. Mohl may have been used throughout, and the study of antiquity carried so far as simply to reproduce an ancient poem as well as an ancient subject'.

It would have been more charitable, perhaps, had the reviewer, before making this goodnatured suggestion, ascertained, by reference to M. Mohl's work, how far it was confirmed by the fact.

The reader, however, is now in possession of the whole of the sources from which I have drawn the story of *Sohrab and Rustum*, and can determine, if he pleases, the exact amount of my obligation to M. Mohl. But I hope that it will not in future be supposed, if I am silent as to the sources from which a poem has been derived, that I am trying to conceal obligations, or to claim an absolute originality for all parts of it. When any man endeavours to *'remanier et réinventer à sa manière'* a great story, which, as M. Sainte-Beuve says of that of *Sohrab and Rustum*, has *'couru le monde'*, it may be considered quite certain that he has not drawn all the details of his work out of his own head. The reader is not, I think, concerned to ask, from what sources these have been drawn; but only how the whole work, as it stands, affects him. Real plagiarism, such as the borrowing without acknowledgment of passages from other English poets—real dishonesty, such as the endeavouring to pass off the mere translation of a poem as an original work—are always certain enough to be discovered.

I must not be led on, from defending the morality of my imitation, to defend at length its aesthetics; but I cannot forbear adding, that it would be a most unfortunate scruple which should restrain an author, treating matter of history or tradition, from placing, where he can, in the mouths of his personages the very words of the old chronicle, or romance, or poem (when the poem embodies, as that of Ferdousi, the tradition of a people); and which should lead him to substitute for these any '*eigene* [sic] *grossen Erfindungen*'. For my part, I only regret that I could not meet with a translation from Ferdousi's poem of the whole of the episode of *Sohrab and Rustum*: with a prose translation, that is: for in a verse translation no original work is any longer recognizable. I should certainly have made all the use I could of it. The use of the tradition, above everything else, gives to a work that *naïveté*, that flavour of reality and truth, which is the very life of poetry.

NOTE 7, PAGE 95

Balder Dead

'Balder the Good having been tormented with terrible dreams, indicating that his life was in great peril, communicated them to the assembled Æsir, who resolved to conjure all things to avert from him the threatened danger. Then Frigga exacted an oath from fire and water, from iron, and all other metals, as well as from stones, earths, diseases, beasts, birds, poisons, and creeping things, that none of them would do any harm to Balder. When this was done, it became a favourite pastime of the Æsir, at their meetings, to get Balder to stand up and serve them as a mark, some hurling darts at him, some stones, while others hewed at him with their swords and battle-axes, for do what they would, none of them could harm him, and this was regarded by all as a great honour shown to Balder. But when Loki beheld the scene he was sorely vexed that Balder was not hurt. Assuming, therefore, the shape of a woman, he went to Fensalir, the mansion of Frigga. That goddess, when she saw the pretended woman, inquired of her if she knew what the Æsir were doing at their meetings. She replied, that they were throwing darts and stones at Balder without being able to hurt him.

' "Ay," said Frigga, "neither metal nor wood can hurt Balder, for I have exacted an oath from all of them."

'"What!" exclaimed the woman, "have all things sworn to spare Balder?"

'"All things," replied Frigga, "except one little shrub that grows on the eastern side of Valhalla, and is called Mistletoe, and which I thought too young and feeble to crave an oath from."

'As soon as Loki heard this he went away, and, resuming his natural shape, cut off the mistletoe, and repaired to the place where the gods were assembled. There he found Hödur standing apart, without partaking of the sports, on account of his blindness, and going up to him said, "Why dost thou not also throw something at Balder?"

'"Because I am blind," answered Hödur, "and see not where Balder is, and have, moreover, nothing to throw with."

'"Come, then," said Loki, "do like the rest, and show honour to Balder by throwing this twig at him, and I will direct thy arm toward the place where he stands."

'Hödur then took the mistletoe, and, under the guidance of Loki, darted it at Balder, who, pierced through and through, fell down lifeless.'—*Edda*.

[Note first published in 1869.]

NOTE 8, PAGE 130

Tristram and Iseult

'In the court of his uncle King Marc, the king of Cornwall, who at this time resided at the castle of Tyntagel, Tristram became expert in all knightly exercises.—The king of Ireland, at Tristram's solicitations, promised to bestow his daughter Iseult in marriage on King Marc. The mother of Iseult gave to her daughter's confidante a philtre, or love-potion, to be administered on the night of her nuptials. Of this beverage Tristram and Iseult, on their voyage to Cornwall, unfortunately partook. Its influence, during the remainder of their lives, regulated the affections and destiny of the lovers.—

'After the arrival of Tristram and Iseult in Cornwall, and the nuptials of the latter with King Marc, a great part of the romance is occupied with their contrivances to procure secret interviews.—Tristram, being forced to leave Cornwall, on account of the displeasure of his uncle, repaired to Brittany, where lived Iseult with the White Hands.—He married her—more out of gratitude than love.—Afterwards he proceeded to the dominions of Arthur, which became the theatre of unnumbered exploits.

'Tristram, subsequent to these events, returned to Brittany, and to his long-neglected wife. There, being wounded and sick, he was soon reduced to the lowest ebb. In this situation, he despatched a confidant to the queen of Cornwall, to try if he could induce her to follow him to Brittany, etc.'—DUNLOP's *History of Fiction.*

[Note first published in 1853. The passage is a brief abstract of Dunlop, composed of select sentences.

In all editions through 1881, 'follow' in last line reads 'accompany.']

NOTE 9, PAGE 166

That son of Italy who tried to blow

Giacopone di Todi.

NOTE 10, PAGE 171

Recalls the obscure opposer he outweigh'd

Gilbert de la Porrée, at the Council of Rheims, in 1148.

NOTE 11, PAGE 172

Of that unpitying Phrygian sect which cried

The Montanists.

[Note first published in 1869.]

NOTE 12, PAGE 173

Monica

See St. Augustine's *Confessions*, book ix, chapter 11.

[Note first published in 1869.]

NOTE 13, PAGE 174

My Marguerite smiles upon the strand

See, among 'Early Poems', the poem called *A Memory-Picture.*

[Note first published in 1877.]

NOTE 14, PAGE 197

The Hunter of the Tanagræan Field

Orion, the Wild Huntsman of Greek legend, and in this capacity appearing in both earth and sky.

[Note first published in 1869.]

NOTES BY THE AUTHOR

O'er the sun-redden'd western straits

Erytheia, the legendary region around the Pillars of Hercules, probably took its name from the redness of the West under which the Greeks saw it.

[Note first published in 1869.]

NOTE 16, PAGE 255

The Scholar-Gipsy

'There was very lately a lad in the University of Oxford, who was by his poverty forced to leave his studies there; and at last to join himself to a company of vagabond gipsies. Among these extravagant people, by the insinuating subtilty of his carriage, he quickly got so much of their love and esteem as that they discovered to him their mystery. After he had been a pretty while exercised in the trade, there chanced to ride by a couple of scholars, who had formerly been of his acquaintance. They quickly spied out their old friend among the gipsies; and he gave them an account of the necessity which drove him to that kind of life, and told them that the people he went with were not such impostors as they were taken for, but that they had a traditional kind of learning among them, and could do wonders by the power of imagination, their fancy binding that of others: that himself had learned much of their art, and when he had compassed the whole secret, he intended, he said, to leave their company, and give the world an account of what he had learned.'—GLANVIL's *Vanity of Dogmatizing*, 1661.

[The passage is an abstract of Glanvil.

l. 6. 'well exercised' in 1853, '54, and '57.]

NOTE 17, PAGE 262

Throughout this poem there is reference to the preceding piece, *The Scholar-Gipsy*.

[In 1868: 'reference to another piece, *The Scholar-Gipsy*, printed in the first volume of the Author's Poems.']

NOTE 18, PAGE 268

Young Daphnis with his silver voice doth sing

Daphnis, the ideal Sicilian shepherd of Greek pastoral poetry, was said to have followed into Phrygia his mistress Piplea, who had been carried off by robbers, and to have found her in the power of the king of Phrygia, Lityerses. Lityerses used to make strangers try a contest with him in reaping corn, and to put them to death if he overcame them. Hercules arrived in time to save Daphnis, took upon himself the reaping-contest with Lityerses, overcame him, and slew him. The Lityerses-song connected with this tradition was, like the Linus-song, one of the early plaintive strains of Greek popular poetry, and used to be sung by corn-reapers. Other traditions represented Daphnis as beloved by a nymph who exacted from him an oath to love no one else. He fell in love with a princess, and was struck blind by the jealous nymph. Mercury, who was his father, raised him to Heaven, and made a fountain spring up in the place from which he ascended. At this fountain the Sicilians offered yearly sacrifices.—See Servius, *Comment. in Virgil. Bucol.*, v. 20, and viii. 68.

[First published in 1869.]

NOTE 19, PAGE 274

Ah! where is he, who should have come

The author's brother, William Delafield Arnold, Director of Public Instruction in the Punjab, and author of *Oakfield, or Fellowship in the East*, died at Gibraltar on his way home from India, April the 9th, 1859.

[Note first published in 1867.]

NOTE 20, PAGE 275

So moonlit, saw me once of yore

See the poem, *A Summer Night*, p. 242.

[Note first published in 1869.]

NOTE 21, PAGE 276

My brother! and thine early lot

See Note 19.

[Note first published in 1867.]

NOTE 22, PAGE 280

*I saw the meeting of two
Gifted women*

Charlotte Brontë and Harriet Martineau.

NOTES BY THE AUTHOR

NOTE 23, PAGE 285

Whose too bold dying song

See the last verses by Emily Brontë in *Poems by Currer, Ellis, and Acton Bell*.

[last lines (1877 and '81) *becomes* last verses (1885).]

NOTE 24, PAGE 298

Goethe, too, had been there

See *Harzreise im Winter*, in Goethe's *Gedichte*.

NOTE 25, PAGE 306

The author of *Obermann*, Étienne Pivert de Senancour, has little celebrity in France, his own country; and out of France he is almost unknown. But the profound inwardness, the austere sincerity, of his principal work, *Obermann*, the delicate feeling for nature which it
5 exhibits, and the melancholy eloquence of many passages of it, have attracted and charmed some of the most remarkable spirits of this century, such as George Sand and Sainte-Beuve, and will probably always find a certain number of spirits whom they touch and interest.

Senancour was born in 1770. He was educated for the priesthood,
10 and passed some time in the seminary of St. Sulpice; broke away from the Seminary and from France itself, and passed some years in Switzerland, where he married; returned to France in middle life, and followed thenceforward the career of a man of letters, but with hardly any fame or success. He died an old man in 1846, desiring that on his grave
15 might be placed these words only: *Éternité, deviens mon asile!*

The influence of Rousseau, and certain affinities with more famous and fortunate authors of his own day,—Chateaubriand and Madame de Staël,—are everywhere visible in Senancour. But though, like these eminent personages, he may be called a sentimental writer, and though
20 *Obermann*, a collection of letters from Switzerland treating almost entirely of nature and of the human soul, may be called a work of sentiment, Senancour has a gravity and severity which distinguish him from all other writers of the sentimental school. The world is with him in his solitude far less than it is with them; of all writers he is the most
25 perfectly isolated and the least attitudinising. His chief work, too, has a value and power of its own, apart from these merits of its author. The stir of all the main forces, by which modern life is and has been impelled, lives in the letters of *Obermann*; the dissolving agencies of

the eighteenth century, the fiery storm of the French Revolution, the first faint promise and dawn of that new world which our own time is but now more fully bringing to light,—all these are to be felt, almost to be touched, there. To me, indeed, it will always seem that the impressiveness of this production can hardly be rated too high.

Besides *Obermann* there is one other of Senancour's works which, for those spirits who feel his attraction, is very interesting; its title is, *Libres Méditations d'un Solitaire Inconnu.*

[Note first published in 1868.

    l. 8. whom they will touch (1868 and '69) *becomes* whom they touch (1877).

    l. 28. is in the letters (1868) *becomes* lives in the letters (1869).

    l. 31. now fully bringing (1868, '69, '77, and '81) *becomes* now more fully bringing (1885).]

NOTE 26, PAGE 306

Behind are the abandoned baths

The Baths of Leuk. This poem was conceived, and partly composed, in the valley going down from the foot of the Gemmi Pass towards the Rhone.

[Note first published in 1869.]

NOTE 27, PAGE 312

Glion?—Ah, twenty years, it cuts

Probably all who know the Vevey end of the Lake of Geneva, will recollect Glion, the mountain-village above the castle of Chillon. Glion now has hotels, *pensions*, and villas; but twenty years ago it was hardly more than the huts of Avant opposite to it,—huts through which goes that beautiful path over the Col de Jaman, followed by so many foot-travellers on their way from Vevey to the Simmenthal and Thun.

[Note first published in 1868.]

NOTE 28, PAGE 313

The gentian-flower'd pass, its crown
With yellow spires aflame

The blossoms of the *Gentiana lutea.*

[Note first published in this form in 1885. In 1867 and '68, the first line only was annotated: 'The *gentiana lutea* of the Alps.'

NOTES BY THE AUTHOR

In 1869, '77, and '81, this same line was annotated by a cross-reference to a note on *Empedocles on Etna*, Act I, scene ii, l. 5.]

NOTE 29, PAGE 313

And walls where Byron came

Montbovon. See Byron's Journal, in his *Works*, vol. iii, p. 258. The river Saane becomes the Sarine below Montbovon.

NOTE 30, PAGE 399

And the kind, chance-arrived Wanderer

Poias, the father of Philoctetes. Passing near, he was attracted by the concourse round the pyre, and at the entreaty of Hercules set fire to it, receiving the bow and arrows of the hero as his reward.

[Note first published in 1885.]

NOTE 31, PAGE 430

And that curst treachery on the Mount of Gore

Mount Hæmus, so called, said the legend, from Typho's blood spilt on it in his last battle with Zeus, when the giant's strength failed, owing to the Destinies having a short time before given treacherously to him, for his refreshment, perishable fruits. See APOLLODORUS, *Bibliotheca*, book i, chap. vi.

[Note first published in 1885.]

NOTE 32, PAGE 436

Ye Sun-born Virgins! on the road of truth

See the Fragments of Parmenides:

.   .   .   κοῦραι δ' ὁδὸν ἡγεμόνευον,
ἡλίαδες κοῦραι, προλιποῦσαι δώματα νυκτός,
εἰς φάος   .   .   .   .   .

[Note first published in 1867.]

NOTE 33, PAGE 444

Couldst thou no better keep, O Abbey old,
The boon thy dedication-sign foretold

'Ailred of Rievaulx, and several other writers, assert that Sebert, king of the East Saxons and nephew of Ethelbert, founded the Abbey of Westminster very early in the seventh century.

'Sulcardus, who lived in the time of William the Conqueror, gives a minute account of the miracle supposed to have been worked at the consecration of the Abbey.

'The church had been prepared against the next day for dedication. On the night preceding, St. Peter appeared on the opposite side of the water to a fisherman, desiring to be conveyed to the farther shore. Having left the boat, St. Peter ordered the fisherman to wait, promising him a reward on his return. An innumerable host from heaven accompanied the apostle, singing choral hymns, while everything was illuminated with a supernatural light. The dedication having been completed, St. Peter returned to the fisherman, quieted his alarm at what had passed, and announced himself as the apostle. He directed the fisherman to go as soon as it was day to the authorities, to state what he had seen and heard, and to inform them that, in corroboration of his testimony, they would find the marks of consecration on the walls of the church. In obedience to the apostle's direction, the fisherman waited on Mellitus, Bishop of London, who, going to the church, found not only marks of the chrism, but of the tapers with which the church had been illuminated. Mellitus, therefore, desisted from proceeding to a new consecration, and contented himself with the celebration of the mass.'—DUGDALE, *Monasticon Anglicanum* (edition of 1817), vol. i, pp. 265, 266. See also MONTALEMBERT, *Les Moines d'Occident*, vol. iii, pp. 428–32.

NOTE 34, PAGE 446

The charm'd babe of the Eleusinian king

Demophoön, son of Celeus, king of Eleusis. See, in the *Homeric Hymns*, the *Hymn to Demeter*, 184–298.

NOTE 35, PAGE 448

That Pair, whose head did plan, whose hands did forge
The Temple in the pure Parnassian gorge

Agamedes and Trophonius, the builders of the temple of Apollo at Delphi. See Plutarch, *Consolatio ad Apollonium*, c. 14.

NOTE 36, PAGE 456

Stol'n from Aristophanes

See *The Birds* of Aristophanes, 465–85.

NOTES BY THE AUTHOR

Of Robin's reed

'Come, join the melancholious croon
　　　O' Robin's reed.'—BURNS, *Poor Mailie's Elegy.*

[Publisher's note in edition of 1890.]

NOTES CANCELLED BY THE AUTHOR
The New Sirens, PAGE 26

In *Macmillan's Magazine*, December 1876, the poem was prefaced by the following note:

I shall not, I hope, be supposed unconscious that in coherency and intelligibility the following poem leaves much to be desired. It was published in 1849 in a small volume without my name, was withdrawn along with that volume, and until now has never been reprinted. But the departed poem had the honour of being followed by the regrets of a most distinguished mourner, Mr. Swinburne, who has more than once revived its memory, and asked for its republication. Mr. Swinburne's generosity towards contemporary verse is well known; and *The New Sirens* may have won his favour the more readily because it had something, perhaps, of that animation of movement and rhythm of which his own poems offer such splendid examples. In addition to Mr. Swinburne, the poem has had also several other friends, less distinguished, who desired its restoration. To a work of his youth, a work produced in long-past days of ardour and emotion, an author can never be very hard-hearted; and after a disappearance of more than twenty-five years, *The New Sirens*, therefore, is here reprinted.　　　　　　M. A.

Stanzas in Memory of the Author of Obermann, PAGE 306

l. 50. ('His quiet home one keeps.') This allusion to Wordsworth was annotated in 1852, '55, and '69: 'Written in November, 1849.' The footnote was dropped in 1877.

Empedocles on Etna, PAGE 406

In 1867 and 1868 the poem was accompanied by the following note: 'I cannot deny myself the pleasure of saying that I reprint (I cannot say *republish*, for it was withdrawn from circulation before fifty copies were sold) this poem at the request of a man of genius, whom it had the honour and the good fortune to interest,—Mr. Robert Browning.'

Act I, scene ii, l. 5. ('Of the sun-loving gentian, in the heat') was, in 1877 and '81, annotated: 'The *gentiana lutea*.'

INDEX OF TITLES

INDEX OF FIRST LINES

INDEX OF FIRST LINES

INDEX OF FIRST LINES

INDEX OF FIRST LINES

PRINTED IN GREAT BRITAIN
AT THE UNIVERSITY PRESS, OXFORD
BY VIVIAN RIDLER
PRINTER TO THE UNIVERSITY